Young Children's Behavior

THIRD EDITION

Young Children's Behavior

Practical Approaches for Caregivers and Teachers

Louise Porter
PhD, MA(Hons), MGiftedEd, DipEd

·P A U L·H·
BROOKES
PUBLISHING CO.®

Paul H. Brookes Publishing Co.
Post Office Box 10624
Baltimore, Maryland 21285-0624

www.brookespublishing.com

Library of Congress Cataloging-in-Publication Data

Porter, Louise, 1958-
　　Young children's behavior : practical approaches for caregivers and
　　teachers / Louise Porter. — 3rd ed.
　　　p. cm.
　　Includes bibliographical references and index.
　　ISBN 978-1-55766-956-8 (pbk.)
　　1. Preschool children—Psychology. 2. Behavior modification. 3.
　　Discipline of children. 4. Early childhood education. 5. Classroom
　　management. I. Title.
HQ774.5.P67 2008
372.1102--dc22

　　　　　　　　　　　　　　　　　　　　　　　　　　　　2007041751

Publisher: Debbie Lee
Publishing Services Manager: Helena Klijn
Edited by Ruth Matheson
Proofread by Pamela Dunne
Design and typesetting by Darben Design
Index by Mei Yen Chua
Printed by Ligare

contents

part 1

Foundations
of discipline

'There is a time to admire the grace and persuasive power of an influential idea, and there is a time to fear its hold over us. The time to worry is when the idea is so widely shared that we no longer even notice it, when it is so deeply rooted that it feels to us like plain common sense. At the point when objections are not answered anymore because they are no longer even raised, we are not in control: we do not have the idea; it has us.'

KOHN (1999, p. 3)

DEVELOPMENTAL TRENDS IN CHILDREN'S BEHAVIOUR

Contrary to the urban myth of the 'terrible twos', 2-year-olds actually display no more frequent behavioural difficulties than they did when younger (Baillargeon et al. 2007). Prior to 2 years of age, parents are mainly concerned with children's eating, sleeping and toileting patterns (Campbell 1995). After that age, adults begin to expect socially appropriate behaviour and (somewhat unrealistically) assume that, now that children are beginning to talk, their behaviour will come under the control of external verbal commands. Thus, past 2 years of age, adults believe that young children's behaviours are intentional and, therefore, begin to hold them accountable for their actions (Zahn-Waxler & Radke-Yarrow 1990).

Beyond 2 years of age, the behaviours that commonly concern parents and other adults are uncooperative behaviour (often termed non-compliance or defiance), high activity levels and aggression (Campbell 1995). With respect to following directives, 14-month-olds have been observed to desist from a desired behaviour (e.g. touching forbidden equipment) 40% of the time, with this figure rising to an average of 85% cooperation by almost 4 years of age (Kochanska et al. 2001). More challenging for children are requests to persist at distasteful tasks, such as packing away toys or sitting quietly during group activities. On persistence tasks, 14-month-olds cooperate on 14% of occasions, while by almost 4 years of age they can do so around 30% of the time (Kochanska et al. 2001). Being a more complex task, voluntary control takes longer to learn, with the result that conflict between parents and toddlers over prohibitions and engagement in activities is common, with one study recording an average of 19 disputes per hour (Laible & Thompson 2002).

The second behaviour that commonly concerns adults is overactivity. In the early years, it is difficult to distinguish normal childhood exuberance from early signs of inattentiveness that will later be disabling. While I address this topic in Chapter 15, it is clear that trend is important: from 3 to 5 years of age, children's activity levels will typically decline (Campbell 1995) and come under self-control so that they are appropriate for the situation. Absence of this trend can signal the need for further investigation.

The third behaviour of young children to concern their parents and other caregivers is aggression. It gains aggressors access to resources and status and, as such, serves a vital survival function. Therefore, it is not surprising that it occurs at high rates in our species. As a result of the emergence of anger, frustration and an understanding of cause and effect, physical aggression appears during the latter half of the first year of life, resulting in its use by around half of all 1-year-olds (Alink et al. 2006, Loeber & Hay 1997). Infants' developing mobility permits more frequent peer interaction, but they still lack language proficiency. The result is that at 1 year of age, half of their interactions are negative (Deynoot-Schaub & Riksen-Walraven 2006, Vaughn et al. 2003). In most cases, negativity is normal and simply signals growing children's attempts at autonomy at a time when their emotional self-regulation is only just emerging.

Physical aggression peaks somewhere between 24 and 42 months, following which it begins to decline steadily in both frequency and severity, as a result of socialisation, the emergence of self-regulation, empathy and moral reasoning (Kochanska et al. 2001), and children's improved capacity to use language to solve conflicts (Baillargeon et al. 2007, Côté et al. 2006, Deynoot-Schaub & Riksen-Walraven 2006, Gilliom et al. 2002, Rubin et al. 2003, Shaw et al. 2003, Tremblay 2004). After 30 months, the number of children's negative interactions decreases and their positive interactions increase in number (Deynoot-Schaub & Riksen-Walraven 2006, Vaughn et al. 2003). This decline is most apparent for girls such that, although the genders have similar rates of aggression up to 3 years of age, thereafter it becomes less common for girls (Loeber & Hay 1997).

Thus, reasonably high rates of uncooperative and aggressive behaviours are normal prior to 3 years of age, but become less common after that age (Côté et al. 2006, Hay et al. 2004, Schaeffer et al. 2003, Shaw et al. 2003). Nevertheless, roughly 10–15% still have moderate rates of aggression, with as many as 60% of those 3-year-olds with *severe* antisocial behaviours maintaining these high rates into the early school years and beyond (Campbell 1995, Campbell et al. 2000).

Almost all behaviours are functional at some time and in some contexts. Therefore, demanding though certain child behaviours can be, they do not constitute a 'problem' unless they:

- are part of a constellation of difficult behaviours spanning oppositionality, negative mood and aggression
- persist beyond the age when they typically begin to decline
- are relatively severe, excessive or are aberrant regardless of age, such as head banging and biting oneself
- are evident in several settings
- are inappropriate in the context, and
- impair children's social functioning or educational progress (Campbell 1995, Campbell et al. 2000, Lutz et al. 2002).

The resulting disruptive acts are considered to be a problem because they violate the rights of the children performing them (by, for example, attracting a negative reputation or limiting their learning) or because they interfere with the rights or needs of surrounding people.

CONTRIBUTORS TO CHILDREN'S ANTISOCIAL BEHAVIOUR

Socialisation is the transmission of values across generations (Kochanska et al. 2003). With discipline as its tool, socialisation teaches children to distinguish right from wrong and promotes their self-control so that they can abide by these values (Smith 2004). Apart from the obvious genetic component (which seems most influential on attention skills rather than behaviours as such) (Campbell 1995), the persistence of children's behavioural problems has been attributed to four causes: characteristics of the children themselves, social disadvantage, family distress and parenting behaviours (or disciplinary styles).

Child characteristics

With respect to children's qualities that cause the persistence of antisocial behaviour, most of the research has focused on their temperament. You might find it useful to think of this as children's 'emotional temperature'—that is, how readily and how hotly they react emotionally to events (Wakenshaw 2002). Children have been variously described, for example, as inhibited or fearful versus bold, as emotionally placid versus irritable and highly reactive, or as flexible versus inflexible. More recently, however, it has become clear that the persistence of behavioural difficulties is not due to children's temperament as such (Aguilar et al. 2000), but whether they learn to regulate their feelings (Eisenberg et al. 2005). In turn, an impairment in regulation of their feelings is a result of parenting quality. The only temperamental quality that remains influential is that children who are irritable, emotional or reactive experience most benefits from warm and responsive discipline (Belsky et al. 1998, Letcher et al. 2004, Shaw et al. 2000).

A second quality of children assumed to affect their behaviour is their overall cognitive abilities and language skills. However, these have less influence on their behaviours than does the presence of childhood aggression (Loeber & Hay 1997) and family adversity (Campbell 1995).

Social disadvantage

Family risk is a more powerful predictor of persistent behavioural problems than is child temperament (Aguilar et al. 2000, Campbell et al. 1991a). Given that everyone starts life with the propensity for aggression, those who are most likely to persist in their antisocial behaviour are boys brought up in disadvantaged socioeconomic and family circumstances (Belsky et al. 1998, Campbell & Ewing 1990, Côté et al. 2006, Fergusson et al. 2005, Miller-Lewis et al. 2006, O'Leary et al. 1999, Romano et al. 2005, Rubin et al. 2003, Shaw et al. 2003, Tremblay 2004).

However, while initial levels of children's aggressive behaviour are affected by their family's socioeconomic status, these problems persist only in the face of insensitive, unresponsive and harsh parenting (Campbell et al. 1991a, 1991b, Diener et al. 2003, McFadyen-Ketchum et al. 1996, National Institute of Child Health and Human Development (NICHD) Early Child Care Research Network 2005b, Parke et al. 2004, Petterson & Albers 2001, Qi & Kaiser 2003). This negative style of parenting is common when parents lack support both within and outside their families (Coolahan et al. 2002, Meyers 1999).

Family distress

Parenting quality declines in families with high levels of conflict, frequent stressful life events and a low degree of social support, when parents themselves display antisocial behaviour and when mothers in particular have low levels of educational attainment and emotional difficulties (Aguilar et al. 2000, Campbell 1995, Campbell et al. 1991a, 1991b, 2000, Smith & Farrington 2004). These stressors cause parents to withdraw, thus becoming unavailable and less nurturant in their parenting which, in turn, leads to a deterioration in their children's emotional, behavioural and academic adjustment (Ackerman et al. 2002, Aguilar et al. 2000, Campbell 1995, Campbell et al. 1991a, 1991b, Dearing et al. 2006, Sturge-Apple et al. 2006).

Disciplinary styles

Thus, the abiding conclusion is that it is not children's characteristics, socioeconomic disadvantage or family distress, but parenting style that determines whether children's antisocial behaviour improves or persists (Aguilar et al. 2000, Belsky et al. 1998, Campbell 1995, Shaw et al. 2000, Smith & Farrington 2004). Mothers' responsiveness can cause angry infants to cooperate (Kochanska et al. 2005) and render ordinarily non-conformist children as cooperative as their more typically well-behaved counterparts (Parpal & Maccoby 1985). In contrast, parents who employ a controlling, hostile and rejecting style of discipline fail to teach their children self-regulatory skills and prosocial means of solving problems, resulting in children's escalating and ongoing antisocial behaviour (Coldwell et al. 2006, Côté et al. 2006, Fergusson et al. 2005, Miller-Lewis et al. 2006, O'Leary et al. 1999, Romano et al. 2005, Rubin et al. 2003, Shaw et al. 2003, Tremblay 2004). The evidence for this effect is detailed in Chapter 2. The next task here is to describe the range of disciplinary styles. Although most adults are familiar with a rewards-and-punishment style of discipline, this is only one of many potential disciplinary styles common across cultures (see Table I.1).

TABLE I.1 The four styles of discipline		
	Warm, responsive, high support for children	**Rejecting, unresponsive, low support for children**
High expectations	Egalitarian, guidance	Controlling, authoritarian
Undemanding	Indulgent, permissive	Disengaged, neglectful

Source: Adapted from Maccoby and Martin (1983, p. 39).

Controlling discipline

Also known as power assertive or authoritarian discipline, controlling discipline values child obedience to adult authority (Brenner & Fox 1999). Controlling parents tend to have unrealistically high expectations of children that are not balanced by responsiveness to the children (Maccoby & Martin 1983). They typically spend little time in nurturing activities, such as reading to their children (Brenner & Fox 1999).

To achieve compliance, this style employs both psychological and behavioural control. *Psychological* control intrudes into the emotional life of children and pressures them to conform by invalidating and shaming them and by manipulating the parent–child relationship through guilt, threats of the withdrawal of love, and constraining the child's interactions with others (Barber 1996). Psychological control can extend to attempts by parents to control even their children's personal habits such as eating, toileting and sleeping, by imposing restrictive routines and regimented schedules. This intrusive form of control reflects the adults' rather than the children's needs and stifles children's autonomy and self-expression. It is associated with less warmth towards children and with actively restrictive disciplinary strategies, such as excessive demands, hostility and the use of threats and criticism (Barber 1996, Coolahan et al. 2002).

A second form of control is *behavioural*. This uses rewards and punishment to pressure children to comply with parents' expectations. Although less detrimental than psychological control, this too is risky for child development and for the parent–child relationship, as discussed in Chapter 2.

Egalitarian discipline (guidance)

Adults employing this style of discipline are flexible and responsive to children's needs. They accept children, offer mutual emotional warmth and engage children in making joint decisions through self-assertion, explanation and negotiation (Brenner & Fox 1999, Coolahan et al. 2002, Grolnick 2003, Grolnick & Ryan 1989). They emphasise proactive discipline, providing a structure that encourages prosocial behaviour (Socolar et al. 1997). They maintain clear expectations of children's behaviour, but the obligation is considered to be reciprocal: parents believe that they are obliged to respond to children's needs and reasonable requests, while requiring children to behave in ways that consider others (Maccoby & Martin 1983).

In terms of reactive discipline, when children act thoughtlessly, adults guide them to correct their behaviour, without using punishments. Low on psychological control or intrusiveness into children's lives, egalitarian adults encourage children's independence and individuality.

For many decades, this approach has been known as an authoritative style but, because that label is easily confused with the controlling or *authoritarian* style, I prefer to call it *egalitarian*. This means that adults and children are considered to have equal rights, although obviously different roles. Even so, the word egalitarian itself is unfamiliar to many, as a result of which throughout this book I usually refer to this method as the *guidance* approach.

No-nonsense discipline

An in-between pattern has recently been described for impoverished families from minority cultures (McGroder 2000). Having qualities of both the controlling and guidance approaches, the no-nonsense style places restrictions on children but, nevertheless, its focus on compliance is seen as nurturing and a necessary response to dangerous environments (Campbell et al. 2000, McGroder 2000). While having fewer detrimental emotional effects than the controlling style, no-nonsense parenting can produce rebellion in adolescents once they are able to escape their parents' strictures.

Indulgent discipline

Indulgent parents may be responsive to their children, but have few expectations, offer few guidelines about their behaviour, and do not follow through on directives (Brenner & Fox 1999, Coolahan et al. 2002). This style can arise from parents' romantic notion of childhood as a time that should not be corrupted by adult interference. Children whose permissive parents make few demands for mature behaviour tend to lack impulse control and self-reliance and have low self-efficacy, which is a sense of being able to influence events in one's life (Maccoby & Martin 1983).

Disengaged discipline

Disengaged or neglectful parents tend to be underinvolved with their children, are indifferent to them and emotionally detached. They are inattentive and minimally responsive towards their children (Brenner & Fox 1999). Parents are preoccupied with their own issues and fail to distinguish their needs from their children's.

This style can be seen when parents have tried and failed to curb their children's antisocial behaviour and have now given up. These parents often convey negativism about their children and respond in kind to their children's disruptive behaviour, bickering with them and becoming aggressive in response to the children's aggression (Maccoby & Martin 1983).

Except for extreme neglect, disengaged parenting is probably the least pure disciplinary style, commonly alternating with exasperation that may escalate into coercion, often comprising capricious restrictions and sanctions. The damage done by the neglect can thus be compounded by the deleterious effects of coercive discipline (Maccoby & Martin 1983).

CONCLUSION

Alfie Kohn's (1999) quote at the beginning of this introduction is referring to the notion that the use of rewards and punishments (i.e. consequences) seems like such 'common sense' that we fail even to question it. The disciplinary styles just described, however, differ fundamentally in their endorsement of consequences. This book describes a guidance approach, which teaches rather than employs rewards or punishments, on the understanding that this will promote considerate behaviour in children.

In advocating a system of discipline without consequences, it might seem that you would need to adopt entirely new practices. However, a guidance approach is grounded in what you already know about teaching children all other developmental skills. When assisting toddlers to learn to walk, we do not punish them for falling over: we encourage them, celebrate their achievements, accept their mistakes as natural, and help them to persist in the face of setbacks so that they become more skilful. So it is with learning to behave thoughtfully.

The purpose of Part I, then, is to set out in Chapter 1 the ideas that underpin a guidance approach. Understanding these ideas and practices will ensure that, when confronted by children's thoughtless behaviour, you do not have to make hasty decisions on the run, but instead can give a reasoned response that reinstates order—and thus meets your immediate needs—at the same time as ensuring that children acquire and apply the principles of prosocial behaviour, both at the time and subsequently. Chapter 2 then presents the evidence for the superiority of guidance compared with controlling discipline. This information provides the foundation for the preventive and interventive practices presented in the remainder of the book.

chapter 1

Contrasting ideas about discipline

'It is widely understood that people learn by example. But adults who are respectful of children are not just modeling a skill or behavior; they are meeting the emotional needs of those children, thereby helping to create the psychological conditions to treat others respectfully.'

KOHN (2000, p. 5)

This book presents a system for guiding children's behaviour that uses no rewards or punishments (which are sometimes referred to as *consequences*) to control children's behaviour, but instead *teaches* children to act thoughtfully, using the same skills that we would employ to teach them to read and write or balance on climbing equipment. Dispensing with rewards such as praise, it instead teaches children to recognise their own achievements so that they strive to become more competent, rather than to earn an external reward. It requires considerate behaviour, but regards mistakes as inevitable and as occasions for teaching rather than punishment. Instead of attempting to control children from the outside by imposing consequences, it teaches and supports children to control themselves.

Gartrell (2003) has termed this a guidance approach to discipline. Although this is a recent label for the approach, the underlying ideas have existed in education for over a century, since the days of John Dewey, Maria Montessori and Friedrich Froebel, the originator of kindergartens.

This guidance approach can be contrasted with a controlling form of discipline in which adults attempt to make children behave in ways we like by giving them rewards such as praise, special treats, or access to a favourite activity. The second tool of controlling discipline is the use of punishments to entice children to change their behaviour. For ethical reasons, there are not many punishments available to parents or educators. Nevertheless, the few in wide practice include reprimands, denying children a favourite activity, and imposing time out (i.e. requiring children to sit apart from others until their behaviour improves). Although some accept the additional practice of hitting children to discipline them, I consider such violence as unnecessary, unproductive and unethical—and certainly inexcusable in professional care or educational settings.

The core distinction between the two disciplinary methods is that controlling approaches use consequences, whereas guidance does not. Behind this variation in practice are some fundamental differences in beliefs about children and their behaviour, the goals of discipline, the effectiveness of external controls, and the role of adults. Understanding these underlying assumptions will help in adopting guidance practices.

BELIEFS ABOUT CHILDREN

Adults' beliefs about children, their behaviour and how they learn are the single most significant influence on the quality of care that they deliver to children (Abbott-Shim et al. 2000, Clarke-Stewart et al. 2002, Maxwell et al. 2001, Vartuli 1999). Our beliefs colour everything that we do with children, both in terms of their education and also when disciplining their behaviour.

With respect to children and their behaviour, differences in beliefs centre on three aspects: the nature of children; judgments about children's skilfulness; and a time orientation.

Beliefs about children's nature

Through the centuries, the human race has evolved in its beliefs about children. From the fourth to the nineteenth centuries, children were considered to be expendable. Infanticide was common until the 1850s, when it was replaced by abandonment into foundling homes, servitude or to wet nurses. These practices resulted in the deaths of more babies than did the combined plague epidemics (Grille 2005). After this era, parents began to keep their children closer, but only under conditions of strict control. Children were seen as 'little devils' whose evil impulses needed to be suppressed. Adult control was imposed through the use of beatings and other punishments, while tenderness was said to 'spoil' children.

By Victorian times, attitudes had softened and, although children were seen as bothersome, at least they were no longer considered to be malevolent. Although severe corporal punishment enforced inappropriate expectations for children's behaviour, some nurturing practices such as breastfeeding were promoted and restrictive swaddling discouraged. Nevertheless, babies were to be fed, toileted and put to bed according to regimented schedules, a practice that survives in some quarters today, often masquerading as a professed 'need' of babies for 'routine'.

Remnants of our earlier suspicions about children remain today. As illustrated in Figure 1.1, their behaviour is regarded through a moral lens that dichotomises 'good' (which equals conforming and obedient) and 'bad' behaviour. Adults are advised not to indulge children's needs for fear of creating dependence. And whereas we no longer think that children are to be seen but not heard, we nevertheless do not take their ideas very seriously (Grille 2005).

FIGURE 1.1 Forms of discipline arising from beliefs about children's nature

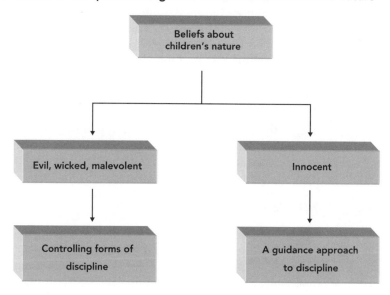

Although today hardly anyone actually believes that children have inbuilt immoral tendencies that have to be driven out of them, we have some habits of language that are based on negative images of children, such as:

- We describe children as 'attention seeking' and 'manipulative', and claim that they are being deliberately disruptive—sometimes even 'to get at us'.
- We say that children 'have got to learn', by which we mean that their present needs are immaterial. Their behaviour has to be suppressed so that they acquire the skills needed to conform in the next setting. My response to this is that although they might have to learn to drive a car in mid-adolescence, this does not imply that we should start teaching them as preschoolers.
- We claim that we have to 'come down hard' on a disruptive behaviour because otherwise it will persist. This assertion reflects an underlying belief that children are not motivated to develop and grow in competence and therefore we must force them.
- We say we have to be firm, have limits and set boundaries because 'if you give children an inch, they'll take a mile'. This signals a basic distrust of children's motives. Rather than imposing limits for children's 'own good', a guidance approach believes that children need structure, not limits or rules, a distinction that will be explained in Chapter 10.
- We tell parents that they must not give into (or 'spoil') their children because 'they'll have won, and you'll have lost'.

Similarly sour views of children are expressed by educators whose credentials might suggest a more informed opinion, such as the following (which I have embellished with italics):

- 'Kids, when they are little, are—in a way—*sort of nuts*! They are not born reasonable and unselfish; they are born *unreasonable* and *selfish*' (Phelan 2003, p. 16).

- 'When students are not given the limits they need, *they will act up* in order *to make the adults around them take notice*' (Canter & Canter 2001, p. 7).
- 'Children are not born good; they have to be disciplined; otherwise they *are a threat to the rest of society*' (Boyson, in Holland 2004, p. 75).[1]
- 'If students are given the freedom to do nothing, that is most likely what they will do' (Wolfgang et al. 1999, p. 173).
- 'Today's youth is rotten to the core; it is evil, godless, and lazy … It will never be able to preserve our culture' (Watzlawick et al. 1974, p. 33).

It would be comforting if these negative views of young people were all, like the last one, written on clay tablets over 3000 years ago but, as you can see, the quotes are far more recent. They clearly assume that children will not choose to put in effort to learn or act thoughtfully unless inflicted with pain and discomfort (Kohn 1996).

Beliefs about children's skilfulness

The second element of beliefs about children relates to their developmental capacities. This feeds into our view of children as learners and, in turn, contributes to our ideas about how they should be taught. The philosopher, John Locke, saw children as bereft of useful knowledge, as *blank slates*, irrational and ignorant (Lee 2001, Montgomery 2003). According to this view, children need shaping, training and controlling—or, in other words, *schooling*. Guided by this top-down model of teaching, the task of adults is to fill children with the information and skills that we determine will be useful to them and to society. To achieve this, we must ensure orderly (i.e. passive) behaviour so that children can absorb the information we impart. Once again, a controlling system of discipline is implied, as shown in Figure 1.2.

FIGURE 1.2 Forms of discipline arising from beliefs about children's skilfulness

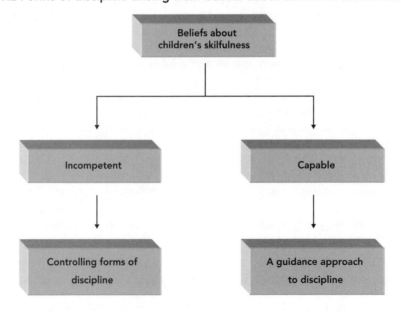

---

1. Sir Rhodes Boyson was an ex-school principal and British Conservative MP advising the government on educational policy, culminating in *The Conservative Education Reform Act* of 1988 (Holland 2004).

Although, in recent times, children have been seen to be more active learners, at the heart of both the passive and active conceptions of children's skills is the notion that children are only becoming adult—in fact, only *becoming human*. They are not yet complete and therefore do not warrant respect (Buckingham 2000, Lee 2001). In comparison, adults (human *beings*) are responsible and fully competent (i.e. stable, complete, 'grown up') and therefore worthy of respect (see Table 1.1). Yet a guidance approach does not regard adults and children as fundamentally different and does not believe that chronological age is an adequate criterion for distributing dignity and worth. It recognises that, like children, adults are still growing towards being all that they can be. Therefore, still being incomplete is not a reason to discriminate against children, as both adults and children have yet to finish their personal growth.

TABLE 1.1 Practical implications of views of childhood		
	Children as threats to social order	**Children as innocents**
Children as empty vessels/ blank slates	Children are untrustworthy They need socialising Adults must censor children's experiences and restrict their movement to prevent them from acting antisocially Top-down teaching model that is focused on training, rather than on education Controlling discipline	Innocence makes children vulnerable Children are incomplete, still *becoming* human Censorship is needed to protect them from premature adulthood Child-focused but adult-directed curriculum (adult is a 'gardener') Mixed disciplinary styles
Children as competent	Children are blameworthy They must take legal and moral responsibility for their mistakes Top-down teaching model Autocratic discipline	Childhood is neutral: children are neither good nor bad, just human *beings* Child-centred (constructivist) teaching model (adult is a facilitator) Egalitarian discipline (guidance)

A time orientation

The third difference between conceptions of childhood is their perspective in time—that is, whether adults focus on children's future or their present needs. The first perspective (often espoused by politicians) is that children are worth investing in, because they are 'our future'. This future focus leads to the concept of adults as gardeners—intervening at each stage of growth, taking deliberate control over the types of plants (children) that flourish, training and feeding them to 'maximise their potential'. The focus is not on children's present needs but on their future. This means, for example, that when they protest an adult directive, their objections can be discounted. What is important is shaping their behaviour for the future ('He's *got* to learn …').

An opposite time perspective looks to the past to generate anxiety—if not episodic hysteria—about the apparent impending disappearance of childhood. It is assumed that children face more serious and varied risks from society at large than in the past (although to the extent that we can judge, it is likely that personal threats to children are, if anything, declining in industrialised societies). Based on a concept of threatened childhood innocence, this view is captured by lay people and eminent educators alike, the latter including David Elkind (2001) who mourns the speed at which children today grow up, pressured by media into consumerism and by ambitious parents seeking to skill them up to compete in a market economy.

However, this nostalgia overlooks the fact that childhood is not a universal or unitary phenomenon. It is experienced differently in suburban Adelaide, Arnhem Land, metropolitan London and the slums of Calcutta. It is experienced differently today from a century ago and, no doubt, a century hence. Thus, Buckingham (2000) believes that what commentators are mourning when they decry the loss of childhood is in fact the decline in adults' *control* over childhood, over what children can experience. Thus, the issue is not one of the loss of childhood itself, only of the change in childhood as we in privileged societies have known it.

A guidance perspective on children

A guidance approach sees adults as caring facilitators who trust children to direct themselves and make appropriate choices when given the autonomy and support to do so. In terms of their *nature*, it believes that children are trustworthy. It anticipates that children will behave well when treated well and poorly when treated poorly. It believes that they strive to please their parents and other adults whom they care about, that they want to surprise us and have us be proud for them. Faced with the choice between thinking of children as inherently wicked and inherently good, given the lack of evidence either way, this perspective chooses to believe in humanity—that people are just as capable of behaving altruistically as they are of behaving selfishly (Kohn 1996).

In terms of their *developmental capacities*, it sees children as skilled and trusts that they are innately driven to grow and become all they can (Raskin & Rogers 2005). This view of children as competent underpins both a constructivist approach to their education and egalitarian discipline. It sees the adult's role as being rather like the conductor of an orchestra (Banks 2005). Although the conductor is a skilled musician and has responsibility for the functioning of the entire ensemble, the individual musicians know their instruments better than does the conductor. Similarly, while adults have an overview of the skills that will be useful for children to acquire and will know how the group needs to function, over time the children will come to know themselves better than will an outsider. This view trusts children to exercise self-direction, rather than imposing controls on them.

Finally, a guidance approach respects who children are *now*, not for what they may become in adult life. It upholds that human beings are of equal worth regardless of any distinguishing features, including age.

BELIEFS ABOUT CHILDREN'S BEHAVIOUR

A sour view of children feeds directly into a similarly negative view of their behaviour. This can be contrasted with a neutral attitude to their developmental errors such as losing their balance when learning to walk, scribbling instead of drawing, or making spelling mistakes. A grade two teacher who notes that a child has misspelled a word is not likely to define that error as 'naughty' or 'misbehaviour'. The teacher is even less likely to correct the error with a tirade such as:

> 'How many times have I told you that for the sound ee, i comes before e except after c. Now look how you've spelt "recieve". Now I want you to go over there, sit

on that chair and think about what you have done wrong. When you're ready to apologise, come over and tell me how you should have spelt it. Then, after today, I don't want to have to talk to you about this again. Am I making myself clear?'

Yet when children act thoughtlessly on occasion, adults will often define that as 'misbehaviour', as inappropriate, naughty or unacceptable. In other words, adults are more likely to become moralistic about behavioural than developmental errors. This contrast is shown in Table 1.2. It is illustrated by the difference between how we respond when children are learning to ride a bicycle without training wheels, versus those who are having difficulty sharing. We would realise that learning to balance on a bike would need many lessons and much practice and would naturally entail many mistakes. But when children are having trouble sharing, we believe that they should not need to be taught how to solve disputes, should never get into conflict with each other, and should be able to solve conflict without rancour. In keeping with these beliefs, we often say such things as, 'I shouldn't have to come over there and sort this out for you ... I shouldn't have to speak to you about this again ... If I have to come over there one more time, I'll take the toy off both of you.'

TABLE 1.2 Assumptions about developmental versus behavioural errors	
Behavioural errors	**Developmental errors**
Children are trying to annoy us; their errors are deliberate	Children try to get things right; their errors are accidental
Children should not explore limits: they should obey them	Learning requires exploration
Mistakes should not happen	Errors are inevitable
When children have behavioural difficulties, *they* should change to meet expectations	When children have learning difficulties, we need to adjust the setting to make it easier for them to be successful

As depicted earlier in Figure 1.1, this moralistic attitude to children or their behavioural mistakes almost inexorably leads us down the path of controlling disciplinary measures. In contrast, a guidance approach realises that behavioural mistakes are inevitable. Children are not seen in terms of good or evil, while their behaviour is regarded as natural expressions of human impulses. When they act thoughtlessly, the response should be to teach more skilful behaviour, rather than to punish them for natural childhood mistakes, as that would amount to punishing them for *being* children.

GOALS OF DISCIPLINE

Another difference between the controlling and guidance approaches is what they aim to achieve. The controlling approach wants children to comply with adult directives and, indeed, defines 'non-compliance' as a behavioural problem. However, there are three reasons not to teach children to do as they are told. First, individual children are endangered when we teach them that they must obey adults, as they will not learn that they can resist adults who are enticing them into an abusive relationship (Briggs &

McVeity 2000). Second, surrounding children are made vulnerable to the group bullying that can occur when children who have been trained to follow others go along with a dominant peer who suggests victimising a less powerful child. Third, whole communities become unsafe when people do as they are told. The defence of most perpetrators of genocide is that they were 'only following orders'. More crimes against humanity have been committed in the name of obedience than out of rebellion (Milgram 1963).

Therefore, a guidance approach does not want children to be compliant, but instead aims to teach them to act considerately. This entails thinking about how their actions affect others or, when they have not been able to do this in advance, to listen when they receive feedback about a negative effect of their actions, and adjust how they are behaving. To achieve this, they will need the following four qualities:

1. Children need an *independent sense of right and wrong*. They need to act considerately because it is the right thing to do, rather than because they are worried at being detected and punished for misdeeds. They need to behave thoughtfully, not out of fear of retribution nor even because they are being supervised, but because they know that it is the right way to act.
2. Children need to learn to *regulate their emotions* so that their outbursts do not disturb those around them. Their ability to control their emotions allows them to learn to resolve conflict peaceably (Rubin et al. 2003); but, even more importantly, children's ability to control their emotions allows them to cope with setbacks in life and ensures that their emotions nourish their lives, rather than impairing their wellbeing. This is the essence of resilience.
3. Given that our species lives and works in groups, we need to guide children to *cooperate* so that the group can complete its tasks and all members can have their needs met.
4. We need to imbue in children a sense of *potency* or *self-efficacy*—that is, a sense that they can make a difference to their corner of the world and, even more centrally, can control their own actions and feelings by staying in command of what they think.

Rewards and punishments cannot teach consideration of others because they focus children's minds on what will happen *to them* if they behave in a particular way: 'Will I get caught? Will I get into trouble? Will I be sent to time out? Will I be told that I'm good? Will I get a special treat?' and so on. This focus on what *they* get from their behaviour distracts them from thinking about how their actions affect *others*.

LOCUS OF CAUSALITY

This rather clumsy term refers to where we locate the cause of our personal wellbeing. If we believe that others 'make' us happy or miserable, or that we cannot be happy until the stars, luck or destiny decree it, we have judged that events outside of us cause our emotional wellbeing, in which case we are said to have an *external* locus of causality.

Controlling discipline believes that outside consequences determine how individuals act. One person delivers consequences to make others change their behaviour. This places control of individuals in the hands of someone outside themselves. Therefore, this style of discipline is said to have an external locus of causality. The problem it generates is that, when we believe that we can control others but our efforts do not work (which a guidance approach finds entirely predictable), we blame *them* and become increasingly coercive (Donovan et al. 2000).

In contrast, a guidance approach says that no one can control others. We delude ourselves if we think it is possible. This is because individuals' actions are triggered by their own needs, not by external consequences. Therefore, it argues that we all have an *internal* locus of causality. In support of this claim, it asserts that if people were controlled by external rewards and punishments, our prisons would be empty; no one ever would give up a job with a high salary in pursuit of greater personal satisfaction; no one would perform voluntary work in the community; and children would never answer an adult's exasperated question, 'What did you do that for? Didn't you know you would get into trouble?' by responding, 'Yes, I knew that. But, gee, it was worth it.' These examples tell us that people are controlled from within, not by others.

It is true that individuals will calculate the potential risks and rewards of acting in particular ways. But if their need is great enough, they will perform a behaviour despite these risks. This means that if they are determined enough, there is virtually nothing we can do from the outside to *force* them to change their minds. (As you will see in coming chapters, we will be able to guide children to make better decisions for themselves, but without using coercion.) Furthermore, even if individuals *can* be manipulated externally, this does not mean that they *should* because, as you will read in Chapter 2, rewards and punishment carry many risks.

ADULTS' STATUS

Believing that no one *can* control anyone else (because human beings do not work that way), and that no one *should* control anyone else (because that is not ethical), might seem to leave you having to tolerate children's thoughtless behaviour. This is far from the truth. A child-focused approach gives children freedom, but not licence (Mintz 2003, Rogers & Freiberg 1994).

It may also seem that, deprived of your power to *make* children behave thoughtfully, you have nothing left to ensure considerate behaviour. However, this belief arises from a misconception that *either* adults are in control *or* children will walk all over them. Instead, guidance replaces bossing with leadership, or being the orchestra conductor. This may seem to give you less power, but in fact you will have more *influence*. Without coercion to rebel against, children will value your good opinion of them and will choose to act thoughtfully, rather than responding to force.

On very rare occasions, a guidance approach will still, however, employ protective force. Just as you would protect children from running onto a road, so too you would protect them from another's aggression and protect the aggressor from developing a negative reputation. Nevertheless, this protective force differs from coercive force, whose aim is merely to gain compliance.

CONCLUSION

This chapter has questioned some of the assumptions behind a controlling style of discipline. When you compare the contrasting ideas as summarised in Table 1.3, you might recognise that you believe the ideas in the right-hand column (corresponding to a guidance approach), but when responding to children's disruptive behaviour, find yourself using controlling methods. This is almost inevitable, given that most of us were brought up under a controlling system of discipline and have little professional training

TABLE 1.3 Summary of differences between the controlling and guidance approaches	
Controlling discipline	**Guidance approach**
Distrusts children	Trusts children
Behavioural mistakes should not happen and should be punished	Mistakes are inevitable and call for prevention by meeting children's needs and for teaching more skilful behaviour
Aims for compliance and obedience	Teaches considerate behaviour
Children's behaviour can be controlled by outsiders (an external locus of causality)	Children's behaviour is governed by their needs (an internal locus of causality)
Adult is a boss, with coercive power	Adult is a leader with expertise and protective power

in an alternative. In fact, as mentioned in the introductory section, the controlling approach is so widely endorsed in so many cultures that it can appear to be 'common sense'. Yet 'common sense' told our forebears that the world was flat. Even though this supposition was unanimous, that still did not make it correct. Similarly, even when beliefs about the use of rewards and punishments to control children's behaviour are widely held, this does not prove that they are true.

While exposing these beliefs to scrutiny might cause us to question them, changing practice also generates a change in belief (Maxwell et al. 2001). The purpose of this book, then, is to describe alternative practices that both honour individual children's needs and still require them to consider others. The solutions suggested by a guidance approach may already be familiar to you, as you will be using them in other aspects of your life, but you might not have thought to use them for children's disruptive behaviour because the dogma of a controlling approach has directed you to be coercive rather than conciliatory.

SUGGESTED FURTHER READING

Biddulph S 1998 *The secret of happy children*, 3rd edn. Harper Collins, Sydney.
Kohn A 2005 *Unconditional parenting: moving from rewards and punishments to love and reason.* Atria Books, New York.
Porter L 2006 *Children are people too: a parent's guide to young children's behaviour*, 4th edn. East Street Publications, Adelaide.

chapter 2

Evidence about disciplinary practices

> 'Any approach to discipline is judged to be a failure not only on the obvious criterion that it fails to establish and affect appropriate standards of behavior, but also if, in establishing such standards, it does so primarily by teaching children to obey rules rather than to make reasoned judgments about what actions are desirable, and about how actually to decide to act in those desirable ways.'
>
> COVALESKIE (1992, p. 175)

A guidance approach has almost as long a history as rewards-and-punishment systems, with evidence of its effectiveness amassing for 50 years. This chapter details that evidence.

EFFECTIVENESS OF PRACTICES

Any disciplinary practices must be effective: above all, they must *work*. This means that a disruption ceases. But it also means more than that. Ultimately, any truly optimal style of discipline must lead to its own demise (Maccoby & Martin 1983): children should out-grow the need for adult supervision. For methods to be thus effective, they must achieve the following outcomes:

- As well as ceasing in the present, disruptions in general and this particular disruption need to be prevented in future.
- The children involved should learn something positive during the process of correction such as how to solve disputes or manage their emotions—not how to

avoid detection, to tell lies to get out of trouble, to deny responsibility, or to blame someone else.

- There must be no unintended emotional side effects on the child, such as feeling intimidated or fearful, or being seen by peers as troublesome and therefore as someone to avoid or victimise.
- Surrounding children must continue to feel safe about how *they* would be treated if in future they were to make a mistake.
- Adults have to feel that they are abiding by their principles and doing a good job.
- The methods that we use must convey our values.
- The adult–child relationship must suffer no harm as a result of how a disruption was handled. Children should be equally willing to interact with you after a corrective intervention, not least because you can have no influence on them if they avoid you.

In other words, we must evaluate the effectiveness of disciplinary practices not only in light of their impact on the target behaviour, but also considering their effects on the recipient, onlooking children, the adults who correct the behaviour, and the relationship between the children and adults.

RESEARCH ABOUT THE EFFECTS OF GUIDANCE

It is not enough to demonstrate that a controlling style can reduce children's non-compliance when programs are directed by doctoral-level researchers and academic psychologists: behavioural interventions have to be practicable in natural settings (Carr 1997, Ervin et al. 2001, Nelson et al. 1999). On that score, parenting using controlling discipline does improve children's aggression and parents' confidence (e.g. Bryant et al. 1999, Connell et al. 1997, Leung et al. 2003, Sanders 1999, Sanders et al. 2000). However, such studies do not examine whether guidance methods would achieve these same results. For this we need comparative research, of which every single study has shown a guidance approach to produce superior results across all domains of children's development.

Behavioural outcomes

Parents' lack of warmth and restrictive control of children results in children's increased aggression, defiance and uncooperativeness over time (Aguilar et al. 2000, Campbell & Ewing 1990, Crockenberg & Litman 1990, Denham et al. 2000, Donovan et al. 2000, McFadyen-Ketchum et al. 1996, Spieker et al. 1999), particularly for those with early high rates of behavioural problems (Denham et al. 2000).

In contrast, parents who provide positive support, structure and emotional warmth (which characterise a guidance form of discipline) tend to produce children who are increasingly cooperative, self-controlled and independent (Aunola & Nurmi 2005, Baumrind 1967, 1971, Denham et al. 2000, Feldman & Klein 2003, Kochanska et al. 2005, Miller-Lewis et al. 2006, Parpal & Maccoby 1985, Rubin et al. 2003, Smith et al. 2004). Toddlers with sensitive, responsive and supportive parents develop more constructive responses to frustration (Calkins & Johnson 1998, Gilliom et al. 2002, Kochanska et al. 2000). Their improved skills at self-regulation lead to fewer aggressive and destructive behaviours, improved cooperation with others and more appropriate self-assertion (i.e. assertiveness that does not escalate into defiance) (Crockenberg & Litman 1990,

Donovan et al. 2000, Gilliom et al. 2002).

These findings have been replicated in centre-based care (Feldman & Klein 2003) and in schools (Rutter 1983). My research in centre-based care found that caregivers using controlling methods endured far higher rates of behavioural disruptions than did those using a guidance approach (Porter 1999).

Morality

More than merely enforcing compliance, discipline aims to teach moral behaviour and to develop children's empathy and moral reasoning (or 'conscience') (Kochanska et al. 2003). In terms of *acting* morally, children are more willing to abide voluntarily by their parents' guidelines when these are not imposed externally, but are self-generated or independently endorsed by the children (Grusec & Goodnow 1994, Kochanska 2002a). This is known as committed compliance, which is the first step towards self-regulation and the integration of parents' values (Kochanska 2002a). *Emotionally*, children are more willing to cooperate when they enjoy interacting with their parents (Kochanska 2002a, 2002b, Kochanska & Aksan 2004, Kochanska et al. 1999, 2005, Laible & Thompson 2002).

With respect to moral *reasoning*, children are more willing to listen and will develop more sophisticated moral thinking when their parents reason and negotiate with them, rather than deliver lectures about their behaviour (Walker et al. 2000). The result is that children whose parents use guidance develop empathy and thus focus on the effects of their behaviour on others, rather than attending to the costs to themselves of violating rules (Maccoby & Martin 1983).

In contrast, controlling discipline may achieve immediate compliance, but at the cost of undermining children's moral reasoning by fostering an external locus of causality ('I'm only doing this because they made me'), anger towards and rejection of the disciplinarian, and rejection of their parents' standards (Kochanska et al. 2003). In short, children who comply with prohibitions simply because they are being supervised or are fearful of reprisals do not develop self-regulatory skills and therefore continue to require adults to oversee their conduct (Kochanska et al. 2001, 2003).

Learning

In terms of their learning styles, adults' controlling discipline generates in children less initiative and persistence (Baumrind 1967, 1971, Grolnick et al. 1984), declining intrinsic motivation (Deci et al. 1993, Leung & Kwan 1998), less engagement in learning (de Kruif et al. 2000, Kim & Mahoney 2004), and greater negativity towards school work (Dornbusch et al. 1987, Ginsberg & Bronstein 1993, Gonzalez-DeHass et al. 2005, Gottfried et al. 1994, Grolnick & Ryan 1989, Maccoby & Martin 1983, Parker et al. 1999, Paulson et al. 1998, Steinberg et al. 1989, 1992, 1994). In turn, these negative learning styles lead to declining academic and social performances (Aunola & Nurmi 2004, Chen et al. 1997, Mattanah 2001). Because parents using controlling discipline have fewer language-rich interactions with their children overall and during discipline, their children develop significantly lower language comprehension skills compared with those whose parents use reasoning and negotiation to discipline (Burchinal & Cryer 2003, Gest et al. 2004, Raviv et al. 2004, Steelman et al. 2002).

Emotional development

Emotionally, compared with children whose parents use a guidance approach, children of controlling parents are more negative, withdrawn, anxious, unhappy, and hostile when frustrated (Baumrind 1967, 1971, Ispa et al. 2004). They have a lower self-esteem (Maccoby & Martin 1983), are lonelier and more depressed (McDowell et al. 2003), and are more emotionally reactive to family adversity (Propper & Moore 2006). These negative emotional effects are particularly evident when parents use psychological control such as guilt to manipulate children (Aunola & Nurmi 2005). Parents' distress or punitive reactions to children's negative feelings teaches children to suppress emotions but, when emotionally aroused, they are more likely to vent their feelings intensely, which leads to antisocial behaviour (Eisenberg et al. 2005, Fabes et al. 2001, Grolnick et al. 1996, Kochanska et al. 2005, Rubin et al. 2003).

In contrast, children and adolescents whose parents use guidance tend to be self-confident and socially outgoing (Baumrind 1967, 1971, Ispa et al. 2004), have high self-efficacy and are better able to regulate emotions such as anger or distress (Dekovic et al. 2003, Eisenberg et al. 2005, Fabes et al. 2001, Gray & Steinberg 1999, Grolnick et al. 1996, Kochanska et al. 2005, McClun & Merrell 1998, Rubin et al. 2003, Steinberg et al. 1989, 1992, Wentzel 1994). They have a healthier emotional adjustment overall and are more resilient when facing adversity (Kaufmann et al. 2000, Propper & Moore 2006, Wyman et al. 1999).

Social outcomes

Sensitive parenting is the most significant predictor of children's social functioning across all settings and throughout the early childhood and school years (NICHD Early Child Care Research Network 2001a, 2003d, 2003b, Steelman et al. 2002). Parental guidance improves children's connectedness to or engagement with parents (Donovan et al. 2000, Ispa et al. 2004), which extends into more positive peer relationships (Russell et al. 1998). Guidance gives children experience of and teaches them the skills for social competence, such as managing their emotions, power sharing, influencing and being influenced by others, making suggestions, negotiation, compromise, collaboration, intimacy and displaying positive emotion.

In reverse, controlling interactions with parents can cause children to develop negative expectations of peers and, in turn, to engage with them in antisocial or less competent ways (Booth et al. 1994, MacKinnon-Lewis et al. 1999, McDowell et al. 2003, O'Connor 2002), including both physical and relational aggression (Casas et al. 2006, Deater-Deckard & Dodge 1997, Nelson et al. 2006). Thus, controlling discipline produces children who are more disruptive in the preschool playground and less prosocial in their peer interactions, with the result that they are less well liked by peers (Hart et al. 1992). Alternatively, passive social behaviours such as withdrawal can result from psychologically controlling parenting (Coplan et al. 2004, Rubin et al. 2002), leaving children vulnerable to being bullied (Ladd & Kochenderfer-Ladd 1998).

Conclusion: outcomes of disciplinary styles

These beneficial outcomes of a guidance approach apply across all developmental domains and all cultures, socioeconomic groupings and various family structures (Amato & Fowler 2002, Aucoin et al. 2006, Chen et al. 1997, Eamon 2001, Grolnick 2003,

Kaufmann et al. 2000, Kilgore et al. 2000, Kim et al. 1999, Nelson et al. 2006). A single exception is found in dangerous neighbourhoods, where controlling discipline may deflect adolescents from a path of delinquency (Lansford et al. 2004), perhaps because they recognise that their parents' high supervision and control reflect the desire to keep them safe, rather than being a sign of parental distrust. Even so, the beneficial effects of parental control in dangerous neighbourhoods are not uniform across all ethnic groups (Dearing 2004).

DISADVANTAGES OF PUNISHMENTS

Despite its widespread use, surprisingly little is known about the effective use of punishment in everyday settings (Johnston 1972, Lerman & Vorndran 2002). Most research has focused on animals being exposed in laboratories to electric shocks, sprays of water, blasts of air, squirts of lemon juice, unpleasant odours and physical restraint, none of which can be used with children. Moreover, to have any effect at all on behavioural rates, these punishments have to be administered immediately (within seconds), intensely and every time the behaviour occurs, which is impossible in natural settings (Holden 2002, Johnston 1972, Lerman & Vorndran 2002, Martin & Pear 2007). Instead, the only punishments available to adults for disciplining young children are verbal reprimands, withdrawal of access to a favourite activity, time out and, for some parents, smacking (or spanking), each of which has its own shortcomings.

Reprimands

In the short term, firm reprimands reduce transgressions more effectively than gentle rebukes, but they also evoke more emotional distress in children and are no more effective in teaching alternative behaviours (Pfiffner & O'Leary 1989). Stern reprimands have been found to be especially aversive within a warm parent–child relationship, possibly because they cause children to fear losing their parents' love. This fear is particularly potent for young children because they cannot yet feel two emotions at once and therefore are not aware that their parents can both be angry and love them at the same time.

Time out

Time out typically entails sitting youngsters on a chair apart from others while their behaviour settles. From a behaviourist perspective, if it allows children to escape a setting or task that they dislike, time out does not act as a punishment—that is, it will not reduce misbehaviour, and may even encourage it (Myers & Holland 2000, Sterling-Turner & Watson 1999). Meanwhile, children who are placed in time out for disruptive behaviour then receive less teaching, leading to a cycle of escalating learning difficulties and behavioural problems (Arnold 1997). As well as these theoretical objections, time out has the following practical difficulties that constrain its use (Myers & Holland 2000, Sterling-Turner & Watson 1999, Wheeler & Richey 2005):

- How do you ensure that the children in time out do not escape? Restraint is the most effective means, but that is not ethical.
- How do you prevent children from damaging the area where they have been placed?

- When do you allow them to leave—after a predetermined time has elapsed or only when they have calmed down? If the former, how can you reasonably allow them to re-enter the group when they are still disruptive? But, if the latter, what do you do when the process of calming down is prolonged?
- If the area is separate from others, how can you maintain adequate supervision and ensure that you do not forget isolated children, unintentionally confining them for extended periods?
- If the area is within easy sight, how do you avoid the public humiliation for children whose peers can see them being shamed?
- How do you avoid punished children developing a negative reputation?
- How do you help punished children resolve their sadness at being isolated? (Wiltz & Klein 2001).
- In group settings, how do you avoid onlooking peers feeling intimidated and fearful that the same thing could happen to them if they commit a misdeed?
- How can you convey an ethos of inclusion when you contradict that by excluding children of whose behaviour you disapprove?

The fact that settings which employ time out typically apply it repeatedly to the same handful of children indicates that, even if time out achieved an immediate cessation of the troublesome behaviour, it is certainly not preventing a recurrence. While in withdrawal, the children are expected to contemplate and thus learn from their transgression, but I am yet to meet any adult who actually believes that this is what they are thinking about. Instead, they are likely to be harbouring resentments and planning how to avoid being caught next time.

Physical punishment

In professional care and educational settings, physical punishment of children is unconscionable. Yet in countries where it is not illegal, it is still practised by the majority of parents (by between 79 and 94% of US parents of 3- and 4-year-olds, and 11% of parents of 5-year-olds) (Deater-Deckard & Dodge 1997, Larzelere 2000). Some parents will ask your thoughts about it, in which event the evidence presented here will equip you to give a reasoned response.

When studies focus on young children with clinical levels of disruptive behaviour, infrequent mild physical punishment accompanied by reasoning achieves improved short-term compliance and reduced aggression; but more typical children experience no positive benefits and only harmful effects, particularly when aged over 6 years, when subjected at any age to frequent use (one to three times a week) (Eamon 2001, Larzelere 2000) and when children are inhibited or fearful (Colder et al. 1997). Detrimental outcomes are most pronounced for frequent and severe physical punishment (Afifi et al. 2006, Fergusson & Lynskey 1997, Straus et al. 1997).

In the long term, this form of punishment has the following negative effects on all domains of children's functioning:

- *Behavioural* effects of physical punishment include escalating aggression, defiance and antisocial acts during childhood and adolescence (Aucoin et al. 2006, Colder et al. 1997, Côté et al. 2006, Eamon 2001, Gershoff 2002a, Larzelere 2000, McCord 1997, Nelson et al. 2006, Straus et al. 1997) and into adulthood (Afifi et al. 2006).

- *Morally*, physically punished children comply simply to avoid consequences and thus fail to develop an internal locus of causality. This results in impaired conscience development, or the failure to internalise parents' values (Gershoff 2002a).
- Children who are subjected to physical punishment show impairments in *social skills* such as social problem solving, with lowered peer acceptance and increased peer dislike. These effects probably come about because their experience of a hostile relationship with their controlling parents causes them to develop similarly negative expectations of peers (Domitrovich & Bierman 2001).
- Physically punished children show diminished *connectedness* to and trust in punitive adults (Bender et al. 2007, Gershoff 2002a). In other words, even when *individuals* show resilience, punishment damages *relationships*.
- At the time, like all forms of punishment, smacking will produce *emotional distress* such as fear of loss of adult approval, anger, humiliation, guilt and sadness (Holden 2002). These emotions are likely, in turn, to block any cognitive appreciation by children of the message behind the discipline (Holden 2002). In the longer term, many physically punished children experience low self-esteem, anxiety and depression and, in adulthood, alcohol dependency (Afifi et al. 2006, Aucoin et al. 2006, Bender et al. 2007, Colder et al. 1997, Eamon 2001, Larzelere 2000, MacMillan et al. 1999, Nelson et al. 2006, Smith 2004). Even when physical discipline is culturally normative, it still reduces children's emotional adjustment and increases their levels of social aggression, albeit to a lesser extent than occurs when the parenting practice is less well accepted culturally (Lansford et al. 2005).
- *Developmental* impairments, such as reduced IQ (Smith & Brooks-Gunn 1997) and language comprehension (Gest et al. 2004), probably arise because parents employing corporal punishment use less reasoning when disciplining.

Even where these detrimental effects cannot be demonstrated, no beneficial effects can be proven either (Lytton 1997). The only positive result ever found has been increased compliance. However, this is a dubious achievement because, as already mentioned, it does not teach children moral reasoning or encourage independent thinking (Bear et al. 2003, Covaleskie 1992, McCaslin & Good 1992, Wien 2004). Furthermore, where smacking achieves compliance, this is evidence that the children are amenable and therefore lesser methods would be equally if not more effective. In other words, it is unnecessary.

Moreover, even behaviourists conclude that punishment is effective for the 95% of children who are mainly cooperative and therefore would respond to lesser methods while, for the remainder with entrenched antisocial behaviour, punishment seldom works (Eslea 1999, Maag 2001). Its disadvantages far outweigh its gains in compliance and, other than signalling who is in charge, it fails to promote any lasting behavioural improvements (Wheeler & Richey 2005).

Conclusion: disadvantages of punishment

Some researchers argue that difficult infants incite parents' coercive discipline and that it is the children's difficult behaviour—and not the parents' disciplinary style—that causes the subsequent emotional and behavioural disturbances (Jaffee et al. 2004). However, this seems not to be the case. Across studies, mothers who use restrictive control are not responding to their child's higher rates of behavioural difficulties, as these do not differ among the children studied (Campbell 1995). Instead, mothers' parenting style has more to do with their own emotional state and history of being nurtured as a child, than to their own child's temperament (Diener et al. 2003, Meyers 1999). Even easily distressed or irritable infants can be soothed by responsive parenting and can thereby learn to regulate their emotions, such that they become more sociable and positive than infants who were initially less reactive (Belsky et al. 1998, Eisenberg et al. 2005, Propper & Moore 2006).

In other words, parents' use of controlling discipline is not a response to their children's difficult natures (Meyers 1999); instead, their children become difficult because of the controlling discipline (Belsky et al. 1998, Donovan et al. 2000, O'Leary et al. 1999, Smith et al. 2004, Snyder et al. 2005). This leads to the conclusion that, while children's behavioural difficulties remain fairly stable over time, this is not due to their difficult natures, but to the fact that irritable and ineffective parenting styles become entrenched over time and perpetuate the children's difficulties (Dallaire & Weinraub 2005, Hastings & Rubin 1999, Kilgore et al. 2000, Nix et al. 1999, O'Leary et al. 1999, Smith et al. 2004, Snyder et al. 2005). This is particularly true for children with moderate to high levels of uncooperative behaviour (Shaw et al. 2003, Smith et al. 2004, Stoolmiller 2001).

Even if parents *were* responding to their children's difficult natures, nevertheless, children's antisocial behaviour improves in response to less coercive disciplinary methods (Collins et al. 2000, O'Connor 2002). That is, controlling parenting exacerbates any existing problems, whereas responsive disciplinary practices produce meaningful improvements (e.g. Connell et al. 1997, Forgatch & DeGarmo 1999, Leung et al. 2003, Marchant et al. 2004, Sanders 1999, Sanders et al. 2000, Scott et al. 2001, van den Boom 1995, Webster-Stratton 1998).

For a summary of the disadvantages of punishment, see Box 2.1.

DISADVANTAGES OF REWARDS

The most common reward is praise, while others include giving children access to a favourite activity such as computer time or outdoor play, or giving them special treats such as a favourite food. Although these sound benign, reward systems always entail punishment—that is, adults must withhold a reward when they judge that the child has not earned it. But the loss of an anticipated reward *feels* like a punishment (Kohn 1999). Furthermore, both rewards and punishments are attempts by adults to make children do things our way, in which case both deny children the opportunity to control themselves. Those spirited children who value their autonomy are likely to react against both forms of manipulation, responding with resistance, rebellion, retaliation and escape (Gordon 1970, 1974). In other words, rewards produce many of the same negative side effects as punishment (see Box 2.2).

Of these disadvantages, the effect of rewards on children's motivation and learning has been the most comprehensively researched. On this issue, it has been found that individuals who seek rewards as evidence that they have out-performed others or to prove their worth become very competitive and, if they cannot win, grow despondent or disengaged (Dweck & Leggett 1988, Sylva 1994). They avoid tasks that carry a risk of failure, are less persistent when faced with challenge, react helplessly to errors, develop more negative views of themselves when they experience failure, and may become disruptive in an effort to avoid or escape task demands (Covington & Müeller 2001, DiCintio & Gee 1999, Elliott & Dweck 1988, Kamins & Dweck 1999, Kistner et al. 2001, Milgram & Toubiana 1999, Mueller & Dweck 1998, Vallerand et al. 1994).

BOX 2.1 Summary of the disadvantages of punishment

To punish children for making natural childhood mistakes would be to punish them for *being* children. Not only is this unfair, but the administration of punishment adds to rather than solves children's behavioural problems.

Limited effectiveness

- Punishment is unreliable at gaining immediate compliance and does not produce long-term self-directed compliance.
- Children learn to behave well only to avoid punishment, rather than developing a conscience.
- It cannot prevent disruptions, only follow these: children must act thoughtlessly before action is taken.
- Adults must be constantly vigilant to detect misbehaviour, and cannot. Failure to identify the full circumstances leads to errors in administering punishment.
- Punishment works only for those who do not need it.

Detrimental effects on recipients

- Punishment can produce negative emotional side effects both at the time and in the long term.
- Aversive consequences can increase antisocial behaviour such as aggression.
- Punishment can teach children to imitate controlling others.
- Children can learn to avoid punishing situations, either by withdrawing or by becoming submissive.
- Punishment can provoke undesirable behaviours such as resistance, rebellion and retaliation, which in turn attract more punishment.
- Punishment can intimidate onlookers even when they themselves are not punished.
- Punishment can attract negative reputations that cause onlookers to exclude children who are punished.

Effects on administrators and society

- Punishment can become addictive and can escalate into abuse.
- Punishment can teach children to ignore adults who threaten but do not deliver punishment.
- Punishment damages relationships, making children less likely in future to want to please the adults who use it.
- Violence in homes and in our social institutions contributes to a violent and unsafe society.

Thus, the delivery of praise or other rewards for achievement reduces children's intrinsic motivation for the task, particularly when they discover that they cannot outdo their peers or earn desired rewards (Deci et al. 1991, 1999, 2001, Ryan & Deci 1996, 2000). This approach to learning causes deteriorating performances when they experience setbacks.

In contrast are those who seek to become competent simply for the satisfaction of acquiring new skills. This is known as a mastery orientation to learning, or growth

BOX 2.2 Disadvantages of rewards

When adults determine which behaviours they approve and when and how they will deliver rewards, they clearly are attempting to control others. The delivery of rewards signifies an inequality of power between adults and children, implying that adults have both the right and some special expertise to judge whether others' achievements are adequate.

Effects on children's self-esteem

- Children will not feel accepted because even positive evaluations signal that they are being judged.
- Children will feel discouraged when they fail to attain expected standards or behave well but are overlooked.
- When ideal behaviours are rewarded, children can learn to expect themselves to 'be good' all the time, lowering their self-esteem when this is impossible.
- Rewards teach children that other people's opinions of them are more important than their own.

Rewards can impede learning

- Rewards cause children to develop external rather intrinsic motivation.
- Striving to earn a reward—in contrast with developing a mastery orientation—causes deteriorating performances when challenged.
- Rewarded children strive to please and therefore avoid making mistakes, becoming less creative and adventurous.

Rewards can provoke disruptive behaviour

- Discouragement about being unable to meet unrealistic expectations can cause children to behave disruptively.
- Many children—particularly those who are spirited or non-conformist—resent being manipulated (even by rewards), resisting this denial of their autonomy by becoming disruptive.
- Rewards do not teach children to monitor their own successful behaviour and thus do not give them the skills to regulate their thoughtless actions either.
- Rewards increase competitiveness between children as they try to outdo others to gain for themselves the limited number of rewards that are available.

Praise can be ineffective

- Children need to be saturated with rewards for these to alter their behaviours. This is seldom practicable in natural settings.
- Praise can be automatic for adults and delivered, therefore, in a meaningless way.
- Adults and their feedback will lose credibility if the children's own evaluations of their performances contradict those of the adults.

Praise can be unfair

- Adults need a high level of technical expertise to use rewards fairly.

(continued)

> ■ While some children 'pull' praise from adults, others do not and consequently receive less recognition than they deserve.
>
> Source: Balson 1992, Chew 1998, Dinkmeyer & Dreikurs 1963, Dinkmeyer & McKay 1989, Dinkmeyer et al. 1980, 1997, Dreikurs & Cassel 1990, Dweck & Leggett 1988, Harrison 2004, Hitz & Driscoll 1988, Kohn 1999, Larrivee 2002, 2005, Nelsen et al. 2000.

seeking (Dykman 1998). Learners with this view see failure not as an indictment of themselves, but as useful feedback about the need to try another approach (Elliott & Dweck 1988). When not subjected to external pressure to excel, they report enjoying tasks more and experiencing less tension while completing them (Deci et al. 1994). They sustain their effort and are more positive about their own capacities, as a result of which their performances improve (Elliott & Dweck 1988).

These findings lead to the conclusion that, both to enhance children's learning and safeguard their self-esteem, children need specific, *informative* feedback that describes but does not judge what they have achieved. The distinction between judgmental and informative feedback is expanded in Chapter 7.

ETHICAL PRINCIPLES

The above debate produces two conclusions. The first is that punishment does not work: not only does it not prevent future transgressions or teach moral reasoning, it also does not even reliably achieve compliance at the time (Gershoff 2002b). Second, even achieving immediate compliance would not be enough to justify its use. Cattle prods or physical restraint would induce compliance—but we do not use these methods because they are not ethical. In other words, while we must judge methods according to their effectiveness, we must also consider their ethics.

A fundamental tenet of early childhood education is that we must treat children and their families in an ethical fashion—that is, we must do what is right, just and good, rather than what is merely expedient, convenient or practical (Katz 1995). This principle implies that, when trying to correct disruptive behaviour, any measures used must be in the children's own interests. That is, they must be aimed at improving the safety or quality of life of young people themselves.

The second principle is that you must do no harm. Given children's lack of power to advocate on their own behalf, you must employ practices that are respectful of and provide security for children and in no way 'degrade, endanger, exploit, intimidate, or harm them psychologically or physically' (Australian Early Childhood Association 1991, p. 4).

The third principle is of inclusion. This means that we cannot scapegoat children because of their disruptiveness, any more than we would discriminate against them on the basis of their sex, culture or religion.

A fourth ethical principle pertaining to children's discipline requires that any intervention be delivered competently by staff with adequate training, experience and supervision. To abide by this principle, you will need to be informed of the full spectrum of options, rather than simply the range of rewards and punishments.

ECLECTICISM

Eclecticism means blending ideas and practices from various approaches. Some people seek to combine both guidance and controlling methods on the assumption that a guidance approach will prevent thoughtless behaviour but is not firm enough to correct it. However, in the evidence just reviewed, *not a single study* found controlling discipline superior to guidance at either prevention or correction and, indeed, while across studies the outcomes of controlling discipline differ in severity, they do not differ in direction: *all* the results of controlling discipline are negative. Therefore, we cannot justify using methods that are ineffective.

The problem with blending incompatible methods is that they will undermine each other, such as when guidance approaches build trust between adults and children but punitive discipline (e.g. time out) then damages the adult–child relationship. In order to be effective, we need to understand the ideas behind the practices, rather than selecting a method merely because it 'seemed like a good idea at the time'. This *atheoretical* eclecticism is not an option for professionals (Young 1992). Corey (1996) calls it sloppy and labels it the worst form of ill-discipline that provides an excuse for failing to engage with ideas and which allows practitioners merely to pick and choose elements of theories that support their preconceived notions.

You can, however, blend those methods that share a common philosophy. This *synthetic* eclecticism is an attempt to integrate compatible ideas, resulting in a more comprehensive set of practices than suggested by any of the original theories alone. Such a hybrid will not create contradiction and confusion, as long as it preserves the principles of the original approaches.

CONCLUSION

Many adults recognise that, while they believe in a guidance approach to discipline, they nevertheless respond to disruptions in controlling ways (Lewis 1997). Commonly, authoritarianism is the only style that we know, because our parents raised us that way and our professional training has not provided information about alternatives. Certainly in group settings, stress can heighten our need to exert control whenever we feel that the demands are escalating.

Or, perhaps more crucial than any of these reasons, it may be difficult to abandon controlling discipline because ingrained in us is a deep distrust of children that has been handed down to us over countless centuries and advocated by those religions which adopt an authoritarian (as opposed to nurturing) conception of their God (Gordon 1991). While it is clear that children need guidance, the evidence presented here allows us to conclude that we can achieve the same—actually, better—behavioural outcomes by means other than rewards and punishments. The upcoming chapters will describe these alternative methods.

SUGGESTED FURTHER READING

A critique of theories of behaviour management

Porter L 2007 *Student behaviour: theory and practice for teachers*, 3rd edn. Allen & Unwin, Sydney. Or, its equivalent title, *Behaviour in schools: theory and practice for teachers*, 2nd edn. Open University Press, Maidenhead, UK.

The disadvantages of consequences

Kohn A 1996 *Beyond discipline: from compliance to community*. Association for Supervision and Curriculum Development, Alexandria, VA.

—— 1999 *Punished by rewards: the trouble with gold stars, incentive plans, A's, praise and other bribes*, 2nd edn. Houghton Mifflin, Boston, MA.

Codes of ethics

Early Childhood Australia 2006 *Early Childhood Australia's code of ethics*. Early Childhood Australia, Canberra.

National Association for the Education of Young Children 1989 Code of ethical conduct. *Young Children* 45(1):25–9.

Stonehouse A 1991 *Our code of ethics at work*. Australian Early Childhood Association, Canberra.

part II

Universal interventions

'We want more for our children than healthy bodies. We want our children to have lives filled with friendship and love and high deeds. We want them to be eager to learn and be willing to confront challenges ... We want them to grow up with confidence in the future, a love of adventure, a sense of justice, and courage enough to act on that sense of justice. We want them to be resilient in the face of the setbacks and failures that growing up always brings.'

SELIGMAN ET AL. (1995, p. 6)

When considering disciplinary practices, we tend to focus on responses to problems that have already arisen. However, this overlooks the fact that by far the largest and most crucial component of any disciplinary program is prevention: it is both more humane and more effective to prevent difficulties than to correct them once they have arisen. A neglect of preventive measures will inevitably lead to failure and frustration (Maag 2001). Thus, as depicted in Figure II.1, your disciplinary measures must encompass three layers of practice, with those at the lower levels predominating.

The first component is *primary* or *universal preventive* practices, which focus on the larger environment and put in place protective mechanisms that safeguard all children and prevent behavioural difficulties in general (Algozzine & Kay 2002, Kerr & Nelson 2006). The aim is for these universal preventive measures to meet the needs of most children most of the time, creating fewer disciplinary issues and thereby releasing resources to direct towards the few remaining difficulties that surface.

Nevertheless, not every incident can be prevented. Therefore, you will also need to plan *targeted* or *supportive* interventions that teach specific skills and provide support to protagonists during a disruptive incident.

FIGURE II.1 Levels of prevention and intervention with children's behavioural difficulties

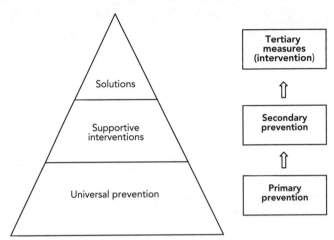

The tertiary and final level of practice is *enacting solutions*—otherwise known as intervention. These methods are designed to solve chronic or ongoing difficulties and will encompass both immediate and longer term solutions.

Fundamental to both prevention and intervention is the requirement that we meet children's basic and emotional needs. This is crucial for three reasons. First and foremost, it is a fundamental human right and is one of the main means of helping children to be well adjusted. Second, by being responsive to children, we are equipping them to consider us in return. Only when they experience empathy can they develop consideration for others. Third, in terms of this book's emphasis on behavioural disruptions, frustration of children's needs would lead to behavioural outbursts.

HUMAN NEEDS

The core guidance principle is that children will be productively engaged and act thoughtfully when what we are asking them to do and how we are asking them to do it meets their needs. A need is innately necessary for an organism's continued growth, integrity and vitality, rather than being an acquired motivation (Deci & Ryan 2000). A need is distinguishable from mere desires on the criteria that it is universal (i.e. found in every culture, even though their relative importance may vary from one culture to another) and leads to *behaviour* designed to satisfy it, *thought* focused on meeting it, and *emotional* benefits from its satisfaction and distress from its non-fulfilment (Baumeister & Leary 1995).

To provide some structure to what could otherwise seem an interminable list of these needs, I propose the model depicted as Figure II.2, which is fashioned on a tree, allowing the emotional needs to be linked. In keeping with Maslow's (1968) conception and as indicated by the upward arrow to the left of the tree trunk, the model is hierarchical, which means that the lower needs have to be satisfied before individuals can focus on meeting their higher needs.

The most basic human requirement—fundamental for all growth and therefore depicted in Figure II.2 as the roots of the tree—is the need for physical *survival*—for food, shelter, warmth and (in adulthood) procreation. When its roots are compromised, the tree cannot flourish; similarly, when individuals are worried about their own survival, they cannot focus on any higher needs.

At the next level are the dual needs for *emotional safety* and *wellbeing*, depicted as the trunk of the tree in Figure II.2. As we know from children reared in orphanages, it is not enough that they simply be fed and watered. Children also need to feel assured that they will be nurtured and that adults will be sensitive to and alleviate their discomfort or pain.

At the next level are the core emotional needs, depicted in Figure II.2 as the tree's three limbs. While different individuals and different cultures may rank these three needs slightly differently, on the whole they are equally vital for our satisfaction with life (Sheldon et al. 2001). The three core emotional needs are:

- *Belonging.* This is the need to love and be loved. Evidence for the need for belonging is both strong and compelling. Infants and parents of all cultures form loving bonds with each other. Thwarting the need to belong leads to many negative outcomes such as higher rates of physical and emotional illness, suicide and delinquency. The development of new relationships elicits joy, while the dissolution of relationships (e.g. in divorce) creates distress. People are more satisfied in relationships characterised by mutual caring and frequent contact, and people think about and seek out new relationships when they feel lonely (Baumeister & Leary 1995).

FIGURE II.2 A model of individuals' needs

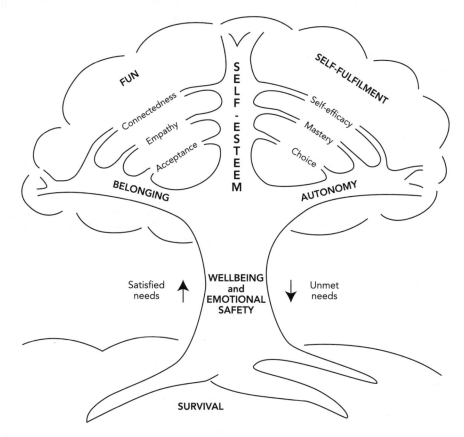

■ *Autonomy*. The need to be self-determining was first posited by Dewey and Piaget (Kamii 1985). We know from Seligman's (1975) work and self-determination theory (Deci & Ryan 2000, Ryan & Deci 2000) that it is a crucial human drive. Seligman found that, across cultures (and even species), learned helplessness results when individuals feel unable to control their circumstances. This helplessness comprises cognitive impairments in the form of an external locus of causality and affective and behavioural responses typical of depression.

■ *Self-esteem*. This is the need to value oneself and to think of oneself as worthy (Mruk 2006). Self-esteem is moderately to strongly related to emotional adjustment (O'Brien et al. 2006) and, indeed, is depicted as the central limb in Figure II.2 because it ranks more highly than all other emotional needs in predicting life satisfaction (Sheldon et al. 2001). However, it cannot exist in a vacuum. Our self-esteem is drawn from our connectedness to others, our sense of control over our own lives, and from feeling competent at the skills we value.

The final level of need is depicted in Figure II.2 as the tree's foliage and encompasses the dual requirements for self-fulfilment and fun. The need for self-fulfilment refers to the drive for long-term growth towards an ideal version of ourselves (Sheldon et al. 2001). It means that people cannot live out others' ambitions for them, but have to fulfil their own mission in life. This does not imply that they will be self-centred, however, as many individuals feel fulfilled when looking after others.

Finally, the need for fun is, according to Glasser (1988, p. 30), the 'intangible joy' that we feel when all our lower needs are being met. As such, fun cannot be mandated, but is found only within contexts that provide for our physical needs (for survival), are nurturing (to meet the need for emotional safety and physical wellbeing), affirming (promote self-esteem), emotionally close (foster belonging), free (permit autonomy), and fulfilling.

CAREGIVING PRACTICES THAT MEET THESE NEEDS

In the coming chapters, I will detail caregiving practices aimed at meeting the needs presented in the above model. The core practices are listed in Table II.1.

TABLE II.1 Core caregiving practices that meet children's needs	
Need	**Caregiving practice**
Survival	Physical caretaking
Emotional safety	Responsive caregiving
Wellbeing	Nurturance
Belonging	Empathy
Autonomy	Guidance
Self-esteem	Authentic feedback
Self-fulfilment	Stimulation
Fun	All of the above

CONCLUSION

In the coming chapters, I present measures for meeting each of these human needs. As that can occur only within the context of a rich and challenging program, a chapter on programming begins this section. This first chapter contends that disciplinary measures must be in tune with educational practice, so that how we respond to disruptions does not undo the educational aims of our wider program. The subsequent chapters focus on how meeting children's basic and emotional needs will prevent behavioural disruptions.

chapter 3

A child-centred educational program

'Teachers' professional capacities to manage the classroom, engage children in instruction, and promote a safe, positive classroom climate are associated with improved academic outcomes for children ... These classroom-level variables encourage a secure environment in which positive relationships can develop.'

BAKER (2006, p. 225)

Home environments that stimulate children's learning produce fewer behavioural problems in children, as well as significant advances in their development (Bradley et al. 2001). The same is true of high-quality centre-based care, which has been shown to improve infants' exploratory behaviours and problem solving (Schuetze et al. 1999) and enhance the overall cognitive, language and literacy skills of toddlers and preschool-aged children, contributing in turn to their adaptive functioning in the early years of school (Burchinal & Cryer 2003, Burchinal et al. 1996, 2000, Clarke-Stewart et al. 2002, Gilliam & Zigler 2000, Gormley et al. 2005, NICHD Early Child Care Research Network 2000, 2003c, NICHD Early Child Care Research Network & Duncan 2003, Peisner-Feinberg & Burchinal 1997, Peisner-Feinberg et al. 2001, Phillips et al. 1987, Rubenstein et al. 1981, Sundell 2000, Sylva et al. 2006, Zaslow et al. 1998). When followed up with responsive educational programs, these gains are maintained through the school years (Andersson 1989, 1992, Reynolds et al. 2004), with the benefits particularly pronounced for children experiencing environmental risks (Hubbs-Tait et al. 2002, Love et al. 2003, Peisner-Feinberg et al. 2001).

CURRICULUM PLANNING

There are two broad approaches to curriculum planning. The first is a *top-down* approach in which adults determine which skills and information are of value to children and then set about teaching these. Such an educational program is largely originated by the adult, although it is not necessarily unresponsive to children's needs. It may be child-*focused* and developmentally appropriate, with adults aiming to meet children's needs by providing activities that they judge will be useful to and enjoyable for the children. However, there will typically be significant amounts of didactic or adult-led teaching.

In contrast, a *bottom-up* approach is child-*centred* or child-*referenced*. In this approach, adults are guided by information about specific children (Kugelmass & Ross-Bernstein 2000) and follow rather than lead the children, responding to and expanding on their expressed interests. Also known as a constructivist approach, this style is based on a view of children as actively constructing their own experiences (Dahlberg et al. 1999). Its view of children as inventive, enriched and vibrant human beings whose need to construct identities and generate understandings of the world is the starting point for, rather than an afterthought in, curriculum planning (Dahlberg et al. 1999, Fraser & Gestwicki 2002). Rather than attempting to instil a predetermined curriculum, a bottom-up approach respects and responds reflectively to the skills and interests of children and their parents. It does not simply indulge these or rely on improvisation or chance, however, but utilises educators' expertise and active teaching skills, while also engaging children's (and parents') competence (Fraser & Gestwicki 2002).

A constructivist approach shifts the educational emphasis away from *telling* children what they should know and how they should behave, towards *listening* and responding to the richness of their present lives. It capitalises on 'teachable moments', when children's behaviour, interests or questions demonstrate that they are particularly receptive to learning from experience (Bailey 2002). By being responsive in this way to the children's interests and needs, the curriculum will not only be developmentally appropriate, but also 'humanly, culturally and individually appropriate' (Stonehouse 1994, p. 76).

Research comparing the two styles shows that children engage in less complex interactions with peers and objects when their teacher directs their activity (Kontos et al. 2002). In contrast, during child-directed social play, children display more persistence, sophisticated thinking and emotions than during teacher-led pretend play (Gmitrova & Gmitrov 2003), with these gains in thinking skills arising perhaps because when they organise the play themselves, they not only have to adopt its roles but also direct the flow of the activity.

In terms of their academic skills, in the years prior to school, children in constructivist or child-focused settings show improved academic and verbal achievement and motivation, fewer behavioural and emotional difficulties and increased self-reliance and engagement compared with those receiving high levels of teacher-directed instruction (NICHD Early Child Care Research Network 2003d, Stipek et al. 1995, 1998, Wiltz & Klein 2001). They also enjoy their educational experiences more (Wiltz & Klein 2001).

Conversely, the need to enforce compliance during teacher-directed instruction generates a negative climate and diminishes children's pleasure and motivation in learning (Maccoby & Lewis 2003, Stipek et al. 1998), particularly for boys (Huffman & Speer 2000). The children become more dependent on teacher directives and approval and more anxious, while achieving less academically than do children engaged in self-directed learning (Huffman & Speer 2000, Stipek et al. 1995, 1998). They display twice as much stress, with disadvantaged children being particularly vulnerable as a result of their higher life-stress levels overall (Hart et al. 1998). The developmental inappropriateness of rote drill to teach young children basic literacy and numeracy causes children to dislike these activities (Wiltz & Klein 2001) and results in increased behavioural difficulties (Stipek et al. 1998).

Teacher-directed instruction also tends to create a competitive social hierarchy, whereas being in a child-centred setting teaches children empathy and reduces peer rejection (Donohue et al. 2003). Not only does this increase the children's tolerance for diversity, but also reduces individual children's behavioural difficulties that otherwise might induce peer rejection (Donohue et al. 2003).

AIMS OF EARLY CHILDHOOD PROGRAMS

A conformist curriculum transmits the dominant culture, social roles and norms but, in so doing, can unwittingly reinforce unequal power (Kilderry 2004). To examine this political stance, you will have to reflect on whether you regard your task as one of helping children *conform* to their culture, of teaching independent thinking skills so the children are empowered to *reform* or advance society, or of challenging social, political and economic inequalities and thus *transforming* the dominant culture (MacNaughton 2003).

Educational goals

The broad aim of reforming and transforming education is for children to grow in knowledge and skills so they can generate understandings of themselves and their world and solve personal and societal problems (Dahlberg et al. 1999, MacNaughton 2003). This general goal can be broken down into the following specific aims (Katz & Chard 1989, NAEYC & NAECS/SDE 1991, Smidt 1998).

Facilitate competence

This involves acquiring and applying a range of skills across all developmental domains. To that end, children need experience and instruction in many areas. Moreover, for children to remain willing to put in the effort required to achieve, they need positive attitudes to learning and to themselves as learners. These attitudes or dispositions can be classified into three cognitive and one emotional orientation to learning, as follows:

- The *creative* dispositions include imaginativeness, being open to new ideas and experiences, having tolerance of ambiguity, curiosity, adventurousness, exploration, being playful and seeking alternatives.
- *Reflective* skills include the use of metacognitive strategies of self-awareness, self-control (including impulse control), and self-monitoring to regulate one's own thinking.
- *Critical* thinking skills include planning, and being strategic, inquiring, investigative, intellectually rigorous and logical (seeking truth, reason and evidence).
- *Emotional* dispositions include the *motivational* cluster such as experiencing interest, confidence and enthusiasm for learning, and goal-directed *behaviours* that include

engagement, persistence, patience, independence, cooperativeness and delay of gratification (Gagné 2003, Goleman 1995, Lambert & Clyde 2000, Perkins et al. 1993, Ritchhart 2001).

Provide emotional support for children

Early years education also aims to support children's emotional development by establishing a safe and caring physical and emotional environment that supports and protects the children's right to learn and grow personally, helping children establish satisfying and successful social relationships, and developing a healthy self-esteem in each child.

Build a supportive community

A final aim is to support children's social networks by collaborating with their parents or other primary caregivers and connecting with their cultures. A supportive climate also cares for educators both personally and professionally.

Goals for discipline

If we proclaim constructivist goals for children's education, these must also apply to disciplinary practices. Children will not profit from being taught to think critically and solve problems while, at the same time, being required to comply behaviourally (McCaslin & Good 1992). Therefore, discipline must aim to educate children in moral decision making, rather than simply imposing conformity to adult standards.

BEHAVIOURAL ASSESSMENT

While assessment for educational purposes is an ongoing and systematic process of gathering information about children's learning levels, styles and skills to inform educators about how best to meet the children's needs (McLoughlin & Lewis 2005), *behavioural* assessment will take both a focused and a wider view of what may be contributing to the behaviours that children are displaying. This analysis will consider the program's environment, content and learning processes that may be provoking children's behavioural difficulties, in interaction with children's additional needs posed by delayed or advanced development or family adversity.

EDUCATIONAL PROVISIONS

Although the focus of this book is on guiding young children's behaviour, the program provides the context for this. A stimulating curriculum is a means of meeting children's physical, psychological, social, intellectual and academic needs (Greenberg 1992). A secondary aim is to engage children so that they do not find alternative, less productive things to do, resulting in disruptions.

Physical setting

The environment refers to the physical structure of a setting, its organisation and its social climate. Within an ecological perspective, the environment is seen as the 'third teacher'—with the first being the children themselves and the second being their social relationships with adults and peers (Fraser & Gestwicki 2002). As Fraser and Gestwicki (2002, p. 100) observe, 'Space does indeed speak'. The first message that buildings can convey to those who use them is that they and the activities that go on there are valued. To that end, the facilities must be well maintained and aesthetically pleasing.

Second, the space communicates a welcome to children, families, educators and visitors, and signals their ownership of the space by reflecting their personal interests and requirements (Fraser & Gestwicki 2002). A well-organised play environment also fosters inclusion of children with atypical development—for example, by minimising noise to aid the communication of children with impaired hearing or by reducing obstacles to assist the mobility of those with vision impairments and to ensure accessibility for those with physical disabilities (Doctoroff 2001).

Third, physical arrangements convey to children and adults what they can do in that space. The level of challenge, attractiveness and fun affects the participation of the children. Therefore, the structure should help children to feel safe, allow them to exercise choice, invite investigation, permit them to use ideas creatively and access materials readily, thus giving them confidence that they can have control of their learning (Fraser & Gestwicki 2002, Robson 1996, Smidt 1998).

Fourth, the physical layout allows the program to flow smoothly—such as by keeping thoroughfares free of congestion, minimising distractions for children who find it difficult to concentrate, and allowing adults to monitor and thus respond to children in a timely manner. Providing sufficient space also avoids the unintentional collisions that can occur when children are in close proximity to each other.

The outdoor play space is of crucial importance, both to the development of children's physical skills and their social interactions (Barbour 1999). It also allows children to express their feelings more exuberantly (Dowling 2005). Equipment needs to provide adequate challenge to attract children with high physical competence, while being flexible enough not to exclude those who are less able physically (Barbour 1999). Too much challenge excludes these children, confers higher social status on those who are able to partake of the activities, and segregates children according to their physical competence (Barbour 1999).

Adequate resources

Most of young children's conflicts arise out of competition for access to toys and equipment, whereas when these resources are plentiful, the children are more likely to engage cooperatively over tasks (Brown 1996, O'Brien et al. 1999). Thus, the most obvious way to prevent disputes over play equipment is to make sure that you have numerous items of the same type so that children do not become frustrated or have to wait too long for a turn.

Flexible routines

The purpose of routines is to give children predictability, allow them to avoid unnecessary delays and confusion during transitions, and to complete self-care tasks successfully. In other words, routines help the day run smoothly, which will ultimately promote the comfort, health and wellbeing of the children. This is true as long as procedures provide for some meaningful choices for the children. However, in some cases, schedules are more about adults' convenience or enshrining the way things have always been done (Wien 1996). The result can be that the children's time is organised inflexibly into fixed segments, with the day looking like a 'production schedule'. This has the following deleterious effects on both the children and adults (Wien 1996):

- Given that adults are the only ones who can read the time and who determine the sequence of events, the program becomes top-down rather than child-centred. A setting dominated by the clock becomes unspontaneous and unresponsive to children's interests and levels of engagement. Thus, centres with inflexible routines tend to offer a lower quality of care (Wishard et al. 2003).
- When children's play is constantly being interrupted for the next segment of teacher-directed activity, the play is not sustained enough for the children to become deeply absorbed, elaborate on its themes, and reach closure.
- When caregivers are constantly focused on the next thing to be arranged, they cannot participate with the children in their present experiences.
- Organisation of the day into fragmented time slots means that there are numerous transitions for the children to navigate. The rigid time allocation means that these have to be conducted efficiently, which typically requires children to line up to come indoors or go outdoors and queue for access to the bathroom. Such practices are not only developmentally inappropriate, but also risky, as they provoke behavioural disruptions.
- The need for transitions to be efficient turns time into a scarce resource, with the result that children have to be hurried through self-help activities such as hanging up their hats and tidying up equipment and therefore do not have enough time to become proficient at these skills.
- Adults who must watch the clock constantly feel harried. Paradoxically, although they are exerting total command over events, they feel that at any moment they could lose control and thus feel stressed.

Instead, to prevent disruptiveness at transitions and during routine tasks, the rhythm of the day must be governed by the children's pace, not by the ticking of the clock.

Physical activity

All children and boys in particular need to release pent-up energy through regular physical activity, alternated with some calming activities so that their behaviour does not become disorganised. Physical activity gives children confidence in their ability to control their bodies, exercises both the body and the brain (thus enhancing development), teaches children that they can meet physical challenges and, as long as it does not become an avenue for competition, offers an outlet for stress.

Adult–child ratio

An accepted canon of early years education is that having fewer children per adult allows for more sensitive care and more responsive adult–child interactions (Sundell 2000), which, in turn, foster children's social and communication skills (Abbott-Shim et al. 2000, Burchinal et al. 2000, Clarke-Stewart et al. 2002, Howes 1983b, Howes & Rubenstein 1985, Phillipsen et al. 1997). This is true, however, only as long as the presence of more adults results in both more and better quality interactions between adults and children, rather than simply increased supervision (Tizard et al. 1976) or increased chat between adults (Goodnow 1989). Furthermore, when extra adults are allocated to assist children with additional needs, it is important not to shadow those children constantly and thus create dependency or act as a barrier between the children and their peers (Hauser-Cram et al. 1993).

Group size

The size of a group will affect the intimacy of interactions between its members and adults' responsiveness to individual children (Ahnert et al. 2006), even when adult–child ratios are held constant. For example, a group of one adult and five children has the same adult–child ratio as a group of three adults and 15 children. Yet members of the two groups will interact very differently, with very young children and perhaps older children with developmental delays being less able to function well in the larger group.

Young children naturally congregate in groups that comprise one more person than the number of their birthdays. Thus, 3-year-olds engage in associative play with three peers plus themselves, and 4-year-olds can play cooperatively with four peers plus themselves, yielding a group size of five children. This tells us that, even when the setting can accommodate a large number, young children are not necessarily able to accommodate a crowd, particularly when the task is demanding, such as during group story time, when their language, concentration and sensory integration skills may be challenged. When both the task and the size of the group are challenging, behavioural disruptions are likely to increase.

Having said this, a large group seems to be most detrimental when caregivers are attempting to impose external controls on the children (Porter 1999). This style of discipline becomes particularly ineffective when there are too many children to oversee, whereas staff using a guidance approach tend to be able to manage a larger group. This might be because guidance fosters autonomous cooperation in the children or because those caregivers who tend to use a guidance approach satisfy the children's curricular and emotional needs, thus avoiding disruptions that arise when these are not met.

It is also worth mentioning that groups can be too small. When only a handful of children do not have a nap or when attendance at a session is low, the children can mill about aimlessly, as if there needs to be a critical mass to spark off a play idea (Porter 1999). Therefore, when numbers are low, adults may need to guide the children to initiate play.

Age mix of the children

The age span within a group strongly predicts the children's intellectual and social outcomes (Sundell 2000). Whereas small age spans (up to 2 years' difference between the youngest and oldest group members) improve particularly the younger children's development over and above a same-aged grouping, groups containing children of widely differing ages (up to 50 months' span) produce poorer outcomes (Sundell 2000).

While the aims of mixed-age grouping are to foster a climate of acceptance of diversity and not to restrict children to developmental timetables (Katz et al. 1990, Lloyd 1997, Mosteller et al. 1996, Roberts et al. 1994, Veenman 1995, 1996), over time, children in mixed-aged settings gravitate towards age mates as play companions, thus nullifying the advantages of the wider spread of ages (Winsler et al. 2002), while perhaps even disadvantaging children as there are fewer age mates with whom to form friendships than there would be if all those in the group were around their age.

Thus, social advantages are few, while groups of widely disparate ages pose some particular challenges for programming (Mason & Burns 1996). For example, the immediacy of toddlers' care needs can interrupt teacher-planned activities for the older children (Sundell 2000). Equipment that is designed for the older children can be dangerous for the younger ones. Therefore, there is a risk of 'dumbing down' the curriculum to make it safe for the younger children. The result can be that the older children are deprived of the advanced activities that they need in order to feel challenged and, with little else to occupy them, can become disruptive. Meanwhile, young children and those with physical disabilities can feel under threat of toppling when bigger children run past them boisterously. They can become tentative in active play and discouraged when object play is too difficult for them.

Mediated learning

Mediated learning—as distinct from direct learning through the senses—occurs when adults interpret the environment for children, reflecting their interests, needs and capabilities (Klein 1992). Although early childhood programs value exploration and discovery, when children are acquiring new skills or concepts, having difficulty becoming engaged or sustaining attention, or requiring remedial instruction, you will need to guide their learning. Once they are engaged, you might need to offer those with learning difficulties extra cues, prompts and encouragement to continue to be involved (McCollum & Bair 1994), and give them additional time in which to respond to your overtures or directives (Wolery et al. 1994). This assistance to become occupied will help them both to learn more and be less disruptive.

When guiding children's task performances, you will invite their ideas and suggestions, provide cues, ask open-ended questions, identify problems, and offer and ask for feedback. These interactions will incorporate the following key strategies (Klein 1992, Kugelmass & Ross-Bernstein 2000):

- *Focus.* You can select salient aspects of the activity and help children to focus on these through accentuation or exaggeration (Klein 1992, Moss 1992). With babies, for example, you might 'dance' a toy to within easy reach. With older infants, you could point out important features: 'Hey, look at this! What do you think it's for?'
- *Meaning.* You can convey your intellectual interest in and emotional excitement about an activity so that children learn to find such activities interesting and develop the commitment that is necessary for sustained effort and success.
- *Expansion.* You can affirm, acknowledge and clarify children's experiences, and expand their awareness beyond their immediate activity by making explicit connections between it and past events and achievements.
- *Feedback.* You can express excitement and satisfaction with children's achievements by, for example, giving explicit and informative feedback about their efforts.
- *Organisation.* You can help children to plan, regulate and monitor their activities by working on tasks jointly until children gradually acquire the ability to use their organisation skills independently, which typically begins from 4 years of age.

Inclusion

Children of either gender and of diverse cultures, abilities and family types have a basic human right to be welcomed and engaged in their educational settings. Although there is extensive information on programming for equity, here I canvass only those issues relevant to children's behaviour.

Culture

The term *culture* encompasses demographic characteristics such as race, gender, country of origin, language and socioeconomic status, as well as less explicit features such as individuals' beliefs, values and attitudes (Sheridan 2000). Some cultural awareness is needed when evaluating children's behaviours, because within the dominant culture's frame of reference, a child's behaviour might be interpreted as problematic, whereas it may be appropriate within the child's family (Ramirez et al. 1998) or be a natural reaction to social disadvantage or disempowerment.

Gender

When gender issues are raised with respect to children's behaviour, boys tend to be the focus (Lee-Thomas et al. 2005) because as young children and throughout life, compared with girls, boys on average are more aggressive, display riskier behaviours, and are more competitive with each other (Fabes et al. 2003, 2004, Geary et al. 2003). While honouring boys' physical energy, boldness and curiosity, these qualities must be directed and channelled productively (Mercurio 2003) so that they do not impinge on surrounding children or attract a negative reputation and peer rejection.

While the *content* of your program can provide activities and materials that challenge sexist stereotypes, the *processes* that you use are even more crucial for ensuring that girls have equal status (Fleer 1998). Your measures will be grounded in the supposition that dominance (the exercise of power) should not be the only route to social status. This stance will require you to apportion time and space equitably between boys and girls, because each time a boy overrides other children during play or conversation, a lack of adult intervention to teach turn taking tacitly gives boys permission to dominate while obliging girls to submit to this (Fleer 1998).

Boys' larger and more boisterous social groupings can dominate the play space, disenfranchising girls and less bold children from participating in the vicinity, intimidating or even physically hurting them (Lee-Thomas et al. 2005). Therefore, although the notion of free play can seem romantic and sacred, it will be necessary to monitor and, at times, redirect children's play when it constrains the activity of those around them (Lee-Thomas et al. 2005).

Even at very young ages, some boys have learned to disrespect women and therefore are unresponsive to discipline from their female teachers (and their mothers). In these instances, I use what I term my make-no-mistake speech: 'Make no mistake. Even though I'm a woman, I expect to be taken seriously.' In delivering this information and following it up with action, you do not have to be stern—only resolute.

Atypical development

Very few disabilities in and of themselves will *cause* disruptive behaviour. When programs are responsive to their needs, children with developmental delays will, on the whole, be able to behave similarly to a younger child of their developmental level. However, they do have from three to four times higher rates of social withdrawal and attention difficulties (Baker et al. 2002, 2003), particularly when their learning difficulties relate to language or sensory integration skills (see Ch 15). When programming to prevent behavioural difficulties, you will need to adjust aspects of the environment, program content and learning processes so that the activities are accessible and invite the children's engagement. The most crucial adjustments to learning processes include reducing the duration of activities, employing smaller groupings in keeping with the children's delayed attention skills, and mediating the children's learning to help them navigate tasks successfully.

Although many assume that the inclusion of children with disabilities requires a willingness or positive attitude on the part of staff, in fact educators are more confident about including children with disabilities when they have the information, resources and support to do so (Devore & Hanley-Maxwell 2000, Mohay & Reid 2006, Soodak et al. 2002). These ensure a successful experience for those with disabilities, their peers and staff, upon which their attitudes to disability will broaden (Guralnick 1994, Stoneman 1993).

EVALUATION

With respect to children's behaviour, in order to judge whether disruptions are being prevented and selected interventions are effective, you will need to evaluate the resources (inputs) being deployed and the processes being used to achieve outcomes (Reid 2004). In terms of inputs, the key question is whether the program makes efficient and ethical use of staff, parents' and children's time, and whether staff have sufficient resources such as professional training, a library, access to consultants and adequate facilities for preventing and responding in planned ways to children's disruptions.

Evaluation of *processes* requires staff members to reflect on how satisfied they are with children's level of engagement and disruptiveness and with their own disciplinary measures. Assessment of *outcomes* will focus on the effects of preventive and interventive measures on individual children, while checking that certain individuals or groups are not being marginalised or disadvantaged by the approaches being used.

CONCLUSION

Ongoing behavioural difficulties are a reminder to adjust your setting so that it is both *possible* for all children to achieve expectations and, by meeting their needs, promotes their *willingness* to do so. This is the 'goodness of fit' principle, which states that when we supply what children require, they will be able to function appropriately. This will prevent most behavioural disruptions and, in turn, free adults and children for authentic teaching and learning.

SUGGESTED FURTHER READING

Arthur L, Beecher B, Death E, Dockett S, Farmer S 2005 *Programming and planning in early childhood settings*, 3rd edn. Thomson, Melbourne.
Dau E (ed.) 2001 *The anti-bias approach in early childhood*, 2nd edn. Pearson, Sydney.
Fraser S, Gestwicki C 2002 *Authentic childhood: exploring Reggio Emilia in the classroom*. Delmar, Albany, NY.
MacNaughton G, Williams G 2004 *Techniques for teaching young children: choices in theory and practice*, 2nd edn. Pearson Prentice Hall, Sydney.
National Association for the Education of Young Children website: http://www.naeyc.org.

Additional needs

Harrison C 2003 *Giftedness in early childhood*, 3rd edn. Gerric, Sydney.

Porter L (ed.) 2002 *Educating young children with additional needs*. Allen & Unwin, Sydney. Or, its equivalent title, *Educating young children with special needs*. Paul Chapman, London; Sage, Thousand Oaks, CA.

Porter L 2005 *Gifted young children: a guide for teachers and parents*, 2nd edn. Allen & Unwin, Sydney; Open University Press, Buckingham, UK.

Meeting children's basic needs

'There are many kinds of safety that are required for children to learn. At the most basic level, there is physical safety … [This] is not enough, however. Safety also means emotional safety—the safety to be yourself, to be vulnerable, to ask for help, and to be warmly supported.'

SAPON-SHEVIN (1999, p. 13)

SURVIVAL

The first and most basic human requirement is for physical survival. Because it is the source of all growth, it is depicted in the model in Figure II.2 as the roots of the tree. Although the need for survival is mostly the responsibility of parents, it has direct programming implications in centres that supply meals. Children's food must meet their cultural and individual requirements and must supply sufficient fuel for their daily activities so that they can engage productively in a program and focus on meeting higher level needs. Early childhood practitioners also play a role in children's survival by reporting to child welfare agencies any concerns they have about possible neglect or abuse of children.

Child abuse

Throughout human history, children have always been considered the property of their parents, to do with as they wished (Grille 2005). This history still casts its shadow on modern life, with studies finding that as many as 16.5% of children are physically or emotionally abused or neglected (Afifi et al. 2006), with the actual rate suspected to be higher still. Unsurprisingly, parents who are most likely to abuse their children emotionally or physically are those who are young, who themselves were abused as children, who have current emotional difficulties such as depression, poor impulse control and low self-efficacy, endure poverty, live with a violent partner, and misuse drugs (Dixon et al. 2005a, Mullen et al. 1996, Thompson & Wyatt 1999). Their lack of knowledge about normal behaviour and parenting strategies and negative attributions about their children induce anger and harsh parenting during disciplinary encounters (Dixon et al. 2005b, Frias-Armenta 2002, Mapp 2006, Nix et al. 1999). This pattern is not inevitable, however. Research and my own clinical experience show that many parents who were abused or subjected to harsh discipline themselves avow never to subject their children to the same and instead develop close, nurturing relationships with their children (Wyman et al. 1999).

Sexual abuse involves the exploitation and coercion of children by someone more powerful than them. Prevalence estimates vary considerably, with one study reporting rates of 15% for girls and 7% for boys (Kim & Cicchetti 2006), and others finding similar rates for both genders (Bromberg & Johnson 2001, Rossman et al. 1998). The peak age of onset of sexual abuse appears to be 7 to 8 years for females and prior to puberty for males (Webster 2001). Sexual abuse commonly persists for in excess of 2 years.

Approximately 20% of adult males and 8% of adult females report having some sexual interest in children, with as many as 7% of males and 3% of females saying that they would engage in sexual activity with children if they could avoid detection (Bromberg & Johnson 2001, Vizard et al. 1995). The factor that translates this high level of sexual interest in children into actual abuse is not the mental illness or prior abuse history of the perpetrator, but simply children's powerlessness. Children trust adults to keep them safe, are not capable of assessing adults' motives and are taught to obey adults (Briggs & McVeity 2000). Thus, most sexual abuse of children (over 85%) is perpetrated by someone known to them, often an adult family member or friend—or, in 20 to 50% of cases, an adolescent perpetrator, often a sibling (Bromberg & Johnson 2001, Metzner & Ryan 1995, Vizard et al. 1995).

Detection of abuse

While having compassion for the emotional outcomes of abuse for children, this book's focus is on its manifestations in the form of behaviours. In that case, when abused children withdraw, they can be ignored in care and education settings and thus deprived of the support that they vitally need (Hoffman-Plotkin & Twentyman 1984). Alternatively, many of the children's behaviours are directed against surrounding individuals and therefore are often regarded as 'problems'. In turn, this makes abused children particularly likely to be the recipients of controlling forms of discipline (Hoffman-Plotkin & Twentyman 1984), thus adding another layer of injustice in their lives.

Given that you will seldom know that a child is being abused, it is imperative that you consider maltreatment as a possible cause of antisocial behaviours and make absolutely certain to respond in nurturing rather than controlling ways to any child displaying a constellation of difficult or distressing behaviours such as those listed in Box 4.1.

BOX 4.1 Signs and effects of abuse and neglect

The following effects of abuse can act as signs that aid its recognition. Many of these occur at the time of the abuse, whereas others have a sleeper effect, not appearing until one or more years after the abuse has ceased. After the termination of the assaults, effects tend to persist longer for younger children and those for whom fewer supports are made available upon discovery or disclosure.

Emotional signs

Neglected and abused children do not learn to trust others, particularly when the perpetrator is a parent. This can have serious emotional effects at the time and in later intimate adult relationships.

- Neglected children in particular, but abused children overall, typically have lowered self-esteem. Parental criticism and insults cause them to see themselves as less worthy and to doubt that their peers will accept them. In turn, low self-esteem causes increasing behavioural problems over time.
- Neglected and abused children are hypervigilant for signs of potential threat.
- They remain emotionally disturbed for longer when witnessing unresolved conflict between others.
- They may not regulate anger and aggression.
- They have few emotional coping strategies.
- They have little understanding of their own or others' feelings.
- Many display anxiety, depression, fearfulness or agitation.
- Most have low self-efficacy as a result of being unable to deflect the abuse.
- Prior abuse can sensitise individuals to subsequent traumas, making them vulnerable to post-traumatic stress.

Social skills

Of all the domains of development, children's social competence is the most impaired by neglect or abuse. Children who experience maltreatment from their parents anticipate hostility from others and will either act aggressively or cope with their distress by constricting emotion. These responses help the children cope with their maltreatment, but are maladaptive in peer settings and contribute to persistent problems in maintaining satisfying interpersonal relationships.

- Abused children often withdraw socially. They may interact little with peers and are less responsive to friendly overtures from adults or children.
- Their interactions are often unskilful.
- Physically abused children in particular have high rates of hostility and aggression towards peers and adults.
- Abused children's abilities to appreciate others' perspectives and be empathic are impaired, being less likely to show concern or offer help to distressed peers and perhaps even delighting in their distress.
- They demonstrate poor social problem-solving strategies and impaired conflict-resolution skills.
- They experience peer rejection.

(continued)

- Some assault or threaten adults in the belief that adults can be dangerous.
- They may not seek comfort from others when distressed.
- Alternatively, abused children can be highly dependent on adults.
- They may 'freeze' in the presence of their abuser.

Behaviours

When the abuse has been occurring for some time, it is difficult to draw a link between it and children's behaviour. However, if the abuse has just begun, you might see a sudden change in abused children's behaviour corresponding with the onset of the abuse. The children's behavioural patterns can resemble attention-deficit hyperactivity disorder (ADHD) or oppositional disorder or their opposite, which has been termed compulsive compliance, whereby children suppress their own emotions to comply with adult demands, modifying or falsifying their feelings to gain adult approval.

- Abused children's behaviour can regress whereby they display some demanding patterns that were typical of them some time ago or they adopt new behaviours not seen before. Some revert to baby talk, bedwetting or being fearful.
- Their behaviour is often impulsive.
- They are commonly hostile and uncooperative with adults.
- They might be reluctant to accompany a particular adult, or adults in general.
- Some inflict injury on themselves (in the absence of severe sensory integration dysfunction).
- Many have disturbed sleep and nightmares.
- Sexually abused children might start talking about secrets or of something nasty that is happening to a friend or a doll.
- Sexually abused children might display sexualised behaviour such as blatant flirting, excessive touching of their own genitals or sexual play with another child.
- Sexually abused children might re-enact the abuse in drawings, play or with their toys.

Learning skills

Children's disorganised home environments, disrupted routines and inadequate supervision disrupt their ability to complete academic work at home or be fully prepared for the school day. Long-term high cortisol levels affect a wide range of brain functions.

- Neglected children are often passive and helpless in their task orientation, give up easily, do not cope well with frustration, are distractable, impulsive and lacking in initiative.
- They are more reliant on adult directions and the administration of external consequences, being less intrinsically motivated.
- Neglect results in a lack of stimulation that causes delays in children's language skills, particularly expression, and impairment of overall intellectual abilities.

(continued)

- Neglected and physically abused children tend to perform at low levels academically. At younger ages, this is most pronounced for reading skills whereas, by late primary school, the disadvantage is across all subject areas.
- Physically abused children's reduced engagement in learning and view of themselves as academically incompetent lead to declines in their school achievement, with the result that they are more likely to be retained in a grade, have high levels of absenteeism and special education referrals, and experience higher than usual failure rates.
- Children experiencing sexual abuse typically achieve reasonably well at school. This is remarkable given that their anxiety levels must make it difficult to concentrate on academic tasks.
- Sexually abused children often display knowledge of adult sexual behaviour that is in advance of their years or developmental level.

Physical signs

Children aged under 5 years are at more serious risk than older children of injury from physical abuse.

- Children enduring physical abuse may have injuries such as bruises, welts, burns or fractures that have no convincing causal explanation.
- They might show little response to pain.
- Those suffering sexual abuse can have injuries or infections to the genital or anal areas or throat.
- Because their immune system is compromised by chronic stress, many abused children suffer long-term somatic complaints.
- Sexually abused girls experience early menarche, sexual debut, 18 months' earlier childbirth and problems with sexual intimacy.

Source: Bolger & Patterson 2001, Bonner et al. 1992, Bromberg & Johnson 2001, Burack et al. 2006, Carrey et al. 1995, Feiring et al. 2002, Fergusson & Lynskey 1997, Flores et al. 2005, George & Main 1979, Glaser 2000, Goodwin et al. 2004, Gowen & Nebrig 2002, Haynes-Seman & Baumgarten 1998, Hoffman-Plotkin & Twentyman 1984, Kim & Cicchetti 2004, 2006, Klimes-Dougan & Kistner 1990, Koenig et al. 2000, Luthar et al. 2000, Maughan & Cicchetti 2002, Mullen et al. 1996, Pollak et al. 2005, Shields et al. 2001, Shonk & Cicchetti 2001, Solomon & Serres 1999, Thompson & Wyatt 1999, Trickett 1998, Vigil et al. 2005, Webster 2001, Zahn-Waxler & Radke-Yarrow 1990.

Report suspected abuse

The sexual assault of children or adults is a criminal offence and therefore must be reported to police. In many jurisdictions, it is a legal obligation to report all other forms of child abuse as well. But even when not mandated legally, you have a moral obligation to protect the children in your care. Therefore, when you see children with unusual injuries, ask them or their parents in neutral tones how these happened. If their explanation is implausible, if the children report an abusive incident, or if a constellation of behaviours (such as those listed in Box 4.1) cause you to suspect that they may be unsafe, report your concerns to your local child welfare agency for their investigation.

Offer reassurance but not secrecy

In the meantime, do not ask children for detailed descriptions of events: experienced investigators are best suited to finding out this information in a way that will not add to the children's distress or contaminate the evidence should there be legal proceedings. Reassure children that help is available, but never promise to keep the abuse a secret or suggest that they should forget about what has happened. Ignoring abuse only allows it to recur, both to this child and to others in the perpetrator's life. As children might have been told not to tell anyone about the abuse, reassure them that it is wrong for anyone to tell them to keep a secret forever, and that they can talk to you about anything. Encourage them to talk, but do not force them to confide in you.

Foster children's assertiveness

Personal safety programs attempt to alert children to potential threat from unfamiliar adults without making them suspicious or, worse still, terrified of 'strangers' (Bonner et al. 1992, Johnson et al. 2005, Jordan 1993). These programs may be necessary, but the real risk comes from adults and adolescents known to the children, in which case protectiveness programs offer little to empower them to resist abuse or to ensure that their assertiveness does not endanger them further (Bevill & Gast 1998, Ko & Cosden 2001). By the time children are having to fend off an attack, protective skills will be too little too late. However, children can be enfranchised in everyday ways within your program by affirming that they are valued, so that they are less likely to collude with abuse in an attempt to gain the affectionate contact with adults that they are not receiving otherwise, and giving them numerous opportunities to be assertive about their needs.

Support the family

After reporting your concerns to the authorities, one aspect of your role is to support the family, even if a family member has been named as a possible perpetrator. The non-offending adults will need immediate emotional support to help them to cope during the investigation (Briggs 1993). It might be useful to give them some reading material or the names of a parent support group, psychologists or family therapists who could assist them (Briggs 1993).

If the perpetrator is outside the immediate family, parents will need your advice not to confront the perpetrator themselves, to take steps to ensure that other family members have not been abused also, to avoid making the child feel guilty either for the abuse or for the turmoil that disclosure has produced, and to reassure abused children that any threats made against them by the perpetrator were lies. You might also encourage parents to gain a medical check for their child, as many sexually abused children want reassurance that they have not been permanently injured physically.

Locate support for yourself

Your outrage and hurt on behalf of a child whose parents are neglectful or abusive will be compounded if it reactivates memories of similar trauma in your own life. You might be tempted to avoid contact with the parents for your own protection, or to collude with the family in order to maintain a working relationship with them but, in so doing, could be disregarding the harm that their child has suffered (Harskamp 2002). Given the emotional climate, potential risk of intimidation and the ramifications of malpractice, you will need to access a colleague or consultant who can support you to maintain productive contact with the parents while their child is in your care. Accessing some personal support will be especially important when the accused person is a member of staff (see Box 4.2).

BOX 4.2 Responding to allegations of abuse by staff

Immediately upon receipt of an allegation of abuse by a member of staff and its notification to the authorities, the centre manager, director or senior teacher will need to take the following steps (Mikkelsen 1997):

- The accused member of staff must leave the premises immediately and cannot return to work until the allegation has been investigated. If the allegation is not credible, this will seem doubly unfair, but is for the protection of all involved, including the accused.
- Consult with your governing body or, if independent, obtain legal advice.
- Cooperate with the investigation in a matter-of-fact manner. Expressing outraged indignation or being defensive may be misconstrued as guilt rather than innocence.
- Without divulging names, to avoid innuendo, gossip and uncertainty as the news spreads on the centre grapevine, within hours write to all parents, advising them of the allegation against a member of staff. In order to check that there have been no other victims, the letter should ask parents to gently inquire of their children if anyone has made them feel bad or scared, touched them in ways that maybe were not usual, or told them to keep something a secret. Parents could also consider whether their child's behaviour has changed recently.
- Call a meeting where staff can discuss the traumatic effects of the allegations on themselves and plan how to fill the staffing gap left by the suspended worker.
- In most cases, parents will withdraw an abused child from the centre. But, if not, staff must be absolutely certain not to discuss the abuse with the child or attempt to convince the child to retract the allegation. Staff may feel so uncertain about how to respond to the child that they avoid interacting with him or her altogether, which is not desirable either (Mikkelsen 1997).

EMOTIONAL SAFETY

After the need to survive, safety is the next most fundamental requirement. Safety encompasses the needs for security, stability, protection and freedom from fear, anxiety and chaos (Prince & Howard 2002). In other words, more than simply being fed and watered, children need nurturing—and to know that they can depend on that nurturance. In the model in Figure II.2 (on p. 35), this need is depicted as part of the tree's trunk, signifying its vital importance.

Adults can choose to take part in activities and to associate with people who bolster our self-esteem, but children are at the mercy of the contexts in which we place them (Katz 1995). This means that they rely on you to create an accepting environment in which they can feel emotionally safe and confident about their ability to meet the demands being placed on them.

Support stressed children

When children feel emotionally unsafe, they can have a reaction that, for want of a better term, we might call stress. Strictly speaking, stress is a physical reaction to feeling out of control, particularly of negative events in life, whereas worries are the cognitive component, and anxiety is the emotional aspect of distress. However, in common usage, the word stress is usually a shorthand way of referring to all three aspects, implying that perturbed individuals have assessed that the demands exceed their capacity to cope.

While ensuring that your program does not itself provoke stress for children, in cases where their stress arises from family adversity, you may feel powerless to help. However, recognising that children are encountering more than the usual difficulties, you can provide more than the usual level of support. Positive experiences out of home can compensate for or directly counter risks posed in other parts of children's lives, insulating them from the detrimental outcomes that are often thought inevitable (Rutter 1999).

Provide responsive caregiving

Children experiencing adversity in their living circumstances will benefit most from high-quality intellectual stimulation and responsive relationships with adults. You can support stressed children, first, by noticing its signs (see Box 4.3) and allowing children to discuss their feelings at the time these behaviours are being manifested. Even when children are displaying some of these signs, however, you must not be too quick to jump to conclusions that these are caused by family stress. You would not blame children's disruptive behaviour at home on your program; similarly, you cannot assume that a child's behaviour in your care is due to events in the family. It is more likely that behavioural outbursts are instigated by events in the immediate environment. The children may respond to these by using antisocial methods that they have learned at home, but the actual trigger is within your setting. This, then, is the place to implement adjustments for stressed children. You will need to ensure that your program itself does not provoke stress reactions by imposing expectations that the children feel unable to meet. Both the content and processes (such as waiting times, duration of activities and balance of active versus quiet play) need to enable children to function adaptively.

Highlight children's resilience

Children who are ill-treated or blame themselves for family adversity often lose sight of their own resources. To counteract this, comment on their strengths and efforts to cope. At the same time as being empathic to the injustices they endure, it is also important to highlight the parts of them that are 'normal' so they do not come to see themselves as fragile, different or damaged, but can use their strengths, interests and passions to experience life in ways that are not connected to their abuse (Berg & Steiner 2003).

Some children become so sensitised to threat that they lose sight of the positive aspects of life. To help them get back in touch with life's positive possibilities and notice that they are enjoying themselves, you might sit beside them and comment that they look to be having fun (Caughey 1991).

BOX 4.3 Signs of stress in children

Children living with adversity have difficulties regulating their emotions. Unlike typical children, their rate of behavioural difficulties does not decline during early childhood, while their emotional difficulties such as depression and anxiety increase. Specific manifestations of this include:

- social withdrawal
- negative peer interaction
- reactive or proactive aggression
- antisocial behaviour (e.g. damage to property)
- anger
- sadness or depression
- distress
- anxiety and fearfulness
- hypervigilance—scanning their environment to detect potential threats
- slowed recovery from stressful events
- increased health problems, and
- disturbed sleeping patterns, which result in fatigue, inattention, hyperactivity and poor performance on learning tasks.

Source: Cummings 1998, Cummings et al. 2003, 2006, El-Sheikh & Harger 2001, El-Sheikh et al. 2006, Katz & Woodin 2002, Maughan & Cicchetti 2002, Peterson & Zill 1986, Shaw et al. 1999, Sternberg et al. 2006a, 2006b.

Foster self-efficacy

Low self-efficacy is transmitted across generations—not genetically, but when mothers respond inconsistently to their children's communications of distress, they teach their children that they cannot secure help, and the children stop trying (Seligman 1975). You will observe this when infants and toddlers do not ask for what they need, do not persist at tasks, or fail to show pleasure at their accomplishments (Jennings & Abrew 2004). Therefore, for all children but particularly those experiencing family adversity, you will need to respond to the children's signals or requests, so that they learn that they can ask for and receive the care they need.

Children who experience family conflict often blame themselves for it or are given or spontaneously take on the job of looking after their stressed parents. The fact that they have no power to fix the problems reduces their self-efficacy. You can establish whether children are bearing responsibility for their parents' welfare by having them draw a picture of their family and asking them who looks after each member. Children who are well adjusted can report that the adults look after themselves, each other and the children, while the children look after their teddy or dolls and help tend the family pets. If instead the children answer that they look after one or both of their parents, you might tactfully draw this to their parents' attention.

Many times, the parents do not realise that their children are worried about them and, once aware, can reassure the children and thank them for their concern but remind them that, as children, their job is to devote their energies to having fun and growing up. The parents might also be able to give the children an explanation for the family's stresses, which absolves them of culpability (Zimet & Jacob 2001). Meanwhile, within your program, you can guide them to attribute everyday occurrences to forces that are internal but controllable, specific and temporary (see Ch 6).

Teach emotional regulation

Early exposure to unmanageable stressors can teach children inflexible and maladaptive coping strategies and poor emotion-regulation skills which, in turn, lead to social difficulties (Evans & English 2002). When they are reacting emotionally, you will need to soothe these children so that they can understand and resolve their emotions and thus learn that feelings are not frightening or likely to get out of control. When children's stress gives rise to emotional difficulties, they are less able to generate and then use effective coping strategies (Halpern 2004) and, therefore, can need guidance to use coping skills. Coping does not mean feeling no symptoms when experiencing stressful conditions. It means using strategies to minimise the impact of the stress on your life, which can entail any of the following responses:

- *Problem-focused actions* involve solving the problem that is provoking stress (e.g. using negotiation to resolve a peer conflict). Finding solutions might entail focusing more intently on the problem until it is solved, which will be a helpful strategy, as long as it does not cause children to ruminate on problems.
- *Emotion-focused strategies* aim to reduce the intensity or duration of our feelings. We do this by seeking comfort from others, soothing ourselves, distracting ourselves from the source of our frustration, adjusting our thinking, or passively accepting an uncontrollable stressor. Distraction will be beneficial as long as it does not suppress appropriate social assertiveness or lead to submission.
- *Behavioural responses* could entail disengagement—that is, avoiding a stressor by withdrawing, or being assertive by asking when an obstacle will be removed (Compas 1987, Diener & Mangelsdorf 1999, Eisenberg et al. 2005, Gilliom et al. 2002, Halpern 2004).

The most adaptive strategy depends on the nature of the stressor. In general, problem-focused strategies are effective when individuals have some control over a stressor, whereas emotional or behavioural adjustments are more suited to issues that they cannot change (Spirito et al. 1991). For acute stressors that are beyond individuals' control, behavioural or cognitive avoidance can be useful, but may be less successful for ongoing or chronic stress, while the least effective strategy is emotional venting (Halpern 2004).

However, as long as children do not rely on ineffective coping mechanisms such as wishful thinking, worrying, blaming themselves, or attempting to ignore a problem (Hunter & Boyle 2004, Lewis & Frydenberg 2002), it does not seem to matter how they cope, but that they have a repertoire of positive strategies to select from and can be flexible in their use (Eisenberg et al. 2005, Rutter 1985, 1999).

Foster children's friendships

Promoting peer acceptance and helping troubled children to develop friendships will protect them from stress (Criss et al. 2002). Not only can you support interactions between children within your setting, but you might also be able to recommend community activities to the parents of children who have an affinity for each other, so that by attending together the children can have contact outside of your setting that cements their relationship within it.

While understanding that maltreated children will view their world as dangerous, you must also suggest an alternative point of view (Caughey 1991) and support the children to react with less aggression towards others.

Support stressed parents

Parents who are impoverished and discriminated against (e.g. racially) can have low self-efficacy as a result of being unable to improve their circumstances (Ackerman et al. 2004, Diener et al. 2003). When this feeling is combined with attributions blaming their children for their behavioural difficulties and with parents' need for power or control over their children, it will translate into harsh or even abusive parenting (Bugental & Happaney 2004). First-time parents may be particularly responsive to your suggestions about child development and parenting (Haslam et al. 2006), while another possibility is to provide a parent lounge in your centre where parents can congregate and mentor each other.

Your everyday chats with parents can support them to meet their children's needs. However, parents with high stress can sometimes overwhelm and become heavily reliant on their children's caregivers or teachers. Given that counselling is not your role, you can ask if they would like information about agencies that could assist them. Meanwhile, to emphasise that your focus is their child, when parents are recounting stressful events, you can direct the conversation to how this is affecting their child and ask what they would like you to do to help their child. For example, when a parent is recounting an incident of family conflict, you could ask questions such as, 'And where was Katy at the time? How did she react? How were you able to look after her while feeling so vulnerable yourself? What do you think she needs from us today?' and so on (Gowen & Nebrig 2002).

WELLBEING

Children who are unwell have higher production of the stress-related hormone, cortisol (Watamura et al. 2003). Chronic ear infections, medication side effects, poor diet, lack of sleep, being overweight or underweight, or food sensitivities, create physical discomfort, with the result that children can seem to overreact to minor irritations. This can appear to be a behavioural difficulty, when instead it is a physical problem.

Around 2% of the childhood population endure repeated and chronic bouts of illness (Ashton & Bailey 2004). When this applies to children in your care, you will need to understand their illness and its implications for their education and health management, both ongoing and in the event of health crises (Ashton & Bailey 2004). While it is important that, as far as possible, your setting provides a venue for the children to be 'normal' and, therefore, does not emphasise their special caretaking needs (Bessell 2001), nevertheless, some program adjustments can be needed. For example:

- Health impairments often weaken the body's immunological system, making children susceptible to other illnesses. Therefore, control of contagious diseases within the setting can be crucial.
- In instances where physical limitations result from their illness, adaptations to equipment may be necessary to ensure children's access to activities (Shiu 2004).

■ A lack of energy can mean that convalescing children need considerable quiet time and passive activities to allow them to recover their energy.

Emotionally, children's misunderstandings of their condition and its treatment, their early encounters with pain, and their concern over the observable strain on other family members can mean that they may benefit from opportunities to talk about their experiences. To ensure that you do not confuse them or undermine their parents during these conversations, you will need to discover what they have been told about their condition, particularly if they are dying (McCarthy 1987).

Socially, unwell children's repeated absences are likely to interrupt and disrupt their peer relationships (Shiu 2001). To foster ongoing contact so that children do not feel like outsiders when they return, during their periods of absence you might be able to coordinate a program of home visits by some of their friends. On their return, their peers might need information about the reason for the child's absence, changed appearance and atypical needs (McCarthy 1987, Tyler & Colson 1994). On the other hand, convalescing children might not want others to perceive them as sick and therefore will not want their peers to be given any information (Dockett 2004, Shiu 2001).

Children's relationships with adults can also be distorted by their experience of relating with medical personnel, which can cause them to direct their social interactions to adults rather than peers. Moreover, the requirements of their management can increase children's dependency on adults. To offset this tendency, you might have to mediate their peer engagement in ways recommended in Chapters 5 and 14.

At the time of initial diagnosis, particularly of a child's potentially life-threatening illness, parents are likely to be in shock, frightened and feeling a sense of powerlessness. During their child's illness and treatment, mothers in particular are likely to have their working lives disrupted (Ashton 2004, Vickers et al. 2004). Your understanding of the competing and often overwhelming demands on them may be a considerable help (Vickers et al. 2004). In practical terms, you might be able to support the family by minimising the disruption to mothers' working lives through offering flexible scheduling of their child's attendance around the child's fluctuating health status and medical appointments.

At the same time, staff will need support also, particularly when children are left with permanent disabilities or are dying. Collectively, you will have to look after yourselves and channel your grief into making the children's lives at your centre as productive as possible.

CONCLUSION

Children's personal coping skills will not be enough to assure their wellbeing in the face of unresolved family stress (Halpern 2004). When for whatever reasons children's families are experiencing adversity, your warm relationship with them can protect them against maladjustment (Luthar et al. 2000). While the troublesome behaviour of stressed children seems to invite further rejection, it will be vital to ensure that you do not scapegoat them or respond to their provocative behaviour with controlling discipline, as that would only entrench their emotional, behavioural and peer difficulties.

SUGGESTED FURTHER READING

Stress and resilience

Linke P 2006 *Managing change with infants and young children*. Early Childhood Australia, Canberra.

Seligman MEP, Reivich K, Jaycox L, Gillham J 1995 *The optimistic child*. Random House, Sydney.

Child abuse

Adams C, Fay J 1992 *Helping your child recover from sexual abuse*. University of Washington Press, Seattle.

Baker CD 2002 *Female survivors of sexual abuse*. Brunner-Routledge, East Sussex.

Bass E, Davis L 1993 *Beginning to heal: a first guide for female survivors of child sexual abuse*. Vermilion, London.

Briggs F 1993 *Why my child? Supporting the families of victims of child sexual abuse*. Allen & Unwin, Sydney.

Briggs F, McVeity M 2000 *Teaching children to protect themselves*. Allen & Unwin, Sydney.

Davis L 1991 *Allies in healing: when the person you love was sexually abused as a child*. Harper Perennial, New York.

Hunter M 1990 *Abused boys: the neglected victims of sexual abuse*. Fawcett Columbine, New York.

Lew M 2004 *Victims no longer: the classic guide for men recovering from child sexual abuse*, 2nd edn. HarperCollins, New York.

Sonkin DJ 1998 *Wounded boys; heroic men: a man's guide to recovering from child abuse*. Adams Media Corporation, Holbrook, MA.

chapter 5

Meeting children's need to belong

'Settings most likely to foster social development will (a) build the child's attachment to the peer group as well as the caregiver; (b) emphasize constructivist rather than didactic teaching; (c) support intrinsic and internalised motivation; and (d) identify a broad, coherent mission that includes social development and emphasizes the creation of group structures to support it.'

MACCOBY & LEWIS (2003, p. 1073)

While the materials and activities made available to children offer them opportunities for discovery and learning, they also shape the interactions that take place (Cassidy et al. 2005, Wishard et al. 2003). The warmth and sensitivity of these interactions are the most crucial influence on children's learning (NICHD Early Child Care Research Network 2003d, Peisner-Feinberg & Burchinal 1997).

COMPONENTS OF SOCIAL COMPETENCE

Two distinct sets of social skills have their rudimentary beginnings prior to 1 year of age. The first is a prosocial cluster comprising exchanging affection with others, which requires skills such as being empathic, altruistic and cooperative (LaFontana & Cillessen 2002). To develop this prosocial orientation to their relationships, children need both a healthy self-esteem and positive attitudes about relating with others (Salmivalli et al. 2005). The combination of these two qualities yields four different social orientations, which are depicted in Table 5.1.

TABLE 5.1 Social orientations according to perceptions of self and others		
	I'm okay	**I'm not okay**
You're okay	Prosocial High self-efficacy High communal goals	Dependency Low self-efficacy High communal goals
You're not okay	Aggression High self-efficacy Low communal goals	Withdrawal Low self-efficacy Low communal goals

Source: Adapted from Salmivalli et al. (2005) whose research confirmed three orientations; the 'dependency' category is my own conjecture.

A second cluster of social skills allows individuals to achieve their goals within social settings at the same time as maintaining positive relationships with others (Green & Rechis 2006, LaFontana & Cillessen 2002). This requires the skills of sharing, using persuasion, negotiation and, occasionally, strategic coercion (Green & Rechis 2006). High status within the group hierarchy helps individuals to meet their own goals. Whereas incompetent children have a restricted repertoire of these behaviours or cannot adjust their approach to suit the circumstances, those who are socially competent can use various strategies depending on which is likely to be most effective (Green & Rechis 2006). Both clusters of social skills are needed for children to perform the specific prosocial behaviours listed in Box 5.1.

BOX 5.1 Prosocial skills

The core social task of the early childhood years is for young children to learn to regulate the intensity of their emotions and control how they express these to others.

A prosocial orientation

Although specific social behaviours can differ at different ages and across ethnic and cultural groups, a prosocial orientation is universal. This encompasses:

- a social *orientation* towards being positive and agreeable
- being *socially perceptive* so that children adjust their actions according to group norms
- choosing *relevant* actions in light of the circumstances and behaviour of peers, and
- *balancing* their interests with the needs of others.

Entry skills

In order to be successful in their bids to enter a group, children need to be competent at employing the following range of entry skills:

- surveillance of a group before attempting entry to ensure that they match their behaviour to the group's
- use of initiations, such as approaching, touching, gaining eye contact, vocalising or using another child's name

(continued)

- positive and cooperative initiations and responses to others' invitations, and
- avoidance of disruptive actions, such as calling attention to oneself, asking questions, criticising the way the other children are playing, introducing new topics of conversation or new games, being too boisterous, acting aggressively, or destroying others' play materials.

Supportive actions

Having gained entry to the play of others, the playmates need to be able to sustain their interaction. This will require them to validate and support each other, through the use of the following strategies:

- *Use of supportive behaviours.* These tell others that one is keen to cooperate and can be trusted. Such actions comprise complimenting, smiling at, cooperating with, imitating, sharing, taking turns and assisting others in play.
- *Diplomatic leads.* Without being bossy, children need to be able to make positive play suggestions to enlist other children in their play.
- *Seeking support.* Children need to be able to ask questions or seek assistance from their playmates. Sometimes, they can frame requests as questions so that these seem less directive.
- *Commenting on play.* Statements serve to remind the players of their play theme, establish common ground, and help the children to function cohesively. To that end, one child might say, 'We're doing this together, aren't we?' To be effective and well received, these comments have to be relevant to the activity and in tune with the other children.
- *Awareness of and empathy towards others.* Children need to pay attention to relevant social cues so that they are sensitive to the initiations and needs of their playmates. In response to feedback from their peers, they need to be able to moderate their behaviour to suit their friends.
- *Self-awareness.* Children need to be aware of how their behaviour will influence other people's responses to them.

Conflict management skills

Most conflict between infants reflects competition over access to resources and space, while for preschoolers it relates to social disputes such as the inclusion of particular children in their play. To resolve conflict peaceably with playmates, children need to:

- be persuasive and assertive rather than bossy
- negotiate play activities
- obey social rules about sharing and taking turns as leader, for example
- suggest compromises when someone's actions have been disputed, and
- not accede to unreasonable demands from playmates, but nevertheless decline tactfully by presenting a rationale for not accepting a playmate's idea or by offering an alternative suggestion.

Source: Asher 1983, Brown et al. 2000, Green & Rechis 2006, Hay et al. 2004, Mize 1995, NICHD Early Child Care Research Network 2001a, Putallaz & Gottman 1981, Putallaz & Wasserman 1990, Trawick-Smith 1988.

ACCEPTANCE

In Figure II.2 (on p. 35), acceptance is the first element feeding children's sense of belonging and self-esteem. The quality of the interactions between adults and children and among the children affects the overall quality of nurturing that the children experience at the time, promotes their social competence, and is the single largest influence on their engagement in and liking of learning (Graziano et al. 2007, Ladd & Burgess 2001). Over time, sensitive caregiving produces in children more prosocial and less antisocial behaviour (Field 1991, Field et al. 1988, NICHD Early Child Care Research Network 2001a, O'Brien et al. 1999, Phillips et al. 1987, Schwarz et al. 1973, Vandell et al. 1988).

Acceptance by adults

While the main purpose of fostering accepting relationships between caregivers and children is for the emotional support and nurturance that this offers children, in the context of this book's focus on disciplinary practices, adults' acceptance of children is likely to increase their willingness to cooperate with our directives. This was shown in one study where preschool children followed 100% of teachers' directives when the teachers' approval rates were high, and only 14% when teachers were disapproving (Atwater & Morris 1988).

However, children who are distractable, disrupt group processes or are aggressive commonly experience adult rejection, receiving four times more negative than positive teacher feedback and fewer positive responses to their constructive participation. They also engage in more mutually angry exchanges with their teachers (Henricsson & Rydell 2004, Stormont 2002, Strein et al. 1999, Tucker et al. 2002). Many of these children receive controlling discipline at home and then are met with more coercion in their care and education settings, which only entrenches their difficulties, causing their antisocial behaviours to persist and prosocial acts to decline (Birch & Ladd 1998, Hamre & Pianta 2005, Henricsson & Rydell 2004, Howes 2000, Reinke & Herman 2002). Repeated reprimands of children with demanding behaviours signals to onlookers that these children are less worthy of their friendship (Schmuck & Schmuck 2001).

In contrast, children's engagement, achievement levels and conduct all improve when they are cared for by emotionally supportive, responsive teachers with whom they experience minimal conflict (Baker 2006, Birch & Ladd 1997, Decker et al. 2007, Graziano et al. 2007, Hamre & Pianta 2005, Ladd et al. 1999, Murray & Greenberg 2000, Pianta & Stuhlman 2004). Children's connectedness with sensitive adults is even more influential for those who are aggressive (Ladd & Burgess 2001), have less self-regulated behaviour (Rimm-Kaufman et al. 2002), for boys (Furrer & Skinner 2003), and for children with devalued minority status (Decker et al. 2007, Meehan et al. 2003).

Peer acceptance

Peer acceptance is a group phenomenon, signalling that the group as a whole values each member's place within it. Even at young ages, peer acceptance protects children from maladjustment arising from family stress (Criss et al. 2002), helps them to overcome reticence (Gazelle & Ladd 2003), feeds the self-esteem of girls in particular (Nelson et al. 2005), deflects aggressive behaviour patterns (Dodge et al. 2003), and improves children's attention, engagement and cooperation and thus performance in school (Flook et al. 2005, Ladd & Burgess 2001, Ladd et al. 1999).

   In contrast, the maltreatment associated with peer group rejection teaches children that peers are unlikely to be friendly and supportive, which leads over time to declining academic participation and achievement (Buhs & Ladd 2001, Ladd & Burgess 2001), and increased levels of both reticence (Flook et al. 2005, Gazelle & Ladd 2003, Spinrad et al. 2004) and reactive aggression (Dodge et al. 2003, Hay et al. 2004, Johnson et al. 2000, Keiley et al. 2000, Stormshak et al. 1999), particularly for children who are predisposed towards aggression or are already vulnerable for other reasons (Hay et al. 2004).

Ensure that the children know each other

Children are more willing to play with someone whom they know and are more likely to form friendships in stable groupings (Howes 1987). Therefore, where possible, maintain a stable group membership and on a daily basis incorporate the likes of name songs in your group sessions so that the children become familiar with each other.

Provide materials that invite social play

Children's social competence is enhanced by their play with peers (Kontos & Wilcox-Herzog 1997a), while their growing competence in all other developmental domains contributes to the development of social play, whose sequence is described in Table 5.2. Children's social play is facilitated by the activities made available to them (Kontos &

TABLE 5.2 Development of social play	
Age	**Play behaviours**
Up to 6 months	Engage almost exclusively with adults
	Begin to explore objects
6–12 months	Begin to explore peers, showing preference for familiar versus unfamiliar companions
12–18 months	Peer interactions are only minimally coordinated, with infants able to repeat each other's actions, take turns and comfort each other
	Toddlers are more willing to share toys than they will be at 2 years of age
18–24 months	Increase in spontaneous and cooperative peer interaction, which is the beginning of peer cooperation
	Strong preference for familiar playmates
	Ritualistic, reciprocal play, such as run-and-chase or hide-and-seek
	High rates of both prosocial and antisocial behaviour
2–3 years	Children can now engage in pretend play, communicating not only its content, but also using their language skills to structure the game itself. This permits active cooperation
	They are now flexible enough intellectually to incorporate and adjust to new and unfamiliar play partners
	The number of children's negative interactions decreases, while their positive interactions increase
3–5 years	Children can differentiate friends from acquaintances
	True reciprocal friendships develop
	They can relate to groups, not just in pairs (particularly boys)
	Sex-segregated play begins

Source: Brownell et al. 2006, Deynoot-Schaub & Riksen-Walraven 2006, Hay et al. 2004, Howes 1987, Vaughn et al. 2003.

Keyes 1999), which indicates the need to provide activities that both entice social play and are more attractive than being alone. For example, computers and small blocks tend to produce solitary engagement, whereas a well-equipped kitchen corner, dress-up clothes, dolls and dollhouses, large blocks, housekeeping materials and vehicles invite social cooperation (Ivory & McCollum 1999).

Initiate cooperative activities

You can actively foster cooperative play between children by instigating activities and games that require joint effort, such as making a group collage or large painting, or navigating an obstacle course in pairs. Structured cooperative games include non-elimination musical chairs, which involves removing a chair—not a player—whenever the music stops, so that all the children end up having to fit on the one remaining chair (Sapon-Shevin 1986).

Facilitate children's social play

To facilitate children's peer acceptance, you can support their social play by adopting the roles of:

- *stage manager* who helps children to engage with materials by making objects available, introducing children to activities, giving suggestions and practical assistance
- *play facilitator* or participant who talks with children about their activities, providing information and feedback to expand on their engagement, and
- *behaviour manager* who oversees children's safety and the fairness of their actions and protects peers by redirecting antisocial behaviour (de Kruif et al. 2000, Kontos 1999).

You can avoid having the children come to rely on your facilitation by enhancing their play *processes*, rather than helping them to craft a better *product* (Harper & McCluskey 2002).

Pairing children

You could deliberately structure an activity that you know will appeal to two children who do not ordinarily play together, or await a natural opportunity to point out to a small group of children that a reticent child appears interested in what they are doing and might want to take part. Although pairing up a withdrawn child with a more prosocial peer can be effective (Greco & Morris 2001), very young children may not have the skills to decide what to do if their playmate does not cooperate, while the inequality of the relationship can lead to dominance by the socially advanced child. Thus, the neglected child might experience a greater quantity of social interactions, but not an improved quality.

Promote the inclusion of isolated children

Appreciating children's and families' diversity not only sends them a direct message of acceptance, but also communicates indirectly to those who are different in less identifiable ways that they will be nurtured within this setting.

The quality of your verbal and non-verbal interactions with individual children creates an expectation about the inclusion of their peers. Positive teacher comments actively help to recruit peer support for excluded children (Schmuck & Schmuck 2001). When children observe you interacting positively with all children and being supportive of disruptive peers, they are likely to perceive their peers as both more competent and more likeable (Hughes et al. 2001) and therefore involve otherwise neglected children in their play (Okagaki et al. 1998).

Children with developmental delays

Children with significantly delayed development will have particular difficulties adjusting to the demands of a peer group (Hay et al. 2004). Although young children express positive attitudes towards children with disabilities, few enter reciprocal friendships with them (Dyson 2005), with the result that many are ignored (or neglected) by peers (Odom et al. 1999). This social isolation comes about because, even compared with younger children, those with intellectual disabilities are less skilled at initiating, leading and sustaining interactions with others and, when their efforts fail, are more likely to withdraw into solitary play (Brown et al. 1999, Guralnick & Groom 1987, Guralnick et al. 2006, Hanline 1993, Harper & McCluskey 2003, Odom et al. 1999, Reynolds & Holdgrafer 1998, Wilson 1999). This pattern is fairly stable over time, limiting not only peer contact, but also reciprocal friendships (Guralnick et al. 2006, 2007).

Children with language impairments and disruptive play behaviour are most likely to be isolated or rejected (Harper & McCluskey 2002), while those who can participate in peer activities are more easily included. For example, children with physical disabilities appear to be well understood, accepted and included (at least at the level of parallel play) in the play of non-disabled children (Okagaki et al. 1998). On the other hand, young children's unsophisticated understanding of disability can cause them to believe that children with disabilities cannot play (Dyson 2005). They tend to overgeneralise about their peer's disability, concluding for example that a physical disability renders the child incapable of thinking. They can also be fearful of catching the disability (Doherty-Derkowski 1995). Therefore, with parental permission, it can be useful to explain to the other children about a given child's disability and allow them to ask questions about it. At times, it will also be important to comment on how the child with a disability is similar to the other children.

Given that children make friends with those who have similar abilities to themselves, children who are isolated because of their disability can sometimes be less lonely when placed with slightly younger children, as long as their size does not cause them to look out of place. The activities can also be better matched to their skills and, if physically unsteady, they can feel safer without bigger boisterous children running around them.

Gifted learners

Giftedness simply means that children are developing at least one-third faster than usual, such that a 3-year-old is as able in one or more developmental domains as the typical 4-year-old. According to this criterion, 3 to 5% of the population are considered gifted, which is the same proportion as are defined as having disabilities.

Gifted learners are typically popular with others, but may not experience peer relationships as deeply companionable. They might develop deep affection for a similarly capable best friend or their parents, but lack a breadth of relationships, making them vulnerable to loneliness and isolated play if their best friend is absent. Thus, despite the fact that their advanced problem-solving skills contribute to social finesse, it can seem at times that they lack the ability to form friendships. The main intervention for these children is to give them access to others at their developmental level, as usually their social success improves and they feel less lonely when they have playmates who can share their sophisticated interests. This may entail moving them up early to the next age grouping or to school, where they can play among older peers. This is usually called 'acceleration', but is really only a case of providing a placement that is developmentally appropriate (Feldhusen 1989).

Children from minority cultures
Children who are in a cultural minority within the group are likely to have fewer peer supports and proportionally more peer stressors such as discrimination or rejection (Ladd & Burgess 2001). This places them at risk of declining achievement, emotional adjustment and social satisfaction. Your acceptance of these and all children can be communicated directly by talking openly with the group about the many differences and similarities between people so that all individuals can be seen to be similar to—and thus potential companions for—their peers (Crary 1992).

Children displaying aggression
A fourth group of children commonly experiencing social isolation are those who frequently behave aggressively. Although these children initially approach others often, their overtures are frequently rejected because their approaches are often boisterous or aggressive, they are less cooperative and their actions disrupt others' play, with the result that over time they initiate less often and become increasingly isolated (Dodge 1983). Measures for improving their aggression and thus peer inclusion are given in Chapter 14.

EMPATHY

As illustrated in Figure II.2, the second quality that feeds both children's self-esteem and their sense of belonging is receiving empathy. Empathy has been aptly described as emotional resonance with others (Frith 2004). It is the ability to appreciate how others feel and to respond in a caring way to alleviate their distress (Swick 2005). It is distinguished from sympathy, which is feeling sorrow or concern *for* another (de Wied et al. 2005). Empathy is the cornerstone of our social development, leading to a quest for justice through altruism, prosocial behaviour and low levels of aggression (Hastings et al. 2000, Young et al. 1999, Zhou et al. 2002). It generates high levels of peer acceptance and the ability to form mutual, harmonious friendships (Clark & Ladd 2000).

Empathy requires both the cognitive ability to see the world from other perspectives and the emotional sensitivity to appreciate others' feelings. Early theories that young children could not be empathic have subsequently been disproved. From a very young age, children who receive empathy can be aroused by another's distress, will endeavour to interpret it, will express concern, and attempt to comfort others (Young et al. 1999). Even in the first days of life, when one infant cries, others will too, reacting almost reflexively to others' distress as if it were their own (Young et al. 1999, Zahn-Waxler & Radke-Yarrow 1990). By 10 weeks of age, infants discriminate and can mirror their mothers' joyous emotions, while averting their gaze from her expressions of sadness (Zahn-Waxler & Radke-Yarrow 1990).

In their second year of life, infants can realise that another's misery is not their own, although they are still confused about the cause of someone else's distress and are uncertain how to help (Swick 2005). By 3 years of age, children are able to talk about emotions and therefore have a better idea about the likely cause of another's distress. Their attempts at consolation are more appropriate to the other's needs—for example, they may console a peer with, 'It's okay. Mummy will be back soon'. Finally, by 4 years of age, children can ask another, 'What's the matter?' rather than assuming that what upsets them will have upset the other person. Their repertoire of helping behaviours has now expanded from a simple hug or pat to helping, sharing, offering verbal sympathy, protecting and defending victims and expressing anger towards the source of their distress (Zahn-Waxler & Radke-Yarrow 1990).

Thus, children's supposed 'egocentrism' is overcome by the age of 4, as long as we teach them about their feelings and how their actions affect others (Swick 2005). Adults' responsiveness to children's distress directly teaches them how to regulate their own emotions without becoming overwhelmed, teaches them empathy and motivates them to act prosocially towards others in distress (Davidov & Grusec 2006). With their personal needs thus satisfied, they are freed up to attend to the needs of others (Swick 2005, Zhou et al. 2002).

Coaching of emotions

Emotions entail physical changes within our bodies. They motivate us to meet our needs or achieve our goals by signalling whether these are being met (Ashiabi 2000). As such, emotions serve a survival function: fear signals the presence of a threat, while sadness tells us to search for a way to be happier. Emotions also serve a communicative function of letting others know how we feel and asking for their help. In infancy, this communicative function of emotions is absolutely essential to survival.

It is probable that all mammals experience the primary emotions of joy, love, hurt, sadness, fear and repulsion (Adler et al. 2004). However, it is less likely that other species experience secondary emotions, which are a combination of thoughts and feelings, such as suspicion, guilt, surprise or disgust. And it is likely that humans are the only species that experiences emotion *about* emotions—for example, when we are embarrassed to show that we are sad, or anxious that we may not be able to disguise nervousness.

Four features differentiate children's emotions from those of adults. First, children are more intense in their feelings. When a 2-year-old drops his or her ice-cream, a 10-minute despair session ensues, whereas adults typically do not react with the same level of distress. Second, children have a limited vocabulary to explain to themselves what they are feeling. Third, they lack experience at resolving emotion. Fourth, children under the age of approximately 8 to 10 years are unaware that one event can engender two conflicting feelings (Harris 1983, Kostelnik et al. 2006). They are what has been termed 'serial emoters': they feel emotions successively rather than in combination. One minute they can declare that they will never be friends again with a peer who has hurt them and then, a few minutes later, will be holding hands in warm communion with that same child. This does not mean that the first emotion was insignificant. In fact, young children's inability to perceive conflicting feelings means that, at the time, the only emotion they are aware of is their anger, undiluted by warmer feelings. This serial emotional experience is also illustrated by the 3-year-old's piteous cry to an angry parent, 'You don't love me anymore, do you?' which signals that, unable to feel two emotions at once, the child is unaware that we adults can feel both anger and love simultaneously.

Together, these qualities mean that children's emotional intensity can frighten them. This can be seen when young children have a tantrum about, say, being denied an ice-cream but, at some point during their protest start gasping, gagging and retching. This hysteria is no longer about the ice-cream, but a signal that they are frightened about having become so out of control. It is a feeling about a feeling.

Children's heightened emotionality, then, makes it extremely important that you appropriately express your own emotions and help children to recognise, understand and express their own. Children will feel safe when they experience neither blame nor scorn nor humiliation for how they feel. When you validate even negative feelings, you will teach children that all emotions are valid—that *they* are valid. Labelling their feelings so that they understand these and supporting them to reduce their emotional arousal will teach them to remain in command of the intensity and duration of their feelings (Eisenberg et al. 1999) and therefore to find them less distressing.

CONNECTEDNESS

In the model in Figure II.2, the third feature which feeds both children's sense of belonging and their self-esteem is connectedness to others. Close adult–child relationships improve children's cognitive and social skills, both at the time and in the longer term (Peisner-Feinberg et al. 2001).

Children's relationships with adults

At under 2 years of age, infants and toddlers in childcare have twice as many interactions with their caregivers than with their peers, with 10-month-olds spending just over 40% of their time interacting with adults and only 6% with peers, and 2-years-olds spending 26% of their time interacting with adults and 11% with peers (Deynoot-Schaub & Riksen-Walraven 2006). This highlights the importance of the children's connectedness to those adults. Guided by Freudian theory, this concept is often labelled as 'attachment', but for the reasons given in Box 5.2, I find this concept unnecessary and confusing and therefore choose to focus on the quality of interactions between adults and children, rather than on diagnosing the quality of children's 'attachment' to those adults.

Whether guided either by this perspective or by attachment theory, research concludes that children's connectedness to adults is fostered by the emotional availability of caregivers whose willingness to respond to, reflect and validate children's experiences facilitates children's engagement in learning, fosters their language development, and teaches them empathy and prosocial behaviour with peers (Clark & Ladd 2000, Graziano et al. 2007, Ladd & Burgess 2001, Landry et al. 2001, Tamis-LeMonda et al. 2001, Tucker et al. 2002). Children with warm adult support are more likely to develop mutual harmonious friendships and receive high levels of peer support, in all likelihood because these children receive empathy and thus learn how to give it (Clark & Ladd 2000) and, with warm support, learn how to regulate their own emotions (Davidov & Grusec 2006).

Give children your attention

Although educators spend the vast majority of their time interacting with children, one study has found that nearly one-third of the children actually receive no individual attention on a given day (Kontos & Wilcox-Herzog 1997b). This signals the need for adults consciously to make contact with individual children who otherwise could be overlooked.

Provide continuity of care

Children are more willing to approach and to be soothed by staff with whom they are familiar (Papero 2005). Thus, continuity of care will not only benefit all children, but will also be especially valuable for those who are unable to soothe themselves and therefore vent emotions in the form of disruptive behaviour (De Schipper et al. 2004). Providing for continuity of care requires that you overcome practical barriers such as staff members' preference or special skills at working with a particular age group, caregiver turnover, space and the timing of transitions (Aguillard et al. 2005, Cryer et al. 2000).

Plan transitions to new groupings

When caregiver continuity cannot be provided, recommended practice is to ease children's transitions to the next grouping (Cryer et al. 2000). Measures include:

- ensuring that children do not move up alone, but with at least one other child with whom they have a close relationship (Vaughn et al. 2000)
- having the children visit their new class ahead of the transition and, afterwards, revisit their old class when they wish to
- for internal moves, ensuring that all children and staff mingle during outdoor play so that all adults, children and environments are familiar to children of all ages, and
- preparing parents for the move by introducing them to their child's new caregivers (Cryer et al. 2000, 2005).

Although these measures will assist children to some extent, it is still likely that for the first month in their new class, at least half will display heightened levels of distress, particularly when they enjoyed a high quality of care in the group from which they recently graduated (Cryer et al. 2005).

BOX 5.2 An ambivalent attachment to attachment theory

Attachment theory is strongly endorsed within the psychiatric and psychoanalytic (Freudian) traditions. It states that children need to form an emotional attachment to a primary caregiver and that this relationship then provides a secure base from which to explore outwards. This attachment is said to determine children's socioemotional functioning both at the time and throughout life.

The theory arose from observations of the maladjustment that resulted when children were institutionalised during World War II. However, based not on any data, but on an *assumption* nested in the Freudian belief in the primacy of infants' relationships with their mother, Bowlby concluded that the orphans' maladjustment arose from the loss of their mother (Birns 1999, Honig 2002), when they suffered many other deprivations as well.

Furthermore, the concept that human babies need *intensive* care exclusively from a *single* caregiver is false. Unlike other species, human infants develop affection for many people—their mother, father, siblings and familiar adults and peers—even when they spend very few of their waking hours in their company (Birns 1999). In other words, children rely on and benefit from an array of relationships (Verschueren & Marcoen 1999, Waters & Cummings 2000).

My concern is that attachment has been misconstrued as an all-or-none phenomenon, whereby babies are thought to have only 6 to 8 months in which to become 'attached', after which it is too late. This places a tremendous burden of guilt on those parents (particularly mothers) who could not be available to their

(continued)

babies in those first few months, perhaps because of postnatal depression, late adoption or when family adversity impaired their emotional availability (Bakermans-Kranenburg et al. 2004, Birns 1999, Morris 2005).

Certainly, a tremendous body of research has linked children's attachment patterns to their developmental attainment (e.g. Moss & St-Laurent 2001, Spieker et al. 2003, Stams et al. 2002) and social and emotional behaviour (e.g. Anan & Barnett 1999, Bohlin et al. 2000, DeMulder et al. 2000, Kerns et al. 1998, Kochanska 2001, Moss et al. 2004, NICHD Early Child Care Research Network 2006, Pauli-Pott et al. 2007, Stams et al. 2002, Verschueren & Marcoen 1999, Warren et al. 1997). Nevertheless, these links are modest in size, which indicates that there are numerous other environmental (not to mention genetic) influences on children's adjustment. Moreover, attachment and emotional wellbeing seem related when both are measured at the same time, but attachment quality in childhood does not reliably predict adjustment in the long term, as the theory expects (Lewis et al. 2000).

This suggests that, rather than children's attachment patterns *causing* their emotional and social wellbeing, instead both could be caused by the quality of children's current relationships with their primary caregivers. This is in fact what the research has found—that attachment quality depends on the sensitivity of parents (e.g. Bakermans-Kranenburg et al. 2004, Diener et al. 2003, Koren-Karie et al. 2002, Posada et al. 1999, Raval et al. 2001) and other caregivers (Howes et al. 1988). When fluctuating family circumstances produce changes in parental sensitivity, there are corresponding changes in children's attachment patterns *and* socioemotional adjustment (Hamilton 2000, Lewis et al. 2000, Moss et al. 2005, NICHD Early Child Care Research Network 2001b, 2006, Seifer et al. 2004, Waters et al. 2000a, 2000b, Weinfield et al. 2000).

Given that attachment patterns change when the quality of children's relationships with their caregivers alters, I question whether we need the concept of attachment as a 'middleman'. We lose nothing and gain clarity by saying simply that children are better adjusted and function better when they are in relationships with people who are tuned into and demonstrate sensitive care towards them. This statement has clear implications for practice in that we already know how to fashion high-quality relationships with children.

Children's friendships

Group acceptance is a collective attitude that provides the climate in which friendships may develop (Schwartz et al. 2000). In groups, the reward for dominant individuals is members' acceptance of their status and power; in contrast, in friendship, the reward is affection (Bukowski 2003). In other words, friendships have a quality beyond mere social acceptance, being an ongoing, voluntary bond between individuals who see themselves as roughly equal, have a mutual preference for each other, share emotional warmth and interact reciprocally (Hartup 1989, Howes 1983b, 1987).

Young children's friendships are just as important to them as to their older counterparts (Johnson et al. 2000) and are fundamental to their satisfaction with their care or preschool experience (Langsted 1994, in Pugh & Selleck 1996). They provide children with a context for skill acquisition, supply emotional and cognitive resources, and present models for their future relationships (Ladd et al. 1996). Children's healthy adjustment does not require a large number of friends, but instead friendships that are of high quality (Berndt 2004, Hartup 1996). Indeed, within the larger and more competitive networks typical of boys, many boys in fact experience little intimacy or friendship (Ladd et al. 1996).

The quality of friendships varies according to their:

- *content*: whether friends engage in prosocial versus antisocial interactions
- *constructiveness*: how well companions resolve conflict between them
- *closeness*, with healthy friendships balancing intimacy with individuality and thus not imposing exclusivity on the partners
- *symmetry*: whether social power is shared, or one partner dominates, and how reciprocated their affection is for each other, and
- *affective qualities*: whether the relationship is supportive and secure or unsupportive, conflict-ridden and unstable (Hartup 1996).

Young children particularly value relationships that affirm their self-esteem, are low in conflict and are intimate (Ladd et al. 1996). Such high-quality or healthy friendships advance children's development across all domains and serve a protective function against maladjustment (Ladd & Troop-Gordon 2003). Compared with their interactions with less preferred playmates, children interact more with reciprocal friends (Vaughn et al. 2001), are less likely to overreact and vent feelings inappropriately, are more conciliatory when in conflict, and are less vengeful or passive in resolving disputes (Burgess et al. 2006, Leary & Katz 2005). In a mutual context, children are more engaged in joint tasks and willing to explore possibilities together; thus their learning improves (Hartup 1996).

Friendships also help children to develop social skills, teach self-control, give them experience at problem solving, provide practice at using language, and allow children to exchange skills and information that they do not readily learn from the adults in their lives (Asher & Parker 1989, Asher & Renshaw 1981, Hartup 1979, 1996, Johnson & Johnson 1991, Kohler & Strain 1993, Perry & Bussey 1984, Rubin 1980). Friends facilitate children's engagement with the wider peer group and are particularly potent at preventing the maladjustment of children who are aggressive (Ladd & Burgess 2001).

On an emotional level, friendships supply affirmation and reassurance, help children develop a realistic self-concept and healthy self-esteem, enhance confidence and reduce fears and worries in stressful situations (Burgess et al. 2006), avoid loneliness, provide fun, and foster individual happiness. Friends also offer practical and emotional support through giving information, advice and counsel.

In contrast, sustained friendlessness alters children's beliefs in their own worth, which leads, in turn, to emotional difficulties such as depression. Friendlessness leads to pessimistic and distrustful expectations of peers and thus causes loneliness, and it exacerbates children's attention difficulties, producing lowered school achievement (Ladd & Burgess 2001, Ladd & Troop-Gordon 2003).

Guide children's use of social skills

Whether aimed at fostering group acceptance or children's abilities to establish and sustain friendships, formal social skills training programs are unlikely to be practicable within everyday care or preschool settings (Odom et al. 1999) and seldom produce enduring improvements in children's social behaviours. Instead, children's social skilfulness is more likely to improve in response to naturalistic approaches that focus on the environment, their everyday interactions and their developmental skills (Strain & Hoyson 2000). Within these natural play interactions, some prosocial behaviours that you can coach in children were listed in Box 5.1.

Assist children's development

High-quality friendships are enabled when the companions are competent at language so that they understand the play themes and can use communication skills to negotiate, sustain and elaborate on their social play (NICHD Early Child Care Research Network 2001a, Rose 1983, Rubin 1980, Trawick-Smith 1988). Similarly, children need the requisite motor skills such as balance, running and ball skills to participate in peers' physical play. Therefore, if individual children appear to have delayed skills in these core developmental domains, recommend to their parents that they seek specialist assessments and, where indicated, intervention to improve the children's developmental skills and, in turn, their social engagement.

CONCLUSION

What children play, they learn (Chick et al. 2002). The function of social play during childhood is to meet immediate needs, master current developmental tasks and prepare for the social roles of adulthood (Geary et al. 2003). Although social play follows a fixed developmental sequence (as described in Table 5.2), children's engagement in complex play, both with objects and with their peers, relies more on the quality of the setting than on characteristics of the children themselves (Kontos & Keyes 1999). Child-centred, sensitive adults provide materials that encourage social play and proffer feedback for prosocial behaviour, while their emotional responsiveness sets the tone for all relationships within the setting, including with peers (NICHD Early Child Care Research Network 2001a).

SUGGESTED FURTHER READING

Dowling M 2005 *Young children's personal, social and emotional development*, 2nd edn. Paul Chapman, London.
Kostelnik MJ, Whiren AP, Soderman AK, Gregory K 2006 *Guiding children's social development: theory to practice*, 5th edn. Thomson Delmar, New York.
Sapon-Shevin M 1999 *Because we can change the world: a practical guide to building cooperative, inclusive classroom communities*. Allyn & Bacon, Boston, MA.

chapter 6

Meeting children's need for autonomy

'The essence of autonomy enhancement is not minimisation of the educator's presence, but making the educator's presence useful for the [child] who strives to formulate and realise personal goals and interests.'

ASSOR ET AL. (2002, p. 273)

The second emotional requirement (after the need for belonging) is for autonomy, which is the need to be self-determining or in command of our own lives—to be the origin or initiator of our own actions. Not to be confused with independence, self-centredness or detachment from others, autonomy is the ability to steer our own course in life, to make choices for ourselves, and to exercise volition (Deci & Ryan 2000, Grolnick 2003, Osterman 2000, Ryan & Deci 2000). It encompasses other concepts such as self-efficacy, potency, or a sense of agency—and is the opposite to learned helplessness. Although emerging in the earliest months of life, the drive towards autonomy becomes particularly apparent around the age of 2, when young children express considerable pleasure at being able to do things for themselves. This contributes to both their self-esteem and their sense of themselves as having the power to act upon their world.

At the core of autonomy is children's ability to regulate their own emotional experience and expression. This skill is the single largest influence on both their wellbeing and social skills, as mentioned in Chapter 5. Children's autonomy will flourish when they have:

- freedom to make choices—that is, to work towards self-selected goals
- intrinsic motivation to achieve mastery or competence
- self-efficacy, which is the belief that one can control events in one's own life, and

- environmental supports, particularly the provision of guiding rather than controlling discipline (Wehmeyer et al. 2004, Wheeler & Richey 2005).

FREEDOM TO MAKE CHOICES

When activities are mandatory, children dislike them and consider them to be work, whereas when they can exercise meaningful choices about their activities and learning processes, they are more engaged in learning and consider it to be play (Wiltz & Klein 2001). In turn, enhanced engagement both advances their learning and reduces disruptive behaviour (Cordova & Lepper 1996, Dunlap et al. 1994, Stipek et al. 1998).

Asking for their suggestions and listening to their preferences tells children that you value them and believe in their abilities to make choices for themselves—as long, however, as the choices on offer are authentic (Assor et al. 2002). Thus, it is important not to *ask* children if they would like to do something that is compulsory, such as wearing sunhats outside in summer. Nevertheless, when there is no choice *whether* to do something, you can still give children options about *how* to do it. For example, you could ask if they would like to wear their red hat or their yellow one. When there is only one hat available and therefore you cannot give them a choice about *how* to perform this compulsory activity, you can instead give them a choice about how to *feel* about it, thus: 'I know that you don't want to wear your hat. But it protects your skin and eyes so you need to wear it in the sun. Now, you can get upset about if you want to. But that just means you will have to stay inside, and I know how much fun you have outside.'

MASTERY

When children engage in learning, they learn not only the content of the activity itself, but also that they can devise a goal and work towards it. In short, they develop self-efficacy.

Foster intrinsic motivation

Chapter 2 reported that children who seek to earn external rewards for their achievements engage with tasks only when they believe that they can excel; otherwise, when beset by obstacles they quickly become discouraged and give up, often becoming disruptive. In contrast, those with a *mastery* orientation to learning—who seek to become more competent rather than to earn rewards—persist in the face of challenge, believing in their own capacity to surmount obstacles and solve problems. They interpret failure not as a measure of their worth, but as a sign that they need to change strategies. Thus, being motivated intrinsically to achieve mastery (rather than being motivated to earn an extrinsic reward) leads to improved engagement and performances over time.

The main means to promote intrinsic motivation is to give children feedback about the skills and qualities that they have displayed, supplying information that is specific enough for them to evaluate their own achievements and decide what their next goal might be. Thus, praise (and other rewards) for achievements is replaced with acknowledgment. I expand on this distinction in Chapter 7.

Teach self-instruction skills

Children will be more able to master tasks and feel in command of their own learning when they can guide their own task performance. For this purpose, they can use self-instruction or self-talk, which is the personal verbal prompts that we use to guide our own behaviour. When a task is new or challenging to us, we talk about it out loud to ourselves; then our self-talk becomes covert; and, finally, we no longer need to self-instruct because we have mastered the task.

You can teach children these steps by completing a task (e.g. a jigsaw puzzle) alongside them, talking out loud to yourself about the choices you make to solve it ('No, I don't think that fits there, because it's the wrong colour … Maybe I could turn it around'… and so on). Then guide the children to talk to themselves as they complete a similar task, first out loud and then silently (Alberto & Troutman 2003). Even if giving themselves instructions is beyond some children, all will be able to evaluate their own performance, which is a second aspect of self-talk. As babies they were able to notice that they had learned to walk and, once older, can notice when something has turned out as they planned.

Promote mastery for children with disabilities

Once mobile, physically able babies see a toy and can approach it to inspect it. This teaches them about whatever they are exploring but, more importantly, teaches them that they can plan to achieve a goal and carry it out. They learn that they can learn. However, children with physical difficulties cannot act on that impulse and therefore are at risk of developing a passive learning style. To prevent this, it is absolutely crucial that they receive physiotherapy in their earliest months. Beyond that, you can safeguard their disposition to exercise control over their learning, emotions and behaviour by offering them numerous opportunities to exercise choice over those things they *can* control.

SELF-EFFICACY

Self-efficacy answers the question, 'How effective, competent or powerful am I in my life?' It results from our previous experience of being able to influence events. As already mentioned, our sense of control over our own actions is crucial to academic success and emotional adjustment. When individuals believe that they have the capacity to influence outcomes (i.e. when they have an internal locus of causality or high self-efficacy), they have a greater incentive to invest effort in tasks and strive for success and, as a result, develop into more persistent and more reflective learners (Knight 1995).

On the basis of past successes—and particularly our experience of failures—we generate explanations (or 'attributions') about what causes these. Such attributions have the following properties (Weiner 2000):

- where we *locate* the cause of events: whether we believe them to be due to internal versus external forces
- whether we see these forces as *durable* (e.g. personal traits such as ability) or *temporary* events (e.g. lack of effort)
- whether the causes are general or *pervasive* (e.g. inability at maths), versus *specific* (e.g. not understanding fractions), and
- how *controllable* we believe events to be.

When individuals believe that they are at the mercy of uncontrollable outside forces that are permanent and pervasive, they develop helpless *thinking*, *emotional* discouragement and disengaged *behaviours* (Weiner 2000, Ziegert et al. 2001). This pattern is known as learned helplessness (Seligman 1975). By the age of 5 years, a sizeable proportion (from one-third to a half) of children have a helpless thinking style, which remains fairly stable thereafter (Burhans & Dweck 1995, Heyman et al. 1992, Kistner et al. 2001, Ziegert et al. 2001).

The helplessness of school-aged children arises because they see their successes and failures as reflecting on their ability. Those who think of ability as a fixed capacity believe that if you cannot do something, there is nothing you can do about that. They interpret failure or the need to expend effort (to 'work hard') as evidence that they are incompetent (Dweck & Leggett 1988, Kavussanu & Harnisch 2000, Pintrich 2000).

Unlike their older counterparts, however, young children have optimistic views of their skills. Therefore, to them, failure does not reflect on their ability. Instead, their concrete thinking causes them to see it as a reflection on their *worth*. They think in simpler terms of 'good' and 'bad'. Thus, young children who feel helpless interpret mistakes as evidence that they are 'bad', inadequate or unworthy (Burhans & Dweck 1995, Heyman et al. 1992, Kistner et al. 2001) and therefore in the face of challenge will lack persistence and experience lowered self-esteem.

To avoid helplessness and encourage children to persist intellectually or emotionally in the face of setbacks, you can teach them to attribute the outcome to their own effort, rather than to uncontrollable factors such as inability or luck.

Correcting faulty internal attributions

The belief that failures are due to incompetence leads to the conclusion that failure is *uncontrollable*. To contradict this, you will need instead to direct children's focus onto something that is internal, temporary, specific and controllable—namely, strategy use (Robertson 2000). Teaching them to attribute their failure to an ineffective strategy transfers their focus from *themselves* as failures to their specific *actions* and assures them that a change in strategy will produce better results.

Specifically, when you hear children blame their *personality* for failings (e.g. when they say 'I'm hopeless at this') or when they assume that the problem is *permanent* ('I'll *never* be able to do it'), you can affirm their disappointment but then gently correct their statements with something like: 'You're right. It hasn't worked out … What could you do to fix it?'

Correcting faulty external attributions

A counselling approach known as rational–emotive behaviour therapy (REBT) upholds that individuals develop emotional difficulties because they believe the common fallacy that events or other people *make* us feel as we do (Ellis 1962). In contrast, REBT claims that emotional upsets arise not from external events themselves, but from how we think about those events (Gonzalez et al. 2004). In other words, the source of our emotions is *internal*. This distinction is illustrated by an example developed by Ellis.

Imagine that as you are driving, you pass a lifelong friend who, upon seeing you, leans out her window and hurls a long tirade of abuse at you for some wrong that you have apparently done but of which you were unaware.

If your friend were leaning out of her car window you would feel distressed and mortified at her vitriol, with no idea what you had done to upset her. However, if she were leaning out of a mental hospital window, you would probably think: 'The poor dear—she's clearly disturbed and in the best place to get the help that she needs.'

Your friend's behaviour was the same—but your emotional response varied according to your *interpretation* or thoughts about what the behaviour meant. This shows that other people's actions might be the stimulus for our feelings, but they do not *cause* these. Our own thinking generates our emotions.

The logical extension of believing that other people make us feel unpleasant things is to conclude that we cannot feel better until they stop it. Our demands often contain the words *must, should* and *should not* (which thinking Ellis provocatively calls *mus*turbating). But because we cannot make others change their behaviour, we feel helpless. We have generated an explanation that says that the cause is now both external *and* uncontrollable.

A third error entrenches our distress. This is that we exaggerate the negative consequences of others' failures to meet our demands. This is termed awfulising or catastrophising or, for children, 'doomsday' thinking (see Table 11.1 on p. 123).

The result of this series of errors in thinking is that, rather than feeling healthy emotions such as sadness, regret, sorrow, annoyance or frustration, we generate feelings that are excessive, illogical, self-defeating and upsetting (Ellis 2005, Gonzalez et al. 2004). To overcome this, REBT teaches individuals to dispute their external, uncontrollable attributions. To that end, adults and anyone aged over 4 can reflect on the following questions, depicted by the acronym AFROG (Kaplan & Carter 1995, p. 407):

- Does this thinking keep me *alive*?
- Does this thinking make me *feel* better?
- Is this thinking based on *reality*?
- Does this thinking help me get along with *others*?
- Does this thinking help me to reach my own *goals*?

For younger children, a simpler version of these questions is to ask them if their thinking is helping them, given that what they are telling themselves gets them upset or into trouble.

Be sure also not to actively teach children to blame external causes for their own errors. With all good intentions, adults sometimes try to distract children from an injury (e.g. by blaming the 'naughty step' for tripping them up). Instead, without confronting children with their mistakes, if you feel the need to comment, you might say something that highlights their own agency, such as: 'Did you forget that the step was there?' or 'Did you forget to get your balance before jumping off?'

ENVIRONMENTAL SUPPORTS

Even when individuals have the capabilities to make choices about how to meet their needs and feel potent enough to enact these, they will not be able to do so if there is little environmental support for autonomous actions. Fundamental to this is egalitarian discipline. This style recognises that autonomy is as vital a human requirement as are belonging and a healthy self-esteem, and that violating children's autonomy needs would be as detrimental to their emotional adjustment as would the violation of those other two needs.

Therefore, guidance teaches children self-regulation, rather than imposing consequences to secure their compliance. This avoids reactive behavioural difficulties—comprising resistance, rebellion, retaliation and escape—which are reactions by children with high autonomy needs against having controls imposed on them externally (see Ch 8). It also teaches children the key self-regulation skill of managing their emotional experience and expression. Failure to achieve this can manifest in social withdrawal in response to anxiety (Eisenberg et al. 2001, 2004a, Henderson et al. 2004), reactive aggression, which is a response to uncontrolled anger (Denham et al. 2002, Frick et al. 2003, Rubin et al. 2003, Vitaro et al. 2006), and proactive aggression, whereby children manipulate their peer relationships using the same psychological controls that are being imposed on them by adults (Brendgen et al. 2005, Casas et al. 2006, Nelson et al. 2006).

CONCLUSION

When we meet children's need for autonomy, they will develop what is variously termed an internal locus of causality, self-efficacy or a sense of personal potency or agency. They will believe in their own ability to shape their lives. This self-belief can be seen when they are self-directed and persistent in their attempts to achieve a goal (Jennings & Abrew 2004). Children who are self-directed accept responsibility for their successes and can recognise when their behaviour is infringing on others. This is the basis not only of resilience but also, in terms of the focus of this book, of learning to behave considerately.

SUGGESTED FURTHER READING

Seligman MEP, Reivich K, Jaycox L, Gillham J 1995 *The optimistic child*. Random House, Sydney.

chapter 7

Meeting children's need for self-esteem

'Self-esteem is not a trivial pursuit that can be built by pepping children up with empty praise, extra pats, and cheers of support. Such efforts are temporary at best, and deceptive at worst. Our children need coaches, not cheerleaders.'

CURRY & JOHNSON (1990, p. 153)

In the model presented in Figure II.2 (on p. 35), the third emotional need (after the needs for belonging and autonomy) is for a healthy self-esteem. Although depicted as central in that model, self-esteem does not develop in a vacuum but, from their earliest days, is an outcome of infants' connectedness to others. Thus, the training ground for a healthy self-esteem is a nurturing adult–child relationship that provides comfort, protection and security. From this, all the basic social skills will emerge (Ashiabi 2000, Young et al. 1999). Children's self-esteem is also fed by how much control they can exercise over their lives— hence, their determined cries of, 'I do it myself'.

THE NATURE OF SELF-ESTEEM

Self-esteem is learned. Adults' reactions to children tell them about the type of people they are and imply the type of people we want them to be. The comparison between these two aspects—the self-concept and the ideal self—constitutes self-esteem, which is a global assessment of our worth (Mruk 2006), and is measured according to whether we achieve our ideals. That is, self-esteem has three parts, as depicted in Figure 7.1.

FIGURE 7.1 Self-esteem as the overlap between the self-concept and ideal self

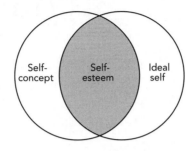

The self-concept

Our self-concept or self-perception is our picture or description of ourselves. We learn this from the feedback that we receive from others and from our efforts at mastery. Young children's self-concept develops first with recognition of themselves (e.g. in a mirror), followed by seeing themselves as separate individuals with their own desires and an ability to assert and act on these (DesRosiers et al. 1999). Next, young children start to be able to describe themselves. This description is fairly basic at first but expands considerably during the early childhood years, becoming more differentiated as children age and learn more about themselves (Marsh et al. 2006). By 5 years of age, for example, they can distinguish their academic from non-academic abilities, and recognise their differing talents across skill areas such as maths and verbal abilities (Marsh et al. 2002).

The self-concept also becomes more abstract, with young children describing themselves according to concrete descriptions of their behaviours (Marsh et al. 1999), whereas, by adolescence, they describe their relationships within and outside the family (which includes ancestors as well as living people), abilities and talents at sport and academic work, temperament, religious ideas, and ability to manage their own lives (Sekowski 1995, van Boxtel & Mönks 1992). These characteristics span five facets— social, emotional, academic, family and physical self-concept—which together form a global or overall self-concept (Pope et al. 1988, van Boxtel & Mönks 1992).

The ideal self

The ideal self is a set of beliefs about how we 'should' be. We learn these standards from actual or implied critical judgments by significant people in our lives or by a process called social comparison, in which we compare ourselves to others (Adler et al. 2004).

Self-esteem

Self-esteem, then, is a judgment about whether our abilities and qualities meet or fall short of the standards that we have learned to value as ideal. A mathematical way of saying this is (Mruk 1999):

$$\text{Self-esteem} \quad = \quad \frac{\text{Perceived attributes}}{\text{Aspirations}}$$

Our judgment about whether our achievements match our ideals has both an intellectual and an emotional component (Pope et al. 1988). How we *think* about our achievements affects how we *feel* about them.

SIGNS OF LOW SELF-ESTEEM

Box 7.1 catalogues the common characteristics of children with a healthy self-esteem. These individuals are realistic about their shortcomings, but not harshly critical of them (Pope et al. 1988). They have a relatively balanced perception of their positive qualities and realistic expectations of themselves. Pictorially, the circles in Figure 7.1 will overlap, although not completely, as we all need ambitions or goals for which to strive.

BOX 7.1 Characteristic behaviours of children with a healthy self-esteem

When children have a healthy self-esteem, they:

- make transitions easily
- approach new and challenging tasks with confidence
- set goals independently
- have a clear sense of self-control
- assert their own point of view when opposed
- trust their own ideas
- initiate activities confidently
- show pride in their work and accomplishments
- cope with (occasional) criticism and teasing
- tolerate frustration when thwarted
- describe themselves positively
- make friends easily
- lead others spontaneously
- accept the opinions of others
- cooperate and behave thoughtfully, remaining largely in command of their own behaviour, and
- make appropriate eye contact (although this will vary across cultures).

Source: Adler et al. 2004, Curry & Johnson 1990.

In contrast with the qualities listed in Box 7.1, children with low self-esteem can display a wide range of less adaptive behaviours. They might constantly try to earn adult approval through being overly helpful, repeatedly declaring affection for others (seeking reciprocation), or overreacting to any real or implied criticism. Socially, children with low self-esteem might not be able to have any fun, can be withdrawn and might be too self-conscious or 'shy' past the usual age. While usually having friends and being well liked, they are less assertive and therefore are vulnerable to being bullied on the one hand, or easily led on the other.

In terms of their learning, children who doubt their abilities often avoid trying something new, avoid taking risks or being adventurous, and give up easily. Instead, they restrict themselves to the same activity (such as playing only in the sandpit) because they fear that they would fail at everything else. Discouraged by their mistakes, they prefer to avoid new challenges. They will lack initiative and be uncertain about making decisions.

In its most extreme form, the low self-esteem of abused children arises from the deeply set belief that they are unlovable (see Ch 4). As a result, even in their preschool years, maltreated children can display self-destructive, risky or self-mutilating behaviours, including having suicidal fantasies.

Contrary to common misconceptions, children with high levels of proactive aggression typically have high self-esteem because their aggression secures their dominance (Salmivalli et al. 2005). Thus, a high self-esteem in and of itself does not ensure considerate behaviour. It also requires a positive view of others (see Ch 5).

FACILITATING CHILDREN'S HEALTHY SELF-ESTEEM

Children can develop low self-esteem when they:

- correctly recognise that they are not competent at something they value
- have many valued skills and qualities, but do not realise it, or
- expect perfection—their standards are too high.

Promote children's competence

Of these three causes of low self-esteem, feeling incompetent is the least enduring, as it improves when individuals become more skilled. Although individuals' self-concept is largely the result of their past successes and failures (Bouffard et al. 2003, Chapman et al. 1990, McCoach & Siegle 2003, Muijs 1997), people have some defence against a history of failure—namely, they decide that they do not *want* to be good at something at which they lack talent. When, however, children are committed to learning a particular skill, this becomes an educational issue. Adults will need to teach them the skill or locate someone who can.

When learning new skills, children will feel best about themselves and their abilities when they are meeting meaningful challenges and putting in some real effort (Katz 1995). Success at something meaningful breeds confidence. Therefore, when children believe that they have failed at something worthwhile, they do not want to be placated with messages that it does not matter. Instead, we need to coach them to achieve their goals so that they *can* feel satisfied with their achievements.

It is also important for children's self-esteem that they acquire self-care skills at an appropriate age. Sometimes, our good intentions to help them mean that we do something for them that they could do for themselves. Instead, let children attempt tasks for themselves—even if they make mistakes along the way—so that they develop faith in their ability to learn and are willing to take risks. Beginning at 30 months, self-regulation of their emotions and behaviour also gives them a skill not only for self-soothing but also about which to feel proud.

Embellish children's self-concept

The second cause of low self-esteem is a lack of awareness of our own personal qualities. Although young children's self-concept is usually positive, school entry brings with it increased feedback, particularly about their academic skills, with the criteria for success (e.g. grades) being more objective and encouraging social comparison (Cole et al. 2001, Marsh et al. 1999, 2002). The result is commonly a deterioration in self-esteem during the first years of school. In most cases, this decline will be to realistic levels, whereas other children highlight their deficiencies and overlook their achievements, resulting in a distorted self-concept.

Acknowledgment

To prevent or repair a distortion in children's self-knowledge, they need information about their personal skills and qualities. They do not, however, need to be judged for their performances, as that would raise their ideals. Therefore, you can acknowledge and celebrate their successes, without praising these. This form of feedback will *verify* their own assessment that they have achieved something worthwhile, *highlight* their successes so that they notice these, and *expand* on what they have achieved—for example, by pointing out that, not only is their block tower very high but also, when it fell down, they had another go: they can persist. This feedback allows children to 'park' information about themselves in their self-concept.

Informative feedback (otherwise known as acknowledgment) differs from judgmental feedback (praise and other rewards) in describing children's skills and qualities, without judging these or implying that children must continue to achieve to that standard in order to be considered worthy. *Information* about their attainments will embellish their self-concept, whereas *judgmental* feedback will raise their ideals, perhaps to a point where they feel that they can seldom attain what is expected of them. Pictorially, the circles in Figure 7.1 will draw further apart.

Acknowledgment differs from praise in the following three ways:

1. Acknowledgment teaches children to *evaluate their own efforts*: 'What do you think of *that*? Was that fun? Are you pleased with yourself? You seem pleased that you did that so well.' In contrast, praise approves of work that meets *adult* standards.
2. Unlike praise, acknowledgment *does not judge* children or their work, although you could offer an opinion of their achievement. For example, 'I'm impressed that you tried something new. I admire that you had another go.'
3. Acknowledgment is a *private* event that does not show children up in public, compare them with each other or try to manipulate other children into copying a commended child. Acknowledgment simply describes in private what the adult appreciated: 'Thanks for sitting quietly today in group time. It helped the other children to enjoy the story', or, 'I appreciate that you helped pack the toys away.'

> ### Guiding principle
> *When you want children to develop a healthy self-esteem, celebrate and acknowledge their efforts. Do not praise them.*

Like praise, however, acknowledgment is not value-free. We *do* know that particular skills and dispositions (such as those listed in Ch 3) will be useful to children now and in the future, and we hope that they will come to value these. But we cannot impose our values on children. Also, as with praise, you can still tell children that they are terrific, although not for doing something that pleases you, but simply because they *are* wonderful. With acknowledgment, you want to share your pleasure in their company; with praise, you want to manipulate them into doing things your way or being a particular kind of person.

Some negative effects of praise and other rewards were given in Box 2.2 (see pp. 28–9). While many of the emotional effects have not been subject to rigorous research and while in practice praise does not always produce these negative outcomes, *it is risky*. It is particularly risky when children are young and forming their personality. If from a young age all they learn is that they must meet others' standards or risk disapproval, they will have no basis for forming their own self-assessments.

Acknowledging children's achievements or considerate behaviour requires no new skills on your part. It requires only the same language that you use for the adults in your life. If a friend gained a promotion, you would not say, 'Good boy', but would congratulate him. When a friend helped you out by picking up your children from school when you were held up at work, you would not comment that she was a good friend but instead might say, 'Thanks. I appreciate it'.

The examples in Box 7.2 illustrating the distinction between praise and acknowledgment avoid one-up-one-down language in which adults adopt the stance of expert with the right to judge others. Instead, acknowledgment allows children to monitor and assess their own performances. This will both allow them to develop a comprehensive picture of their own skills and qualities, and to apply their self-management skills to regulating their own behaviour.

BOX 7.2 Examples of praise versus acknowledgment

The following scenarios provide examples of various forms of acknowledgment that *verify* children's own evaluations, *highlight* their achievements, and *expand* their awareness of their skills.

Action:	A child has helped to pack up the play equipment.
Praise:	You're a good helper.
Acknowledgment:	Thanks for your help.
	I appreciate your help.
	Thanks. That's made my job easier.
	Thanks for packing away so quickly. Now there is more time to play outside.
	Thank you. I know you weren't in the mood to pack up and I appreciate that you did it anyway.
Action:	After much effort, a child has built a tall tower of blocks.
Praise:	Well done! That's terrific!
Acknowledgment:	Congratulations!
	Wow! Look at *that*!
	Hey, you did it!
	You look very pleased with that!
	I'm impressed that you kept trying when the blocks fell over so often.
	I admire that you figured out that the bigger blocks had to be at the bottom.
	You look very proud of that. I agree with you. I think you deserve to be.

(continued)

Action:	A child who has completed a painting comes to you asking, 'Is this good?' while looking pleased with it.
Praise:	Hey, that's great! Good for you.
Acknowledgment:	You look delighted with that! I agree with you. I think you should be pleased.
	Looks like you enjoyed doing that.
	It looks to me like you planned your painting very carefully. What's *your* favourite part?
Action:	A child who has completed a painting comes to you asking, 'Is this good?' while looking dispirited.
Praise:	Hey, that's really good. You've done well.
Acknowledgment:	I can see you're disappointed with it.
	What don't you like about it?
	How come it didn't turn out as you'd hoped?
	Do you want to fix it, or just leave it for now?
Action:	A child has reluctantly shared an item of play equipment with a peer.
Praise:	Good boy for sharing.
Acknowledgment:	Thanks for sharing with Sam. She looked sad that she had nothing to play with.
	Sam seems really grateful that you let her have a turn.
	I appreciate that you gave Sam a turn. That way everyone can have some fun.
Action:	A child thanks you for giving him a drink that he requested.
Praise:	Good boy for using your manners.
Acknowledgment:	You're welcome.
	It's a pleasure.
	I hope you enjoy it.

Authentic feedback

If you were to comment on children's products, it would be difficult for your feedback to be authentic or honest, as you are seldom going to tell children that their performances are inadequate. Therefore, comments that they are excellent can lose credibility. Moreover, focusing on the outcome highlights the skill differences between children. Instead, when you focus on the *processes* that the children have used, every child can receive equal feedback because all learners, be they with a disability or particular talents, can concentrate, plan, persist, solve problems, and so on. The processes that you might care to highlight were listed as 'dispositions' in Chapter 3.

Activities that expand children's self-concept

Sometimes, it can help vulnerable children to supplement everyday feedback with a formal activity for expanding their self-concept. To that end, one option is to jointly generate a list of all the things they can do. Over the course of a few days, this can accumulate to document any skill that they have ever displayed. A single instance is enough to tell you that they can do something, even if they do it rarely. When listing the children's skills, be sure not to qualify the achievements with 'sometimes' or 'when tries' or with descriptions of how well they perform the activity. If they insist that you write down, for example, that they can run fast, you make that two items: 'Jake can run' and 'Jake can run *fast*'.

Teach children to evaluate negative feedback

At times, everyone will fail at something and will be snubbed or rejected by others. It is important that individuals notice this sort of negative feedback, especially when it is valid. But it is also important that we not let a single failure define ourselves as failures in general, or take other people's opinions of us more seriously than we take our own (Katz 1995). Therefore, when children are disappointed in themselves, your first response is to listen and accept what they feel. They will think that you do not understand them if you insist on reassuring them that things are not that bad, or that they should cheer up (Ch 9 explains that reassuring others blocks communication with them).

On the other hand, if children are reacting to an invalid criticism or are expecting unrealistically high performances from themselves, you might gently ask whether they are being realistic, without giving advice or chastising them for what they feel. You could, for example, comment, 'You seem disappointed with your drawing. But I'm wondering if you expect to be able to draw like the bigger children. Do you think that *your* drawing is like a 4-year-old's? Isn't that all you can expect when you're still 4?'

Encourage realistic ideals

The third cause of low self-esteem listed earlier was having standards that are just too high. Although a certain degree of perfectionism is functional in that it is the engine that drives high achievement (Silverman 1994), perfectionism becomes dysfunctional when children are not satisfied even with excellence.

Accept yourself

If you console children when they are disappointed in themselves, but contradict this by reacting critically to your own mistakes, they will not be convinced by what you say to them but will copy how you handle your own achievements and failures. When you can be philosophical about your own mistakes, surrounding children will learn from you how to be similarly gentle with themselves. To teach children how to acknowledge their own successes, it can sometimes be useful to say positive things about yourself in their hearing: 'I've been really organised today ... I'm a star! ... One thing I like about me is ... I'm really good at ... I'm pleased I chose that book to read. You all seemed to enjoy it.'

Prohibit put-downs

The topic of put-downs and exclusions by peers is addressed in Chapter 14. Here I want to highlight that adults sometimes unintentionally talk to children in ways that demean them. We may do so to discipline them by adding critical comments to simple commands, such as: 'Give that back. That's very selfish.' Such negative labels or disparaging comments or nicknames for children can become self-fulfilling—or like seeds in their minds—that grow into a negative self-concept (Biddulph 1998).

We might also incite children to fail by giving instructions that tell them what *not* to do ('Don't fall'), instead of what they could do: 'Walk slowly. Take small steps.' Or we encourage behaviour that will limit them in the long run—for example, by calling shyness 'cute', or commenting in children's hearing that they are not very capable at something.

Using *emotional blackmail* to induce a change in children's behaviour will also lower their self-esteem. One form of this is *using guilt to control children*: 'It makes me sad when you do that.' Sometimes, such negative messages are reinforced by *ridicule* if children become upset: 'Don't be silly. I didn't mean it. Don't be a baby.'

Finally, we adults have copied some habits that devalue children, such as not introducing them when we introduce adults, speaking about children in front of them as if they cannot hear or do not care what we are saying, or denying their requests because their wishes seem frivolous. Although we do not intend to cause hurt, such carelessness inadvertently tells children that we do not value them.

Encourage safe risk taking

Two factors discourage girls in particular from being adventurous and thus extending their skills. First, despite their lower accident rate, girls are hovered over and protected from harm more than are boys (Gilbert 2000). Second, girls are more likely to have an external locus of causality (or low self-efficacy). They receive more judgmental feedback than do boys, from which some learn that they are worthy only when they please other people and get things right. The result is that girls fear failure, and do not develop the confidence to persevere and surmount challenges. To encourage persistence and a healthy self-esteem in children of both sexes, you can express your faith in their ability to work at and solve a problem, rather than cautioning them that a task is difficult.

Accept mistakes

Children often believe that being competent means not making mistakes. But if they are not making any errors, this means that they already knew how to do the task at hand, in which case that is not called learning: it is *practising*. Some will need you to explain this distinction. Then, when they have not been as successful as you or they would have hoped, comment on what they *did* achieve. And do not require them always to correct their errors: children cannot do 'their best' all the time, any more than adults can.

You can also teach children to live by the following self-affirming statements:

- Strive for excellence, not perfection.
- On worthwhile tasks, strive to *do* your best, not to *be* the best.
- Have the courage to be imperfect.
- Don't let failure go to your head.

Some make-a-mistake games can invite inhibited children to experience getting things wrong and discover that the world does not end as a consequence. You can jointly make up a disgusting colour of playdough, or try to outdo each other to fail at getting a ball in a hoop, or you can direct children to make deliberate (but safe) mistakes and see if you can detect these.

Finally, as mentioned in Chapter 1, accepting mistakes refers not just to developmental errors—when children put their shoes on the wrong feet or write their letters backwards—but to behavioural mistakes as well. Children will not profit from the mixed message to be adventurous and creative when learning, but to conform and do as they are told when behaving (McCaslin & Good 1992). Mistakes in either domain—learning or behaviour—are inevitable and need to be seen as an occasion to teach children more skills, rather than instigating a punishment.

CONCLUSION

Toddlers get very excited when they walk for the first time. This is evidence that, even at that young an age, they know how to notice when they are successful. At the other end of the age range, we adults need to sustain ourselves by evaluating our own efforts. But, in between these ages, external rewards (commonly in the form of praise) train children out of noticing for themselves when they do well.

Yet self-esteem is literally that—*self*-evaluation. Children might doubt other people's opinions of them, but they will believe their own. Therefore, we need to give children opportunities to assess their own achievements and to set realistic standards for themselves. Being able to do this will directly help their self-esteem at the time and throughout life. Subsequently, their self-monitoring skills can be applied to their behaviour such that they will be able to notice when their actions are negatively affecting someone else. This is the basis of learning to be considerate.

SUGGESTED FURTHER READING

Berne PH, Savary LM 1996 *Building self-esteem in children*, expired edn. Crossroad Publishing, New York.

Biddulph S 1998 *The secret of happy children*, 3rd edn. Harper Collins, Sydney; Free Spirit Press, Minneapolis, MN.

Curry NE, Johnson CN 1990 *Beyond self-esteem: developing a genuine sense of human value*. National Association for the Education of Young Children, Washington, DC.

For academic readers

Kernis MH (ed.) 2006 *Self-esteem: issues and answers: a sourcebook of current perspectives*. Psychology Press, New York.

part III

Supportive interventions

'The process of acquiring a set of rules, values, and, ultimately, principles, as well as using such standards as guides for behavior, takes place over the entire course of childhood and adolescence.'

SROUFE (1996, IN GOWEN & NEBRIG 2002, p. 191)

The model presented as Figure II.1 in the introduction to Part II (see p. 34) signified that by far the majority of our disciplinary techniques must focus on the prevention of disruptions. This is done by making every attempt to meet children's basic and emotional needs. Nevertheless, these efforts cannot prevent every disruption; therefore, we will need at our disposal a range of measures for responding during a disturbance. This section presents these techniques, beginning with the presentation of a model for determining what might be instigating children's behaviour, followed by chapters that offer a series of graded responses from the everyday to more targeted interventions for chronic or ongoing difficulties.

All of the recommended methods are based on my research findings that a controlling style of discipline generates cycles of escalating adult coercion and child resistance, exacerbates and prolongs each disturbance at the time and, in the long term, perpetuates high rates of behavioural problems, both by individual miscreants and the group as a whole (Porter 1999). Other researchers have shown similarly that children are less likely to comply with adult directives when adults use controlling commands (Wachs et al. 2004) and, conversely, children display fewer behavioural problems when experiencing warm relationships with their teachers (Peisner-Feinberg & Burchinal 1997). In light of these findings and the extensive evidence presented in Chapter 2 for the superior outcomes of a guidance approach, my conclusion and that of other researchers is that when adults use less controlling behavioural guidance strategies as part of a more responsive relationship, children's behaviour improves.

This guidance approach accepts that children have rights but, equally, surrounding individuals do not have to suffer their inconsiderate behaviour. It also accepts that making behavioural mistakes is a natural part of learning and, as the quote above states, it will take a long time for children to learn to act considerately. In the meantime, although we must teach children how to behave thoughtfully, we cannot punish them for their mistakes, as these are a natural childhood event.

chapter 8

Origins of inconsiderate behaviour

> 'Mistaken behavior is a natural occurrence, the result of attempts by inexperienced, developmentally young children to interact with a complicated, increasingly impersonal world.'
>
> GARTRELL (1998, p. 40)

The controlling and guidance styles of discipline differ markedly in their beliefs about the causes of disruptive behaviour. Controlling discipline believes that, as all behaviour is a response to outside rewards and punishments, therefore disruptive behaviour too is triggered by outside consequences. According to this perspective of the world, consequences can have one of two effects on others' behaviour. The first is due to a lack of rewards. This view says that, given that children are inherently evil by nature, if we fail to reward them sufficiently for good deeds, in the resulting vacuum they will revert to type by acting antisocially.

The second effect arises from incorrect punishment. This explanation says that disruptive behaviour persists because adults are inadvertently reinforcing (i.e. rewarding) it. The most common explanation on this last theme is that children are being given attention for behaviour. (I dispute this concept later in this chapter.) In contrast, a guidance approach is built on the notion that children act as they do in order to satisfy their needs.

GUIDANCE EXPLANATIONS FOR DISRUPTIVENESS

As illustrated in Figure 8.1, I propose a layered series of explanations for children's disruptiveness, loosely based on the hierarchical structure of children's needs (as illustrated in Figure II.2 on p. 35).

Transient discomfort

Young children's behaviour can become disorganised very easily in response to fatigue, illness or overstimulation. Children have very limited tolerance for minor physical discomforts such as hunger or exhaustion and require immediate relief of these conditions.

Developmental inexperience

Everyday disruptive incidents can arise from children's lack of experience at solving problems. For example:

- Children are naturally exuberant. They will occasionally become elated and excited about simply being alive and will engage in rowdy behaviour that unintentionally irritates or inconveniences surrounding individuals.
- Children learn by exploring both their physical and social environment. They will behave in particular ways to discover what adults stand for, and what they will not stand.
- Young children's language skills and problem solving are still emerging and will not be automatic during times of stress. Conflict with peers, for example, can provoke aggression, even in otherwise verbal children.
- Children can act unskilfully when they have learned inappropriate behaviour displayed by others, such as when those who are raised aggressively become violent with their playmates.
- While children may know how to behave considerately, they can become overly emotional and temporarily lose control of themselves. This is termed a tantrum.

The four 'tantrum' patterns

To receive the care they require to survive, babies have to act on every feeling they experience by communicating what they need. Their survival *demands* that they express emotions. They *have* to tell their parents when they are tired, hungry, in pain, and so on. Therefore, it is no wonder that young children still occasionally indulge their emotions and lose self-control. Even adults sometimes have lapses of self-control, such as when we eat a prohibited food when on a diet.

Signs that children are emotionally overwhelmed manifest in the form of what I call 'tantrums', of which I have observed four patterns, two active and two passive. The active tantrums are obvious to anyone, while the passive tantrums are more subtle and therefore can be more confusing to deal with. Despite the outward differences, however, they both signal the same loss of emotional control and can be responded to in very similar ways (see Ch 11).

The first active tantrum takes the form of *protest* at a denial of something that children want. For preverbal children, this cannot be considered a tantrum, as they have

FIGURE 8.1 Causes of children's behavioural difficulties

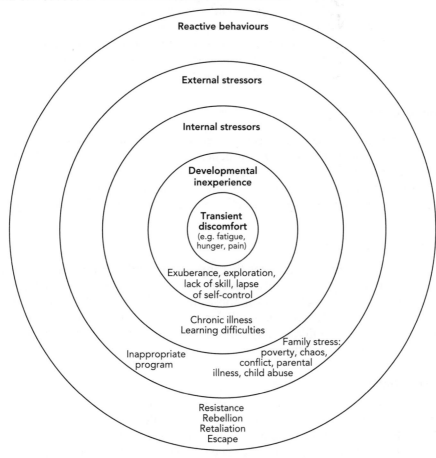

no other means to communicate their disappointment. What defines protesting as a tantrum is when children who are capable of expressing themselves verbally get so overwrought that they cannot use words but instead cry, scream, hit or kick others, or hurt themselves (e.g. head banging). Although we have all seen—or experienced—this protesting tantrum in shopping centres, it is nevertheless uncommon beyond the age of 3 years, partly because children's skills mature and partly because adults recognise a protesting tantrum for what it is and generally deal with it successfully.

A second active tantrum is *social*. This comes in two forms: the reactive explosion of anger and aggression towards a companion, which signals that the aggressor is overwhelmed by emotion; and proactive or instrumental aggression aimed at dominating companions or getting one's own way in play. Either pattern can entail verbal abuse, refusing to share or take turns, bossing others at play, bullying, name calling, and generally not being friendly. However, the reactive form signals an *inability* to control one's emotions, while the proactive, calm, form represents a *choice* not to control one's impulses. Sometimes during play, two playmates have both lost control, in which case both can be said to be having a social tantrum.

Now to the passive versions. First is the behaviour that tends to replace protesting tantrums—namely *whingeing* (or whining in US terms), sulking or nagging. Although quieter than its protesting cousin, whingeing and whining tell us that children's disappointment—not their knowledge about considerate behaviour—is driving their actions. They cannot get past their frustration or disappointment.

The fourth and most common pattern of behaviour that signals that children are not managing their feelings is *uncooperative* behaviour. They do not follow directives because they do not want to, and think that this is justification enough not to do as asked.

Internal stressors

Children's behaviour can become disorganised when they have particular disabilities such as language impairments, attention deficits, the autism spectrum of disorders or sensory integration difficulties (see Ch 15), were exposed in utero to neurotoxins, alcohol or other drugs, or have food intolerances. Unlike the transient discomforts that are a part of everyday life, these chronic stressors can produce ongoing behavioural difficulties.

External stressors

The significance of external stressors is that they thwart children's needs, in reaction to which the children may behave in antisocial ways. Depending on the nature of the stressor, the needs being violated span all those illustrated in Figure II.1 and discussed in previous chapters—namely, survival, wellbeing, emotional safety, belonging, autonomy, self-esteem, fun and self-fulfilment. These stressors can be provoked by the immediate setting or by children's life circumstances.

Program features

Up to two-thirds of teachers in schools blame children's behavioural disruptions on their home life, with 30% blaming characteristics of the children themselves, and only 4% concluding that aspects of the program might be inciting the behaviours (Bibou-Nakou et al. 2000, Croll & Moses 1985, in Miller 2003). The absurdity of this is clear when we consider that, when children behave disruptively at home, their parents do not blame their childcare or preschool program for causing it. Similarly, we cannot assume that home factors cause behaviours that occur in our centres. It is far more likely that children's behaviour is a reaction to their immediate circumstances. Their choice of solution (acting prosocially versus becoming aggressive) may well be a pattern that they learned in their family and elsewhere—and more appropriate responses may need to be taught—but what incites their arousal is nevertheless the events in your setting. Thus, the first step is to adjust any aspects of the program that might be stressing children.

Family adversity

The wellbeing of children is inextricably linked to the wellbeing of their families. In my experience, troubled and isolated children have troubled and isolated families. Stable families of all types—be they single parent, dual working parents, gay or lesbian parents, teen parents or stepfamilies—raise well-adjusted children (Bornstein et al. 2006, Golombok et al. 2003, MacCallum & Golombok 2004, Macmillan et al. 2004, McGroder 2000, Spence et al. 2002). However, families experiencing turmoil as a result of poverty, parents' emotional difficulties or drug abuse are less able to meet the needs of children. While the majority of children growing up within such adverse family circumstances ultimately achieve normal emotional and behavioural wellbeing (Spence et al. 2002), those enduring the following forms of adversity typically receive less responsive parenting at the time, which delays their emotional development and leads to behavioural manifestations of stress (such as those listed in Box 4.3 on p. 58):

- *Chaos.* Environments that are noisy, crowded, and low in routine and organisation stress all family members and result in less communication between parents and children (Coldwell et al. 2006).
- *Poverty.* Poverty has a toxic effect on children, affecting all domains of their functioning, largely because chronic economic pressure can lead to insensitive, unresponsive and harsh parenting (Diener et al. 2003, NICHD Early Child Care Research Network 2005a, Parke et al. 2004, Petterson & Albers 2001, Qi & Kaiser 2003).
- *Untreated parental mental illness.* Mothers' depression during pregnancy results in higher cortisol and disturbed neurotransmitter levels in their babies causing, among other things, irritability, fussing, crying and stress, and increased activity levels in the infants (Cornish et al. 2005, Diego et al. 2005, Field et al. 2001, 2004, Hay et al. 2003, Lundy et al. 1999, Sohr-Preston & Scaramella 2006). Subsequently, severe and ongoing depression in either parent disrupts responsive parenting, with the result that children do not receive the soothing care they need to learn to regulate their arousal levels. As a result, many display disproportionate rates of emotional and behavioural difficulties through childhood and beyond (Field et al. 2003, Gartstein & Fagot 2003, Lundy et al. 1999, Marchand et al. 2004, NICHD Early Child Care Research Network 1999, Papero 2005, Sohr-Preston & Scaramella 2006, Spence et al. 2002).
- *Parental drug use.* Without doubt, the two most dangerous drugs for parents to ingest during pregnancy are nicotine and alcohol. Exposure to these and to illicit drugs in utero results in decreased blood and oxygen reaching the fetus, causing stunted growth and increased risk of miscarriage, premature birth, low birth weight, stillbirth and sudden infant death (Bendersky & Lewis 2000, Friend et al. 2004, Howard et al. 2005, Wunsch et al. 2002). Meanwhile, indirect effects of drugs can be due to the chaotic home circumstances prevailing when a parent is an addict.
- *Parental conflict.* Intense and unresolved conflict between parents causes them to withdraw, thus becoming unavailable and less nurturant in their parenting which, in turn, leads to a deterioration in the children's emotional, behavioural and academic adjustment (Ackerman et al. 2002, Dearing et al. 2006, Sturge-Apple et al. 2006). Children's reactions to witnessing their parent being attacked can be similar to those of being abused themselves (Bogat et al. 2006), particularly when they feel to blame for their parents' disputes or feel responsible for solving these (Ackerman et al. 1999, Cummings et al. 2003, 2006, El-Sheikh & Harger 2001, Jenkins et al. 2005, Zahn-Waxler & Radke-Yarrow 1990, Zimet & Jacob 2001).
- *Child abuse.* In Chapter 4, I described the many deleterious effects of child neglect and abuse. Of all the domains of development, maltreated children's social skills are the most impaired (Luthar et al. 2000), manifesting as a lack of empathy (Shields et al. 2001, Zahn-Waxler & Radke-Yarrow 1990) and high rates of aggression resulting from their inability to regulate their emotions (Bolger & Patterson 2001, Flores et al. 2005, Maughan & Cicchetti 2002, Shields et al. 2001, Shonk & Cicchetti 2001).

Reactive behaviours

Reactive behaviours are children's reactions to being controlled. When adults attempt to force compliance, children will react with resistance, rebellion, retaliation or escape attempts (Gordon 1970, 1974), thus inciting another round of adult coercion. These reactive behavioural problems tend to be blamed on individual children—who may be diagnosed with the likes of oppositional defiance disorder—but the problem is not with the child, or even with the adults, but with the adult–child *relationship*.

An example of a recursive cycle of correction and resistance is given in Box 8.1. Although such behaviours are highly disruptive, they are a natural and adaptive attempt by children to assert their autonomy in the face of threats against it (Campbell 1995). Given that the need for autonomy is equally as vital as belonging and a healthy self-esteem—and that we would expect violation of those two needs to produce poor

---

BOX 8.1 An example of reactive behavioural difficulties

During a prolonged group time, Katy was becoming bored, restless and fidgety, and was reminded numerous times to sit quietly and listen until, finally, her caregiver told her that, as she was not listening, she had to go and sit on the chair until she was ready to do so. This is a form of punishment known as time out.

Upon this, Katy refused to leave the group, flopped onto the floor on her tummy and started complaining at increasing volume. This is *resistance*. When the adult who was helping to manage the group tried to lift Katy off the floor, she flopped out of her arms, returning to the floor and again refusing to move. This is *rebellion*. Subsequently when, to avoid disrupting the entire session, the adult attempted to drag Katy over to the chair, Katy hit out at her in protest. This is *retaliation*. To defend herself, the adult let Katy go. Now that Katy was free, she ran away, whereupon the caregiver pursued her. This is *escape*.

With the other children clearly taking more interest in this circus than in the prospect of another verse of *Twinkle, twinkle*, the group leader abandoned the group session and she too gave chase. Realising that she was about to be cornered, Katy climbed under a trestle table that she discovered at the back of the room, refusing to come out, scratching and spitting at the adults whenever they tried to retrieve her. She remained there for 30 minutes, distressed, crying and whimpering.

A controlling approach to discipline would interpret this as evidence that Katy had a behavioural problem. She was inattentive and defiant, and this needed to be punished. But a guidance approach would interpret her original restlessness as normal exuberance and, honouring that she was only 4 years old and could not concentrate for longer than is possible for people of that age, would have invited Katy to leave group time once her behaviour signalled that she had had enough. Instead, the imposition of time out was an attempt to punish her, and every behaviour after that—crying, refusing to comply, hitting the adults, running away—were all a response to being punished. These actions were far more disruptive and prolonged than her original inattentiveness had been, and were caused by adults' attempted solution to that behaviour, not by the ill-natured intentions of Katy herself.

outcomes—violating children's need for autonomy can equally be expected to have negative results.

In my research into behavioural guidance in centre-based care, I observed that these reactions by children were the most common source of disruptions, making up approximately three-quarters of the incidents that drew caregivers' responses (Porter 1999). Reactive disruptions were typically more prolonged, severe and distressing than the original behaviour, leading me to conclude that the controlling measures that had been sold to adults as solutions to children's behavioural problems were instead its causes.

It is true that, for some children, behavioural controls seem to work (to the extent that the children obey adults). These are the children who want you to like them and who rarely offend with their behaviour. Although there is no research evidence of this, these children might constitute as many as 80% of the population. They draw most of their self-esteem from satisfying their need to belong. (You might picture the central branch in Figure II.2 as leaning to the left.) For these obliging children, punishments are unnecessary, however, because the children will mostly govern themselves and spontaneously correct their errors.

In contrast, the other 20% of children—whom I call spirited or non-conformist—are prepared to risk your displeasure to prove to you that you cannot make them comply. They would rather risk condemnation than sacrifice their free spirit. These are the very children whose behaviour most needs correction, but the more you try to control their behaviour, the worse it gets (Porter 1999, Wachs et al. 2004). The main source of these children's self-esteem is their autonomy. (You might visualise the self-esteem branch in Figure II.2 as leaning to the right.) For these spirited children, you cannot use punishments or rewards, as these only engender escalating defiance.

RESPONSES TO THE BEHAVIOUR TYPES

Table 8.1 summarises adults' options for responding to these categories of disruptions. On the principle that we should use the simplest solution first, you would work outwards

TABLE 8.1 Responses to children's behaviours	
Behaviour type	**Responses**
Considerate	Acknowledge
Transient discomfort	Satisfy children's physical needs
Exuberant or exploratory behaviours	Understand Be assertive if the behaviour becomes intrusive
Skill deficits	Teach a more mature skill Explain how the skill will be useful
Lapse of self-control	Soothe the children
Internal stressors	Make program adjustments and provide extra support so that children can circumvent any learning difficulties
External stressors	Change the demands Help children to cope Support families
Reactive behaviours	Use guidance, not controls

from the innermost circle in Figure 8.1, beginning with scanning to ensure that a child is not discomforted.

At the next level, behaviours arising from children's developmental inexperience are natural and, indeed, necessary for their learning. Yet, like beauty, 'misbehaviour' is in the eye of the beholder. That is to say, there is considerable variation in which behaviours adults regard as normal and which they label as 'misbehaviour'. In one preschool study, for example, the researchers counted an average of 49 instances of 'misbehaviour' every 15 minutes (Arnold et al. 1998), while in another study, teachers of 4- to 7-year-olds reported that fully 16% of their young charges had 'definite' behavioural problems, while grade one teachers identified one-third of their students as having either mild or definite problems (Miller 2003, Roffey & O'Reirdan 2001).

When adults label so many behaviours as problems, this raises questions about whether we truly understand which behaviours are natural for children. In saying this, I am not suggesting, however, that adults should be patient with disruptiveness, certainly not in the sense of showing excessive forbearance (Weber-Schwartz 1987). When children's actions are limiting others in some way, we need to be assertive about that rather than patient, because tolerating unfair behaviour would allow them to develop an antisocial habit and would be unjust to those having to endure it.

Guiding principle
Inconsiderate behaviour calls for understanding, but not patience or excuses.

In instances when children know how they should be acting but are too overwhelmed to use this knowledge, your response will be either to adjust the demands or help to soothe them so that they can resume thoughtful behaviour (see Ch 11).

Internal stressors—that is, when children lack skills because of a disability or disorganised nervous system—are mainly an educational issue. Disruptive behaviours need to be avoided through appropriate programming and the provision of extra support to help the children to circumvent their learning difficulties.

With respect to pressures that are external to children, while you must look broadly and entertain the possibility that children's stressed behaviours could be a response to strained family circumstances, you must also examine whether aspects of their program could be more immediate stressors.

Finally, reactive behavioural difficulties can be avoided by guiding the children when they first disrupt, rather than punishing them. As reported in Chapter 2, children are more likely to cooperate with adults who have previously cooperated with them.

THE ATTENTION-SEEKING MYTH

Despite virtually unanimous opinion that children behave thoughtlessly to 'get attention', I have discovered not a single shred of research evidence verifying this claim. The idea originated almost a hundred years ago when Alfred Adler declared that children sought *affection*. Subsequently, his disciple, Rudolph Dreikurs transformed this into the *attention*-seeking explanation that persists to this day. To my mind it seems absurd to claim that, 'For some children, attention for negative behaviour is better than no attention at all' (Roffey & O'Reirdan 2003, p. 41), when adults would prefer to be ignored than reprimanded. Surely, children cannot be so deranged that they actually *prefer* to be rebuked.

Certainly, when children act disruptively, this commonly attracts adult attention. But it is not the *attention* that influences the children's subsequent behaviour: it is the quality of the adult's *teaching* during the disciplinary encounter. The notion of 'attention-seeking behaviour' confuses children's *intent* (which we do not know, as we cannot read minds) with the *outcome*. That a child is given bandaids for injuries sustained when falling off a bicycle does not mean that falling off was 'bandaid-seeking behaviour', any more than a criminal who ceases breaking the law after a prison term was formerly engaging in lawlessness as a form of 'prison-seeking behaviour'.

Furthermore, the concept that children are attention seeking advises adults to ignore them. I repeat: adults are being advised not to give children something (attention) when they ask for it. Even when their request takes a less than ideal form, the notion that we should deny children something they need is ethically questionable.

Aside from its ethics, the practice of ignoring thoughtless behaviour is monumentally unsuccessful. Particularly when the behaviour is an entrenched habit, it can grow to the point of being so dangerous, disruptive or intrusive that you cannot ignore it any more. In the interim, the child has learned to persist with inconsiderate behaviour, while surrounding individuals have had to tolerate a violation of their rights.

It is true that when adults are busy, children will occasionally behave inconsiderately, perhaps believing that they can do so with impunity. However, instead of regarding this behaviour as a quest for attention, it will be more useful to think of it as a message that the children are uncertain that, despite having other duties, nevertheless you will still insist that they act considerately. Because you cannot do two things at once—you cannot execute one task and manage their behaviour at the same time—you will need to become single-minded and give the disruptive behaviour your full attention, in the process clarifying how you require the children to act.

Many of us do not think to do this because we believe that the children will have 'won' by receiving the attention that they were seeking. However, when you do interrupt what you are doing and clarify what you expect of children, their behaviour improves. Thus, if you wanted to think in terms of winning and losing, you win by reinstating considerate behaviour.

CONCLUSION

In some respects, it is irrelevant whether a child's disruptive behaviour is caused by events beyond your control, such as a disability or family strain, because it is your task to adjust the demands and strengthen available supports to make it possible even for stressed children to function in your setting. But the core message of this chapter is that the behaviours over which you have most influence—and whose avoidance would vastly reduce your workload—are the reactive behaviours that are protests against controlling forms of discipline. These can be prevented by the guidance methods to be described in the next chapters.

9 chapter

Communicating to solve problems

'At the level of needs there are no conflicts … Conflicts occur when we think that there is only one way or one person to meet a need. Conflicts also occur when the strategy chosen to meet a need means that some other important needs will not get met.'

HART & HODSON (2004, p. 63)

In the previous chapter, I declared that all human behaviour is designed to meet our needs. The model of emotional needs that formed the basis for Part II upheld that these needs are universal. Therefore, needs cannot be in conflict, as everyone shares the same requirements. Nevertheless, the *behaviours* that each of us selects to meet our needs can interfere with someone else's requirements at the time. Inevitable as this is, when our goal is to satisfy everyone, rather than to prove ourselves to be in the right, communication becomes a tool for connection rather than judgment (Hart & Hodson 2004). To achieve this, you will need to employ the following core communication skills:

- *listening* to others when their behaviour is signalling that their needs are not being satisfied
- being *assertive* when someone else's behaviour is interfering with your own needs or those of other children in the group, and
- most common of all, *solving a problem collaboratively* when both your own and another's needs are being frustrated by a behaviour.

LISTENING

Rosenberg (in Hart & Hodson 2004, p. 51) states that, 'A need is life seeking expression'. To listen to this expression will require, first, that you give others your attention. This means stopping whatever else you are doing, as portrayed in the following motto.

Don't just do something: stand there (Rosenberg 2003, p. 91).

Once attending, you can invite children to tell you how they feel, or you can listen with your eyes and describe what their behaviour signifies about their feelings: 'You look a bit sad' or 'You seem excited'. You might add: 'Do you want to tell me about it?' and then wait quietly while they decide if they want to talk, and what they want to say.

Once they have begun talking, you might say very little—maybe just 'mm-hmm', 'oh' or 'really?' —or you could repeat back the last few words that they have said, to encourage them to carry on. When listening, it pays to ask very few questions—especially ones that call for a yes/no answer—because questions will direct, rather than follow, what the children are telling you. Questions can make others feel that they are being subjected to an inquisition, rather than being listened to.

The next component of listening is reflecting others' feelings. This can be a particular challenge when children are expressing strong emotions, even positive feelings such as joy or excitement, but can be especially confronting when they are expressing anger at us. But, as Ginott and colleagues (2003) write, emotions, like rivers, cannot be stopped— only channelled. Like first aid for a physical injury, reflection is a first-aid measure for hurt feelings. You can reflect the content, the feeling, or the meaning behind what others are telling you by paraphrasing or summarising what it seems they are saying (Bolton 1987). Identifying young children's emotions can be difficult because they do not yet have a wide vocabulary to describe how they feel. However, when they experience being listened to and you help them to understand their emotions by labelling what they are feeling, they develop emotional literacy.

Often we believe that we are listening when instead our responses discourage others from talking to us. Box 9.1 lists 12 common conversation habits that Gordon (1970) called 'roadblocks to communication'. Of the three categories he identified, giving advice (or 'sending solutions') is probably the most common because we all want to help children to feel better. But it has many disadvantages. First, because you did not wait to hear what was the real problem, it tells children that you will not listen to them. Second, giving advice tells others that you think they are not capable of finding their own solutions and it does not give them any practice at doing so. But at the same time, giving advice makes it unlikely that children will do as you suggest because it was not their idea. Therefore, not only will others feel resentful if you impose a solution, but also you will have to supervise them to ensure that they carry it out.

Subsequently, Robert Bolton (1987) added a thirteenth communication roadblock to Gordon's 'dirty dozen'. He says that accusing other people (blaming them) or feeling guilty ourselves for using the communication roadblocks is itself a communication stopper. With this in mind, rather than feeling guilty for using some of the communication roadblocks described here, you might divide a page vertically down the middle and write down some of the comments that you hear yourself saying in the course of a day. Then, in a reflective moment, you could translate these into true listening responses. This way, you can plan ahead what to say next time, without having to pause when in the midst of a conversation to construct a genuine listening response.

BOX 9.1 Roadblocks to communication

The following list of 'roadblocks' is accompanied by examples of how each one might unwittingly be used with young children.

Judging

It is important to accept *that* children feel something, even when you do not understand *why* they feel as they do.

- *Criticising or blaming* children for feeling something ('Don't be silly—it's not that bad') is a clear message that we do not accept their feelings. We might, for example, tell them that they would not have got hurt if, instead of running, they had obeyed the rule to walk on the path. This does not communicate any empathy for their pain, which they will think is unfair.
- *Praising children* tries to talk others out of their feelings, as when we say to a child who is reluctant to eat her lunch: 'You're such a good girl. I know you will eat up properly.'
- *Name calling* is much the same and has similar effects to criticising and blaming children.
- *Diagnosing or interpreting* what children are feeling is an attempt to tell them what their 'real' problem is and ignores their view of it. 'You don't want to do a painting because you got all messy when you did one yesterday.'

Sending solutions

Sometimes, when we believe that we are listening, instead we are attempting to tell children what they should do about their problem.

- *Directing children* to stop what they are feeling or doing ('I don't care what you want—you're doing this *now*') tells them that their needs are not important.
- *Threatening* imposes your solution on children: 'If you don't get ready *right now* for nap time, I will make you stay in bed longer.' This makes children fearful, resentful and liable to test you to see if you will carry out your threat.
- *Preaching* explains to children why they should feel differently: 'You should come for your nap now; otherwise, you'll be too tired later to play.' Preaching is patronising because it treats children as if they did not know this already.
- *Interrogating* asks a series of questions to try to get to the root of the problem. With separation protests, for example, you might inquire: 'Didn't you have a good time yesterday?' Probing suggests that you are about to find a solution for children, instead of trusting them to find their own.
- *Advising* is an attempt to impose a positive solution: 'Perhaps you can play with Alice, so that you have some company.' Although the solution is meant to be positive, it still tells children to get over their feelings before they are ready.

Avoiding the other person's feelings

A third group of communication roadblocks tries to take the heat out of children's feelings, perhaps because these distress us.

(continued)

- *Distracting* children from their worries, without letting them resolve these might take the form of blaming a 'naughty step' for causing a fall. Sometimes, the children are in a frame of mind to enjoy the humour, but if we ignore their real distress often enough, they will learn to stop talking with us about things that matter to them.
- *Logical argument* sends the message 'Don't feel—Think'. 'You actually like vegetables when you taste them. You know you do.'
- *Reassuring* tries to change how children are feeling. It tells them that they are not allowed to feel badly and thus ignores the depth of their feelings, providing evidence that you do not understand them. We often tell children who have hurt themselves not to cry, for example, when instead we need to acknowledge that it hurts. Only when their pain has been recognised will they be willing to hear that it will get better.

Source: Gordon (1970).

Non-verbal listening

Listening validates children's feelings and communicates that you accept these and the children themselves. Your own non-verbal behaviours can let them know this too, when you maintain appropriate eye contact while they are talking with you, use a courteous tone of voice with even the youngest of children, and make sure that you chat about things that interest them, instead of interacting mainly to deliver instructions.

A final non-verbal message that tells children that you accept them is not interfering with what they are doing. Letting them do a task their way tells them that you believe in their abilities. Although we want children to improve their skills, in many cases they will learn more if we let them discover things for themselves than if we tell them the answer.

ASSERTIVENESS

Assertiveness is necessary when others' behaviour frustrates your own needs or those of other children in your care. Generally, you will be aware that this is happening because it will provoke what is sometimes called a 'negative' emotion. Although we would prefer to feel only 'positive' emotions all the time, these 'negative' feelings are messages that our needs are being violated (Hart & Hodson 2004). Therefore, they serve an important function of alerting us that something has to change so that we can receive something we value.

The cornerstone of assertiveness is accepting responsibility for our own feelings and needs. This means that we must avoid victim language that blames others for how we feel and obscures recognition that we make our own choices. For example, we often claim that we 'have' to or 'must' do something (as if someone is threatening execution at dawn if we do not comply) or that we 'cannot help' our behaviour, perhaps because of uncontrollable impulses, or our role ('I have to wipe down the tables because I'm the most junior staff member here').

We also use words that appear to describe our feelings, when in fact they are interpretations of others' actions. Examples include when we say that we are feeling manipulated, pressured, overworked, oppressed or taken for granted (Rosenberg 2003). Instead, words that express our actual *feelings* rather than others' actions (or lack of them) include: annoyed, bitter, disappointed, disgruntled, tired, frustrated, irritated, overwhelmed and resentful.

At its most basic, avoiding victim language means that we cannot say to children, 'That makes me angry' or 'You've made me sad'. Instead, we must accept that our feelings are created by our own thoughts—by how we interpret (i.e. think about) someone else's actions (see the discussion in Ch 6 about the link between thinking and emotions).

Manage anger

It is both natural and human to be angry on occasion at children's behaviour, particularly when one child has hurt another in your care. However, being such a strong emotion, anger takes careful management and should not be indulged. It is *not* okay for us to become abusive just because we are outraged.

To regulate anger, it can help, first, to recognise that it is not the first emotion that you feel but is a response to an earlier feeling, usually being hurt or frightened. Saying that you were scared or hurt will be more effective than telling children that you are angry at them.

Second, when children act disruptively, we are usually not angry at them so much as angry with ourselves for not knowing how to respond. Therefore, it would be foolish to display our anger to them, when we are its source.

But third and most important is the recognition that anger indicates that we are analysing or judging—the children or ourselves—and instead need to focus on which of our needs is not being met (Rosenberg 2003). Thinking angry and resentful thoughts makes it less rather than more likely that our need will be satisfied. Instead, we need to harness the energy behind the anger and channel it into expressing our feelings and needs.

Construct I-messages

When someone else's actions are interfering with meeting your needs, you will have to tell them so, by describing what you need, not their behaviour. Telling children about themselves ('You're naughty') or about their behaviour ('That was very naughty') is called a 'you' message and is aggressive, not assertive. Instead, assertiveness involves that word 'I': 'I need a moment to help Jasmine with her sore knee' or 'I need to know that you will keep yourself safe by not climbing up there'. Assertive messages to children will avoid any hint of accusation, because otherwise they will feel guilty and react negatively.

The basic I-message has the following components:

- how we *feel* about the behaviour we are seeing
- the *needs*, values or wishes that are creating our feelings, and
- what we would like the other person *to do* that would meet our needs.

Taking each aspect in turn, when disclosing how you feel, it is important to be accurate about the strength of your feelings. Rather than saying, 'I worry when you hit the babies' you will need something like, 'I get terrified when I see you hitting Sam like that. I was frightened that you'd split his little head right open. And I get angry to see a big person hurt someone so small.' It can pay not to qualify your message with words such as 'really', 'pretty' or 'a bit', as these water down the feeling word. On the other hand, do not overstate how you feel. Other people will learn to ignore you if you exaggerate.

During the second part of the assertive message, it can be difficult to detect and name the need that is giving rise to your feelings, especially when you have been trained never to ask for what you require. Therefore, when analysing why you feel as you do, it might help to recall the list of human needs that guided Part II of this book (survival, emotional safety, wellbeing, self-esteem, belonging, autonomy, fun and self-fulfilment) and identify which of these is not being met. Naming the need that generates the feeling gives us a better chance of being understood, as many listeners—and children in particular—may not be able to guess why we feel as we do.

The third part of the assertive message asks others to do something to meet your needs. When doing so, it is important not to *tell* children what they should do, as that will invite either submission or rebellion (Rosenberg 2003). Your goal cannot be to ensure compliance, but to build better understanding. You can determine if you are making a demand rather than a request by observing how you respond if they do not do as you ask. If you blame them, lay on guilt, or punish them for not complying, that is a demand. In contrast, a request is signified by a display of empathy for the other person's objections to your request (Rosenberg 2003).

Having described these three components, there are five specific types of assertive messages that can be useful (Jakubowski & Lange 1978). For each, there will be two phases to their delivery: first, saying what you require and, second, *listening* to the recipient's reaction.

'I-want' statements

This first type of assertive message asks someone to meet our needs. However, sometimes when we tell others what we want, they misinterpret this as a demand instead of a request. To prevent this, you can qualify your statement in some way. One option is to ask how willing or able the other person is to do as you ask. For instance: 'I would like a few minutes to select today's book. Can you wait while I do that?'

A second way to qualify a request is to rate how strongly you would like it: 'I want you to all to sit on your bottoms so the people behind you can see. This is a number eight want' (on a scale of 1 to 10). If the children are too young to understand numbers, you could use gaps between the fingers ('th-is much') or between outstretched arms ('th…i…i…is much') to illustrate how strongly you need something.

A third approach is to state what your request means and does not mean: 'I would like everyone to leave the computer and play outside for a few minutes while the sun is shining. You can come back inside once you've had a run around' (letting the children know how long they will be deprived of the computer).

'I-feel' messages

This second type of assertive message tells people about your feelings. Most people who have read anything about assertiveness are familiar with the 'I-feel' statement in the form of: When you (*do such and such*), I feel (*whatever*) because (*my rights are being violated in this way*). However, in my experience, this kind of statement is not very successful. It tends to provoke defensiveness, as listeners can feel blamed and criticised, with the result that they produce a non-verbal or verbal response along the lines of, 'I'm sorry, but you've mistaken me for someone who cares!'

Aside from the resistance they can provoke, a second problem with I-feel messages is that we often mistakenly use them to express thoughts rather than feelings. You can tell if you are doing this by noticing whether 'I feel' is followed by words such as *that*, *as if* or *like*, with pronouns (*I, you, she, they* or *it*) or by a person's name (Rosenberg 2003). Examples of the distinction are given in Table 9.1.

TABLE 9.1 Distinctions between thoughts and feelings	
Thought	**Feeling**
I feel that you should help tidy up.	I am frustrated at this mess.
I feel like a failure.	I am disappointed in myself.
I feel that I have to do everything around here.	I resent being overworked.
I feel that she is being bossy.	I am angry at being denied the chance to make my own decisions.

Therefore, to avoid resistance and to ensure that you talk about *feelings* rather than thoughts, you can name the need that leads to your feelings. This follows the format: *I feel … because I need …* This message is more likely to receive a compassionate hearing from others. As an example, instead of, '*When you* don't sit quietly at group time, *I feel* frustrated *because* I know that the other children cannot listen', your statement of need would become: 'I feel disappointed that you're kneeling up, because I need everyone to have a fair turn at seeing the book.'

Empathic assertion

Like the *When you … I feel … because* formula, an empathic assertive message also has three parts, but it begins by expressing understanding of others. This is powerful as it conveys that the children's behaviour is not 'naughty' but, coincidentally, happens to frustrate satisfaction of your need. This avoids listeners becoming defensive at a perceived accusation. Second, by listening to them first, you build goodwill and therefore make it more likely that they will listen to you in return.

Having expressed understanding, the second part of an empathic assertive message is to tell children about your need and, third, ask for a joint resolution. For example: 'I can see that you're enjoying yourself, and I know that it's fun to run and make noise with your friends. I am worried, though, that you will crash into the younger children. So what would you like to do? Would you like to find a quieter game to play or should we find you somewhere else to run where it will be safe for the little ones?'

Mixed feeling statements

In this fourth type of assertive message, you name more than one feeling and explain why you feel each. For example: 'I appreciate that you helped by playing quietly outside when the babies were asleep this morning. I'm disappointed now, though, that you are playing the musical instruments outside their window and might wake them up.'

Confrontive assertion

This is useful when children have violated a prior agreement about their behaviour. The confrontive assertive message has the following parts:

- describe in a non-judgmental way what the two of you agreed to
- describe what the child did, and
- request what you want to do about that.

For example: 'We agreed that you would play by yourself until you were ready to share in a friendly way with Dimitri. I see that you have come back to the sandpit and taken the bucket he was using. I would like you to give Dimitri back his bucket and find somewhere else to play. Do you need me to help you get started?'

Listen to others' reactions

After you have stated what you need, others sometimes respond negatively, perhaps by becoming aggressive, defensive, crying, withdrawing, sulking or—especially for 3-year-olds—complaining that it is not fair. Another common reaction is debating the issue with you. When children react in these emotional ways, rather than blaming yourself or them, listen for the feelings and needs hidden in their responses. That they have become emotional tells you that *they* now have the problem. Therefore, give them some time to digest your statement and their feelings, and then reflect back the emotion behind their reaction. For example: 'You think it's not fair that I asked you to help tidy up when you didn't make the mess.' Or, with tears: 'Seems that you're too upset now to talk about it. We'll speak again later.' Or: 'You're sad at what I said.' With sulking: 'You're not saying anything, so I imagine that you're just thinking about it at the moment. Let's talk again later to decide what we'll do about it.'

Finally, repeat your assertive message, stating again your feelings and the unmet need that gives rise to them. It can take from three to ten assertive messages before other people are willing to change their behaviour. Therefore, you will need to persist. And of course if you notice even a hint that they are willing to do as you ask, reflect this back: 'Sounds like you'll be happy to put some of the toys away. Thanks. That'll be a help.'

Conclusion: advantages of assertion

Being assertive about what you need is likely to be more successful than simply hoping that someone else will guess what you require. It helps others to know and understand you as an honest human being and to act thoughtfully once they realise what you need. It demonstrates that you respect yourself and communicates that you believe others are mature enough to handle your message. Being assertive is also a better option than waiting until a problem has festered into simmering resentments, or caused you to vent your anger or to impose controls on children in an effort to make them stop a behaviour that impinges on you.

Even so, it will not solve every problem every time. Sometimes, even after an assertive message, children do not desist. This can come about when their feelings are beyond reason, in which case they will need soothing before they can heed your message (see Ch 11).

COLLABORATIVE PROBLEM SOLVING

The third communication skill is needed when the needs of two or more people are being thwarted by a given behaviour. Conflict of this type between individuals is both inevitable and productive in that it signals that individuals' needs are not being met and therefore can trigger a search for a solution. In the process, resolution can build greater understanding of each other. Therefore, rather than looking for someone to blame for a violation of our needs, our goal will be to craft a solution that allows both people to meet their needs without impinging on others.

Guiding principle
Look for a solution, not a culprit.

Whether solving a conflict between yourself and a child, or assisting children to resolve a dispute between themselves, the collaborative problem-solving process entails six steps:

1. Agree to talk it over.
2. Listen to what other individuals need and tell them assertively, but without aggression, what you require. Keep in mind that you are both attempting to meet your needs. The conflict is merely about the strategies you each have chosen.
3. Together, come up with ideas of what you *could* do to meet your needs. At this stage, do not evaluate how practical these suggestions are; just brainstorm all possibilities, even silly ones. If it helps, write down your ideas.
4. Next, decide which of the options you *will* do. Do not choose a compromise that satisfies no one, but instead persist until you find a solution that meets both your needs.
5. Decide when and how to carry out your chosen solution.
6. Once a solution is in place, check whether it is working.

With simple, everyday problems, the steps do not have to be this regimented, although solving even minor issues will always entail the basic component of listening to each other.

Collaborative problem solving improves the chances of finding a high-quality solution, because two heads are always better than one. Moreover, having contributed to devising a solution, the children will be more motivated to abide by it. Meanwhile, helping to decide what should be done develops their thinking skills.

On the other hand, collaborative problem solving will not work when there is true time pressure to get something done or when children are in danger, such as being about to run in front of traffic. In these instances, you will need to take charge without consulting them, perhaps explaining your reasons later. This is the protective use of force, designed to protect children from harm. By contrast, a punitive use of force is intended to secure compliance (Hart & Hodson 2004, Rosenberg 2003).

CONCLUSION

Communication skills are not solutions to problems, but they are the tools for solving them. Effective communication enhances relationships, such that children are more likely to consider and cooperate with those who have considered and cooperated with them. Nevertheless, assertiveness and negotiation will not work when children are out of command of their feelings and thus beyond reason. In that case, you will need to guide them to calm down (in ways recommended in Ch 11) prior to attempting negotiation.

SUGGESTED FURTHER READING

Bolton R 1987 *People skills*. Simon & Schuster, Sydney.

Faber A, Mazlish E 1999 *How to talk so kids will listen: and listen so kids will talk*, 2nd edn. Avon, New York.

Hart S, Hodson VK 2004 *The compassionate classroom: relationship based teaching and learning*. Puddle Dancer Press, Encinitas, CA.

Rosenberg MB 2003 *Nonviolent communication: a language of life*, 2nd edn. Puddle Dancer Press, Encinitas, CA.

Website for the Center for Nonviolent Communication: www.cnvc.org.

Everyday responses to disruptions

'Often, anger, irritation, and frustration seem to motivate externalizing behaviors (e.g. reactive aggression); [while] other people's negative responses to [these] behaviors ... may also elicit frustration and anger from the child.'

EISENBERG ET AL. (2005, p. 193)

This quotation signals that, while we will repudiate behaviours that hurt others, nevertheless we must respond to perpetrators in ways that do not provoke in them further negative reactions. The list given at the beginning of Chapter 2 of the criteria by which we can judge the effectiveness of disciplinary methods indicated that not only must the disruption cease, but future recurrences should be prevented, the miscreant and onlookers must feel safe about how adults will treat them, we must not damage the adult–child relationship through our choice of disciplinary method, and our methods should convey our values so that the children learn something positive from their mistakes.

INSTITUTE GUIDELINES, NOT RULES

Many adults proclaim that rules are necessary to prevent disruptiveness and to give children the security of knowing what is expected of them (see, for example, Arthur et al. 2003). In other words, the claim is that children 'need' rules, limits or boundaries. However, rules usually forbid children from doing something and often come with a predetermined sanction for their violation. Children do *not* need this.

The assumption behind the contention that children 'need' limits is that they will misbehave unless we impose rules to prevent it. In practical terms, the problem with having rules is that it instigates the need to police these, which entails controlling discipline with all its disadvantages (see Ch 2). Even if this worked to ensure that children obeyed, it would not teach them how to think morally (Bear et al. 2003, Covaleskie 1992).

For these reasons, a guidance approach employs no predetermined rules or consequences, but instead uses problem-solving techniques when a conflict arises. (See the example in Box 10.1.) This approach acknowledges that, in a social world, there *will* be occasions when two people want different things or when children lose control of themselves and make a mistake. These circumstances need solving. But they would not be prevented by teaching rules of the 'be nice to each other' variety, and intervention would not be made any easier or more effective by imposing some predetermined consequence for misdemeanours.

BOX 10.1 The redundancy of rules

Wanting to keep routines consistent for the children, a relief preschool teacher asked her young charges about the rules in their centre. Despite her framing the question in various ways, the children seemed puzzled by her questions and could not answer. Finally, she decided that being specific would help: 'What about the toilet? What's the rule for using the toilet?' One of the children was now delighted to be able to answer, 'I know!' he declared, 'When you go to the toilet, you do a wee'.

The regular teacher had no need for rules. She had only ever used conflicts or disturbances to activate problem solving. Therefore, the children experienced these events as exercises in finding solutions, not occasions for reciting rules and imposing consequences for infractions.

GIVE POSITIVE INSTRUCTIONS

When you hear yourself using the word 'if', take that as a sign that you are trying to control children: '*If* you pick up the toys, you can have some computer time.' Instead, a less directive way of delivering the same information is, 'There will be time to play on the computer after the toys are all packed away.' Rather than trying to manipulate children into tidying up, this message recognises that quick completion of the chore will free up extra time.

Name the action you want, not the one you do not want

A second aspect of giving positive instructions is that you will need to tell children what *to* do rather than what *not* to do. When I say, 'Don't think about pink elephants', you cannot help but think of them. Similarly, if a child is balancing on a high platform, rather than saying, 'Don't run', you could say, 'Take small steps'. Otherwise, the human brain hears the word 'run', making it more likely that this is precisely what the child *will* do.

Use visual language for visual learners

Although all of us with intact senses can process information in various modes, we can also have preferences for one mode over another. Infants are attuned to auditory stimuli and thus those with intact hearing learn by listening, rather than by watching the world. However, at around 4 years of age, they convert to being better able to process visual information, while not yet having the mature skills to process both at once (Robinson & Sloutsky 2004). Children who learn by listening tend to think logically, attend to details, respond well to verbal instructions, plan ahead and are organised. Because language presents a sequence of sounds and ideas, they become proficient at sequential tasks.

It is suspected, however, that some children—perhaps as many as one-third— have a genetic preference for visual processing. These children will include those whose parents have selected into occupations that require three-dimensional visualisation, such as architects, engineers, motor mechanics, air-conditioning installers, and so on. A second, smaller, group may become visual by default following prolonged bouts of hearing impairment. These two groups can differ in their ultimate processing abilities. However, they all learn by forming visual images of concepts. They cannot hear you when watching the television; in their focus on the bigger picture, they miss the details; they tend not to be able to follow long sequences of instructions; cannot be reasoned with verbally, especially when distressed; and find it difficult to change tack once they have a fixed plan of action in their minds (Silverman 2002).

If you are an auditory-sequential learner, you might misconstrue these behaviours as a lack of cooperation. It can appear that the children are being obstinate in defiance of verbal instructions, when instead they need to be able to picture what you are asking them to do. The following strategies can help:

- Before giving an instruction, make sure you have eye contact with visual children (where culturally appropriate). Hold up your pointer finger in their line of sight and bring it towards your face, or stand between them and the object of their gaze. Then, having attracted their attention, give them a brief moment to change out of picturing and into listening mode. That way they can take in what you are about to tell them.
- Use visual language when giving instructions. Rather than saying, 'Go to your bag and get your hat' you could try, 'Can you picture where your hat is at the moment? Okay, get it.'
- Sometimes, these children have a fixed picture in their mind of something they need to complete (such as a block construction), but this conflicts with an imperative that they go home. With children who are nearing school age, it can help to explain to them about changing channels on the television. With televisions, you can switch from one program to another, but the first program continues. So it is with the pictures in their heads. They can switch to their movie about going home and then, next time they come to the centre, can change back to their other picture and continue their construction.
- Where relevant, use visual signals, cartoons or photographs to remind them of behaviours that you need them to perform.

CHANGE THE DEMANDS

Sometimes, for unknown reasons or because of transient physical needs (see Ch 8), children cannot enact what we are asking them to do. In these circumstances, rather than trying to change the child, it can be wise to recognise the child's limitations and instead alter the demands or, conversely, increase your supports to make it easier for the child to achieve what is needed.

Change your mind

When children are protesting at your refusal of their request, you can change your mind if, on reflection, you realise that doing so would not interfere with your rights. This is not the same thing as spoiling or 'giving in' to children. *Spoiling* means that you indulge an unreasonable request when you do not want to, just to keep the peace. Being *flexible* is simply taking into account the new information that what they have asked for means so much to them.

When a child's request is unreasonable or cannot be accommodated, you can explain why you cannot grant it. When children know that you usually try to meet their needs, they will accept the occasional rebuff. Most of the negative reactions we see when children's requests are not granted are a reaction against being controlled, rather than a reaction to being denied. Therefore, within a guidance approach to discipline, the occasional denial will seldom provoke resistance.

Help children to start

Sometimes, children do not cooperate because they do not like what you have asked them to do. In Chapter 8, I labelled this as an uncooperative tantrum. But sometimes, uncooperativeness comes about either because children (aged under 4) cannot interrupt their train of thought on command, or (aged under 30 months) cannot translate a verbal instruction into an action. In these cases, repeating a verbal instruction is unlikely to work given that it has not thus far. Instead, you can help them to change the focus of their attention so that they can enact a verbal command by moving across to the children and helping them to get started. For example, you could hold their hand and guide them towards the door so that they receive help to start leaving the room.

Adjust the task

On occasions, it can help to adjust an activity to make considerate behaviour easier for children to achieve, rather than expecting children to change how they are acting. It might be that you cease group time once the limits of children's attention span appears to have been reached. In this way, changing elements of the activity ensures that difficulties that are brewing never eventuate. A second example is that, when children are whizzing down the path on bikes at such speed as to endanger themselves or others in the playground, you could create an obstacle course that both prevents accidents by slowing the children down and makes their game more interesting. This allows the children to meet their need for fun, while you satisfy your need to provide a safe environment.

Negotiate reciprocal contracts

By their very nature, contracts are reciprocal: if I buy your house, I pay you the asking price and you give me the title deeds to the property. But most behavioural deals or contracts with children (particularly in schools) specify how the children must behave, and what consequence it will attract if they do not. This is not a contract, but a lecture that has been committed to paper. Instead, you can negotiate a deal with children, the first part of which arrives at a description of how you need them to behave and the second part specifies what you will do to help them achieve that. This is an acknowledgment that you are asking them to do something that is not easy and therefore that they deserve your support to help them achieve it. During story time, for example, while asking children to sit reasonably quietly, you could help them to do so by providing fidget items, having them choose a book, bringing in a favourite book from home, or turning the pages, and so on.

AVOID ESCALATING CONFRONTATIONS

Reactive behavioural problems come about because children are resisting our attempts to control them. The following measures can deflect confrontations, and in so doing avoid turning a small issue into something much bigger.

Ask children about their actions

A guidance approach is based on some fundamental beliefs about children, one of which is that they have reasons for acting as they do. They are rational creatures. Therefore, on this assumption and, recognising that people choose behaviours that they think will meet their needs, ask children how the behaviour works for them, as illustrated in Box 10.2. When you adopt a curious rather than confused or judgmental stance, there is every chance that they will confide in you.

BOX 10.2 Why is Liam making baby noises?

A 5-year-old who was extremely advanced in his maths skills (being already capable of multiplying fractions) was nevertheless given the same maths tasks as all the other new school entrants in his class. This might entail, for example, rolling two die on the floor and adding up the dots on the upper faces. After some weeks of this and similarly unchallenging tasks, his behaviour in class became such that he was referred by the school to a psychologist for assessment of what his teachers deemed to be an emotional disturbance, manifested as crawling around the floor, sucking his thumb and making baby noises.

After preliminary greetings, I asked him about this. 'Liam, I hear that you're making baby noises in maths class. What's that about?' His prompt reply was derisory, 'Well, if they're going to give me baby things to do, I might as well make baby noises!'

The child and family would have been saved an unnecessary drive and consultation if the adults at school had assumed that Liam was a rational human being and had asked the same question.

A subsequent step to asking children about the reasons for their actions is to ask them to suggest how you should respond. Not only does this provide you with some valuable information for resolving the issue, but having them act as your consultant enhances their stature, defining them as having more qualities than just their troublesome behaviour. It also seems a little cheeky, which amuses them.

Use strategic ignoring

If a behaviour is not actively interfering with anyone's needs—such as the chanting that is popular with 4-year-olds—it is wise to ignore it. Sometimes, telling children that you are pretending you cannot hear them lets them know that you are monitoring and will step in if the activity becomes bothersome. In the meantime, they need to have fun.

Educate children about the effects of their behaviour

When children do something thoughtless, you can dispassionately explain the effect of their actions. When one child had fallen off his bike and nearby children laughed, a caregiver simply said: 'It hurts Max's feelings when you laugh at him when he hurts himself.' This informative message has a reasonable chance of being effective, in contrast with the ineffectiveness of a judgmental message of outrage such as: 'Well! That's not very nice, is it? How would you like it if Max laughed at you if you fell off your bike? How would you like it if I laughed at you? Would you like me to push you off your bike, so you can see how it feels?'

Give permission for the behaviour

The more you try to talk individuals out of acting a certain way, the more they want to persist. Therefore, if children are resisting your attempts to end a disruption, you can give them permission to carry on with the behaviour, but in a way that does not inconvenience anyone. For example, as long as you can do so safely, you could move children who are in the throes of a protesting tantrum to a more comfortable area, or invite sad children to keep crying, explaining that people who are sad are allowed to cry and, therefore, they can take all the time they need to feel better.

Let children save face

As children's self-esteem is vulnerable to feelings of failure and, as discouragement can provoke further disruptions, it is important to give children a way to save face after a mistake. To that end, you could say:

- 'Sometimes people forget to think first. You'll probably remember next time. What do you think?'
- 'Looks like that was an accident. What could you do next time to stop it happening again?'
- 'I've explained that what you did was wrong. I'm sure you wouldn't have done it if you had known that. Now that you know, I reckon you won't do it again.'
- When a very young child has picked up a dangerous item, you could say, 'Thank you for finding that. Would you put it over here now please?' In this way, you do not have to chastise the child, while still ensuring the child's safety.

Do not coerce an apology

In order to preserve children's dignity, do not force them to apologise for their mistakes. If you respond with understanding, they may voluntarily choose to say sorry. But if they are not ready to do so, it will not help to force them to say something they do not mean. In cases where one child has injured another, you could console the injured child with, 'I think that Henry is sorry that he hurt you. He's probably too angry to say so now, but he might be able to say so later.' You can follow this up with apologising on behalf of the perpetrator. (See the section on aggression in Ch 14 for more detail on consoling victims without humiliating perpetrators.)

CONCLUSION

The everyday responses suggested in this chapter will be useful as long as children are not in the midst of an emotional outburst, when they will be beyond reason. In that case, the children will need to calm down before explanations will help.

Guiding principle
You cannot reason with people while they are being unreasonable.

These everyday responses are also less useful when you find yourself repeating the same injunction over and over again to the same children, to little avail. On such occasions, it pays to ask yourself how often you would need to tell these particular children where you had hidden some sweets or chocolate biscuits. If they could remember the location of these treats with only two explanations, this means that after a similar number of explanations about their behaviour, they will equally be able to recall what is required of them. Listen to how often you repeat reminders to 'Use your words, not your fists', 'Keep the sand below people's eyes in the sandpit' or 'Be gentle with the babies'. When you have issued these reminders more than twice, this indicates that the issue *cannot* be that children have forgotten what is required, but simply that they have temporarily lost command of themselves. They do not, therefore, need more information—but instead need support to regain self-control. This, then, is the subject of Chapter 11.

Teaching children emotional self-control

'Caregivers who talk about emotions and foster this ability in children enable them to express optimal patterns of emotions, and to separate impulse and behavior ... Affectively balanced, integrated emotional development is promoted when caregivers assist the child in maintaining a positive affect and tolerate the child's negative affect as valid and worthy of regard and concern.'

ASHIABI (2000, p. 81)

Whereas every emotion serves a useful function and can nourish our lives, feelings become debilitating when they are too intense or prolonged. Therefore, although at birth we are programmed to communicate our emotions, by the age for school entry, children need to be developing skills for regulating or managing their emotions. This is necessary because surrounding individuals have a right not to be disturbed by children's angry outbursts. But, far more important, managing their feelings ensures that children's dysregulated emotions do not upset their own emotional balance and disrupt their ability to solve problems. Being able to understand their own feelings and express emotion appropriately contributes to their personal wellbeing and resilience, social problem-solving skills, social acceptance and the ongoing quality of their relationships (Ashiabi 2000, Bohlin et al. 2005, Denham et al. 2003, Eisenberg et al. 2003, 2004b, Fabes et al. 1999, 2002, Maszk et al. 1999).

Children will particularly need emotional regulation skills when provoked by confrontations with peers, at which times the protagonists need to be able to respond in constructive and competent ways that both resolve the conflict and preserve their relationship. I must emphasise, however, that controlling emotions does not mean denying our feelings. Children who are compelled to suppress emotions such as sadness and anger later commonly vent them inappropriately when their feelings mount up and overwhelm them. As for sadness, as Michael White counsels, 'If you are crying on the inside and not on the outside at the same time, you will drown your strength' (White 1989, in Payne 2000, p. 1).

Thus, rather than outright suppression or denial, controlling emotional expression entails managing the intensity and duration of our emotional reactions and controlling the outward expression of our feelings (Eisenberg et al. 2004a, Murphy et al. 1999). Using these internal and external coping measures allows the underlying emotion to become a constructive force that enhances our problem solving and helps us meet our goals, rather than disrupting or disorganising our responses to challenges and thus hindering goal attainment (Denham et al. 2003, Eisenberg et al. 2000, 2001, 2003, 2004b).

Children develop self-managing capacities from an early age, with distressed babies sucking their pacifiers or fingers, or turning away from a stress source (Maccoby & Martin 1983). Past the age of 2, the challenge for children is to learn additional ways to manage their arousal levels and subsequent responses when emotionally provoked. This is *the* developmental task of the early childhood years.

DEMONSTRATE EMPATHY

Even when children's emotional distress has triggered antisocial behaviour, they need you to validate and label what they are feeling and support them until they are composed once more. This process will teach them how to recover from strong emotion and will protect surrounding children from further outbursts.

TEACH COPING STRATEGIES

You can teach children to apply the three coping methods that were described in Chapter 4: problem-focused actions, emotion-focused strategies, or behavioural responses. Children need to be flexible in applying these strategies, as each can be most adaptive in different circumstances, whereas rigid responses will make it difficult for children to solve problems constructively and rebound from setbacks (Eisenberg et al. 2005). In order for them to learn these methods, you must not intervene pre-emptively, but instead within a supportive relationship give children the chance to take charge of their own emotions (Calkins & Johnson 1998) and persist in the face of frustration (Eisenberg et al. 2005).

EXPLAIN GROWING UP

Growing up is a process of learning how to be boss of our feelings. Adults (mostly) have learned that we cannot act on every impulse; in contrast, young children believe that if they feel something, it is okay to act on it. This is part of normal development. However, as they are approaching school age, they need to be beginning the lifelong process of learning how to be in charge of what they do.

To teach this to children who inappropriately vent their emotions, I explain that while their body—their outside—is getting taller, bigger, stronger, and so on, their insides may have forgotten to grow up. Their feelings boss them around and get them into trouble or get them upset (as the case may be). As they are growing up to be a school person shortly—or will be *this* old at their next birthday—now is the right time to start *thinking* about growing up on the inside as well.

You cannot talk children into growing up, or they would not want to do it. Also, you cannot give them suggestions of how to achieve it. Instead, caution them that it will take them a long time to think about. The purpose of this warning is to restrain children from making an impulsive decision to change, as resolutions that are made in haste are broken just as quickly. However, you can express your faith that part of them knows how to do it. After all, they have grown up on the outside so successfully that this shows that they know how to do it! Finally, you can advise them that while they are thinking about how to teach their feelings to grow up, you will help them when they get out of control (see the sections below).

TEACH CONSTRUCTIVE THINKING

As described in Chapter 6, our thoughts generate our feelings. That children are becoming overwhelmed by their emotions or venting these outwardly tells you that their thinking is not helping to regulate what they feel. Having taught them that these emotions are due to how they are talking to themselves in their heads, you can guide them to identify which dysfunctional thinking patterns they use (as listed in Table 11.1). Once children are aware of the patterns they use, you can coach them to think in new, more productive ways that, in turn, will lead to more balanced emotional responses.

TABLE 11.1 Children's common dysfunctional thinking patterns			
Inaccurate style	**Common theme**	**Examples**	**Resulting emotion**
Robot thinking	It's not my fault	I can't help it: I've got ADHD	Feelings of failure
I'm awful	It's all my fault—I can't do anything right	People are mean to me because I'm no good	Avoidance of risk
You're awful	It's all your fault	I'd behave better if you weren't so mean	Belligerence
Fairytale thinking	It's not fair	I wish they wouldn't be mean to me	Hurt, anger
Wussie (defeatist) thinking	I can't stand it	Performing in front of others is scary	Anxiety, shyness, overreaction to threats
Doomsday thinking	Things are always awful and they'll never get any better	I'll never have any friends	Depression

Source: Adapted from Roush (1984, in Kaplan & Carter 1995, p. 396).

In my conversations with children on this topic, I have found that defeatist (wussie or wimpy) and doomsday thinking patterns are common to those whose emotions get out of control. Both of these thoughts are often accompanied by one of the other four types; therefore, you will need to explain more than one pattern to emotionally reactive children. Defeatist thinking is clearly inaccurate as individuals can 'stand' (i.e. survive) all sorts of things—even very negative events. And doomsday thinking is inaccurate because *nothing* ever happens always and so things can improve, particularly when children learn to recognise the part they play in their own problems and can change how they are acting by staying in command of what they think.

This method, however, cannot be used when children are upset. It would be about as useful as being told during one of your tirades that you are sounding more like your mother every day. This point is encapsulated in the following guiding principle. Instead, during crises, you will need to help children to calm down.

Guiding principle
*When a person is drowning that is **not** the time to give swimming lessons* (Faber et al. 1995).

SOOTHE CHILDREN

There are two approaches for calming children, both of which will be very familiar to you. The first uses the same method that you would use for babies who have become hysterical. The second uses the approach that you will occasionally have applied to yourself when you have become worked up emotionally.

Bring children in close

When babies become upset, our natural instinct is to bring them in close to us and soothe them. But often our first impulse with older children is to send them away to sort themselves out alone, perhaps because we consider that their behaviour is deliberate. To ask young children to calm down without support, however, is unfair and is too big a task at such a young age. (It is even too big a task for many adults.)

Therefore, when young children have shown you by their behaviour that they are out of command of their emotions (by displaying one of the tantrum types described in Ch 8), instead of sending them away from you, bring them in close, either physically or emotionally. Cuddle them; soothe them; tell them you understand how badly they are feeling; let them cry for as long as it takes for them to feel better. Meanwhile, on the grounds that you cannot reason with people while they are being unreasonable, say very little. Do not try to hurry them into feeling better nor explain yourself or the problem. That can come later, if at all.

Staying with children in this way tells them that you are willing to help them, even when their behaviour is antisocial. However, sometimes they are too angry to want a cuddle or even your company. In that case, you can still reflect their feelings (see Ch 9) to communicate that you understand that they are feeling badly, but can withdraw physically. You might offer to stay nearby, at a location where you can continue to tune into their needs while still supervising the other children, or you might withdraw completely with the promise of returning shortly.

For those steeped in a controlling system of discipline, this approach *feels* like a reward for poor behaviour. However, the goal under a guidance approach is to teach children how to get back in control of their emotions. Remaining close is not intended to do that task for them, but it does give them the support they need to achieve it. It provides a safety net for those times when they feel out of command of themselves.

Sometimes, when you bring children in close to you, their feelings escalate into a protesting tantrum (see Ch 8). If it is appropriate and you are able to cuddle young children (aged 3 and under) in a nurturing manner, they might go through a series of emotions before resolving their feelings. Typically, they alternate between anger, sadness and bargaining with you (i.e. reporting that they are alright now, when they clearly are not yet) until, finally, they will become truly calm. However, if they do not want this level of closeness, or if they are thrashing about wildly and could injure you, you must withdraw and return to them when they are calmer.

Protesting about being comforted is less common than you might expect, however. If your talk to that point has been non-accusatory, has sympathised with how upset the child is feeling and asked the child's advice about how you can help, it is less likely that you will provoke a protesting tantrum, as it is, after all, only a reaction against being dominated.

Provide time away (sanctuary)

The first method for soothing someone who is distressed is to give them some emotional support. Sometimes, however, you cannot or do not want to accompany children while they calm down. In these cases, you can offer some soothing solitude. Physically, this is similar to time out in that the child withdraws to a quiet part of the room, but emotionally is vastly different because it communicates your regret that the child feels so overwhelmed and allows the child to withdraw until feeling better. Although both approaches ensure that children's outbursts do not impinge on others, time out punishes children for becoming upset, whereas time away recognises that everyone loses the plot sometimes and therefore gives children some time and space to recover their emotional balance. The children receive the message that it is upsetting to get distressed and they need to do something soothing and enjoyable until they feel better.

The sanctuary area will have chunky cushions, wonderful books, a child-proof CD player with headphones, a view to the outdoors or of an aquarium, and an A-frame with a blanket draped over the top or large cardboard box for the children to climb under and into, to filter out disturbing stimuli. Some will prefer to enjoy these soothing activities in solitude, while others may want to take a friend with them to talk through what has caused them to be disgruntled. (You can allow this only as long as no aggression ensues between them.)

While time out may be familiar, so too is time away—because it is the strategy that you use for yourself when you have become riled over a rotten day. To help yourself recover your temper, you might talk the problem over with a friend, go for a walk, listen to music, turn on the television, have a sleep, or perhaps read a good book. Whatever method you choose, it is a safe bet that you *do not* place yourself on a chair in the bathroom facing a wall in the hopes that this will improve your mood! So it is with children. When they have become distressed, they need to do something pleasant to help them regain their emotional balance.

The two soothing approaches described so far—gaining emotional support from someone else, or doing something enjoyable to calm yourself—are the only two methods known to human beings for recovering from intense emotion (Goleman 1995). However, to those steeped in a tradition of rewards and punishment, both methods can seem as if you are giving children a reward for thoughtless behaviour. A guidance perspective on the world has three rebuttals to this view. First, it does not believe that people act as they do to earn rewards, but instead to meet their needs. No one *needs* to become upset to be fulfilled. Indeed, we would all prefer to avoid it.

Second, the task of a leader is not to manipulate children into compliance, but to teach them. In this case, you are not teaching them the facts of how they should be behaving because, given that you have told them this before, they will have remembered that information. (They would remember if you had told them an equal number of times where the chocolate biscuits or sweets were hidden.) Therefore, they do not need a lecture about their *behaviour*, but they clearly need to learn how to regulate their *feelings*. And there are, as I have said, only two ways that people do this: by gaining support from someone else, or by doing something soothing. It is that simple.

Third, given that children are indeed more intensely emotional than adults, we cannot punish them for becoming overwhelmed—because to do so would amount to punishing them for *being* children. Behavioural mistakes are an opportunity for teaching, not for punishment.

Guidelines for soothing children

When teaching children to manage their own emotions, you will be most successful when you can adhere to the following guidelines.

Offer support early

In my experience, when children frequently display active tantrums (the protesting or social types), they usually exhibit one or both passive versions (whingeing/whining or uncooperativeness) beforehand. Sometimes, therefore, it is possible to deflect a confrontation while they are still in passive mode, before their emotions escalate into a full-blown active tantrum.

Accept children's feelings, but not their actions

Advise children that it is quite okay for them to feel angry. Do not tell them to calm down and be quiet. The issue is not that they are angry, but that they have acted on that feeling in inconsiderate ways. You could help them to begin to discriminate messages about them versus about their actions by saying that you like them but not their behaviour. At such young ages and during an emotional upset, this message is unlikely to convince the children, however—although hearing yourself say it can help you to keep your own feelings in check.

Use minimal talk

When children are out of control of their feelings, they are already too stressed to listen to explanations. It will only make matters worse if you try to reason with them during outbursts. Therefore, when soothing them, use a broken record technique of repeating similar words: 'I know you're upset. I'll stay with you until you feel better … I'm sorry that you're sad. We'll wait here together until your tears are all gone … I can see that you're angry. I'll keep you company until you feel better.'

Once they are calm, there is seldom a need to explain what they did wrong, as they knew it at the time and still know it afterwards. The issue is not a lack of information, but a lapse of self-control. Now that they have overcome their feelings, they do not need a repetition of information that they already know.

Keep children comfortable

It is difficult for overwhelmed children to calm down if they are uncomfortable. Therefore, offer them a cool facecloth for their temples or help them to remove their outer clothing so that physical discomfort does not add to their distress.

Reassure distressed children

Reassure children that you believe they can do it: they *can* calm down. When I have talked with children beforehand about growing up, I've mentioned all the things that they have already learned to do, and told them that I have faith that they can learn to manage their feelings as well. Then, while I am supporting them to settle, I say things like, 'Take your time. I know you'll be able to calm down when you're ready. I *know* you can do it. I believe in you.'

Go the distance

Unless interrupted by other imperatives, be certain to last out until the children are truly calm so that they have had enough time to get back in command of their feelings. Otherwise, their churning emotions will get them into more trouble immediately. I am often asked how long this takes, which is like asking the length of a piece of string. Nevertheless, as a rough guide, I have seldom found children that can calm down from an aggressive outburst in under 20 minutes and, typically, it is nearer double that. (The longest period that I have needed to sit with a 3-year-old has been 3 hours.)

Do not punish

If you attempt to force children to regain their composure, be warned: it does not work. Your response must be nurturing, so that the children learn that emotions are not terrifying, that they do have the skills to overcome their distress and that they will receive support when they need help to do so.

Get medical advice

If children have an illness such as a heart condition or asthma that is aggravated by emotional stress, you will need medical advice about how to manage them if they become hysterical.

CONSISTENCY

If you were able to soothe children every time they lost control of themselves, they would quickly learn how to regulate their feelings and impulses. (I typically find that, with daily practice, most children aged under 5 can learn it within 2 weeks.) However, the reality is that you will not be available to help children every time they become overwhelmed. Another child's injuries will need tending; your shift will end; you will need to speak with parents. However, it is not a problem if you cannot help on any given occasion, as explained in the following guiding principle.

Guiding principle
Consistency is unnecessary—but repeated practice helps.

As an example, if you wanted children to learn to swim, daily lessons would teach them to swim at age level within 2 weeks. But when they cannot have daily lessons and instead receive lessons once a month, they will still learn to swim, but it may take a year. The more practice that children get when learning a new skill, the more quickly they will learn it, but, even with sporadic practice, they still do learn.

Therefore, you do not have to be consistent. Yes, you have to be steadfast and resolute in your determination to protect everyone's rights by insisting on considerate behaviour—but when a disruption occurs, you can adjust your response to suit the circumstances at the time. If on any given occasion, you cannot give overwhelmed children your support to calm down, rest assured that there will be other opportunities. They will lose the plot again another day, and you can guide them to learn self-control then.

The reason that we believe that consistency is imperative is that, indeed, rewards and punishments are so ineffective that, to have any influence at all on behavioural rates, they must be delivered each and every time that the child displays the target behaviour. In contrast, a guidance approach recognises that the more practice children get, the sooner they will learn a new skill, but sometimes the circumstances mean that you cannot supply that practice.

This principle also means that consistency between caregivers and between your setting and home, while no doubt beneficial, is also not essential. Under school age, children's verbal skills are as yet unsophisticated and therefore they rely heavily on non-verbal messages to understand their world. They can discern what is required in each setting, and can figure out who requires what from them in each. It certainly would give them more practice at self-control if they were encouraged to exercise it in all the locations where they spend time but, nevertheless, they do adjust to the unique requirements of each place.

CONCLUSION

In their early years, children are still developing an understanding of their emotions. Up till school age, they progressively develop the language and social skills to govern how they behave when emotionally aroused. The natural developmental progression is towards improved self-regulation (Gilliom et al. 2002, Murphy et al. 1999), with infants and toddlers already displaying an array of effective strategies designed to manage their feelings (Diener & Mangelsdorf 1999). The level of support that they receive during these years has a significant influence on how competent they become at managing their own internal states and the behaviours they display when emotionally challenged (Diener & Mangelsdorf 1999).

By being dependable, responsive and empathic when children are emotionally overwhelmed, adults teach children that feelings are not scary and can be controlled (Ashiabi 2000, Fabes et al. 2001). When adults are not punitive in response even to those emotions that trigger antisocial behaviour such as aggression towards peers, but instead offer support to perpetrators for regaining their emotional balance, over time the children will develop the ability to regulate their own emotions independently. In this way, whereas punishment seeks retribution for past misdeeds, guidance aims to prevent future ones, which it achieves by teaching children the skills to regulate themselves.

chapter 12

Finding solutions to chronic difficulties

'You cannot solve the problem with the same kind of thinking that has created the problem.'

ALBERT EINSTEIN (IN DE SHAZER 1993, p. 84)

It is obvious that problems persist because the attempts to solve them have not worked. This does not necessarily mean that those attempts were misguided. They might have worked with another child, a different behaviour, or at some other time. But, for some reason, they are not working now. Rather than blaming the individuals involved, a solution-focused approach understands that the person is not the problem: *the problem is the problem* (Winslade & Monk 1999, p. 2). Problems indicate that people are stuck, rather than sick (Murphy 2006).

When a problem worsens, those involved try harder to solve it, but the harder they try, the worse it gets (Murphy 2006). This leads to a recursive cycle of problems and attempted solutions whereby the child disrupts, you attempt to correct the behaviour, the child resists your correction, you escalate your coercion to suppress the child's resistance, against which the child rebels … and so on. You each get caught up doing 'the same damn thing over and over' (de Shazer et al. 1986, p. 210). This is no one's fault: it just *happens*. The problem is not the dancers, but the dance.

A solutions orientation recognises that those children with the most disruptive behaviour receive the most punishments, and yet their problems have not remitted. Therefore, it is time to change methods. This might not necessarily mean generating yet another new intervention, but *amplifying* present responses that already work, even partially, *viewing* the problem differently, or *doing* something differently (Murphy & Duncan 1997).

AMPLIFY PRESENT SOLUTIONS

The fact that no problem occurs all the time proves that a solution is already in place. At least some of the time all individuals, no matter how stuck, are doing something to prevent a problem from occurring and all environments, no matter how bleak, are supporting them to do so. Looking for solutions that are already being used is powerful because it relieves you of the responsibility of being the expert with all the answers and of having to generate a completely new approach.

Instances where the problem is not occurring or is less severe than usual are known as *exceptions*. Your task is to identify these occasions and then to discover what those involved do to bring them about. In other words, rather than looking for what is wrong and how to fix it, a solution orientation searches for what is right and how to use it (Berg & Miller 1992, in Davis & Osborn 2000).

Phase 1: Describe the problem

Your first task is to describe what happens when the problem occurs and identify who does what in response to it.

Phase 2: Articulate goals

Those involved in responding to the child's disruptions need to enunciate positive goals that state what they want to see happening, rather than negative goals stating what they want stopped. Their goals also cannot focus on someone else's behaviour as we cannot control others, but instead should specify what *they* can do to influence the problem. The 'miracle question' is useful in this regard (de Shazer 1988). This asks those involved to imagine that tonight, while they were sleeping, a miracle happened and the problem was fixed. They are to reflect on what will have changed and who will be doing what differently. This question can be less formal by asking, 'If tomorrow turned out to be a good day, what would be happening?' (Ajmal 2001). The answers of those involved will disclose what is important to them—that is, what they value. This is their goal.

Once goals are framed in concrete terms, scaling questions can ask the adults involved to rate the present problem on a scale of 1 to 10 (with 1 being the worst it has ever been and 10 being the day after the miracle), so they can assess how close they already are to achieving their goal. If children are involved in this discussion, a pictorial representation such as the illustration of a thermometer can help make the scale concrete for them. The following questions can be useful (Kral & Kowalski 1989, Rhodes 1993, Wagner & Gillies 2001):

- At what number is the problem at the moment?
- How happy are you with that number? (This will tell you how motivated they are to change.)
- What number would you prefer?
- What will life be like at $x + 1$? What will you be doing differently?
- Has the problem ever been at $x + 1$ before? If so, what was happening then?
- What do you think are the chances that you will reach (the goal number)? (This allows you to gauge how confident everyone is about the possibility of change.)
- How will you know that you are making progress? What will be the first sign?
- When this problem is entirely solved, what will be happening that is different from what is happening now?

Phase 3: Explore present solutions

Once you have identified instances where the problem could have occurred but did not, or was less severe than usual, your next task is to examine what those involved did to bring about these exceptions. You can begin your search by looking out for those solutions that have been tried, have failed, have succeeded even partially, or may have been recommended but were not attempted, perhaps because they seemed too outlandish (Murphy & Duncan 1997). Finding out what has failed tells you what not to try again, while finding out what has worked even partially gives you the clue to what may work in future. It helps you to recognise what strengths the children or adults involved have already brought to bear on the problem and therefore could use again.

Specific questions that will identify what the children or adults involved have done to generate these exceptions include (Carey & Russell 2003):

- Are you aware of how you got that to happen?
- Did you take any steps leading up to it?
- What did you do to pull that off?
- What were you thinking at the time that helped you do that?

Phase 4: Expand on solutions

There are three paths for responding once you have examined how the exceptions come about. First, if you have been able to identify what is working, the task is simply to repeat those solutions. The notion of 'positive blame' can be useful here. In remarking on the times when children *have* behaved considerately, you can ask them, 'How did you get that to happen?' (Kral & Kowalski 1989). Next you can invite them to do more of that.

Second, when children claim that the exceptions are 'flukes', to heighten their awareness that these are not in fact mere accidents but happen as a result of something *they* do (Carey 1999), you could inquire about their heroes and then ask: 'What do you think (their hero's name—for example, Superman) would do about this? Would that be something you'd be willing to try?' (Murphy 2006). Alternatively, you could set up a game where on any given day they could *pretend* that their miracle, solution or goal has been achieved, and you have to guess whether they are pretending or are 'for real' (Durrant 1995).

Third, when those involved feel hopeless and helpless, believe that they are not in control of their own behaviour (the robot thinkers), or are so despondent that they cannot even picture the miracle scenario, you can invite them to reflect on what they are doing to prevent the problem becoming even more serious (Molnar & de Shazer 1987). Alternatively, you could activate children's problem solving by having them act as your consultant, asking questions such as, 'What advice would you give to someone else having this kind of problem?' (Murphy 2006) or, 'If I have another child in my group who gets upset the way you do, what do you suggest I could do to help that child?'

Phase 5: Notice progress

Once solutions are being enacted deliberately, your task will be to notice improvements. In a process represented by the acronym EARS, you need to *e*licit exceptions, *a*mplify these, *r*einforce (celebrate) children's successes, and *s*tart again by asking about other exceptions (De Jong & Berg 2002), as follows:

- *Elicit exceptions.* As those involved recount changes, it is crucial to notice even those that do not appear to be related to the problem or its solution. Each improvement needs to be appreciated for its own sake, not just as a step towards further advances.
- *Amplify the changes.* Do this by investigating the ripple effect whereby changes in one person's behaviour have altered the behaviour of others (Sklare 2005).
- *Reinforce the changes.* In examining these improvements, you will highlight the skills that children or others have used to bring them about, not out of any attempt to flatter them, but in an effort to help them recognise their own skills. Questions such as 'Where did you get the idea to do that?', 'Did you know you could do that?' or 'What did you tell yourself that helped you do that?' can allow children to appreciate their own successes.
- *Start again.* You can help children to recognise additional changes through questions such as, 'What else is better?' or 'What else have you done to be friendly to the other children?' or by mentioning a new behaviour that you have noticed.

When there appears to all those involved to have been no change or even a deterioration in the problem, you will need to listen to their despondency. Having acknowledged their discouragement, you can then compare bad days with worse days and ask what creates the difference (McLeod 1989). Ask resiliency questions such as how come they have not given up, what keeps them hanging in there and trying, or how come the problem is no worse than it is. A lack of progress could also signal the need to externalise or reframe the problem so that it seems more manageable (see the sections below).

Phase 6: Develop a plan to maintain progress

One specific way to reduce the chances that old habits do not take hold again is to engage children in planning how to cope with the occasional setback, and to help undo their negative reputation by communicating to their peers, parents and other team members the changes that they are achieving. For the reasons given in Chapter 2, this must be done without judgment, but as a way to celebrate and acknowledge success (see Ch 7).

VIEW EVENTS DIFFERENTLY

A second category of change instigators involves *viewing* things differently. This entails either reframing problems (i.e. thinking about them in new ways) so that a new solution can be found, or externalising problems, which is a process of naming them as if they were a separate entity. Using this approach, the children's task becomes one of restraining this entity, rather than trying to discipline some personal defect.

Reframe your understanding of the problem

The technique of reframing is based on the notion that your response to children's behaviour will depend on what you think causes it. The fact that your responses are not working suggests that perhaps your explanation of the behaviour is not helping. Therefore, to find a new solution, you will need to find a new way of looking at the problem. In a reference to how an old painting can look quite different in a revitalised picture frame, this process is termed developing a *reframe*. Reframing is performed in the following steps:

1. *Describe what is occurring.* Note what the children do and when they do it.
2. *Describe present corrective attempts.* Describe who gets involved in trying to correct the behaviour and what their responses entail. Identify the usual effects of these measures.
3. *Identify your present explanation for the behaviour.* Explanations that do not work usually comprise one of two ideas: either that the children are 'doing it deliberately' (perhaps even 'to get at you'), or that they cannot help themselves (because of their personality, disability, family circumstances, or events in the past). The first explanation of deliberate vindictiveness will have caused adults to try to make the children stop it. The second, helpless, explanation will have led to being too permissive and avoiding making demands on children, alternated with exasperation, neither of which is very effective. The fact that you cannot change the past or external causes of children's disruptive behaviours leads to a sense of hopelessness.

Guiding principle

Focus on present conditions that maintain the problem, not past causes—because the past cannot be changed.

---

4. *Generate a new explanation.* A new view of the problem will look at what is maintaining the behaviour *now*, rather than what might have triggered it originally. For example, when children experience distress at separation from their parents, a former view might have been that this signalled developmental immaturity, when a new view could be that they are trying to look after stressed parents, for which duty they cannot be apart. This view regards them as exercising *too much* responsibility, rather than too little. A second example is that children might be unclear that you will insist on thoughtful behaviour when you are busy, so instead of regarding their inconsiderate behaviour at these times as 'attention seeking' and ignoring it, you can regard it as an attempt to clarify your expectations, which you can do by correcting it.
5. *Change how you respond.* The new view of the problem will enable you to let go of an ineffective solution so that you can try another instead (Fisch et al. 1982).

When you are reframing, keep in mind that you cannot read minds and therefore cannot diagnose the intent behind children's behaviour. You are simply looking at the *effect* of their behaviour. Realising that behaviour would cease if it were ineffective, you can assume that it is being maintained because it works in some way. For example, a child who disrupts group story time might be the 'group barometer'—that is, the one who signals when everyone has had enough.

Another simple example of reframing is when children are accustomed to intimidating or manipulating adults. If this has been happening, it can help to tell them firmly, 'You don't scare me'. A clear gaze and a calm voice while delivering this surprising message can be a very powerful way to let the children know that you will steadfastly insist on considerate behaviour.

Externalise the problem

A second way of viewing a problem differently is to 'externalise' it. This approach recognises that children's whole image of themselves can become saturated with examples of their problem behaviour. Thus defined as defective individuals, they have no confidence that they can improve their own behaviour. One way to turn around this negative self-perception is to avoid locating blame *within* children by giving their problem a name and speaking about it as if it were its own entity that was *external* to them. Narrative therapy calls this *externalising* the problem. It can be particularly useful when the problem seems to have a life of its own, or when children report feeling helpless to control it, as heard in the plaintiff cry, 'I can't help it'.

Together with the child concerned, you will decide on a name for the problem, using the child's language or having the child select from a list of potential labels that you generate, such as calling outbursts of anger Temper, Trouble, or the Rage; sadness might be labelled as the Misery; for those with concentration difficulties, it could be that Squirmies make listening difficult (Huntley 1999). And sometimes these problems have allies that team up with them and cause further oppression, such as Self-doubt or Self-criticism (Morgan 2000), which, for younger children, you might label as 'Name calling'.

Your questions then become, 'What did you do to deserve being spoken to like that?', 'How do you feel when Rage pushes you around and gets you into trouble?', 'Do you think that's fair?', 'Would you like to tame Temper so that it stops bossing you around?', and so on. Once the children express the desire to conquer or tame their problem, you might suggest some specific skills and strategies they can use. This might involve teaching constructive self-talk to assist children to weaken the influence of the problem when it is trying to divert them from their goal, or teaching emotional regulation or conflict management skills so that they do not inflame peer conflicts, for example.

RESPOND DIFFERENTLY

The third way to deflect chronic problems is simply to change how you respond during incidents. Given that, in most cases, controlling discipline will have been employed in response to severe and ongoing behavioural problems, *doing* things differently requires instead that you use guidance methods.

Repair damaged relationships

When children's behaviour has been a problem for some time, their relationships with peers, caregivers and parents can all become conflicted. Building a more constructive relationship with these children can provide them with support for making improvements and can disrupt the negative cycle of coercion that typically surrounds them. To that end, make frequent efforts to greet, welcome and include chronically disruptive children and to acknowledge something positive or neutral about their behaviour, without focusing at all on the problem (Molnar & Lindquist 1989).

Check your preventive measures

Working from the outer to inner circles in Figure 8.1 (on p. 97), your first task when analysing the potential causes of ongoing behavioural difficulties will be to examine if they are being triggered as reactions against controlling discipline. Instigating guidance methods will repair these behaviours.

Second, external stressors could be the culprit. The first class of these are elements of the program that might be thwarting children's needs and therefore provoking emotional outbursts, such as an aggressive peer group, too little physical activity, long waiting times, too large a group, or adult-led activities being too prolonged. These and the array of other causes listed in Chapters 3–7 will signal the need to adjust the program to make it easier for children to function adaptively.

The second class of external stressors includes child neglect or abuse or family adversity for which the child feels responsible. Although family distress is beyond your control, its existence can activate problem solving with parents (see Ch 17) and can signal the need to provide affected children with more than the usual levels of emotional support within your program.

Moving further inward on the circles in Figure 8.1, with all previous causes eliminated, you will need to consider whether children are experiencing internal stressors. Those listed in Chapter 8 included atypical development or a nervous system that is disorganised by the likes of ADHD, prenatal exposure to toxins, or food intolerances. If your observations cause you to suspect such internal triggers, you will need to recommend that the parents seek a relevant assessment.

Finally, while you need to consider developmental reasons such as children's immaturity, lapses of self-control or transient discomfort, these typically result in occasional outbursts of antisocial behaviour, but seldom produce chronic patterns of disruptiveness. Therefore, your interventions are likely to focus on more long-term causes.

Start with an easier behaviour

When children display many disruptive behaviours, common sense might suggest intervening in the one that is most troublesome. But I suggest that instead you start with an easier behaviour, get some success with that, and then deal with the next, if it remains a problem. Sometimes, in dealing compassionately with the first behaviour, the children come to value your good opinion of them and self-correct the other problems. Even if you have to attend to the original issue after all, at least you and the children have developed some confidence about your successes so far. An example is beginning to deal with uncooperative behaviour during play time, rather than at sleep time when children's protests would interrupt those who are sleeping.

Interrupt the pattern

A guidance perspective assumes that children are rational, which is to say that they have reasons for what they do. They are not deranged. Even when we do not understand *why* they behave as they do, we must accept that there *is* a reason. The behaviour is an attempt to meet a legitimate need, which we cannot frustrate. Nevertheless, we *can* insist that the resulting behaviour is less disruptive.

There is an old saying that a chain is only as strong as its weakest link. With this in mind, you can disrupt the chain or sequence of events that surround problematic behaviour. This is known as pattern interruption. To disrupt the old, dysfunctioning pattern you could (Durrant 1995):

- change the location of the behaviour
- change who is involved
- change the sequence of the steps
- interrupt the sequence in its initial stages ('derailing')

- introduce random starting and stopping, or
- increase the frequency of the behaviour.

Without detailing all the options, possibilities for interrupting a disruptive behavioural pattern include:

- when children throw themselves down on the floor in a tantrum, as long as you can do so safely, you could move them to some cushions so that they are more comfortable (thus changing the location)
- you could invite children who often fight over their toys in the sandpit to argue now before they go outside so that they do not miss out once outdoor play time begins (changing the sequence or introducing random starting)
- you could soothe children during their passive tantrums (whingeing and not cooperating) before their emotional arousal escalates into an active tantrum (interrupting the sequence in its initial stages), or
- you could let children know that it is okay to cry when their parents leave and that they can continue to cry for as long as it takes for them to feel better (increasing the frequency of the crying).

Try a reversal

If all else has failed, try doing the opposite of what you have been doing so far (Amatea 1989), even if you do not understand in advance how that could help. This use of reversals is based on the belief that, if present solutions were going to work, they would have by now. Given that they have not, you will need to 'change a losing game' (Fisch et al. 1982, p. 88) or, more simply, obey the self-evident truth that if something is not working, you should stop doing it and try something else instead. For example:

- If you have been ignoring the behaviour, give it your attention.
- If you have been sending overwhelmed children away to sort themselves out, bring them in close to you and give them your support to get back in control of themselves.
- If you have been trying to talk them out of a behaviour, give them permission to continue with it—with adjustments so that it does not bother others.
- If you have been thinking that they cannot help themselves, notice the times when the behaviour does not occur, and expect them to do more of what causes those exceptions.

Give up (using coercion)

When those involved declare that they have 'tried everything' to solve a chronic problem, beware: 'tried everything' means *tried everything to make the behaviour stop*. But the more you try to *make* children stop acting in a particular way, the more responsible *you* become for their actions, and the less responsible *they* have to be. Meanwhile, your attempts at coercion excite—particularly in spirited children—resistance, rebellion and retaliation, thus setting off another round in the cycle of disruption and coercion. When this cycle is operating, it is time to give up, to abandon the idea that you *can* control someone else's behaviour and instead place responsibility for solving the problem back on the child.

The first step in this process is to detail to the child that you and everyone else who has been involved (and you can list each adult individually) have tried everything you can think of to make the behaviour stop—and you realise that this is not working, so are giving up trying.

Next, explain that the behaviour still has to stop, and someone has to think how it can—but you (individually and collectively) have run out of ideas. The clear implication is that the *child* will have to be the one to solve it.

The third step is to separate aggressive children from their victims, as surrounding children have a right not to be intimidated. You would explain this by saying that you would not let other children hurt them, and likewise you cannot let them hurt other children. You might cite the guideline that, 'When you can't play in a friendly way, you can't play'.

This isolation can take many forms. With children in centre-based care or preschool, the perpetrator can play alone or accompany an adult, who is kind, chatty, non-lecturing and carries on business as usual—with the single exception of not allowing the child to be in contact with the other children. Every now and then or in answer to complaints from the child, the adult can say things such as, 'I know you want to play. But I need to keep the other children safe. So we have to stay together until someone thinks of a way to keep the others safe.' Again, the implication is that the 'someone' will not be you.

This separation can take hours, days or even (possibly) weeks. In group care or educational settings, the child can be handed over to another member of staff as the need arises. The process can be as flexible and as prolonged as needed. It ends when the child commits to changing the behaviour.

A common objection to this method is that the isolation is no different from punishment. I concede that it comes perilously close, but it is an instance of the use of protective force, as opposed to coercive force. The distinction lies in the intent of the adults. Your aim is not to isolate aggressive children to *force* them to stop the aggression, as that would lead to rancour between the two of you. Instead, your intent is to protect aggressors from developing a negative reputation and safeguard surrounding children from injury. In recognition that there truly *is nothing you can do* to control another person and that there will be a reason for the aggression even though you cannot discern it, you will be supportive to the aggressor, kindly, interested in the child as a person but, equally, firm in your resolve that others have to be protected. You will give the child all the time he or she needs to resolve whatever is maintaining the behaviour.

Guiding principle

The intention behind the protective use of force is to prevent injury or injustice. The intention behind the punitive use of force is to cause individuals to suffer for their misdeeds (Rosenberg 2003, p. 161).

In the final stage, you will need to plan how to respond when the child volunteers to stop the behaviour. At this point, you have to apply the brakes—because a resolution made in haste is abandoned just as quickly. So you would congratulate the child for coming up with an idea, but explain that the difference between a goal and a dream is that a goal has a plan. The child will just have to keep thinking until you hear a plan.

The communication skills outlined in Chapter 9 are essential for negotiating this plan, but you must wait until the child initiates the problem-solving process. The final agreement will span two aspects: how the child is to behave, and how you or other adults will help the child to achieve that.

Once you are satisfied with the child's determination and that you have jointly arrived at a plan that has a chance of being successful, the child can resume social play. If subsequently there is a serious breach in behaviour, this just means that you misread the child's resolve, or that the plan is proving to be unworkable. In that case, you would reimpose isolation until the child can suggest a new or amended agreement.

Have fun

By the time children's behaviour is serious and enduring, life has become very earnest. Adults feel frustrated—even desperate—and, because you are human, might dislike the children who cause you to feel that way. Meanwhile, the children feel victimised by being told off all the time. One thing is for sure: no one is having any fun. Therefore, if nothing else has worked, at least you can have some fun. When a child is throwing a tantrum, you could perform an ethnic dance, have a tantrum yourself, sing at the top of your lungs, or do a handstand—whatever. There is not a child worth his or her salt who can carry on with a tantrum while you are clowning around. And if it does not fix the behaviour, at least you have lightened the mood.

Collaborate with colleagues

It can be necessary for all members of the team to meet to plan a solution to chronic disruptiveness. Whereas most case conferences merely confirm children's negative reputation and entrench adults' feelings of hopelessness through their almost exclusive focus on problems, solution-focused case conferences will instead focus on present interventions, identifying which of these has worked by highlighting exceptions. Discussion will highlight what the adults are doing at those times when the child is not behaving disruptively, and then plan to do more of what is working.

Each adult can rate the child's behaviour on a scale of 1 to 10 before, during and after a planned intervention. The different ratings by various adults and by the same adult in different contexts helps identify what contributes to the higher ratings, can clarify what goal is realistic ('What rating would you settle for?') and, later, can document progress (Harker 2001).

Refer on

If a well-targeted and executed intervention is not successful, you will need to reflect on whether children's troublesome behaviours could be instigated by difficulties outside your setting. As these will be beyond your control, your only ethical option is to recommend to parents that they seek the guidance of a relevant specialist.

CONCLUSION

When something is not working, it is very foolish to do more of it in the hope that this will improve matters. If your present solutions were going to work, they would have by now. So dismiss notions from the controlling approaches that you should do something unsuccessful more consistently—and instead try a new approach, even if at first you do not know how that could help. In the words of de Shazer and colleagues (1986, p. 212), *doing* something differently obeys the maxims:

- If something works, do more of it. (Look for exceptions.)
- If something is not working, stop it. (Do less of the same.)
- If something is not working, do something else. (Do something different.)

SUGGESTED FURTHER READING

Although no texts are written specifically for early childhood on solution-focused interventions, the following texts describe the method and illustrate it with older children.

Solution-focused approach

Berg IK, Steiner S 2003 *Children's solution work*. Norton, New York.

De Jong P, Berg IK 2002 *Interviewing for solutions*, 2nd edn. Brooks/Cole Thomson, Pacific Grove, CA.

Durrant M 1995 *Creative strategies for school problems*. Eastwood Family Therapy Centre, Sydney; Norton, New York.

Murphy JJ 2006 *Solution-focused counseling in middle and high schools*. Pearson Merrill Prentice Hall, Upper Saddle River, NJ.

Selekman MD 1997 *Solution-focused therapy with children: harnessing family strengths for systemic change*. Guilford, New York.

Sklare GB 2005 *Brief counseling that works: a solution-focused approach for school counselors and administrators*, 2nd edn. Corwin Press, Thousand Oaks, CA.

Narrative therapy

Freeman J, Epston D, Lobovits D 1997 *Playful approaches to serious problems: narrative therapy with children and their families*. Norton, New York.

Morgan A (ed.) 1999 *Once upon a time … Narrative therapy with children and their families*. Dulwich Centre Publications, Adelaide.

Morgan A 2000 *What is narrative therapy? An easy-to-read introduction*. Dulwich Centre Publications, Adelaide.

Winslade J, Monk G 1999 *Narrative counseling in schools: powerful and brief*. Corwin Press, Thousand Oaks, CA.

Websites

www.brieftherapysydney.com.au
www.brieftherapy.org.uk
www.sycol.co.uk
www.brief-therapy.org
www.solutions-centre.org

Solutions to common behaviours

'As well as choosing my actions, I can choose where I put my focus. If I focus on thoughts of who's right and who's wrong, what's fair and what's not, who's bad and who's good, I will spend my time analysing, judging, blaming and criticizing … If, instead, I think in terms of the needs people are trying to meet in every action they take, I am more likely to feel compassion.'

HART & HODSON (2004, p. 57)

Part IV applies the guidelines and general recommendations given in previous chapters to some behavioural challenges that are common in the early childhood years. Many of these are typical for young children, which means that the children do not need 'fixing', as they are not broken (Gowen & Nebrig 2002). Moreover, as reflected in the above quote, the recommendations in the coming chapters choose to focus on solutions rather than on finding a culprit.

In keeping with the model in Figure II.1 (p. 34), the recommended strategies span universal preventive measures, targeted responses and, finally, specific solutions. As mentioned in Chapter 12, some solutions might already be in place and simply need amplifying, while others will require a change of strategy. For the most part, this change will encompass reversing controlling discipline and instead enacting guidance.

chapter 13

Disruptions during routines

'In order to change what teachers do, the structuring of their time must be changed. Constraints in time may prevent the teacher from perceiving other possibilities. There is no time in which to conceive it differently, because the teacher is harassed by too much to do within available time.'

WIEN (1996, p. 391)

Children who attend childcare have more regular schedules and enjoy increased opportunities to interact with peers compared with children who are at home full time (Ahnert et al. 2000). Environments with only moderate levels of noise, adequate space, organised traffic flows, and physical and temporal structure have been shown to improve children's engagement, motivation and cognitive skills (Wachs et al. 2004). Thus, establishing child-friendly structures or routines allows children to be self-governing, because the demands on them become predictable.

Nevertheless, children need choice and control over their routines. From a surprisingly young age, while they grant adults the right to guide their behaviour, children reserve the right to make personal decisions for themselves over issues such as what to eat, where to sit, what to wear, and when to rest (Killen & Smetana 1999). Yet in the name of maintaining routines, many of these choices may be taken from children and instead dictated by the adults (Killen & Smetana 1999), resulting in children's protests at this violation of their need for autonomy.

MEAL TIMES

In terms of behavioural disruptions, hungry young children are less likely to cope with the demands of their day. Therefore, their meals need to give them enough fuel. However, food is more than fuel for children's physical, social, emotional and cognitive development. It is also a human rights issue in that children deserve food that meets their nutritional and cultural requirements and satisfies their preferences.

Meal times are also an ideal time to offer language stimulation, to hold conversations with children about personal topics and to cement relationships. The social and emotional atmosphere at meal times shapes children's food acceptance patterns (Birch et al. 1995). Therefore, to encourage sound eating habits and to facilitate children's interactions with each other and with adults, meal times have to be pleasant and comfortable.

Enjoyment

Enjoyment is the first vital quality for meal times. Eating is an important source of satisfaction for most adults; children should similarly find meals pleasant. Therefore, you must avoid allowing your concern for children's nutrition or use of manners to intrude on the pleasure of the occasion (National Childcare Accreditation Council 1993).

Choice

The second criterion for high-quality meal times is that the children be given choice about their food. The highest level of choice is allowing children to determine when they feel hungry and therefore when they want to eat. This can be accomplished by having a series of sittings for meals, whereby perhaps two tables with four placings each are served, with those children who feel hungry invited to eat first. Once they are finished, you can replenish dishes for the next round. This might not be manageable for all hot meals, but could certainly be possible for snacks. It ensures, first, that children eat in response to hunger rather than some external stimulus such as the time, and that those who are deeply engaged in play do not need to interrupt it simply to abide by a meal time schedule. If we value play, we must honour when children are engaged in it.

A second level of choice is allowing children to select how much and what type of food to eat (obviously from a restricted range). This can be done by placing a bowl in the centre of each table and allowing the children to serve their own portions.

Interaction

The third criterion for a high-quality meal time is that it permits interaction among the children and with staff. To that end, in line with the advice to offer choice where possible, children could be permitted to choose where to sit. However, when all the children are eating simultaneously, this can raise three problems: first, they can spend a good deal of time in dispute over who will sit next to whom; second, there can be a lot of milling about as individual children try to locate a place to sit; third, particular pairs or groupings of children can disrupt each other throughout the meal and therefore might be better to be separated.

One possibility, therefore, is to have a series of sittings for meals, as described above. Alternatively, you could allocate a group of children a particular table, perhaps clustering friends together or asking the children with whom they would like to sit, while allowing the children to select their particular seat.

To foster communication between caregivers and children, adults should sit with the children at meal times. This provides some supervision and, more importantly, allows adults and children to chat about topics of interest to the children. This relationship building is, of course, valuable in its own right, but is also useful for discipline in that the children are more willing to please an adult whom they know and who takes an interest in them.

Meanwhile, the adults should eat with the children. Perhaps in an attempt to save on food costs, some centres do not allow staff to eat the food that has been prepared for the children. However, allowing staff to do so avoids having hungry adults attempting to rush children through their meals so that the adults can get their own lunch. And when the adults eat the same food as the children, this communicates that it is enjoyable. (If the adults do not like the fare on offer, this should signal a change of menu.)

Fussy eating

Even when the meals you provide are culturally and individually appropriate, there will be times when individuals refuse to eat what has been prepared for them. Throughout the development of the human race, being suspicious of new foods has ensured our survival (Birch et al. 1995). It is possible, for example, that children's preference for sweet food might be part of our species' make-up as, in the wild, sweet things are seldom poisonous (Birch et al. 1995). This means that it is natural for young children to be suspicious of unfamiliar tastes.

In order to educate their taste buds, you might ask the children to taste the set meal. However, do not attempt to force them to eat it, as that can make them more resistant. If they cannot be encouraged to try the food that is on offer, provide a substitute (within reason), simply because children have a right not to go hungry. However, if individual children continually demand an alternative, perhaps it is reasonable to ask their parents to provide this. If refusals are common to many children, a change in the menu is indicated, not least to satisfy the children but also because wasted food is an unnecessary expense.

Be alert for possible food intolerances

Another reason not to force children to eat the prepared food is that sometimes they refuse food because it upsets their body, even though they cannot tell you so. This can result in refusing a certain class of foods or to their becoming anxious about any but a very restricted range of foods. These children are likely to be small for their age.

The opposite pattern comes about because food to which we are intolerant provides a pick-me-up, but this is followed by a let-down. To avoid this withdrawal effect, the children need another dose of the same food. The pattern, then, is that they will choose the same food or a restricted range of foods over and over, will ask for particular foods when tired as these will pick them up, and might be constantly eating, resulting in becoming overweight.

Three categories of foods are the most suspect. The first involves children with a family history of allergies (such as asthma, eczema or migraines) who can be sensitive to whole foods—namely, dairy products, eggs, wheat, corn, cereals, and caffeine in chocolate, coke, tea and coffee. The second class of triggers for food sensitivities are additives such as colourings and preservatives. The third class are naturally occurring chemicals and foods such as sugars, salicylates, MSG (chemical number 621), phenolics and amines.

If you notice either of these patterns of fussy eating in individual children, it might help to talk with their parents to see if they want to investigate possible food sensitivities. If found, it will be necessary to accommodate the child's particular dietary requirements, as this will avoid medical complications and also erratic behaviour arising from a reaction to particular foods.

Another possibility is that the children are copying their parents' attitude to food. If a parent is constantly on a diet or has anorexia, for example, their children can learn that food is dangerous and will avoid eating. Again, this is a subject that you could raise tactfully with parents if you think this might apply to a child in your care.

Discuss inside growing up

Some children who are fussy eaters have simply never exposed themselves to different foods often enough to learn to like them. For these children, you might introduce the idea that, although their outside has grown up to be the age they are in years (let's say, 4 years old), their tummy has forgotten to grow up so that it can eat 4-year-old's foods. See Chapter 11 for more details on this approach.

Do not use rewards

You must avoid praising or otherwise rewarding children for eating, or chastising them for not eating. Using these external controls to shape children's eating will undermine their ability to regulate their food intake according to their body's (internal) needs. You might ask them, 'Is your body not hungry right now, or just not hungry for pasta?' If children say that they are not hungry, perhaps you could set aside a bowl of food for them to eat later. If they are not hungry for this particular meal, offer a substitute.

It has been a common practice to use children's favourite food (such as dessert) as a reward for eating foods that they dislike. This is unwise, as rewarding children for eating non-preferred foods makes these appear even *less* attractive (Birch et al. 1995).

SLEEP TIMES

Sleep is essential for the integrity of the immune system, for physical growth, to maintain energy and a positive mood, to permit intellectual focus, and to allow individuals to adapt to events (Siren-Tiusanen & Robinson 2001). Sleep deprivation is signalled by behaviours that are the opposite of these.

By the end of the first year of life, infants sleep for 14 to 15 hours a day, with their longest awake period being 3.5 to 4 hours (Siren-Tiusanen & Robinson 2001). Just as the duration of wakefulness is important to their wellbeing, so too is the duration of their sleep. To gain the restorative benefit from naps, children need to remain asleep long enough to complete a cycle of REM (rapid eye movement—dreaming) and non-REM sleep (Siren-Tiusanen & Robinson 2001). This means that children need unbroken sleep time, and therefore that inducing waking is to be avoided.

Managing sleep times is always going to be a challenge. If you do not ensure that tired children have a sleep, they are likely to be disruptive later out of sheer exhaustion. If, however, you force them to sleep, you are in for a prolonged period of issuing commands that might destroy your rapport with the children and thus undermine your subsequent disciplinary efforts.

Maintain home routines

The timing of naps is crucial for their restorative value and, therefore, it is important to allow children to have their nap at the same time that they have it at home (Siren-Tiusanen & Robinson 2001). It can also help to use the same forms of assistance (such as patting or low music) that parents use at home and allow children to bring in a favourite soft toy, pillow or pacifier from home.

Minimise numbers

An effective way to ensure that you are not trying to get all the children to go to sleep simultaneously is to schedule sleep time immediately after lunch. As the children will finish eating at differing times, you can give support to each one individually when he or she first comes to lie down.

Make rest time a comfort zone

It can help to place the children in the same location each day so that they develop a sense of comfort with the area where they are being asked to rest. Minimising background noise and other disruptions can help them to calm down enough to nap.

Do not force children to sleep

You can require children to have a rest, but have no power to force them to sleep. If individual children seem unable to go to sleep with the usual assistance, you might have to give them permission simply to rest, maybe while looking at some books or fiddling with a fidget item. Once they are beginning no longer to require afternoon naps, you will need to decide in collaboration with parents when to stop insisting on these. But even during this transition phase, it will be important to allow children to sleep if they report being tired, lest they become overstimulated for the remainder of the day.

Use disciplinary measures at other times

Sometimes, children's refusal to sleep is part of an overall pattern of uncooperative behaviour. However, it is difficult to deal with this while other children are trying to get to sleep, as the ensuing noise will disturb them. It can pay, therefore, to deal with the uncooperative behaviour at more convenient times. Once the children have learned to take your directives seriously at all other times, they will be less resistant at nap times also.

Provide for the non-sleepers

Physically separate the children who do not need a nap from those who are sleeping. This avoids disturbing those children who are getting to sleep and also prevents the non-sleepers from having to be too restrained in their play. Meanwhile, non-sleepers continue to need active supervision and mediation of their play, as otherwise they might wander around aimlessly and not engage productively with the activities.

GROUP-TIME DISRUPTIONS

Reading aloud to children is intended to teach them about the act of reading and about how to make sense of story sequences (Conlon 1992). However, compulsory group story and song sessions (or 'circle time') attract many difficulties. The first is that these sessions are largely teacher-directed and mandatory, which deprives children of choice and causes them to dislike the sessions and regard them as 'work' (Wiltz & Klein 2001). The result is that, while the sessions might be teaching particular content, at the same time we might unwittingly be teaching children that language activities are dull.

Second, if the sessions are compulsory, children who prefer not to participate disrupt others by touching or by attempting to escape. Third, children with language difficulties, limited concentration span, or sensory integration difficulties can find it impossible to learn within the large group setting. As Dowling (2005, p. 151) observes: 'The most demanding level of movement for a child is to stay still.' Many children cannot sit still *and* listen, for reasons described in Chapter 15.

Fourth, group sessions commonly overextend children's concentration. Disruptions from disengaged children become more likely the longer sessions continue (Porter 1999, Wiltz & Klein 2001). For adult-directed activities (in contrast with self-selected ones), children's concentration span can be calculated to be 3 minutes multiplied by their age in years. When adults are passionate and fascinating, the children can be so enthralled that their concentration span doubles—but this will not be possible for everyone in the group and certainly not when the session is dull.

Reading aloud with children is also intended to satisfy their emotional needs for closeness and conversation (Conlon 1992). This is impossible to achieve in large groups. Moreover, children are most comfortable in groups with one more member than they have had birthdays—in other words, four children per group of 3-year-olds or five children per group of 4-year-olds (Fields & Boesser 2002). It is possible to exceed this group size when the children are fascinated by the activities but, again, not every child will be able to cope in a large group and consequently may become disruptive.

One single solution will avoid teaching children that language activities are 'boring', will avoid interrupting their play (otherwise known as self-directed learning), prevent the behavioural disruptions posed by reluctant attendees, keep group sizes manageable for the children, and prevent children having to wait as a group assembles. This solution is to make group time voluntary. Incidental group sessions would look like this: a caregiver would approach one or two children who were not deeply engrossed in play and would ask if they would like a story. Once it was under way and the children became captivated, others would join the group also. If the group was already too large, other children might elect to wait until the next story session. When children know that they can leave, those who stay will voluntarily manage their own behaviour.

These sessions would occur four or five times a day, with session leaders noting on a card who attended. Over the course of a week, you would find that most children would be participating. Those children who routinely do not take part may have compromised development, specifically:

- the language is either too simple for gifted children or too advanced for those with overall developmental delay, language impairments or with English as their second language
- the children have concentration difficulties, or
- the children have sensory integration difficulties (see Ch 15).

Once your observations of these children have indicated a potential developmental concern, you could recommend that their parents obtain an assessment and, in the meantime, offer one-to-one or very small group reading sessions for these children.

Some adults resist voluntary sessions because they pose scheduling challenges, and others say that we have to insist on compulsory group time to prepare children for school. However, although young people will be ready to drive a car in mid-adolescence, we do not expect them to learn it during early childhood. Most children will mature into school routines, but they are no more—and perhaps even less—likely to do so if we force them before they are capable.

If there is no way to avoid conducting story and song sessions with large groups, you can ensure that the children are *willing* to function in this unnatural setting by:

- responding to the children's interests
- being fascinating, passionate and compelling in the activities that you offer
- placing those who are overwhelmed by the movement of others on the fringes of the group
- giving restless children fidget toys so that they can move unobtrusively while listening
- limiting the duration to an absolute maximum of 20 minutes, and
- inviting children to leave once their interest and concentration have waned.

TOILETING

It is uncommon for children to be toilet trained successfully before the age of 2 years and 3 months and, even at this age, they are really 'toilet timed', responding to frequent reminders from adults to go to the toilet, rather than deciding for themselves that they need to go.

Minimise pressure on training

Sometimes, when adults become anxious about toilet training or want their child to be trained by a certain date, the child picks up on their anxiety and in turn refuses to be trained at all. Therefore, it is important to avoid toilet learning becoming a major focus of your program (Greenman & Stonehouse 2007). If you feel that individual children are under a little too much pressure to learn toileting, perhaps you could tactfully suggest to their parents that everyone back off for a few weeks, and start again later.

Explain inside growing up

In the meantime you could explain to children that they are growing up on the outside, which tells you that they will soon be ready to grow up on the inside as well, by learning to do a wee like a big 3-year-old (or whatever age they will be at their next birthday).

Expect setbacks

Some children acquire toileting skills quite successfully until they turn 3 and then they have a series of accidents again. This comes about because, now that they are 3, they can concentrate for a longer time and therefore do not experience as many natural interruptions during which they could notice that they need to go to the toilet. You might deal with this by reminding children that needing to do a wee can sneak up on them and so they will need to think extra hard to remember to be boss of their sneaky wees. You can also revert to the earlier toilet-timing method of suggesting that they go to the toilet at natural breaks, until they regain control of their toileting for themselves.

Do not use rewards or punishments

It is important not to punish children for toileting accidents. On the other hand, do not praise or reward successes either (e.g. with a sweet or stars on a chart). If we tell children that they are 'good' girls or boys when they use the potty or toilet, this implies that they are 'bad' when they have an accident. Furthermore, reward systems such as star charts make you more responsible for their behaviour than they are and, as with all rewards, children can come to resent being manipulated. Rewards also take the focus away from the fact that the children are becoming more competent, shifting attention instead to the reward. Therefore, acknowledge children's successes, giving informative but not evaluative feedback (see Ch 7).

SEPARATING FROM PARENTS

Children's reactions to separating from their parents will differ according to their prior experience with doing so, the coping strategies they have developed, and their age (Robbins 1997, Waters 1996). Timing is important. Infants adjust more easily when separations from their parents begin early in the first year (before stranger anxiety appears at around 7 months), rather than later (Harrison & Ungerer 2002). Separation distress peaks between 10 and 18 months (Honig 2002), with toddlers aged 1 year to 20 months showing higher levels of the stress hormone, cortisol, for the first 2 weeks in a new setting, with lesser elevations enduring even for some months (Ahnert et al. 2004). Nevertheless, while preschoolers adapt more readily on the whole, not all are better equipped to separate than their younger counterparts (Robbins 1997).

Children will display various patterns of distress upon separation. Some will be settled during their initial days in the new setting but then develop problems once they realise that the arrangement is permanent; others experience separation distress from the outset that persists for some weeks (Robbins 1997). Sometimes, a new stage of cognitive development signals a new understanding of being left in care, in which case separation difficulties begin unexpectedly after some months (Greenman & Stonehouse 2007).

It is important to keep in mind that children are not only being asked to leave a parent, but also to engage in the program, which will be easier for them to do when it is inviting. Thus, the quality of the setting influences whether children's protest at separation turns into despair (Ahnert et al. 2004).

Preparation

At enrolment, talk with parents about how they would like you to respond to any separation difficulties and how they plan to handle these themselves (Greenman & Stonehouse 2007). Ask how their child has responded to previous separations and what they think will work for their child if separation problems occur, and also pass on your suggestions.

A staggered start, with frequent visits before their actual start date can help, but many parents do not find or do not use childcare until the last minute before they return to paid employment, with the result that some children are introduced into care abruptly.

You can ask parents to bring in their child's favourite comforter from home, and try to give the child some favourite activities and foods, especially in the early days. If it can be arranged, it can also help to introduce the child into a small group first.

Allocate a primary caregiver

To help settle new or distressed children, you can allocate one person to be their primary caregiver, and then move the children on to other adults gradually once they have formed a close relationship with their primary carer.

Suggest parent–child time

Suggest that the parents join with the child before they leave. In the busy-ness of getting out of the house, parents are not always able to give their children the emotional closeness they require to get through the day. Therefore, it can help if the parent and child find a quiet corner in which to have a close hug so that they join emotionally before separating.

Recommend brief farewells

Suggest that the parents state briefly and calmly that they are leaving now, and hand the child over to a familiar caregiver. Encourage parents to leave once they say they are going, and not to return (Greenman & Stonehouse 2007). If this means that parents have had to leave a distressed child with you, invite them to call you later to check on the child.

A structured goodbye routine can be useful. This might be that the children put their bag in its place, are helped by their parent to begin an activity, have a hug, and then the parent leaves. It can sometimes help to make the children active in saying goodbye, perhaps by opening the door for the parent (Greenman & Stonehouse 2007).

Ensure that parents *never* sneak out on children when they are leaving, even if warning the children that they are going produces an emotional outburst. If children have no warning signals to distinguish when they have to be self-reliant versus when someone is available to comfort them, they will be anxious all the time.

Finally, suggest that parents *tell* their child they are leaving. If they *ask* if that is okay, the child is likely to say 'no', leaving everyone miserable and the child feeling betrayed when the parent departs despite the child's lack of consent.

Join with the children

Rather than pointing out the attractions of your program (i.e. asking children to find what you offer interesting), instead, ask the children to bring in something from home that interests them and make an effort to become engaged with the children over whatever fascinates them. Another option is to have them bring into the centre a compact disc that they were listening to in the car and play that until it ends. In this way, there is some continuity between home and the centre.

Explain exactly when the parent will return

Do not tell young children that 'Daddy will be back soon' when 'soon' can mean anything from a few minutes to many hours (Greenman & Stonehouse 2007). Instead, explain that their dad will be back after a particular activity.

Accept children's feelings

Normally, you will have tried to reassure children that there is nothing to be upset about, tried to soothe their feelings and generally distract them from their distress. However, children will continue to communicate their distress until someone says 'Message received'. Therefore, tell them that you understand that they are sad. Explain that when people their age are sad, they need to cry. Find them a comfortable corner where they can be sad for as long as it takes—all day if necessary. If they stop crying, you can remind them that they do not have to stop if they still feel sad. Once they believe that you understand them, they will not need to keep letting you know how they feel.

Make the children responsible for a solution

Having listened to children's feelings, ask if there is anything they would like to do to help themselves feel better. They might begin a favourite activity or ask one of the other children to play. But do not rush them into finding a solution. First, give them time to resolve their feelings.

Communicate your faith that children can cope

You can tell children that you know that they will find a way to feel happier. You might learn from the parents about other times when the children have overcome their feelings (such as being scared of the dark), and remind them of these occasions, expressing your faith that they can take charge of their present sadness in much the same way.

Interrupt the pattern

In Chapter 12, pattern interruption was suggested as a solution to chronic problems. With respect to separation difficulties, this can mean changing the sequence of events. The usual sequence is that the parent and child arrive, the parent leaves, and the child becomes upset. It could help to rearrange this sequence so that it is less upsetting to everyone, so the children can be soothed by the person dearest to them (namely, their parent), and the workload for caregivers is reduced. For example, you could tell children that their parent is about to leave and they should become upset now, while their parent is still here to comfort them. Then, once they are calm, the parent can depart. If parents have inflexible working hours, this might require forward planning, such as arranging for them to arrive 15 minutes earlier until the child's distress is resolved.

The rationale for this suggestion is that when children have a long history of separation problems, they can become upset not so much that their parents are leaving, but that they feel so out of control of their distress. When children become hysterical, they need their parents—not relative strangers—to reassure them.

Check that children are not feeling responsible for their parent(s)

Some children have taken on the job of looking after their parents, but they cannot perform this role unless they are together, and therefore they refuse to separate. In my experience, this is most common to eldest children in large families who feel responsible for helping their parent with the younger siblings, youngest children who fear that their parent will be lonely if they are apart, and children whose parents are stressed.

This form of separation distress will not improve unless the children are convinced that their parents do not need them to look after them, and they can see the parents taking care of themselves. Even if stressed and not sure how they will solve their present problems, the parents need to reassure their children that they are working on finding a solution and are still available to look after all the children in the family. It might be that you need to recommend some support agencies that can assist the family.

Recommend another placement

Centre-based childcare does not suit every child. Therefore, to safeguard a child's wellbeing, you might have to recommend a home environment such as family daycare for those who even after sensitive handling cannot settle in a larger group setting.

REUNIONS

Even those children who separated reluctantly from their parents at the beginning of the day might be off-hand when their parents return to collect them. Ignoring the parents might simply reflect the fact that they were certain that their parents were going to return and are happy to stay on.

A second pattern is that some children resist going home. Greenman and Stonehouse (2007) explain that these reactions do not mean that the children prefer their care setting to home. Instead, their reluctance to leave can be an attempt to involve their parents in this important part of their lives.

Alternatively, the children might see their parents and experience renewed sadness that they have been parted all day and so become distressed or in their excitement could 'show off' with disorganised or silly behaviour. This is both natural and can be due to exhaustion.

When parents reunite with their children, suggest that they avoid telling them that they miss them, in case the children think that their parents need their company and so refuse to separate in future. Instead, they can tell their children that they are glad to see them, which is what they mean anyway.

Children who are picked up later often experience mounting distress as they see others going home before them. It can be useful to reserve some special activities for this time of the day and to make use of the improved adult–child ratio to give these children some extra closeness with you (Greenman & Stonehouse 2007).

TRANSITIONS BETWEEN ACTIVITIES

Making children wait is disrespectful. It wastes their time, and is an invitation to behavioural problems (Fields & Boesser 2002). This makes it important for you to manage transitions between activities so that the children who are ready early do not become restless while they await latecomers. It can help to:

- give warning of an impending change in activity so that the children can disengage in time
- allow children to finish an activity in which they are engrossed, even if that means that they will have to start the new one late, and
- break the group into smaller groups for activities such as hand-washing.

PACKING AWAY EQUIPMENT

Planning how to tidy up a whole area of toys in logical steps can be too difficult for youngsters to do without help. (It is like having to tidy up your kitchen on the morning after a party.) The following are some suggestions that could help children to participate:

- *Assist with planning.* Help the children to plan how to go about tidying up, or ask if they would like some suggestions.
- *Turn packing away into a game.* Turn tidying up into a game that helps organise the task—for example, 'Simon says, put away everything that's red ... and now, everything that has wheels' and so on.

- *Help children to tidy up.* Like most activities that children do, they are happiest performing them when they have some company. Therefore, participate in the clean-up yourself, as they will be more likely to accompany you.
- *Give them a day off.* If individual children generally help to pack away and today's refusal is uncommon, give them a day off. Let children know that you appreciate that they usually help and that everyone has a 'slack attack' sometimes, and express your faith that they will feel like helping next time. On the other hand, treat persistent uncooperativeness as a passive tantrum. If children's refusal to assist with packing away is just one of many uncooperative behaviours, you could treat that as a passive tantrum and deal with it as recommended in Chapter 11.

CONCLUSION

The times when children are acquiring self-care skills are not routines to be rushed through in order to get to the 'real' curriculum. They are times to provide responsive care so that children learn that they are worth caring about (Greenman & Stonehouse 2007). Moreover, they are opportunities for children to practise many valuable skills—both content and process—and, in turn, to feel proud of their growing independence and competence. Therefore, although one purpose of routines will be to make these times manageable for caregivers, the main purpose is to make them enjoyable and achievable for the children. Disruptions that occur along the way need to be responded to with awareness that disturbances are inevitable given the demands of the tasks and the maturity of the children performing them.

Through their participation, the aim is for children to discover who they are and what they can do—not to learn your rules and what they cannot do. Routines provide some rhythm to the day, which young children need because they cannot use the time of day as a marker for events. Their function is to help children to navigate tasks with minimal, rather than intrusive, external guidance.

SUGGESTED FURTHER READING

Greenman J, Stonehouse A 2007 *Prime times: a handbook for excellence in infant and toddler programs*, 2nd edn. Redleaf Press, St Paul, MN.

chapter 14

Guiding prosocial behaviour

'The objective … is not to change people and their behavior in order to get our way; it is to establish relationships based on honesty and empathy which will eventually fulfill everyone's needs.'

HART & HODSON (2004, p. 91)

As reported in Chapter 5, young children's ability to regulate their emotions and thus inhibit inappropriate behaviours contributes significantly to both their social competence and acceptance by peers (Brophy et al. 2002, Coplan et al. 2004, Fabes et al. 1999, Hay et al. 2004, Hughes et al. 2000, 2001, Maszk et al. 1999, Riggs et al. 2006). While it can be difficult to detect children's inability to manage internal feelings such as anxiety, outwardly hostile emotions and resulting behaviours come to adult attention much more readily.

When determining whether children's social skills call for an intervention, it is worth bearing in mind that, particularly when you are new to the field, young children's social skills can seem remarkably tactless. Therefore, your best guide is the reaction of the recipient of the behaviour. With the exception of outright aggression, if the recipient does not object, you probably do not need to intervene.

SOCIAL WITHDRAWAL

Solitary play is the natural play mode of babies and toddlers. Only past 3 years of age do children develop associative and cooperative play skills. Even once capable of these more sophisticated forms of play, children of all ages need some time to be alone—to rest, reduce tension, reflect, prepare for the next activity, enjoy some privacy, and have a break from having to react to external stimuli (Galanaki 2005). It is vital, therefore, that you never use isolation in the form of time out as a punishment, because this turns solitude into a noxious state, when it needs to be seen as a positive time for nourishing the spirit.

In this section, I examine the following types of social withdrawal:

- introversion
- shyness
- reticence, and
- disengagement.

This section also discusses selective mutism as a less typical form of withdrawal.

Introversion

Introverted children participate appropriately in social encounters when they want to (Coplan et al. 2004), but also enjoy extended periods alone, often being actively occupied in exploratory or constructive activities such as drawing or building. Most introverts are as happy with their level of social engagement as are more outgoing children (Coplan et al. 2004), perhaps because while they may not have a breadth of relationships, they typically develop deep friendships. Their isolated play is not a problem unless the activity is better done in company (Perry & Bussey 1984) or if it causes peers to see the child as aloof or unfriendly and thus leads to peer neglect or rejection (Coplan et al. 2004).

The main response to introverts is to honour their need for solitude by providing quiet activities and an area where they can find sanctuary from the bustle around them.

Shy (or 'slow to warm') children

Shyness is a disposition that leads to inhibited and awkward social behaviour, particularly in the presence of new acquaintances (Young et al. 1999) and can cause children to be characterised as 'slow to warm up'. It results from children's reduced positive emotions and overcontrol of their expression of emotion, particularly anger (Spinrad et al. 2004). Shy children maintain minimal involvement with others by remaining on the periphery of groups, which allows them to avoid the frustration and anger occasioned by conflicts with others. Because they do not inflame confrontations, they tend to be well liked by peers (Spinrad et al. 2004).

In the early childhood years, shyness is benign, particularly when it wanes with increased familiarity with the setting and children become more socially engaged over time (Ladd & Burgess 1999, Spinrad et al. 2004). In the meantime, however, shy children lack access to peer support and the intimacy of friendships and as a result can feel insecure and lonely and experience lower self-esteem (Chen et al. 2000). Therefore, it is worthwhile to intervene.

Improve children's self-esteem

Shyness is a fear of being negatively evaluated by others (Greco & Morris 2001). Therefore, it can be worth letting children (and their parents) know that what other people think of us is none of our business. You will need to give substance to this message by using acknowledgment rather than praise, and thereby avoiding judging children so that they learn to form their own self-assessments, rather than being reliant on other people's opinions of them.

Normalise shyness

Acknowledge that at times we all feel unsure of ourselves (or 'shy'). It is normal. This saves children from worrying about themselves and therefore reduces the problem.

Express confidence in the children

When adults express understanding of the children's anxieties, but equal confidence in their ability to be sociable despite these, with support the children manage to overcome their inhibitions (Shamir-Essakow et al. 2004).

Give children time to recover themselves

When young children become self-conscious as they all do, do not encourage this by calling it shyness ('Ooh, have you gone all shy?'). Instead, avoid comment and give them a moment or two to recover their self-possession. For example, you might insist that they greet others, but not necessarily immediately upon arrival when everyone is focusing on them.

Expect socially assertive behaviour

Children's acceptance within the peer group recovers when their social assertiveness improves (Haselager et al. 2002). Therefore, guide them to practise social skills (such as those listed in Box 5.1 on pp. 64–5). Sometimes this can be as simple as telling girls that being shy and cute will not cut it for the modern woman in the modern world. (Many have gleaned the opposite message from the many ditsy female characters in television sitcoms and elsewhere.) Another option is to suggest that they *pretend* that they do not feel shy, on the grounds that no one will be able to tell if they are pretending or actually feeling confident.

Make children responsible for a solution

Talk with children about being boss of the shy feelings that sometimes overwhelm them. Just as other fears are a product of their imagination, fears about what others think of you are too. Express your faith that they will be able to take charge of these thoughts (see Ch 11).

Highlight previous successes

Instead of focusing on instances of problems, you can comment on those times when shy children have been socially involved and ask them what they thought or did at the time that helped them act less shy. What does this say about them?

Have fun

If nothing else has worked, you could prescribe the shyness—perhaps by telling shy children not to say 'hello' in greeting, because you would get such a fright and fall down in a faint. This exaggerates how silly their shyness is, making it obvious that nothing dreadful would happen if they overcame it.

Reticence (not joining in)

Reticence is the behavioural manifestation of extreme shyness and is detrimental to children's social, emotional and cognitive skills (Nelson et al. 2005). Reticent children play by themselves, but not by choice. Unlike introverted children who focus on their selected drawing or construction activity, reticent children are preoccupied with watching the rest of the group, hovering on its outskirts, but not becoming engaged with others or generating activities for themselves (Henderson et al. 2004). Despite being of an age to engage in associative or cooperative play, they either do not play at all or play only in parallel (Coplan et al. 2004).

These children tend to be passive and unspontaneous. Their wariness, reduced initiations of social contacts, lack of assertiveness, non-responsiveness to others' invitations, inhibited empathic responses to others' distress, and visible discomfort and anxiety can cause them not only to be neglected or ignored by peers but also to be actively rejected, even taunted or bullied (Findlay et al. 2006, Rubin 1998). Peer rejection may be especially likely for boys (Chang 2004, Coplan et al. 2001, 2004, Gazelle & Ladd 2003, Ladd 2006, Nelson et al. 2005, Rubin & Coplan 2004, Rubin et al. 2006, Spinrad et al. 2004), particularly when reticent behaviour is uncommon in the group (Chang 2004). In turn, this entrenches the children's anxious interaction style and lowers their self-esteem, thus exacerbating their social difficulties (Gazelle & Ladd 2003, Ladd 2006).

Children's reticence is due to anxiety that persists because they cannot regulate their emotions, particularly in unfamiliar surroundings (Eisenberg et al. 2001, 2004a, Henderson et al. 2004). This anxiety can be reflected in higher levels of the stress-related hormone, cortisol (Sims et al. 2005, Watamura et al. 2003). It is exacerbated when adults chastise children because of their own embarrassment at the behaviour or in frustration at the children's dependence on them (Rubin et al. 2002, Shamir-Essakow et al. 2004). Alternatively, becoming overly protective will shield children from manageable challenge and thus from developing coping skills (Bayer et al. 2006, Coplan et al. 2004, Rubin & Coplan 2004, Shamir-Essakow et al. 2004).

Another source of persistent social withdrawal is the nature of the setting, of which two aspects are relevant. The first is that a conflict-ridden environment and the presence of dominant children causes unassertive children to withdraw in self-protection (Hawley & Little 1999, Howes 2000). Second, an inclusive climate reduces children's social withdrawal over time, whereas reticence is intensified within rejecting settings (Flook et al. 2005, Gazelle & Ladd 2003, Spinrad et al. 2004). This indicates the need to intervene with the group rather than necessarily with withdrawn individuals.

Adjust the program

Children will wander around aimlessly not only when they lack social skills, but also when their program does not interest them or match their developmental level. Therefore, check that the activities on offer are attractive and developmentally achievable for reticent children and assist them to engage in those that they cannot perform independently.

Encourage non-aggressive peer group norms

Reticence and peer rejection are both more likely in groups with high levels of aggression. Therefore, prevent aggression and respond to its expression in ways to be covered later in this chapter.

Ensure children's connectedness with adults

Children who feel connected to their caregivers gain the confidence to overcome their social inhibitions and to manage the misgivings brought about by each new social encounter (Bohlin et al. 2005). With repeated experience, the dependability of your support will teach reticent children to expect the best rather than the worst from their social interactions and thus will encourage them to engage.

Check children's health and developmental skills

Children with chronic otitis media (middle-ear infections) and those with language impairments are more likely to play alone and to initiate less verbal contact with others (Benasich et al. 1993, Doctoroff et al. 2006, Vernon-Feagans & Manlove 2005). Similarly, children's inability to engage can result from not being able to organise their attention and thus may be an early sign of an attention-deficit disorder (Olson et al. 2002). Therefore, it can be wise to recommend that parents have reticent children's hearing, language and, if indicated, developmental skills checked.

Match children's developmental levels

Children with significantly delayed or advanced development may play alone because the surrounding children are at markedly different developmental levels from themselves. Because children choose companions who share their interests and skills, those with atypical development might need to be placed in groupings not according to their age but instead their skill level.

Assist children to enter a group

If individuals seem unable to negotiate entry into the play of their peers, begin by ensuring that the children know each other's names. As mentioned in Chapter 5, you could pair up a reticent child with someone who was more socially outgoing, or lead activities involving a reticent child and one other, then adding two, and then more children as the target child became more comfortable in larger groups (Greco & Morris 2001). However, keep in mind that, for the reasons given in Chapter 5, imposing a formal peer-mentoring role on very young children may be unwise. You could also initiate cooperative activities.

Teach emotional self-control

Unlike the overcontrol characteristic of shyness, reticence or withdrawal are signs that children cannot manage their feelings of anxiety. The methods given in Chapter 11 can help to teach them to regulate their emotions.

Teach accurate self-evaluations

In general, neither shy nor reticent children have social skill deficits, although many *believe* that they do (Cartwright-Hatton et al. 2003). Therefore, ensure that your feedback offers information that highlights the social skills that the children use and invites their own evaluations—for example, 'How did you get the other children to let you play?' or 'What did you do that helped them to say "Yes" when you asked them?'

Disengagement

Prolonged lack of engagement either socially or with activities can be caused by delays in children's language, motor, concentration or overall developmental skills. Children with overall delays may engage only briefly with activities, followed by lengthy periods of disengagement as they recharge their batteries and select their next activity (Linn et al.

2000). Given that this down-time can be productive, within reason, give children some breathing space to plan their own activity so that they can exercise some initiative (Linn et al. 2000). However, if their disengagement is prolonged or habitual, help them to re-engage by mediating their learning and social play (see Chs 3 and 5).

In the meantime, if you suspect that a developmental delay is the reason for their solitary play style, conduct some observations, particularly of their language, motor and concentration skills. If these observations confirm your misgivings, recommend to parents that they gain an assessment from a relevant specialist.

Gifted children can also be socially disengaged when there are no peers in the group who share their capabilities and interests. These children will often seek out adults or play alone but, when matched with similarly able children, display appropriate social skills. This form of disengagement, then, is a placement issue, suggesting the need to place gifted learners within a group of older children who will be more able to play at sophisticated levels.

Selective mutism

Despite being sufficiently capable of talking, selective mutes do not speak in the presence of unfamiliar adults or peers, particularly in settings outside of home (Black & Uhde 1995, Dummit et al. 1997, Ford et al. 1998, Steinhausen & Juzi 1996). Most speak more freely with peers than with adults (Black & Uhde 1995, Kolvin & Fundudis 1981). The syndrome also includes children who speak reluctantly, infrequently, with less spontaneity, or too quietly to be heard (Ford et al. 1998).

Girls are more likely to display this pattern than boys (Black & Uhde 1995, Dummit et al. 1997, Kristensen 2000, Steinhausen et al. 2006). Although insidious shyness is commonly noticeable from the children's earliest social encounters, mutism itself typically emerges around 3 years of age, with clinical referrals peaking in the early years of school (Black & Uhde 1995, Dummit et al. 1997, Ford et al. 1998, Kolvin & Fundudis 1981, Kristensen 2000, Steinhausen & Juzi 1996).

Known in the UK and formerly in the US as elective mutism, the change of title signals that these children do not *elect* to be silent out of wilfulness but, because of extreme shyness and anxiety, are *selective* about where and to whom they speak (Steinhausen & Juzi 1996). Because not communicating is seen as provocative, however, the children are often regarded as being controlling and manipulative (Kristensen 2000). Nevertheless, while they can be obstinate and uncooperative, this is mainly in an effort to avoid their anxiety at being pressured to engage socially (Dummit et al. 1997, Ford et al. 1998).

There are four subgroups of selective mutism, each with its own causes and recommended interventions. The first is *transient* mutism, in which children are reluctant to speak for the first few weeks (or perhaps months) after entering a new setting such as preschool or school, but whose difficulties subside spontaneously (Kolvin & Fundudis 1981).

A second subgroup is *migrant children*. Many bilingual children merely lack confidence in speaking in English, which abates as their English communication skills improve. Nevertheless, some migrants do develop the third type, persistent mutism, at a rate almost eight times higher than for native English speakers (Dummit et al. 1997). I am not aware of evidence on this issue, but I suspect that this pattern may reflect post-traumatic stress.

A third group, comprising perhaps 20 to 30% of selective mutes, is children whose mutism is *secondary* to other conditions, such as developmental delays, speech and language disorders or Asperger syndrome (Ford et al. 1998, Kolvin & Fundudis 1981, Kristensen 2000, Steinhausen & Juzi 1996). These children's speech avoidance reflects their awareness that they have communication difficulties.

The final cluster is represented by those with *persistent* mutism. Their symptoms typically last for 3 or more years. Prevalence for this subgroup is considered to be around 0.8 per 1000 in 7-year-olds, and lower in older children (Dummit et al. 1997, Kolvin & Fundudis 1981, Kristensen 2000, Steinhausen & Juzi 1996), although this form of the condition is so rare that such figures are really just estimates. Compared to those whose mutism is transient, these children are likely to be more anxious overall (rather than simply in social settings) and also to have difficulties separating from their parents. Most nevertheless do well academically, although teachers tend to underestimate their skills (Cunningham et al. 2004, Ford et al. 1998).

Recommend an assessment

Once individual children's reluctance to talk has persisted for more than 2 months, recommend to their parents that their child's speech and cognitive abilities be assessed to determine if the mutism has developmental causes (Kristensen 2000). At the same time, assessment also aims to ensure that the children are *not* given remedial education for disabilities that they do not have, but rather focuses on their core issue—which, for non-disabled children, is their anxiety (Dummit et al. 1997).

Adjust the demands

If children's mutism is an effort to avoid unattainable challenges, adjust task demands to raise their confidence and ensure their success (Kristensen 2000).

Resist imposing consequences

Selective mutism is not a manipulative behaviour problem (Kristensen 2000). Therefore, attempts to punish children by ignoring them or imposing time out or other punishments will be ineffective, as attested by former selective mutes themselves (Ford et al. 1998). More likely to be effective are strategies designed to assist them with their anxieties, which for older children may even include medication (Ford et al. 1998).

Take children out of the spotlight

When children first enter a room, we often put them under a social spotlight: everyone watches them. Under this public glare, it can be more difficult for them to talk. Therefore, allow them to delay greeting you until others are no longer watching.

Indirect communication

Another option is to have them talk through a toy—perhaps a doll, teddy or hand puppet—to your equivalent toy, or to sit back to back to them while they talk to you. This allows them to communicate without losing face at appearing to 'give in' to adult expectations that they be sociable.

Encourage children to retain their cultural language

Sometimes, I have met bicultural children who refuse to use English out of loyalty to their parents and their home language. If you suspect this, you might ask the parents to reassure their child that they are happy for him or her to use both languages.

Have the children generate a solution

Speak with children about other fears that they have managed to surmount, such as giving up their comfort rug or pacifier. Ask them how they did that and, even if they do not answer, ponder out loud if they can use the same skills to be boss of their worries about talking.

Refer on

I like a narrative counselling approach for this type of problem, as it highlights individuals' strengths. Under this approach, the mutism can be externalised and named and, in being given a separate identity, distances children from blame while still expressing confidence that they can tame their fears. You might, therefore, recommend a narrative therapist to parents.

EXCESSIVE RELIANCE ON OTHERS

When children are new to the setting, they may become overly reliant on one relationship with a particular adult or child but, after a settling-in period, can venture out to explore other sources of companionship. Others fail to branch out, remaining overly reliant for prolonged periods.

Reliance on adults

In the early stages of reliance on adults, allocate a primary caregiver so that dependent children receive the extra connectedness they need in their early days in a new setting. You might encourage them to gravitate to others by giving them activities to do, first jointly with you, then in parallel with you, and then on their own or in a pair with another child. Once other children become involved, introduce the children to each other and tell them about an interest they have in common, even if it is simply that they are the same age. Once they are engaged together, stand back a little. When the target child appears comfortable, withdraw briefly, and then for increasing lengths of time so the child becomes able to play without adult support. Make sure that children do not just transfer their dependence from you to one other child by introducing a series of different children to their play (Mitchell 1993).

Excessive reassurance seekers

These children become dependent on adults because they doubt their own worth. They frequently approach adults for reassurance but, once given, are not satisfied, knowing that others may declare affection for them insincerely or out of pity (Joiner et al. 1999). Furthermore, when children incessantly request declarations of affection, most adults grow irritated and terse, which contradicts their affirming verbal message. The main intervention for these children is to enhance their self-esteem by ceasing all praise and instead offering authentic acknowledgment (information) about children's genuine achievements (see Ch 7). At the same time, when the children declare affection for you, you can thank them and then, later, when they have not asked for affirmation, say something sincere and positive about them. When it is not pulled from you, and when it offers information rather than a judgment, your feedback will be more credible and, therefore, will need fewer repetitions.

Reliance on peers

Some children are extremely reliant on one particular playmate. This can come about when they are not yet socially mature or flexible enough to adjust to the play styles of less familiar children (see Table 5.2 on p. 67). This can be assisted by teaching social and other developmental skills (see Ch 5). Parents might be able to help their child to become more flexible by inviting home a series of compatible children from your setting.

A second style entails possessiveness or jealousy, where children seem hurt when their friend wants to include others. You can teach these children that belonging *with* does not mean belonging *to*, and explain that, even though they have a favourite food, they would soon tire of it if they ate it daily. So it is with friends. No one person can provide us with all the companionship we require. Therefore, we need to supplement best friendships with good friendships and acquaintances.

A third pattern is those who seek to dominate or control their peer by dictating that they *must* play exclusively with them. This is a form of bullying or social tantrum. Whenever it occurs, require perpetrators to sit out until they remember 'to play in a friendly way' or to take turns at being in charge of the play. Chapter 11 expands on ways to teach children control over their social actions, while the section to come in this chapter on relational aggression offers some additional suggestions.

Whether children adopt an assertive or submissive style will depend on the characteristics of their companion at the time (Hawley & Little 1999). They become more fixed in their dominant or submissive role when with a familiar companion (Hawley & Little 1999). Therefore, it might help subordinate children to pair them occasionally with a less familiar playmate whose personality is less dominant so that they can practise expressing their own views, rather than always submitting to the demands of a domineering peer.

PHYSICAL AGGRESSION

Aggression is the intent to inflict harm on another. Contrary to expectation, it is not the opposite of social competence, as individuals who are most dominant are also the most socially competent. Although they employ domineering behaviour strategically to gain access to scarce resources and social influence, they also display high levels of prosocial behaviour (Vaughn et al. 2003).

This section will address five common forms of aggression: instrumental aggression by infants, reactive aggression by children aged over 3, proactive aggression, bullying and callous behaviour.

Instrumental aggression by infants

Most aggression by infants occurs when they are in competition with a peer over a contested toy or access to space. As mentioned in the introduction to Part I, prior to the age of 2 years, hitting or biting peers are common behaviours in response to conflict. They typically decline from 30 months of age onwards, as the children naturally acquire language and emotional self-control. In the meantime, you will need to guard against attributing their behaviour to any malevolence on their part and therefore responding punitively.

In the immediate circumstances, you might say 'No' or 'Stop' firmly to aggressors. (I reserve the word 'No' for dangerous behaviour, and avoid it for simple mistakes.) Next, in the presence of aggressors, check on and soothe victims, expressing your empathy for their injury and hurt feelings. In this way, aggressors learn the effects of their behaviour, without being blamed or shamed.

When infants bite, check that they are not uncomfortable in the mouth because of teething. With parental permission, you might administer medication such as paracetamol for acute pain, and offer teething rings to soothe low-grade pain. Even without pain as a trigger, you could offer the child something else to bite or eat, explaining, 'Teeth are for chewing. Here is something you can eat' (Mitchell 1993). Even if the children are too young to understand your words, nevertheless they realise that they are being given an explanation, which can mollify them.

Reactive aggression by children aged over 3

Like the baby's instrumental aggression, reactive aggression occurs in retaliation against some real or imagined provocation or threat and arises from feelings of anger or frustration (Hubbard 2001, Prinstein & Cillessen 2003, Vitaro et al. 2006). However, beyond the age of 3 years, children should be starting to develop self-control and language skills to use in place of hitting out at others. That they have not reflects difficulties managing their own emotional arousal (Denham et al. 2002, Frick et al. 2003, Rubin et al. 2003, Vitaro et al. 2006).

Despite their aggressive exterior, these children have been described as 'brittle' in the sense that they are more easily distressed, are overly sensitive to threat, have low tolerance for frustration, poor problem-solving and coping skills, and elevated levels of hostility (Camodeca & Goossens 2005, Crick et al. 2002, de Castro et al. 2002, Little et al. 2003, MacKinnon-Lewis et al. 1999, Prinstein & Cillessen 2003, Vaughn et al. 2003). They have an external locus of causality (low self-efficacy), and therefore they blame others for provoking them, while underestimating and failing to take responsibility for their own aggressiveness (Lochman et al. 2006, Miller et al. 1998, Nelson et al. 2006, Yoon et al. 2000). These children exaggerate the consequences of affronts to their dignity, employing the defeatist thinking pattern described in Chapter 11 and Table 11.1 (see p. 123).

Unlike withdrawn children whose reticence can be specific to their situation, these dysregulated children tend to display behavioural difficulties across settings (Eisenberg et al. 2005). Although with initially lower and declining rates of aggression over time compared with the proactively aggressive children to be discussed next (Little et al. 2003), nevertheless this group is more isolated because their actions are directed against others (Bukowski 2003) and because they become disorganised when provoked. The result is that they display emotions inappropriately (both distress and glee at, say, defeating a playmate), and disengage or otherwise behave oddly in social settings, which their peers regard as age and situationally inappropriate (Hubbard 2001, Leary & Katz 2005). Therefore, their peers usually dislike them (LaFontana & Cillessen 2002, Prinstein & Cillessen 2003).

Proactive aggression

A third type of aggression is proactive. It does not require anger or provocation, but is an attempt by children to gain access either to resources (toys) or to secure or cement their social dominance (Vitaro et al. 2002). Those who are physically aggressive proactively are taught via parental controlling discipline to value using aggression, find it easy to do so, have an inflated view of their own capacities and thus expect to be successful at achieving their goals, which accounts for their stable rates of aggression over time (Camodeca & Goossens 2005, Coie et al. 1999, Egan et al. 1998, Vitaro et al. 2006). Despite being unpopular, their social self-esteem is high because they value dominance, and their aggression helps them achieve that (Frankel & Myatt 1996). As they are not being provoked, children's frequent use of proactive aggression past their fourth birthday signals not that they are out of control of their emotions, but are failing to regulate their *behaviour,* particularly their impulses (Frick et al. 2003).

These children tend to form friendships with similarly proactive aggressors, who then reinforce each other's antisocial behaviours (Poulin & Boivin 2000). Although their friends provide them with emotional support, their friendships also have more negative elements and are more fraught (Hay et al. 2004). Within these aggressive relationships, each child anticipates that the other will be hostile and therefore makes a pre-emptive strike that is justified by the supposed threat of the other (Coie et al. 1999). Thus, both children's high rates of aggression are maintained by mutual suspicion (Coie et al. 1999).

Proactive aggressors are of two types. The first group are those 'tough' boys and dominant girls with socially valued characteristics such as physical attractiveness or athleticism whose aggression is accompanied by high rates of prosocial behaviour. Even from the toddler years, they are more active and engaged and more socially and cognitively mature than less assertive youngsters, and therefore have the social finesse to gain access to activities, while also being able to use aggression strategically (Hawley & Little 1999). As a result, others defer to them and they acquire the status to become central and influential members of prominent cliques, which position they are then able to use to dominate others. However, while seen to be 'cool', these youngsters are nevertheless disliked (Cillessen & Mayeux 2004, Farmer et al. 2003, Rodkin et al. 2000).

The second group are the 'troubled' aggressive children with low social skills and limited prosocial behaviour who tend to be disliked by their peers, particularly in groups where aggression is uncommon (Chang 2004, Hay et al. 2004, Johnson et al. 2000, Rodkin et al. 2000, Stormshak et al. 1999). They may initially approach others often, but their overtures are rejected because they are less cooperative and their actions disrupt others' play. As a result, over time these children initiate less often and become increasingly isolated from prosocial peers and therefore either solicit high levels of (often negative) teacher engagement (Coplan & Prakash 2003) or gravitate towards other socially marginal children (Arnold et al. 1998, Dodge 1983, Farver 1996, Hartup 1989, Hartup & Moore 1990, Hay et al. 2004).

Bullying

A common form of proactive aggression is bullying. This is where individuals oppress others who are typically younger or weaker than themselves in gratuitous, unjustified, deliberate and repeated attempts to dominate and inflict hurt (Kochenderfer-Ladd & Ladd 2001, Rigby 2006, Slee 1995a, 1995b, Slee & Rigby 1994, Smith & Sharp 1994). By this definition, bullying is unlikely in children aged under 5 because they will lack the premeditation required for targeting specific individuals (Crick et al. 2001). Common to this age range, however, are exclusionary manoeuvres which, although intended to hurt, are nevertheless typically an immediate reaction to a peer's perceived transgression (Crick et al. 1999, Porter 1999). See the section below on exclusion of peers.

Callous behaviour

Callous behaviour in which children deliberately inflict pain on another person or an animal comes about when the emotional aspects of conscience are impaired, the children are insensitive to prohibitions, lack empathy for or even enjoy others' distress, and are fearless about consequences and insensitive to cues of impending danger (Frick et al. 2003). As young children, however, they can have similar levels of empathy to their more prosocial counterparts (Hastings et al. 2000). A subsequent decline in their concern for others can be prevented by showing them empathy even when their behaviour is abhorrent, avoiding criticism while still insisting that they regain self-control, teaching them more prosocial behaviour, and supporting their parents to use guidance rather than controlling discipline (Hastings et al. 2000).

Interventions

You will have four aims when responding to aggression. First, you will seek to comfort recipients at the time and, in the long term, to protect them from actual harm and from the social isolation that can accompany being a recipient of aggression (Ostrov et al. 2004). Second, aggressors need protection from developing a negative reputation because, once in place, reputations are resistant to change even when the children's behaviour improves (Johnson et al. 2000). Third, the group as a whole needs protection from contagious aggression, which will both intimidate reticent children in particular and exacerbate the aggression of prone individuals. At the same time, onlooking children need reassurance that they will not be dealt with harshly if in future they were similarly to lose control of themselves. Finally, you have a right to have fewer conflicts to handle.

The basic premise guiding your responses is that non-violence is better than violence at solving problems (Slaby et al. 1995). The following strands of response can be necessary:

- adjust the program
- manage group dynamics
- comfort victims
- intervene with perpetrators, and
- support parents.

Program adjustments

Most reactive aggression in the form of biting or hitting peers is an immediate reaction to present events. Therefore, to prevent recurrences, ensure that children are not crowded and competing for too few toys. Create more space, avoid large group activities, and avoid placing repeated biters near their favourite victim (Greenman & Stonehouse 2007). Ensure that the program is engaging so that children do not become aggressive for entertainment.

Manage group dynamics

Given that aggression is less common within stable, cooperative groups, it will be important to foster cohesion within the peer group in general (Farver 1996). Establishing group norms of non-aggression will also ensure that peers do not emulate each other's aggressiveness and do not escalate their aggression in response to hostility from others (Stormshak et al. 1999). When children are habitually aggressive, it can be valuable to shadow them to observe when they are becoming emotional and to intercept passive tantrums (whingeing and uncooperativeness) before these escalate into a social outburst.

Comfort victims

After an incident of biting or physical aggression, take the perpetrator and victim aside, perhaps holding the hand of the aggressor. Address the victim, not the perpetrator, reflecting his or her feelings: 'That hurt you, didn't it? It hurt your arm and your tears tell me that it also hurt your feelings. Shelley forgot to use her words. She must have been very angry.'

Do not require perpetrators to apologise. If you shame them into doing so, you might provoke another incident. Instead, you might apologise on their behalf. 'I know when Shelley calms down, she will feel very sorry to have hurt you. I'm sure she will want to say sorry then. But she's probably too angry now, so I will say it for her. I am sorry that Shelley hurt your arm and I'm sorry that she hurt your feelings.' This validates the victim's physical and emotional pain without confronting perpetrators with their mistakes.

Next, nurse the recipient's injuries, inviting (but not forcing) aggressors to help, to encourage them to take responsibility for their actions.

In the longer term, teach recipients of aggression how to be assertive and to negotiate with rather than to reject an aggressor, so that peer rejection does not provoke further outbursts of violence (Arnold et al. 1999). Step in immediately if physical aggression is brewing (Arnold et al. 1999), but otherwise give typically subordinate children an opportunity to be independently assertive (Farver 1996). Teach victims how to ask you for help, rather than to tell tales—and be sure to follow up their requests for help to ensure that an aggressor desists (see Ch 15).

Intervene with perpetrators

Aggressive children will need to learn more constructive ways to meet their needs and solve problems.

Build a close relationship with aggressive children

Children's aggression typically alienates their parents, educators and peers (Blankemeyer et al. 2002). This disconnectedness from others will only exacerbate their antisocial behaviour. Therefore you will need to build a warm relationship with them.

Educate aggressors about the effects on recipients

Tell babies and children that their companion is not enjoying their touch. Show infants how to touch gently and perhaps direct their interest to an alternative activity. Even when they do not understand your words, they will realise that they are being given an explanation and are less likely to persist in reaction against a prohibition.

Assess aggressive children's developmental skills

As many as two-thirds of reactively aggressive children have learning impairments, cognitive processing problems such as attention and concentration difficulties, impulsivity and problem-solving deficits, and language difficulties, including auditory working memory impairments (Dionne et al. 2003, Ripley & Yuill 2005, Schaeffer et al. 2003, Vitaro et al. 2002). Any or all of these can result in both poor achievement and a limited repertoire for solving social dilemmas. To identify any learning difficulties, conduct your own observations and, if these confirm your concerns, recommend to parents that they seek assessments from a psychologist and speech pathologist.

Use guiding discipline

Reactive aggression arises from coercive discipline, which fails to teach children emotion regulation (Casas et al. 2006, Romano et al. 2005, Vitaro et al. 2002, 2006). Therefore, after an aggressive incident, perpetrators will need support to learn how to take charge of their own behaviour. Guidance will entail refraining from delivering rewards or punishments. This is because the aim for aggressive children in particular is that they become intrinsically motivated to build friendships and not to aggress. The administration of consequences would only entrench an external locus of causality, with the result that aggressors would require constant supervision of their behaviour.

The core practice for perpetrators of aggression is to help them to calm down. As described in Chapter 11, draw them in close to you or, if for any reason that is not practicable, impose time away until they are calm enough to play 'in a friendly way'. Even if they protest at this imposed isolation, aggression presents one of the rare occasions when the use of protective force is justified—protective in the sense of keeping surrounding children safe, but also protecting the aggressor from the social costs of his or her actions.

While explaining that, 'I wouldn't let them do that to you, and I can't let you do that to them', insist that they take time to calm down until you know that 'the other children will be safe'. As described in Chapter 11, this time can be spent in a solitary occupation such as reading or listening to music, accompanying you as you go about your other duties, or in a soothing hug until the children's emotions are settled. Throughout this time, you do not have to talk to them about their aggression, as they have heard it before and their actions were not the result of a lack of information but due to a lapse of self-control.

This support is aimed at teaching reactively aggressive children to manage their emotions and, in the case of those with proactive aggression, to discipline their impulses. Once the children are calm again, they might need your help to engage in a new activity (Slaby et al. 1995).

Teach prosocial skills

To ensure their social inclusion, both reactive aggressors and their victims need support within peer relationships (Ostrov et al. 2004). Toddlers who react aggressively or who bite might need guidance about how instead to use words to express their needs. Older children might need coaching in how to enter a group without disrupting its ongoing activity (see Ch 5). As reactively aggressive children are more likely to interpret their peers' accidental behaviours as intentionally hostile and therefore respond aggressively, some will need coaching to make more accurate interpretations of others' intent and to overlook occasional mistakes by playmates (Asher 1983, Katsurada & Sugawara 1998).

With proactive aggressors, the hurdle you must overcome is that they value aggression as it secures them status. You can ask these children about their goal: 'Do you want to have a friend, or do you want to be boss?' If they say that they want to have friends, you can ask whether they think that their present behaviour (being bossy, not taking turns, not helping others, or whatever) helps them to make friends, or causes other children to dislike them. You can guide their assessment of this by asking them to reflect on their peers' verbal and non-verbal feedback to them.

If they tell you that they want to be boss, you can ask whether they think that bossing other people makes them a better person. If so, you can feign puzzlement when you ask:

- Where did you get that idea?

- What makes you think that you are not already a good person, whether you are the boss or not?
- How many people do you have to boss around before you will have enough proof that you are okay—this group, the whole centre, the whole city, everyone in the country … or all the world? How likely is that?

While insisting (through imposed time away) that these children control their impulse to boss others around, it can also be useful to give them prosocial opportunities to lead and exercise autonomy so they are less invested in exerting control antisocially.

Be alert for signs of child abuse

High levels of aggression are a common result of child abuse (Bolger & Patterson 2001). Therefore, examine whether an aggressive child is displaying other signs of victimisation (see Box 4.1 on pp. 52–4) and, where indicated, report your concerns to the relevant child welfare authorities.

Support parents

Without telling the victim's parents the name of the perpetrator (although their child will probably do that for you), notify the parents of both children about an aggressive incident. In doing so, however, be clear that you have responded and do not need them to take further action. In those rare cases where you suspect that an aggressive child could receive punishment at home for something that happened in your setting, the child's need for safety might override your obligation to inform parents and therefore you might choose not to tell them of the incident.

In 25 years of practice, I have never yet seen a well child from a well-resourced, well-functioning family displaying repeated aggression. Troubled and isolated children have troubled and isolated families. In other words, chronic aggression in children is a sign of stress in a family. Moreover, children's aggression is likely to be most severe at home (Little et al. 2003), thereby adding to parents' stress. As a teacher or caregiver, your role may not be to support families directly, but it can be possible to recommend agencies to assist them to improve their living circumstances, so that their stress levels are lowered and they can parent more responsively.

You could also encourage parents to provide additional opportunities at home for the children to practise prosocial skills in relationships with family acquaintances or peers from your setting (Hartup & Moore 1990).

Recommend an alternative placement

If your conscientious disciplinary efforts and program adjustments ultimately prove unsuccessful, on the grounds that surrounding children have a right to feel safe in your care, it may be necessary to ask the parents of an unrelentingly aggressive child to withdraw him or her from your setting, while recommending to them some alternative placements. Some authors repudiate excluding children in this way on the grounds that it contradicts inclusive practice (Strain & Joseph 2004). However, there are three arguments for its use in rare cases. First, I believe that aggressors' behaviour is a sign of stress, in which case it is a kindness to find the child a less stressful environment. Second, although expulsion sounds harsh, it can be therapeutic in that it could impel the parents into gaining help for themselves and their child. Third, the alternative can be that some of the victims will be withdrawn from your setting, which seems unfair, given that they are not at fault and therefore should not be the ones to have their care or education disrupted.

EXCLUSION OF PEERS

Introverts, shy children and those reticent children who play alone out of anxiety isolate themselves from the group. This section addresses those children who wish to be engaged with the group, but it excludes them. As a manifestation of peer rejection, exclusion may be less extreme than physical aggression, but chronic exclusion is just as debilitating to victims' academic, emotional and social adjustment (Buhs & Ladd 2001). It comes about for a range of reasons, each of which implies slightly different interventions.

Lack of flexibility in play

Sometimes children deny a new player entry to their play because they have already structured their game and, given their developmental immaturity, are not flexible enough in their thinking to adjust to include a new entrant. In these circumstances, you can ask them about their play and whether there is room for one more child. Complaints such as, 'Matthew wants to be the baby and we already have a baby' could be met with suggestions that this family could have twins, or that Matthew could adopt some other role.

If the children reject these suggestions, you could explain, 'Well, it looks like there isn't room for you in this game just now, Matthew. Children, how long do you think you'll be playing this game before you can let Matthew join in your next one? How long will Matthew have to wait?' This gives a certain end to their exclusion of the hopeful entrant and lets him know that it has to do with the demands of the game, rather than himself.

Pairs of friends sharing intimacy

A second instance when children might deny a child entry occurs when two close friends are sharing some intimate moments in communion with each other. As discussed in Box 14.1, Paley (1992) contends that children cannot share private time in a public place (the playground). But I liken this situation to being out at a restaurant for a special anniversary dinner with our romantic partner. Amidst the candlelight and champagne, we are unlikely to welcome another restaurant patron who asks to join us. Similarly, we cannot require two children who want to appreciate their special bond to open that up to others on every occasion. They might have no other opportunities outside this public setting to enjoy their intimacy.

In this case, I believe that the children's affection for each other needs to be honoured by telling a child whom they have refused entry that the exclusion is temporary and will be over at a specified time. To that end, you can guide the children to say that they will play later with the prospective entrant but that, for now, they want some quiet time together.

Relational aggression

A third form of exclusion is relational aggression, which entails threatening to damage a relationship if the recipient does not do as directed. It can also be an attempt to manipulate the group hierarchy (Prinstein & Cillessen 2003) or to cement group coherence by excluding children who are seen to be different in some way (Bukowski 2003). In the school years, manoeuvres to control others become covert and increasingly subtle (Shute et al. 2002), although they can be reasonably sophisticated even in young children, encompassing:

- blocking a child's access to play
- prematurely terminating play once a particular child enters
- restricting children's access to other peers or to play equipment
- restricting or threatening to restrict a peer's access to social events, as in, 'You can't come to my birthday party'
- dominating or bossing peers during play
- placing constraints on the friendship: 'You can't be my friend unless ...'
- gossiping
- telling secrets or spreading rumours about others
- expressing disapproval of peers or their behaviour
- using hurtful nicknames that parody a child's personal characteristics, and
- manipulating group acceptance by invoking a third party to collude in exclusion, as in, 'We're not playing with her, are we?' (Crick et al. 2001, Deater-Deckard 2001, Ostrov et al. 2004).

Relationally aggressive children tend to be popular in the sense of being highly visible and having high status because their subordinates share the affiliative goal of sustaining group coherence (Bukowski 2003). At the same time, they are personally disliked by their peers (Cillessen & Mayeux 2004, LaFontana & Cillessen 2002, Ostrov et al. 2004, Prinstein & Cillessen 2003, Rose et al. 2004). For their part, victims of relational aggression tend to be socially withdrawn and rejected (Ostrov et al. 2004).

In the years prior to school, most relational aggression is directed at victims in reaction to a perceived injustice or misdemeanour. Without intervention, by the ages of 5 to 7 years, this reactive aggression can be converted into proactive, relational bullying, with the result that the rates of both bullying and victimisation come to resemble the incidence for older children (Alsaker & Valkanover 2001, Kochenderfer & Ladd 1996). To prevent this, intervention will span the measures listed for physical aggression:

- Adjust the program so that children have enough to do and do not engage in manipulating relationships out of boredom.
- Manage group dynamics so that the group does not endorse relational aggression. This will entail banning time out, because you cannot teach the children to include all their peers while reserving the right to exclude those who displease you.
- Support submissive children to be assertive about their rights to play where, with whom and with whatever equipment they like. They have a right to a fair and reasonable turn.
- Explain to perpetrators the effects of relational aggression on its recipients.
- Use guidance to teach perpetrators to control their impulses. This is essential because children's use of relational aggression is common when their parents use psychological controls such as love withdrawal or the induction of guilt or shame. Children will transfer relational aggression from home to their peer relationships when their parents model relationally manipulative behaviours (Brendgen et al. 2005, Casas et al. 2006, Nelson et al. 2006) or fail to check the high rates of older siblings' relational aggression to their younger brothers or sisters (Ostrov et al. 2006, Stauffacher & DeHart 2006).

BOX 14.1 A debate about the 'You can't say "You can't play"' rule

Paley (1992) recommends instituting a blanket rule that 'You can't say "You can't play"'. The aims of doing so are to foster a safe, accepting social climate; to protect excluded children from isolation; and to shield the excluders from the ordeal of deciding who can join them and of feeling badly about being mean (Paley 1992).

Asking children to forfeit their freedom to choose their playmates is such a serious matter that it needs evidence that it works. Research on the effectiveness of this intervention is sparse, with one study finding that children reported that they liked to play with each other more following a year-long institution of the rule but, while it appeared to change their attitudes, it seemed not to change their actual social behaviour (Harrist & Bradley 2003).

Meanwhile, the more skilled children typically remain dominant, while those with low status might become more submissive as a result of their unsuccessful interactions at close quarters with the rest of the group (Jules 1991). When the rule is in operation, these rejected children's perceptions of their acceptance appears not to improve, perhaps because they recognise that they are being included only on sufferance, rather than out of any preference (Harrist & Bradley 2003).

A further problem is that, having included non-preferred children, the rule does not address how to handle their subsequent unskilled or antisocial behaviour (Harrist & Bradley 2003). Paley recommends that the group remind antisocial children to play nicely. Paley expects that, realising that being able to play is a privilege, aggressive children will soon learn not to jeopardise their inclusion by behaving aggressively. Furthermore, their aggression can result from being excluded and therefore, once included, it should abate.

Paley contends that philosophical objections and practical issues can be resolved through group discussion and through resolution of disputes at the time they arise. Questions that can emerge include:

- What do you do if so many people join in that the game gets ruined for those who set it up?
- Do the authors of the game have the right to direct it by controlling who can join in and, if not, do they get to dictate or impose how the game proceeds? Is that just a licence to be bossy?
- If they cannot refuse others entry, do they instead have the choice to leave if they no longer enjoy the game? If everyone leaves except the new entrant, is that inclusion?

I wonder if some of the problem is that adults want children to pretend that if only everyone were good, kind, nice and fair all the time, the world's problems would be solved. As if driven by such romanticism, I have often heard adults say to children, 'We're all friends here at kindy'. But this is not true, any more than all of your work colleagues are your friends. Children know this, as reflected in the following exchange:

Teacher: Frank, we don't hit our friends here at preschool.

Frank: I know that. But he's not my friend.

(continued)

> Maybe it is time to be honest with children. Admitting that we are not friends with everyone honours the true friendships that children do have (Howes & Ritchie 2002). At the same time, we can still appreciate the companionship of less intimate relationships and insist that everyone refrains from hurtful comments and actions towards all others.

Prejudice and discrimination

A final reason that some children exclude certain peers is as an expression of prejudice, which is commonly racial. Stereotypes are assumptions that individuals will possess particular attributes as a result of their group membership. Prejudice is a negative judgment about those attributes and individuals, while discrimination entails actions that arise from prejudicial beliefs (Aboud 2003, Brown & Bigler 2005, Myers 2005). Children begin constructing—and being taught—views about race from their earliest years. As with other observable differences (such as gender), they notice differences in skin colour. By the age of 1 year, children can visually recognise members of differing racial groups; by the age of 3 years, can reliably label gender; and, by the age of 6 years, can reliably label race (Brown & Bigler 2005). Children develop an interest in making social comparisons, with the result that by the age of 3 years, they are knowledgeable about gender stereotypes and are aware of racial stereotypes by the ages of 4 or 5 years (Brown & Bigler 2005).

Thus, stereotyping is perhaps an inevitable reflection of young children's natural tendency to classify. Nevertheless, knowledge about stereotypes is different from actually endorsing these (Brown & Bigler 2005). It is *not* inevitable that stereotypes degenerate into prejudice and that children learn to define differences as deficiencies. Negative evaluations of others arise when individuals lack contact with those who differ from them, when children are taught that differences signal deficiencies, and when children lack empathy. The result can be prejudice and discrimination. However, when children from minority cultures are obliged to accept that they are not allowed to play because of their race, they feel unworthy and their self-esteem and cultural pride is damaged. They also feel that they do not belong, that they are outsiders and that, because their race is immutable, this exclusion is permanent (Elswood 1999).

Establish inclusive group norms

You can foster an expectation within your setting that individuals will help each other out (Nesdale et al. 2005). This can be formalised in a written antibias policy that you supply to all new parents at enrolment. While you cannot demand that others share your values, you can expect that they and their children *behave* considerately in your setting.

Inclusive values can be lived through a multicultural curriculum that does not focus on other cultures' exotic customs, but uses books, visiting speakers and natural events to introduce children to and celebrate differences between people (Crary 1992, Saifer & Clark 2005). Follow up these measures by establishing general principles of using words that do not hurt other people (Saifer & Clark 2005) and of not excluding others from play for reasons of their race, gender or disability.

Foster empathy and highlight moral considerations

Children are less likely to denigrate others when they empathise with them (Nesdale et al. 2005). Therefore, you can foster empathy in ways mentioned in Chapter 5, and question the morality of excluding peers on the basis of their gender or race. From 60 to 90% of preschoolers judge that doing so is unfair and hurtful (Killen et al. 2001, Theimer et al. 2001). Therefore, when they attempt to exclude someone and you explain the morality of this, most children can be readily persuaded to change their minds (Killen et al. 2001, Theimer et al. 2001).

Encourage assertiveness

Teach victims of sexist or racist taunts to be assertive, using general statements such as, 'Don't say those things to me. I don't like it', or more specific rebuttals such as, 'That is not friendly. I won't play with you if you're not friendly' or 'That's not true. I'm not (whatever the other child accused them of being)'.

Mediate problem resolution

When an incident of sexist or racist abuse has occurred, withdraw recipients and offenders together. Talk to *recipients* of the insult. Listen to them and say that you understand that it hurt their feelings. Meanwhile, allow the offender to hear this conversation, without being lectured to or shamed. Apologise on the perpetrator's behalf and, once the recipient is mollified, as long as you can do so without preaching, give the perpetrator some simple information that clarifies a stereotype or misconception (Crary 1992).

Give perpetrators opportunities to exercise power prosocially

Demeaning others can be some children's way of gaining influence in situations where otherwise they feel powerless (Prinstein & Cillessen 2003). Therefore, ensure that perpetrators of discrimination feel accepted and can exercise autonomy in everyday ways within your setting. Ensure that you offer many opportunities for authentic choices and for making real contributions, and that you acknowledge—but do not praise—children's achievements so that they learn how to value themselves and each other.

Balance gender participation

In mixed-gender groups, boys attain most access to resources, with girls frequently deferring to their higher status by withdrawing (Green & Rechis 2006). Even in same-sexed groups, the distribution of resources is inequitable, with the dominant members using both prosocial and coercive means to meet their needs, sometimes at the expense of others (Green & Rechis 2006). So that both genders and children of all races have a fair share of play time and equipment, during disputes you can guide the children to generate and self-monitor a system for sharing equitably, hold discussions with children about fairness, and structure group activities that require both cooperation and sharing of limited resources, such as staging a puppet show (Green & Rechis 2006).

Boys' status and thus access can be enhanced compared with girls through biased interactions with adults. For example, boys attract more adult attention than girls and receive more feedback about their physical prowess, whereas adults tend to comment more on girls' appearance, thus reinforcing boys' active nature and girls' submissive one (Crick et al. 2002). Girls are referred to with endearments (e.g. honey or sweetheart), whereas boys are called by macho nicknames. Avoid these behaviours as they can entrench children's stereotypes about the genders, which is a platform from which prejudice can develop.

ROUGH-AND-TUMBLE PLAY

Play fighting is used to establish and test dominance in a group without violating social norms by being truly aggressive (Geary et al. 2003, Hay et al. 2004). Being three to six times more common in boys than girls, it emerges at about 3 years of age, peaking at 8 to 10 years (Geary et al. 2003). Partners who can de-escalate the play when it becomes too arousing teach each other how to regulate their emotions (Carson & Parke 1996). This is a particularly important lesson for males, which ensures that, as adults, they can step back from the brink of violence. This protects their partners from abuse (Biddulph 2003).

Some children use rough-and-tumble play as a way of greeting or inviting another child to play with them. They do not mean to be aggressive, but their play partners may not interpret these boisterous invitations as friendly and may have difficulty choosing an appropriate response within such a fast-paced interaction (Hart et al. 1992). For their part, the initiators might not notice the other child's protests. In these cases, you can:

- Remind children to use words when they want to invite another child to play.
- Provide a mat for tumbling and other physically active games, and lead cooperative games that allow children to touch each other safely.
- Reflect how the unwilling recipient is feeling about unwanted touch. For example, 'Milly, Rhys said that he wanted you to stop. What do you think he meant?' If, after these reminders, the instigators of rough play do not change their behaviour, this is a lapse of self-control that can be dealt with as described in Chapter 11.

SUPER-HERO PLAY

Some children will carry over into their play the violent themes of popular television programs that depict power and subordination. This super-hero play can help children resolve issues of good and evil and power and powerlessness (Saifer & Clark 2005). Or, the play can simply be an imitation of what they have seen, in which case it is merely ritualistic and does not help children to make sense of their world (Gronlund 1992).

Given that violent play helps children to understand their world, we cannot ban it (Dawkins 1991). An attempt to do so would only make it covert. On the other hand, violent play has some significant disadvantages. First, it can mean that children whose play is often violent are not experimenting enough with their play themes. Second, super-hero play can deteriorate quickly into outright aggression (Gronlund 1992). Third, children who were not originally involved in the violent play can imitate the other children's aggression both at the time and later, although this effect mostly occurs for children who were already aggressive (Dawkins 1991). Fourth, the violence of the play can intimidate onlookers. Fifth, victims of the make-believe violence usually do not enjoy it (Bergen 1994). These disadvantages give rise to the following suggestions for limiting the potential negative effects of play that has violent themes.

Give children other opportunities to resolve issues of power and powerlessness

Give children opportunities to make choices and take responsibility so that they feel powerful in their own lives. This necessitates ensuring that girls as well as boys can participate in the games and discussions about power and safety. Within the curriculum, explore issues of power and safety by using alternative topics such as dinosaurs, space adventures or nightmares. Protectiveness training can also address safety issues for young children.

Become familiar with the programs

Become familiar with the currently popular programs so that you understand their attraction for the children (Cupit 1989) and to incorporate their themes into your educational program. This will moderate any negative effects the programs can have on the children (Dawkins 1991) and, by taking an interest in their issues, we increase the likelihood that they will take an interest in our educational endeavours.

Let the children teach you about their heroes so that you can share rather than disparage their interests (Gronlund 1992). This communicates that you accept their experiences and feelings, allows you to ask questions that help them to be critical of what they see on television, gives you credibility when you discuss aggression with them, and ensures that their violent play does not become surreptitious. More important, however, it allows you to provide support for the children as they work out scary feelings and reach their own conclusions about hurting other people (Gronlund 1992).

Redirect the play

Have available a range of attractive dramatic play materials that can encourage the children to play alternative games. Ensure that there is enough time and equipment for gross physical activity, so that the more active children are able to use their energies without needing to play super-hero games exclusively.

Restrict the play

You could cordon off a section of the outside play area for super-hero play, so that the remaining area feels safe to uninvolved children. Another form of restriction is to insist that the play has to be pretend play, and that no one is to get hurt. Gronlund (1992) recommends teaching children that on television, the real actors use stunt men and women who practise the moves carefully to ensure that no one is injured, and therefore the children also need to practise making the moves safely.

Alternatively, you could set a time limit on the super-hero play. It might be easier to use natural changes of routine—such as fruit time—as a signal to stop the play and settle into another activity.

Finally, you can check with participating children that they still want to play the game. It is important to suspend the game if any of the children are not feeling safe (Bergen 1994).

Extend the scripts

Help the children to extend their super-hero play scenarios into more positive themes by suggesting alternative scenarios that do not involve violence but which still give children power (Saifer & Clark 2005). You can begin with their script but add new parts and new conclusions that are more positive (Gronlund 1992). For example, you could move the danger source from a person to an event, and have the children conquer the danger—for example, by tracking down a wild animal or extinguishing a fire. This avoids the play being a simple repetition of someone else's script and thus teaches children dramatic play skills.

Teach critical skills

If you watch television as part of your day, teach the children to be active viewers rather than passive recipients of what they see. Once they have learned to evaluate what they see on television, they can begin to make judgments about the violence they are emulating (Dawkins 1991).

Enlist parental support

Finally, it can be useful to talk with parents whose children do not seem to be growing out of the super-hero phase. The parents might not know that their children are obsessed with the violence and, once aware of the issue, might decide to limit their television viewing. It can also be useful to encourage parents to buy open-ended toys that allow for creative play rather than television-related toys that have only one purpose (Gronlund 1992).

UNWILLINGNESS TO SHARE

It strikes me that we often expect children to be better at sharing than we adults are. Just like us, children need some territory that is theirs alone and they have the right to choose with whom to share. With this said, some ways of promoting sharing include the following.

Prevent disputes

Have available enough toys to avoid repeated disputes over equipment. Meanwhile, it might be useful to ask children to bring to the centre only those personal toys that they are happy for other children to touch. (The exception will be soft toys for sleep time, which no one has to share.)

Give children permission to finish playing with a toy

Give children permission to finish playing with a toy before being expected to relinquish it for another child. This allows them some control over sharing, which increases the likelihood that they will be willing to share appropriately.

Help the children to structure their own turn taking

When children have to wait for turns on equipment, an egg timer can help them to be aware of the passage of time and respect that it signals the next person's turn. Another option is to have the children write their names or place their name cards on a 'waiting list' so that they do not have to hover idly near the desired equipment, which wastes their time and puts pressure on the children who are using the equipment to defend their place. Be sure that, on the whole, the children are responsible for negotiating these systems. Otherwise, you will have to oversee them perpetually and act as judge and jury in a constant stream of disputes.

Explain that it is friendly to share toys

Explain non-judgmentally that it is friendly to share toys with others and acknowledge or thank (but do not praise) children for sharing.

Encourage restitution

When a baby has snatched a toy from another child who is not protesting, ignore this (Greenman & Stonehouse 2007). If the other baby is protesting, help them both to locate a toy that interests them. When older children have snatched a toy from another child, you could give them a restricted choice—for example, 'You can give that back to Tim, or you can put it down over there'. This allows the perpetrator to save face, while still returning the contested item.

Support bereaved children

Children who have suffered a profound emotional deprivation, such as the loss of a parent through a death or separation, tend to be less able to share and often hoard items that they do not even require. It is as if they have learned early to grasp anything that is available, because they never know when they will be deprived of it. It can help to let these children bring some precious items to the centre without having to share these, to support them in their grieving (see the section on bereavement later in this chapter), and to respond firmly but with kindness, so that the children gain confidence emotionally in the adults who remain caring for them.

Avoid being moralistic about stealing

Some children take home or hide items that are not theirs, in order to avoid having to share these. In response, you could explain that the centre needs all of its toys so that there is something for the children to play with, or that another child will miss a personal item if it is lost. As young children do not fully comprehend ownership and sharing, treat this not as a misbehaviour—that is, do not refer to it as stealing—but regard it as a lack of knowledge on the child's part.

SEXUALITY

It is tempting to assume that the topic of sexuality is irrelevant to early childhood (Robinson 2002). However, sexuality is not limited to romance and intercourse but, more broadly, is about relationships, life choices, dispositions, play, and family, all of which affect children and adults equally (Robinson 2005). Our sexual identity fundamentally organises our human experience, identity and development (Carver et al. 2004), and starts to define us even prior to birth. Children recognise the two sexes by 9 months of age, can label them by 2 to 3 years (which coincides with the beginnings of sex-segregated play), and show strong and rigid stereotyping of the sexes and sensitivity to gender issues from 4 years of age (Fabes et al. 2004).

Gender conformity

During early childhood, children are already actively constructing their sexual identity— that is, ways of being male or female through games such as mothers and fathers, doctors and nurses, holding mock weddings, kissing games and gendered play (Robinson 2002).

Some children are excluded from particular roles within this play according to what is considered appropriate to their gender (Robinson 2005). Social pressure to conform to prescribed patterns of masculinity or femininity disallows boys any attraction towards 'feminine' skills or interests (Kerr & Cohn 2001). A 'boy code' states that not only will boys be boys but also, more insistently, that 'boys *should* be boys' (Kerr & Cohn 2001). Thus, homophobia is not only discrimination against and harassment of the minority who are homosexual, but comprises attempts to limit any heterosexuals who are seen not to be conforming to rigidly prescribed gender roles (Robinson 2002).

Nevertheless, the goal of gender equity is not to have the two genders acting the same, but to promote optimum development of all children. This will entail challenging the binary or categorical view of what constitutes masculine versus feminine behaviour, so that individuals can adopt multiple roles and ways of being female and male (Lee-Thomas et al. 2005, Robinson & Jones Díaz 2006).

Cross-gendered play

Around 14% of preschool-aged boys like to dress up as girls, with this number declining to 6% by the age of 9 years (Gilbert 2000). This cross-gender play tends to raise parents' concerns about their son's gender identity. However, pretending to be a member of the other sex is quite different from longing to be one (Gilbert 2000). On the other hand, a steadfast preoccupation with effeminate play *might* be an expression of a tendency to homosexuality or transsexuality in adulthood. These children will not experience low self-esteem over their lack of conformity to their gender role unless they are pressured to conform. This pressure conveys to children that they are accepted only conditionally and results in their projection of a false self (Carver et al. 2004, Egan & Perry 2001, May 2005).

Sexual orientation

In the process of gender construction, children are also constructed as heterosexual beings (Robinson 2005). From their earliest years, children absorb messages that heterosexuality is not just a statistical majority, but is the norm, natural, unquestioned and indeed compulsory (Robinson 2005). There is complete silence about alternatives, with gay or lesbian families seldom discussed and rarely represented in children's literature.

Although their sexual orientation will emerge during adolescence, children as young as 5 or 6 years can already have some awareness of their sexual preferences, with their first sexual attraction (whether to the same or the other sex) occurring by the age of 10 (Carver et al. 2004, Maguen et al. 2002, Peterson & Rischar 2000). Again, while not emerging until later, young people with a homosexual or bisexual orientation endure not only double the usual rate of interpersonal bullying, but also mobbing by unknown assailants within community settings (Murdock & Bolch 2005, Rivers 2001). Continuous sociocultural harassment of gay, lesbian and bisexual people and overt and covert negative messages about their sexual orientation contribute to a homophobic social climate that by adolescence leads to declining self-esteem, poorer academic performance and increased behavioural difficulties in young people with a homosexual or bisexual orientation (Henning-Stout et al. 2000, Murdock & Bolch 2005).

Around 10 to 15% of adults will engage in homosexual activity, with perhaps 3% identifying themselves as exclusively homosexual. Even at an early age, this diverse range of sexual orientation needs to be recognised. While not discussing sex itself, you can discuss its visible manifestations in the form of families with two fathers, two mothers, one of each, or one parent (Saifer & Clark 2005). Not only does this honour that children grow up in diverse families and may have adult friends who are gay or lesbian, it also communicates acceptance to their parents. While gay and lesbian parents may not always be visible consumers of early childhood care, this does not mean that they are absent (Robinson 2002).

Further, gay and lesbian adults will be employed in childcare centres and preschools. These adults deserve acceptance within the staff team and by parents. Prejudice against homosexuality leads many to assume that homosexuals are also paedophiles, whereas attraction to adults of the same sex has nothing to do with being attracted to children. Indeed, most child abuse is perpetrated by heterosexuals.

Last, in Australia and elsewhere, the law requires professionals not to discriminate against individuals on the basis of their culture, gender or sexuality (Robinson 2002). Social justice principles require us to promote children's ability to be critical of injustice and discrimination in all its guises, not selectively.

Self-stimulation

As babies are soothed and cared for physically, become increasingly mobile, and acquire toileting control, they are learning about and delighting in their bodies (Klass 1999). Once they are able to remove their own clothes and their arms grow long enough to reach the end of their trunk, they will inevitably discover the extra sensitivity of their genitals. However, it is a mistake to think of touching the genital area as 'masturbation', as children do not experience adult-like sexual pleasure from such explorations (Klass 1999).

Some children will use genital touching to soothe themselves. As this is normal, you can communicate acceptance of it at the same time as teaching children about privacy and the need to reserve some activities for when they are alone. If children are engaging in this form of self-calming excessively, it could be worth exploring whether they are unduly stressed or have sensory integration difficulties (see Ch 15). If they attempt to engage other children in sexualised play, it may be that sexual activity is being imposed on them—that is, they are being sexually abused—in which case, a referral to a child welfare agency is indicated.

Sexualised play

As mentioned in Chapter 4, one of the signs of child sexual abuse is sexualised play. On the other hand, some forms of children's sexual interest are normal and healthy as they explore and learn about how their bodies work (Essa & Murray 1999, Rothbaum et al. 1997). The distinction between unhealthy and healthy sexual play rests on its context and content (Essa & Murray 1999, Rothbaum et al. 1997), with an unhealthy interest being signalled by:

- sexualised play that is part of an overall pattern of behavioural difficulties, especially social difficulties and poor impulse control
- children's anxiety, tension, guilt or shame about their sexual play or, alternatively, lack of emotionality about it
- furtiveness about their sexual play, in contrast with openness or lack of self-consciousness

- disproportional, preoccupied or compulsive interest in sexual play compared with other play interests
- inability to redirect children to other forms of play
- eroticism in sexual play (in contrast with sensuality and curiosity), as eroticism signals an advanced understanding or knowledge about sexual behaviour
- purposeful self-stimulation rather than a mere attempt at self-soothing
- approaches to unfamiliar children rather than friends as sexual play partners
- coercion of or aggression towards partners
- large differences in age or size of selected play partners
- complaints from other children about the child's play
- penetration of any bodily orifice with a foreign object, and
- children's heightened knowledge of sexual matters compared with peers from a similar economic, social and cultural background.

When the play appears natural, nevertheless calmly set limits on it and redirect the children to another activity (Kostelnik et al. 2006). If the behaviour is due to some misinformation about socially acceptable sexual behaviour, correct children's knowledge (Kostelnik et al. 2006). If, however, the children's play is itself abusive or suggests that the instigator might have been subjected to sexual abuse, report your concerns to your child welfare authority and respond as suggested in Chapter 4.

FEARS

Some children report being frightened of a variety of inoffensive objects such as balloons, the sound of a toilet flushing, the sound of the hand drier, or going outside. As these fears restrict their activities and social inclusion, intervention is required.

Listen

First, listen to children about their fears. If there is a good reason for their anxieties, try to remove its source. But even if you do not agree that their fear is warranted, understand that they are fearful. Even if the fear seems ridiculous, do not tell them to 'stop being silly'. Such a message would cause them to worry that they cannot hide their fear and that no one will help them. These two feelings make the original problem worse than it was.

Take the panic out of being afraid

Normalise what they are feeling. You might explain that everyone gets frightened at times. Alternatively, teach children the difference between being frightened of something, versus disliking it, versus being surprised by it. Sometimes we appear to be afraid of a cockroach, say, when we really have been surprised at its unexpected appearance. Being surprised or disliking something is not as scary as being frightened of it.

Have faith that children can overcome their fears

Equipped with information from their parents, tell children stories about other times they have overcome fears and express your confidence that they can do so again. Many children believe that bravery means not being scared, when in fact that is boldness, not courage. Instead, it is brave to attempt to overcome your fears even though you feel vulnerable.

Make children responsible for a solution

Ask children how they plan to overcome their fears. As these are a product of their own imagination, only they can change their thinking. You might explain that their fears are sneaking up on them and that children who are growing up on the inside as well as the outside will find a way to out-sneak them. Once they have decided to become boss of their fears, you could offer to be their 'fears adviser'. You know about magic spells that can expel fears, and they know about their own brain and, therefore, because young children believe in magic, together you could invent a magic spell that will make the fears go away.

CHILDREN WHO HAVE BEEN BEREAVED

Young children grieve at the same losses as do adults: lost contact with a friend (perhaps who has moved up to the next age grouping, on to school, or to another centre); at the death of a relative, friend or pet; moving house or losing the family home to a natural disaster such as fire; having a new sibling; hospitalisation; or the separation of their parents, to name a few (Wakenshaw 2002). The most serious of these losses, naturally, is the death of a parent. This can lead to fear of abandonment by the surviving parent, not least because that parent will be absorbed in his or her own distress and therefore may be less emotionally available to the child (Wolchik et al. 2006).

Loss can be especially confusing to young children because they will not be aware that it is final and irreversible (Willis 2002). They lack experience of loss, of their own emotions and of coping strategies, and therefore are unlikely to understand their own feelings (Willis 2002). Anger and protest can be a natural outcome of both the loss and their confusion about it (Wakenshaw 2002). This will be intensified in the case of the death of a parent or sibling, as the deaths of young people are likely to result from an accident and thus be sudden, providing no time to prepare for the loss.

Expect children to react

Just as a physical injury takes time to heal, emotional pain needs a recovery period too. In the grieving process, as adults we experience an array of emotions over many months, spanning *shock* and numbness, *depression* and loneliness, *panic* about whether we are going crazy, *anger* at ourselves, at the person we have lost, and at anyone who may have contributed to that loss, *guilt* for what we did or did not do that might have contributed to the loss, and, eventually, gradual *hope* because we can now remember the person we have lost without the searing pain that memory used to bring and can begin to conceive once again of being happy, albeit not perfectly secure. Along the way we might get physical symptoms of our distress and can have unsettling emotional outbursts.

Children can experience a similar assortment of emotions. Across the age ranges, they will feel lonely, which is a sadness or longing for intimacy (Galanaki 2005). However, this may be the first time they have experienced this emotion and therefore they may not know what it is.

Babies will have no appreciation of their loss, but are attuned to the feelings of those around them and therefore can show erratic, sad or withdrawn behaviour in reaction to loss. They can also be confused by the disruption to their routines engendered by a family bereavement (Willis 2002). Toddlers can feel confused at the dead person's sudden absence or at their parents' distraction with their own grief, and might wander off. Preschoolers will not realise that death is permanent and so can seem to be callously ignoring their bereavement but then later become bewildered at the continued absence of the person who has died or left the family. Children in the 5- to 8-year age group who once said in anger, 'I wish you were dead', are likely to think that they caused the other person's death and might try to behave especially well to bring the person back to life. Children over 9 years of age will experience the same adult-like reactions as already described, and will be interested in the spiritual aspects of death. Finally, adolescents are likely to want to talk about their loss with their peers, while still needing their parents to be available to them also.

Talk openly with bereaved children

When young children in your care have been bereaved, it is almost inevitable that in the natural course of events they will talk with you about it, or their repetitive play on the theme of death will alert you to their preoccupation with it. In either case, you will need to discover from their parents what they would like you to say to their child. When talking about it, keep in mind that children cannot cope with a lot of facts at once, but instead need to be 'drip fed' small amounts of information often.

Limit your information to the physical facts of a death, as this is not the time to try to impart new spiritual understandings. The children will need concrete facts. For example, many are not aware that dead people no longer feel, think or sense. It can be crucial to explain these facts to them, as otherwise they can become hysterical about the burial or cremation. They will need facts and honest answers to their questions about the circumstances and cause of the death. Otherwise, they will fill in missing details with their imagination, which can be even more frightening than reality. You will need to explain that the person who has died did not choose to leave them, but that the person's body was too sick or injured to keep working. (For suicides, tell children that the deceased person's brain was playing tricks on him or her, convincing the person that other people would be happier if he or she were gone, and the person did not realise how much others would grieve.)

It is not unusual for children to repeat the same question in an effort to receive a different answer (Willis 2002). This may signal that, naturally, they do not like the facts or that they are unclear because we have cloaked our answers in euphemisms (such as that the deceased has 'gone to sleep'), which are frightening or confusing them.

If the children ask where the person goes, it might be best to suggest that they ask their parents (so that this information is in line with their religious views), but you can comment that the spirit of the deceased person, or the love that they felt for that person, lives on in their heart and memories, which will always be there.

Allow the children to play out their feelings

Emotionally supportive caregiving can shield children from extraneous stressors, freeing them to handle their bereavement (Wolchik et al. 2006). Even though you might feel distressed yourself, it will be important to listen to children's feelings and to reassure them that they and their family will get through their sadness. Alongside this reassurance, some therapeutic play activities include (Wakenshaw 2002):

- trace children's body outline on a large sheet of paper and have them choose colours for areas where they feel various emotions
- make up some large dice with pictures of their family members or pets on each face (including the one who has died), and when they roll the dice, invite them to tell you how they feel about that family member

- use play telephones or puppet play to talk with the children about their experience of loss, and
- use the sandpit with figurines and ask the children to create something they have been thinking about, then talk with them about their creation (dollhouses and family pictures can generate similar discussions).

Recommend stability to the family

If changes in the child's care, educational or living arrangements are necessary, advise the parents that, where possible, they delay these so that the child's loss of one family member is not compounded by the additional loss of friends, peer group, caregivers and routines.

Recommend that children be involved in the rituals surrounding death

Advise parents to include their children at the time of a death and funeral service. It is more frightening for children to be separated from their parents than to attend the funeral and, if kept away, they might assume that they are to blame for the person's death and are being punished for it. If the time of the funeral is past, parents could instead involve children in a memorial to the person they have lost, such as by planting and tending a tree in the person's memory. They might keep a memento of the deceased person on them at all times, which they can show you and talk to you about when they are keenly feeling their loss.

CONCLUSION

It is important that antisocial behaviour has begun a downward trend by school entry, as problems thereafter can become entrenched. Early childhood provides an ideal opportunity for supporting a decline in young children's aggression, as at this age children are inherently motivated to socialise with others. The free play setting also provides many natural occasions for supporting their use of social skills and for guiding their behaviour.

SUGGESTED FURTHER READING

Diversity

Dau E (ed.) 2001 *The anti-bias approach in early childhood*, 2nd edn. Addison-Wesley, Sydney.
Derman-Sparks L, The ABC Task Force 1989 *Antibias curriculum: tools for empowering young children*. National Association for the Education of Young Children, Washington, DC.

Prosocial behaviour

Slaby RG, Roedell WC, Arezzo D, Hendrix K 1995 *Early violence prevention: tools for teachers of young children*. National Association for the Education of Young Children, Washington, DC.
Sprung B, Froschl M, Hinitz B 2005 *The anti-bullying and teasing book for preschool classrooms*. Gryphon House, Beltsville, MD.

Sexuality

Hauschild M, Rosier P 1999 *Get used to it: children of gay and lesbian parents*. Canterbury University Press, Christchurch.

May L 2005 *Transgenders and intersexuals: everything you ever wanted to know but couldn't think of the question*. East Street Publications, Adelaide.

Death

Fitzgerald H 1992 *The grieving child: a parent's guide*. Fireside, New York.

McKissock D 1998 *The grief of our children*. ABC, Sydney.

McKissock M, McKissock D 1995 *Coping with grief*, 3rd edn. ABC, Sydney.

Wakenshaw M 2002 *Caring for your grieving child*. New Harbinger, Oakland, CA.

Wells R 1998 *Helping children cope with grief: facing a death in the family*. Sheldon, London.

Westberg GE 1992 *Good grief*, revised edn. Fortress, Melbourne.

15 chapter

Disruptions associated with atypical development

'It is not just, as some assume, that one should fit the intervention to the child, but rather that one should fit the intervention to the goal.'

JORDAN (2004, p. 4)

While children's behavioural difficulties—aggression in particular—detract from learning time, the reverse is also true: learning difficulties give rise to frustration, lowered self-esteem and peer rejection, which escalate children's antisocial behaviour (Arnold 1997, Miles & Stipek 2006, Trzesniewski et al. 2006). Therefore, intervention requires a focus on both.

In contrast, gifted learners have a lower than usual incidence of behavioural difficulties (Cornell et al. 1994, Gallucci 1988), particularly when their atypical educational and socioemotional needs are being met. Because they are able to anticipate outcomes at young ages, they tend to be less impulsive and thus less accident-prone than age mates. Nevertheless, some have heightened activity levels that cause them to seek constant stimulation, which can be demanding on their caregivers. Their high self-expectations can lead to outbursts of frustration at failure, and if the educational program is not challenging for them intellectually, they might flit from one activity to another, never really becoming engrossed in the activities on offer. These can appear to be behavioural issues but, as with children with delayed development, they require an educational, not a behavioural, response.

DELAYED OR IMPAIRED COMMUNICATION SKILLS

As depicted in Figure 15.1, there are three aspects to language (or verbal communication): *receptive language* or *comprehension* refers to how much children can understand; *expressive language* or *speech* refers to the ability to put thoughts into words; and *articulation* refers to how clearly individuals can form speech sounds. Expressive language also entails the less well-known aspects of voice quality and prosody.

When children acquire communication skills more slowly than usual, their skills are said to be *delayed*. Alternatively, when their development occurs out of the usual sequence, it is said to be 'disordered' or *impaired*. Children with impaired communication skills might understand some complex language and thus seem to be developing at age level, yet they confuse seemingly easier concepts. Their resulting failure to follow directives can be misconstrued as a deliberate lack of cooperation.

FIGURE 15.1 The components of communication

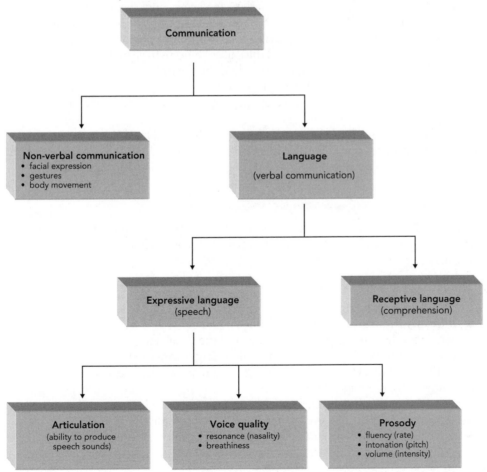

Source: B Burnip 2002a, 2002b, p. 156.

Children can experience delays or impairments in any one or a combination of language, speech or articulation skills, with delays in comprehension (language) being the most significant in three ways. First, the children are less able to understand instructions and therefore can seem to be uncooperative, when in fact they simply have not understood what was being asked of them. Second, those with expressive difficulties can become frustrated at their inability to communicate their own needs and desires. Their impairments will also interfere with establishing and maintaining supportive peer relationships.

Third and, perhaps even more importantly with respect to their behaviour, children who have difficulty with language *do not talk to themselves*. Self-talk or inner speech is needed to regulate their emotions, direct their task performance (e.g. figuring out where to place puzzle pieces) and to guide their own behaviour. Because they are less able to think through and anticipate the outcomes of their actions, their behaviours can seem impulsive and risky. Their impaired self-talk can also lead to some less obvious problems with the likes of toilet training (as the children cannot talk to themselves about the sensations that signal the need to use the toilet), and packing away toys, as this has to be planned logically: 'That's a truck, so it goes in the basket with all the other vehicles.'

Nevertheless, associations between language delays and behaviour problems are modest (Plomin et al. 2002), with only 11% of 4-year-olds and one-third of 8-year-olds with language impairments also displaying behavioural problems (Benasich et al. 1993). Those least likely to develop behavioural difficulties tend to have higher general cognitive ability and have resolved their language problems by the time they start school (Benasich et al. 1993, Snowling et al. 2006). Language problems that persist into the school years are more detrimental than are severe language difficulties that are resolved early (Snowling et al. 2006).

The range of behavioural and other difficulties displayed by children with delayed or impaired communication skills is listed in Box 15.1. These difficulties are often labelled as a behavioural problem, while the underlying language deficit is overlooked.

BOX 15.1 Indicators of speech or language impairments

Many of the following characteristics of children's speech or language are normal at young ages. They indicate delays or impairments only when they persist beyond the usual age.

Speech and language use
- delayed vocabulary acquisition
- difficulty finding words to express ideas
- sentences that are ungrammatical beyond the usual age
- prolonged use of immature word endings (e.g. runned-ed)
- difficulty with articulation at an age when unfamiliar adults typically can understand their age mates
- echolalic speech (i.e. repeating the last word or phrase just spoken by another)
- repetition of questions even when these have been answered
- topic fixation: talking about one topic exclusively, even in the midst of a conversation on an unrelated topic

(continued)

- repetition of the same comment in the same circumstances, and
- communication about immediate ('here and now') events only.

Attention to language

- inattention to or avoidance of language sessions
- watch other children to know what to do during active songs, and
- have difficulty following a short sequence of instructions.

Learning difficulties

- attention difficulties
- reading delays
- impaired overall academic performance at school, and
- delays in acquiring self-help skills such as packing away toys, toileting, dressing or grooming, because of deficient self-talk to guide their performance of these tasks.

Social skills

- elevated levels of solitary play
- use of physical contact rather than words to greet others
- difficulties initiating friendships
- even greater difficulties maintaining friendships
- problematic interactions with other children (e.g. repeated aggression), and
- inability to use language to solve social conflicts.

Emotions

- poor frustration tolerance
- heightened negative emotion, and
- later in life, higher rates of anxiety disorders, particularly social phobias.

Behaviours

- impulsive and risky behaviour, arising perhaps because of an inability to anticipate the consequences of their actions.

Source: Beitchman et al. 2001, Benasich et al. 1993, B Burnip 2002a, 2002b, Caulfield et al. 1989, Dionne et al. 2003, Doctoroff et al. 2006, McCabe 2005, McClelland et al. 2000, Snowling et al. 2006, Trzesniewski et al. 2006.

Stimulate language development

Three settings are particularly potent for assisting children to acquire and practise language: story and song sessions, children's play, and snack and meal times. All necessitate the proximity of teachers and children and all require (as separately advised in earlier chapters) small groups so that adults' conversation does not become managerial, but instead can entail sophisticated communication. In such settings, you can promote the following levels of language:

- *concrete* language that labels and locates events (e.g. 'Where is the crocodile in this picture?')

- *integration of perception* that describes and recalls events (e.g. 'What did we use to make our playdough?')
- *analysing*, summarising, defining, comparing, contrasting and judging events (e.g. 'How do you think Spot felt when he found his mother?'), and
- *reasoning* about perception: making predictions, solving problems and explaining events (e.g. 'Why do you think Spot's mum was worried when she could not find him?') (Massey 2004).

Young children need success with the more basic forms of language before they will be capable of the higher level language skills. Therefore, use levels one and two in conversation approximately 70% of the time and the last two levels for the other 30% (Massey 2004). Massey recommends recording your story-reading sessions and other conversations so that you can play back your conversations and listen for the quality of the language that you use. This will allow you to embellish your conversation, as its quality—rather than the provision of play objects in the environment—most advances children's language skills (Massey 2004).

Simplify instructions

If your instructions exceed children's comprehension levels, they can appear to be uncooperative, when in fact they simply have not understood what you were asking them to do. To help, you can simplify what you say. For example, if you tell children with language difficulties that there will be cake for afternoon tea, they will hear the word 'cake' and think that you are offering it now. Disappointment and confusion will arise when it does not appear immediately. In the same vein, limit your instructions to one or two parts. Rather than saying, 'I want you to go to your bag, get your teddy and lie down', you could say, 'Time to get teddy and lie down'. If you add extra words into your instruction, children sometimes remember only the first thing you said, might go to their bag, forget what they were there to retrieve, wander off and then get chastised for not following instructions.

When children's understanding is uncertain, you can ask them to repeat back what you have said, keeping in mind that those with echolalia can do this and still not appreciate the actual meaning behind the words.

When children cannot translate what you are saying into an action, help them to get started. Guide them to where they need to be and initiate the physical action, such as picking up a block and dropping it in its container to help them to get started with packing away toys. For repeated lack of cooperation, use the strategies mentioned in Chapter 11 for helping children to regain command of their feelings.

Be alert to otitis media (middle-ear infections)

Middle-ear infections are the most common childhood illness, particularly in children's first 2 years of life when their eustachian tubes are horizontal and therefore do not as readily drain fluid from the middle ear (L Burnip 2002a, 2002b). Although signs of pain such as pulling at the ears and effusion from the ears can signal an active illness, half of all middle-ear infections are not detected because the children show no symptoms (Feagans et al. 1994). Infants with chronic otitis media can have impaired hearing for just over half of their first year of life and just under that in their second year (Paradise et al. 1997, Roberts et al. 1998). The fact that sounds appear only half as loud makes it necessary for the children to concentrate to hear, which will tire them.

Even so, this degree and persistence of hearing loss appears not to result in permanent language delays except in unstimulating or low-quality environments. In these settings, because children who do not hear well are less responsive to language, adults and peers tend to converse with them less—and this lack of language stimulation in turn leads to language and cognitive delays (Roberts et al. 1998, Vernon-Feagans & Manlove 2005). Moreover, disorganised settings pose more distractions that will cause children to be less attentive to language (Feagans et al. 1994).

Model correct articulation

Many articulation errors are normal in young children. In the year prior to school entry, many are still not yet accurate with saying the single sounds th, r, l, sh, ch and s, and have difficulty with blends containing r, l and s (such as 'tree', 'play' and 'spoon'). Difficulties will also depend on whether the sounds come in the beginning, middle or end of a word. Multisyllabic words (such as animal, hospital and ambulance) are often still difficult for children up to school age. Most substitutions for these sounds are developmentally normal; others indicate an articulation difficulty.

When young children are learning to talk, do not explicitly correct their articulation errors or force them to say it 'properly'; instead, simply demonstrate the correct sound. For example, when a child has called a cat a 'tat', you can respond positively with, 'Yes, that's a cat'. Detecting the difference, they will ultimately learn how to say the word correctly.

Similarly, when they make grammatical mistakes such as using 'runned' instead of 'ran', you might naturally be able to use the correct form yourself without naming the error: 'Yes. He ran away, didn't he? I saw him too.'

Given that articulation delays can impair others' understanding of children's speech and can signal poor awareness of the sounds of language (which is termed phonological awareness), early intervention is wise to prevent social difficulties and later reading problems. If in doubt, therefore, recommend to parents that they seek a speech pathology assessment.

SOCIAL APPLICATIONS OF LANGUAGE

While all language is social, children's apparent inappropriate use of language in social encounters often raises concerns about how we can respond.

'Baby talk'

Four-year-olds often revert to baby talk as they experiment with their voices. They will also chant, trying out rhyme and rhythms. This is necessary for their language development and therefore should not be discouraged. However, if it becomes intrusive, you could use empathic assertion, as in: 'I know that it's fun to play with your voices and with words. But it will be time to find another game soon, because the noise is bothering those of us playing over here.'

Asking repeated questions

Children learn how to make statements before they learn how to ask questions. But once they have mastered the question format, they realise that asking one gets you to speak to them, even if they already know the answer. This is normal and can be responded to by answering them once or twice and then asking them what they think the answer is.

However, asking repeated questions can also be a sign of impaired communication skills. In this case, children can seem to be using language appropriately—such as asking, 'What you doing?', while you are preparing a snack—but they do not absorb the answer or appear to notice that you have replied. At home, they will ask, 'Where we going?', when in the car, not because they are inquiring about their destination, but simply because they have learned that this is what you say when in a vehicle. If this pattern causes you to suspect delayed or impaired language skills, recommend to parents that they gain a speech pathology assessment.

Use of manners

At a restaurant, when you thank the waiter for delivering your meal, you do not expect the response, 'Good girl for using your manners'. It would be patronising. Likewise, children do not need to be patronised when they thank you for giving them something they have requested. You can respond as would the waiter with, 'You're welcome. It's a pleasure' or 'I hope you enjoy it'. Children will copy this natural use of the social graces, with only a few reminders when they occasionally forget.

Telling lies

There are three types of lies: antisocial lies to deny culpability and get oneself out of trouble, social or 'white' lies to avoid hurting others, and trick lies which are told for fun (Bussey 1999). These trick lies can be annoying to the deceived listener, but they are really just fantasies or wishes. You can handle these 'tall stories' by going along with and extending the fantasy. Alternatively, you can ask gently or playfully whether what children are saying is a wish or hope rather than the truth.

When children tell lies to get themselves out of trouble, they sometimes merely mean to say that they did it, but did not mean it to turn out so badly. In the heat of accusation, this concept can be difficult for them to convey. Therefore, do not demand confessions. Instead, look for solutions to problems rather than culprits. React reasonably, because if you punish children for confessing, they are more likely in future to deny responsibility in order to avoid punishment.

Telling tales

Children will often approach you with a description of what another child is doing wrong. This comes about because young children go through a natural stage of having excessive reverence for rules or because adults have relied on rewards and punishments in their discipline.

You can respond to repeated tale telling in two ways. First, explain the rationale for safety rules so that children can distinguish these from less serious breaches, and approach you only to disclose safety violations.

Second, teach children to ask for help, rather than complaining of a violation. Once children have asked a peer to stop a particular behaviour, but the peer has not desisted, teach them to come asking for help, rather than to report the misdemeanour: 'We need help. Jamie is throwing sand at us. We've asked him to stop and he won't.' This is a clear message that you need to follow up.

Expressing anger at adults

Children will often say that they hate you because, although they actually mean that they are angry, they do not have enough words to describe their feelings accurately. To expand their vocabulary, you can respond with, 'You're angry at me at the moment', or you might even reflect the first feeling such as frustration, disappointment or hurt that caused their anger. Often this listening will be enough to validate their feelings and allow them to calm down. If not, you could ask them what they need to feel better.

Resist the temptation to tell angry children that you still love them, as this might cause them to feel guilty for being angry at you. Likewise, this is not the time to say that you like them but do not like their behaviour, because that is too difficult a concept for young children to grasp in times of stress.

Swearing

There are three forms of swearing: swearing at someone (name calling); using swear words in place of adjectives (as found on building sites); and swearing in frustration. The first is verbal abuse and is a sign that individuals are out of control of their feelings and needs to be dealt with accordingly (see Ch 11). The second and third types might respond to the following measures.

Ignore first occasions

The first time you hear an offensive word, it can pay to ignore it. You might tell the child that you are doing so.

Permit chanting

Almost all 4-year-olds go through a stage of chanting, and will choose swear words or body language (e.g. 'sham-*poo*') so that they can experience what it feels like to be a bit wicked. Because this is normal, you might choose to tolerate it for a while, but to let them know when it stops being amusing.

Pretend to complain

I find it useful to do some mock complaining about children's fascination with wicked words: 'Oh no! Do I have to put up with this for a whole year, do I? Can I run away until it stops?' This accepts that all children play with language and recognises that it does not harm anyone.

Be assertive

If you truly find their language offensive, or if you are concerned that surrounding children might copy it, you could respond in one of the following ways:

- Tell the children that someone has taught them the wrong words to a song they are chanting, and that you will teach them the right ones.
- Assert your rights (e.g. 'I don't like to hear that word'). If the children argue that other people use these words, you can simply state that other people might not mind them, whereas you do, and you have a right to ask them to respect your needs.
- Ask them to desist on the grounds that if surrounding children learn those words and use them at home, they might get into trouble.

Expand their vocabulary

You might ask children if they know what the word means and say that it is better not to use words we do not understand. Alternatively, you could replace the swear word with another, more interesting word: for example, when they tell you about a 'bloody big dog' you can agree that, yes, it is *enor*mous.

Avoid punishment

Punishing children will not stop them swearing. Instead, they will repeat the words under their breath as evidence that other people cannot control them.

SENSORY INTEGRATION DIFFICULTIES

The second most common disability after communication delays and impairments is sensory integration difficulties. Despite their prevalence, sensory integration difficulties are often unrecognised because they span a bewildering assortment of symptoms (as listed in Table 15.1). Children with sensory integration difficulties have problems processing or organising information that they receive through their senses and producing an efficient or meaningful response to that information (Kranowitz 1998). They have problems filtering out irrelevant sensory information and making sense of relevant input.

The affected senses can span a combination of hearing, vision, touch, taste, smell, the vestibular (the balance mechanism in the inner ear), and the proprioceptive senses (which provides information from our joints about the position of our body). Some children take in too much information and overreact to stimuli and therefore become alarmed or too alert (which is akin to the state we get into when we are already late for an appointment and have lost our keys). Other children take in too little information through their senses. Therefore, they underreact to sensory information and seek more stimulation. A third group do either at various times or across the different senses, with their resulting behaviours being very confusing, as sometimes the children need more stimulation and sometimes less, or they might seek more stimulation but then be unable to handle it (Kranowitz 1998).

The behavioural and emotional effects of sensory integration difficulties are often misinterpreted as deliberate disruptions or emotional overreactions. Instead, they are a reasonable response by the children to feeling overwhelmed or stressed. Affected children tend to be:

- excessively irritable
- unable to calm themselves by the usual methods (e.g. thumb sucking)
- inflexible and controlling
- intolerant of changes to routines
- uncomfortable with making transitions between activities
- easily frustrated
- impulsive and prone to accidents
- susceptible to marked variations of mood
- prone to emotional outbursts or tantrums, and
- in need of extensive help to get to sleep.

TABLE 15.1 Signs of sensory integration difficulties

Oversensitive (overreactive)	Undersensitive (underreactive)
Touch	
Avoid touching or being touched by objects or people	Unaware of touch, pain, temperature or how objects feel
Fuss over clothing and footwear	Constantly hurt themselves or others without realising it
Sensitive to slight bumps or knocks	
Pull away from light touch	Touch objects constantly
Avoid getting messy hands	Messy eater and dresser
Are distracted by touch sensations	
Movement (vestibular sense)	
Avoid moving, are fearful, hesitant	Crave fast, spinning, bouncing and jumping movements
Anxious when tipped off balance	
Cautious when climbing stairs with alternating feet (past the usual age)	Constantly move and fidget
Low activity levels	Use too much force with toys or when touching other children
Get nauseated from movement	Hang upside down constantly
Feel vulnerable when their feet leave the ground, fearful of heights	Dart from one activity to another
Dislike active running games	Take foolhardy risks when climbing
Difficulty catching a ball	Rock or bang their head when stressed
Easily fatigued	Move without caution or with poor coordination
Difficulty learning new motor skills (e.g. riding a push toy or tricycle)	Weak muscles (low tone)
Difficulty using tools such as scissors, eating utensils, crayons, pencils	
Walk on toes, to minimise contact with surfaces	
Body position (proprioception)	
Are physically rigid, tense, stiff, uncoordinated	Movement is clumsy, inaccurate
Anxious when tipped off balance	Slump and slouch over tables
	Deliberately bump into objects
	Deliberately fall over
	Jump off unsafe heights
	Difficulty dressing
	Prefer tight bedding and clothing
Visual skills	
Become overly excited when there is a lot to look at	Touch everything to learn about it, as cannot interpret visual cues
Shield eyes from visual input	May misread others' facial expressions and gestures
Avoid eye contact	
Overreact to bright light	Difficulty coordinating eyes for following (tracking) moving objects
Irritable in crowded, visually noisy places (e.g. supermarkets)	Stare intently at objects or people
Look away from tasks	Difficulty naming or matching colours, shapes and sizes
	Difficulty completing puzzles
Auditory (listening) skills	
Cover ears to close out sounds or voices	Ignore voices
Distracted by sounds that go unnoticed by others	Difficulty following verbal instructions
Distressed by noises	Uncertain of the source of sounds
Taste	
Object to certain textures and temperatures of foods	Mouth inedible objects
Smell	
Object to strong odours (e.g. ripe banana)	Ignore unpleasant odours
Notice odours that are imperceptible to others	

Socially, because underreactive children lack understanding of pain, they can have less empathy for others. At play, they tend to wander around aimlessly, without becoming engaged in purposeful activity or they engage in repetitive play for extended periods of time. They often prefer to play with objects rather than people. As a result, these children can be neglected or ignored by peers.

Overreactive children also have difficulty getting along with peers, particularly in crowded conditions, when they become disorganised and therefore may choose to withdraw. This is interpreted as unfriendliness, which leads to social neglect, while their alarm and resulting aggression when touched results in peer rejection.

The behavioural outbursts that result when children are overwhelmed by sensory input are an educational issue, not a behavioural one. The behaviours are not volitional. That is, they are not due to a failure of self-control, any more than children with a significant vision loss can control that they do not see obstacles. For children who are blind, we would remove the obstacles or teach the children where these were. So too for children with sensory integration difficulties, we need to adjust their sensory load (or 'diet') to make it less overwhelming and teach the children strategies for managing their emotional reactions to overload.

Calming activities

Those children who are too alert (who overreact to stimulation) need help to settle their nervous systems. Useful activities include rhythmical linear movement (as with swinging, or jumping forwards and backwards over a line, rope or on a trampoline); giving deep pressure massage; having the children perform heavy work tasks such as sweeping or wheeling a laden wheelbarrow; placing a wheat bag on their laps during quiet activities; or using earplugs or headphones for those who overreact to auditory input (Soden 2002a, 2002b). These activities can both calm children down and give them experience of benign sensations so they no longer interpret these as threatening and therefore can cease overreacting to them.

At times when children are required to sit still and listen, those who are overly alert will be able to achieve this only by repeatedly telling themselves to keep still. However, with this constant stream of self-talk going on, they will be unable to hear their teacher. To overcome this, you can give them a fidget toy. This will allow them to move subtly, thus stimulating an automatic response in their brain to limit their movement. The result is that they are free to listen. (If many children want such a toy, you could give one to each child, or ask the children's suggestions for how to organise turns.)

To prevent these children's nervous system becoming too aroused during group activities, they need to sit on the outer edge of the group or, in line-ups, stand at either end of the group so they are not unexpectedly jostled. (There is no justification for insisting that young children line up anyway, so that practice could be abandoned altogether.) Finally, if the children do become overwhelmed, they need permission to withdraw to a quiet area to calm themselves.

Alerting activities

Those who underreact to sensory input need extra exposure to a range of physical and tactile experiences so they learn to be aware of these and to discriminate various sensations. Alerting activities include sucking thick liquid through a straw, identifying an unseen item in a feely bag, massage, messy play, swinging by their arms, trampolining and swimming (Soden 2002a, 2002b). Those children who are tactile defensive (who overreact to touch) can be helped to participate in finger painting or clay moulding by covering the substances with plastic wrap until the children become desensitised.

Occupational therapy

Sensory integration therapy from a specialist occupational therapist can be useful. Young children gain the most benefit from this therapy, as their nervous systems are still developing and thus are highly responsive to treatment.

Behavioural guidance

Children with sensory integration difficulties are not being deliberately disruptive. They simply *cannot* calm their nervous system by willpower alone. Of the strategies already mentioned throughout this book, the key ones include the following:

- Express your empathy for children's distress and courage at constantly having to deal with a frightening and confusing world of sensations (Kranowitz 1998).
- Provide structure and routines to help children with sensory integration difficulties to organise themselves.
- If your relationship permits and the children appreciate it, give them some physical comfort such as a hug or hand holding when they become overwhelmed.

The children can benefit from activities such as being wrapped firmly in a towel or rug, having them squeeze into a small space, curling up under an A-frame with a blanket draped over it or climbing into a large cardboard box. Relaxation activities can also be useful.

THE AUTISM SPECTRUM

The autism spectrum of disorders is characterised by a triumvirate of impairments that are essentially social:

- impairment of social interaction and reciprocity
- impaired verbal and non-verbal communication (across all the aspects depicted in Figure 15.1), and
- impairment of social imagination, flexible thinking and imaginative play (Cumine et al. 1998, Gillberg 2002, Keane 2004).

Because children with the autism spectrum of disorders fail to reference social events, they do not know how to react to novel items or occurrences, resulting in distress at changes of routines, circumscribed interests that are restricted to the non-social sphere, intense preoccupation with particular activities, and repetitive and stereotyped patterns of behaviour (Jordan 2004, Macintosh & Dissanayake 2004). Their accumulation of knowledge in their interest areas relies on rote memory rather than deep understanding (Gillberg 2002).

Children with autism commonly also have severe language disabilities such that many do not develop expressive speech at all. Around 75% also have an intellectual disability, with 40% recording IQs below 50 (when the average IQ is 100 and intellectual disability is represented by scores below 70) (Howard et al. 2005). Across the spectrum, many also show severe inattention and impulsivity characteristic of attention-deficit hyperactivity disorder (ADHD) (Gillberg 2002). Many also have delayed motor skills, with poor coordination or clumsiness, and delayed self-help or adaptive behaviours (Gillberg 2002, Macintosh & Dissanayake 2004).

Although not yet verified by research (Rogers & Ozonoff 2005), children with the autism spectrum can have acute awareness of sensory information (particularly of sounds), be tactile defensive and sensitive to the taste and texture of foods (Keane 2004). In other words, they have sensory integration difficulties (Siegel 2003). Some overreact to sensory input by becoming distressed or covering their ears against noise, while many underreact and attempt to generate more sensory input (Rogers & Ozonoff 2005). Both overreactivity and underreactivity can manifest as spinning their bodies and twirling items or flapping fingers near their eyes (Siegel 2003). These sensory integration difficulties are not unique to the autism spectrum, but are certainly a common feature (Rogers & Ozonoff 2005).

One Danish nationwide study found an incidence of 8.7 children with autism out of every 10,000 (Lauritsen et al. 2005). The condition has a strong genetic component (Gillberg 2002), with siblings of children with autism being 22 times more likely to have it also (Lauritsen et al. 2005) and 95% of identical twins with autism both having the condition (Siegel 2003).

Children's overall cognitive abilities and language skills at age 3 predict outcomes at age 7. Some children improve in the interim while others show increasing symptoms, leading to greater diversity in the population of children with autism as they age (Charman et al. 2005). The ability of adults with autism to live independently largely depends on their having an IQ above 70, useful speech, low levels of ritualistic behaviours (or, put another way, high levels of adaptive behaviour), and adequate social supports (Howlin et al. 2004, Szatmari et al. 2003). Nevertheless, few are self-supporting, not least because of their lowered occupational status and thus low incomes (Howlin et al. 2004).

Asperger syndrome

There is a continuous spectrum of autistic features, with around 2% of 7- to 9-year-olds displaying some characteristics, although these are not necessarily clinically significant (Posserud et al. 2006). More severely affected are children with Asperger syndrome (with the *g* pronounced as in *get*, not as in *gem*). Some reports suggest prevalence rates ranging from 11 to 45 per 10,000 (Gillberg 2002), up to as many as 60 per 10,000. This amounts to one in 160 children (Jordan 2004, Keane 2004).

In the years prior to school, Asperger syndrome is distinguished from pure autism by children's better language skills and higher intellectual functioning. Children with the syndrome typically acquire language at around the usual age, although their language is pedantic or formal, with disturbed non-verbal behaviours such as eye contact (Cumine et al. 1998). Despite these differences across the spectrum, it now seems clear that Asperger syndrome is a milder form of autism, rather than being a distinctly different condition (Dissanayake 2004, Frith 2004, Macintosh & Dissanayake 2004, Ozonoff et al. 2000). Nevertheless, some argue for retention of its separate label on the grounds that it is more palatable to parents and is useful for practice by signalling a different constellation of needs from pure autism (Leekam et al. 2000).

Asperger syndrome is commonly recognised later than pure autism, both because its symptoms are less severe and because the children's social impairments are not identifiable until they are being expected to engage in more complex social interactions

(Jordan 2004). These children lack empathy. Their obsessive interests alienate their peers and adults alike, resulting in rejection and a four-fold elevation in victimisation from bullying (Attwood 2004). Those with Asperger syndrome may be more interested but no more able to establish and maintain friendships than children with pure autism (Macintosh & Dissanayake 2004). Both groups spend considerable time alone and their friendships are of a poorer quality, as a result of which they describe themselves as 'lonely'—but they do not report feeling sad about their isolation. In other words, they understand loneliness in a cognitive but not affective sense (Bauminger & Kasari 2000).

Many children with Asperger syndrome have high levels of anxiety. Because of this and the fact that their relatively high levels of intellectual functioning mean that they seldom qualify for special education support in schools, they can be more disadvantaged than those with pure autism. Yet their anxiety and rigid or hyperactive behaviour can lead to isolation from peers, while their adaptive functioning can dissipate in novel or stressful situations (Frith 2004).

Treatments

Although identification of the autism spectrum has vastly improved in recent decades, little is known about the most effective interventions (Siegel 2003). Those children with sensory integration difficulties need their educational setting to manage their sensory 'diet' so that they do not become overwhelmed by sensory input. This means providing a balance of alerting, organising and calming activities to match individual children's nervous system needs (Kranowitz 1998).

In addition, the children will need remedial education. This would include special education for their learning difficulties, occupational therapy for self-help training and their sensory integration skills, and speech pathology for their language impairments (as long as their verbal skills fall below their intellectual level, because speech cannot exceed thought).

Those who are more intellectually able can benefit from specific training in social skills to facilitate everyday social interaction (Gillberg 2002).

Once of school age, some children are so anxious that specifically prescribed anti-anxiety medications, anti-depressants or other medications either separately or in combination can relieve some of their more distressing emotions.

Although rewards and punishments are the most common strategy for managing the disruptive behaviours of children on the autism spectrum, I am not convinced that these children respond any better than others to outside controls. Despite the severity of their difficulties, I advocate the guidance methods detailed throughout this book in combination with educational adjustments such as those suggested in Box 15.2.

THE ATTENTION-DEFICIT DISORDERS

There are two basic types of attention-deficit disorders. ADD involves inattentiveness only and ADHD combines inattentiveness *and* hyperactivity. (Strictly speaking, there is a third diagnosis of 'hyperactive only' type, which is reserved for children who are too young yet to be expected to pay attention, but it is seldom applied in practice.) Both terms are replacement labels for a condition that was first identified in 1902 as a lapse in 'volitional control' and which subsequently has variously been called minimal brain

---

BOX 15.2 Teaching adjustments for children with autism spectrum disorders

- *Precise instructions.* Give precise instructions because the children's literal interpretation of language can lead to confusion about what they are being asked to do.
- *Beginning activities.* Their compulsivity, perseveration and perfectionism can mean that they find it difficult to get started on an activity. Use rehearsal to prepare them.
- *Stopping activities.* Again, the children's obsessiveness can make it difficult for them to stop a task. Give them advance warning of an impending change, or circumscribe their compulsive interests to a specific time, location or number of repetitions. Be sure to schedule these activities after others, as that can motivate engagement in a less favoured activity or at least ensure that the children do not become absorbed in their obsession and therefore fail to engage in other activities.
- *Adaptive behaviours.* The children's perseverative qualities can be useful for drilling them in rituals for gaining adults' attention, asking for help, or making social contact with peers.
- *Sensory hyperacuity.* The children can become suddenly and inexplicably disorganised in reaction to sensory information such as the sound of a distant and almost imperceptible siren. Be alert to such possibilities.
- *Fatigue.* The stress of coping in a world that they do not understand can lead to extreme fatigue and, therefore, relaxation exercises and rest periods can be vital.

Source: Cumine et al. 1998.

---

dysfunction, hyperkinesis and hyperactivity (Anastopoulos & Barkley 1992, Campbell et al. 2000). The criteria for diagnosis are listed in Box 15.3.

Nature of the attention-deficit disorders

Despite the longevity of the conditions, some writers (e.g. Jacobs 2005) claim that ADD and ADHD do not exist at all and that the labels are simply a form of oppression in which those with power (namely, parents, teachers and doctors) try to enforce child compliance and, when they cannot, will do so chemically. Jacobs is not alone in arguing that it is not children's non-compliance which is the problem, but society's intolerance of diversity (Conrad 2006).

However, most assert that these conditions are not behavioural, but instead represent a cluster of disabling and distressing learning impairments from which children deserve some relief (Karatekin 2004, Olson et al. 2002). Extensive research is concluding that the learning difficulties underpinning ADD or ADHD are deficits in the brain's executive functions (Glanzman & Blum 2007). These processes control or regulate our thinking and problem solving, deficits in which produce inattention, lack of self-awareness, and poor planning, judgment, organisational skills, reflection and coordination abilities. Children with the conditions are less able to divide their attention between aspects of the task (Karatekin 2004) and take less time to plan ahead before initiating a response (Papadopoulos et al. 2005), perhaps because they cannot retain a long sequence of steps

---

BOX 15.3 Diagnostic criteria for ADD and ADHD

Attention problems

The child must display at least six of the following signs for at least 6 months to a degree that is maladaptive and inconsistent with the child's developmental level:

- failing to give close attention to details or making careless errors
- difficulty sustaining attention
- often appearing not to listen
- not following through with instructions or failing to finish tasks, not due to resistance or lack of understanding
- difficulty with organisation
- avoidance of tasks that require sustained mental effort
- losing things necessary for tasks or activities
- being easily distracted by extraneous stimuli, and
- forgetful in daily activities.

Hyperactivity–impulsivity

A child must demonstrate at least six of the following symptoms:

- fidgeting with hands or feet, or squirming in seat
- being unable to sit during periods of time when remaining seated is expected
- for children—running about or climbing excessively in inappropriate situations; for adolescents or adults—restlessness
- difficulty playing quietly
- on the go constantly
- talks excessively
- blurts out answers to questions
- interrupts others, and
- difficulty waiting.

To be diagnosed, symptoms must:

- have an onset prior to 7 years of age
- continue for at least 6 months and for longer in preschool-aged children
- be present in at least two situations, and
- not be the result of other conditions.

Source: Goldstein 1995, pp. 58–9.

---

in their working memory and thus have to get started prematurely. They know what to do, but cannot do what they know—that is, they do not lack knowledge, but have difficulties performing or enacting what they know (Purvis & Tannock 1997). Their resulting inability to sustain a planful approach to tasks is manifested in impulsive behaviour.

These deficits in executive function lead to problems across many domains. The first is in verbal skills (Clark et al. 2002). In expression, children with ADD and ADHD have problems organising and monitoring their conversation, making it difficult for listeners to follow their train of thought; in comprehension, they have problems organising a sequence of ideas and checking their information recall (Purvis & Tannock 1997). In short, they are both misunderstood by listeners and misunderstand speakers (Clark et al. 2002).

To overcome the disorganisation of their thinking, these children talk out loud to themselves more than usual (Berk & Landau 1993, Berk & Potts 1991, Diaz & Berk 1995, Kopecky et al. 2005). This can lead to constant reminders to be quiet. When their hyperactivity is verbal rather than in motor skills, the children are insatiable. Once they get an idea in their minds, they talk incessantly about it (Green & Chee 2001).

Attention difficulties (but *not* hyperactivity) also lead to reading impairments, because the children miss out on early instruction (Clark et al. 2002, Lonigan et al. 1999, McGee et al. 2002, Rabiner et al. 2000, Spira & Fischel 2005). Subsequently, their reading failure leads to progressive declines in attention skills and academic attainment (McGee et al. 2002, Spira & Fischel 2005). Even when the children do not display learning disabilities as such, their academic achievement is compromised (Glanzman & Blum 2007).

Children with the attention deficits have difficulty regulating their emotions and actions in order to select a socially appropriate behaviour (Clark et al. 2002). They also lack self-awareness, having inflated evaluations of their social performance and thus fail to moderate their actions in response to others' negative feedback (Hoza et al. 2000). These social problems exceed those of children with pure behavioural difficulties alone (Clark et al. 2002). The children's attention deficits produce socially intrusive and disruptive behaviours that generate such significant social problems for them that these really should be included in the criteria for diagnosis (Hoza et al. 2000). Their inappropriate social behaviour leads both to acrimony at home and difficulties with establishing friendships and, even more importantly, with sustaining friendships—except perhaps with other children who are experiencing similar difficulties (Barkley 1988).

This has an emotional cost. Children whose attention deficits give rise to social difficulties suffer associated emotional problems, including low self-efficacy, depression and anxiety (Hinshaw 2006, Hoza et al. 2000, Shelton et al. 1998, Young et al. 2005). While these emotional difficulties may be caused by their problems with emotional self-regulation (Lengua 2003), they are almost certainly also a result of their social difficulties.

In terms of motor activity, unlike normally boisterous activity, ADHD activity levels are excessive, task irrelevant, developmentally inappropriate and pervasive across settings (Anastopoulos & Barkley 1992). In short, children with ADHD fail to regulate their motor activity to suit the context. Their impulsiveness also results in a high rate of accidental injuries.

For unknown reasons, they experience a higher than usual rate of health problems such as incoordination, sleep disturbances, middle-ear and upper respiratory infections, asthma and allergies (Anastopoulos & Barkley 1992). Some of these health outcomes may be related to maternal smoking during pregnancy (Rodriguez & Bohlin 2005, Vuijk et al. 2006).

Finally, ADHD in particular often occurs in association with aggression and oppositional behaviour (Glanzman & Blum 2007). These behavioural problems tend to increase over the early school years (Snyder et al. 2004), but, nevertheless, are considered a by-product rather than a defining feature of the attention deficits. Children with attentional difficulties but without hyperactivity tend not to develop aggression (Loeber & Hay 1997).

Prevalence

Australasian and US research has found that around 2% of preschool-aged children have ADHD (Lavigne et al. 1996, McGee et al. 1991), rising to 3 to 5% during the school years once children's attention difficulties become apparent in the more structured school setting (Spira & Fischel 2005). As with most learning disabilities, more boys than girls are identified, with little variation across socioeconomic groups (Barkley 1988), although children from middle-class families may be rated more poorly by their teachers because of being compared to a more capable peer group (Lonigan et al. 1999).

There is widespread concern that ADHD in particular is overdiagnosed. This does happen, but underdiagnosis is also a concern, especially for girls who, among a mixed-sex group, may stand out less but can be quite disadvantaged compared to their same-sexed peers (Arnold 1996).

Causes

Inattentiveness appears to be due to children's difficulties controlling or restraining their own behaviours, while hyperactive–impulsive and antisocial behaviours could arise from impaired control of emotions which, in turn, seems to be a result of coercive discipline within a stressed environment (Campbell 1995, Martel & Nigg 2006, Spira & Fischel 2005). Attention deficits are thought to result from immaturity in how various parts of the brain function, including the frontal lobes (Glanzman & Blum 2007). The identified areas are responsible for planning and impulse control.

Early signs of children's attention difficulties and impairment in self-regulation appear well before their behavioural difficulties emerge (Olson et al. 2002), which indicates that there is a genuine neurodevelopmental impairment underlying the conditions. However, the exact cause of these impairments is uncertain. Genetics are clearly implicated (Auerbach et al. 2005, Glanzman & Blum 2007, Groot et al. 2004, Hinshaw 2006, Stein et al. 2002), as is mothers' health during pregnancy (Anastopoulos & Barkley 1992, Barkley 1988). Two known risk factors are stress and, to a lesser extent, maternal smoking in the first half of pregnancy, when nicotine alters the fetus's serotonin production and brain cell growth (Monuteaux et al. 2006, Rodriguez & Bohlin 2005, Vuijk et al. 2006).

The constellation of difficulties experienced by children with ADD and ADHD generates family stress (Sheridan et al. 1997). Both parents and teachers are more negative in interacting with these children, but become more positive when the children's behaviour improves, perhaps in response to medication (Whalen et al. 1981, Wodrich 1994). While this suggests that the conditions contribute to adults' negative disciplinary styles, the reverse is also true. Given the high genetic component of the conditions, many parents will themselves have elevated rates of symptoms and, perhaps, shorter fuses when parenting (Whalen et al. 2006). While having little impact on children's *attentional* difficulties, coercive discipline is likely to exacerbate their *behavioural* problems (Hinshaw 2006). Thus, while negative parenting does not cause the conditions, it can perpetuate and exacerbate their behavioural elements.

Outcomes

Approximately 65% of children diagnosed with these conditions in their early childhood years still meet the criteria in adolescence (Glanzman & Blum 2007, p. 351). Their symptoms are likely to remain relatively stable through the school years into adolescence, with children with ADD experiencing ongoing academic (particularly literacy) difficulties and those with ADHD continuing to experience academic plus behavioural problems (Fischer et al. 1990, McGee et al. 1991, 2002, Spira & Fischel 2005). The symptoms do typically improve during the first year or two of school, after which inattentiveness remains stable, while hyperactivity and impulsive behaviours continue a slow decline (Hart et al. 1995). However, while it can appear that the children have outgrown the condition because their overt agitation improves, their inner restlessness often remains into adulthood.

Perhaps only one in four no longer displays ongoing problems into adolescence (Hart et al. 1995, McGee et al. 1991). Nevertheless, most adults make better adjustments to their workplace than they did to school (Barkley 1988). Those with the most favourable adjustment in adulthood have at least average intelligence and language skills, are able to develop and maintain friendships during childhood, are emotionally stable, are not aggressive, and have well-adjusted parents with low levels of family stress (Barkley 1988, Fischer et al. 1993, Goldstein 1995, Greene et al. 1997, Hart et al. 1995, Shaw et al. 2005, Spira & Fischel 2005). The severity of inattentive symptoms appears *not* to make affected children any more prone to behavioural problems in adolescence, unless they were aggressive and oppositional in childhood (Broidy et al. 2003, Nagin & Tremblay 1999) and experience socioeconomic disadvantage (McGee et al. 2002).

Assessment

Most children show their first signs of the conditions between 3 and 4 years of age, when their activity level, impulsivity, intense temperaments and cognitive inflexibility become evident (Glanzman & Blum 2007). Nevertheless, the conditions tend not to be formally identified until school age, in response to the children's emerging social and academic difficulties with sustaining attention, listening, following directives, work accuracy and organisation (Glanzman & Blum 2007). By the school years, ADD is more prevalent than ADHD, but is referred to specialists less often because, while debilitating in terms of learning, it is less disruptive (Hinshaw 2006).

Behavioural observations

Despite the fact that the conditions are intellectual, children's *behaviours* (as listed in Box 15.3) will be the first signal of underlying cognitive impairments. These behaviours are most noticeable when the children are tired, expected to concentrate for long periods and are in a group rather than one-to-one situations, when the activity is boring or repetitive, and when movement is restricted (Anastopoulos & Barkley 1992). Affected children have most trouble when having to plan and monitor their behaviour independently, compared with having an adult supervise them (Clark et al. 2002).

However, the diagnostic criteria are vague, qualified by the word 'often' (e.g. '*often* fidgets'), with no objective criteria to determine how much is 'often' (Jacobs 2005). In the early childhood years in particular, it is difficult to distinguish normal childhood exuberance from ADHD, making accurate diagnosis difficult (Glanzman & Blum 2007). Diagnosis on the basis of observations is also complicated by the fact that the children's behaviour varies according to the circumstances. This requires that symptoms be displayed in two different locations, one of which should not be a clinical setting, as children seldom misbehave in clinicians' offices (Barkley 1988, Hinshaw 2006).

Developmental assessments

Given that ADD and ADHD are intellectual impairments, children's attention, intellectual and language skills must be assessed, with results on formal testing compared to observations by the practitioner (e.g. psychologist or speech pathologist), caregivers or teachers and parents in order to determine whether there is a significant discrepancy between children's measured intellectual abilities and their ability to apply their intelligence in their daily lives (Shelton et al. 1998). Other potential developmental problems must also be excluded (American Psychiatric Association 1994). The precise nature of children's attention deficits will need to be established, as these could encompass problems with *focus*, maintaining attention over time (i.e. concentration or *attention span*), *selective* attention (i.e. ignoring distractions), or *dividing* their attention between tasks in order to manage more than one activity at a time (Sternberg 1999).

Medical assessments

One of the main barriers to children's being diagnosed with ADD and ADHD is that their parents seldom request medical assessments (Sayal et al. 2006). Such assessments will be useful to gain an understanding of any associated health conditions and to exclude other potential health problems that could account for the children's behaviours and developmental skills (Anastopoulos & Barkley 1992).

Treatment

Given the above litany of cognitive deficits and their impacts on children academically and socially, it must be asked how an educational problem comes to be defined as a medical one. Conrad (2006) reports that children are typically referred to doctors for diagnosis of ADHD when their parents and teachers have 'tried everything', but have failed to contain the children's inattentiveness, impulsivity or hyperactive behaviour. However, 'everything' typically means every behaviourist sanction they know of (such as time out, lectures by the principal, case conferences with parents), when instead interventions for an educational problem need to be *educational*.

Educational interventions

Surprisingly little research has been conducted on how best to remediate the learning difficulties of children with ADD and ADHD (Raggi & Chronis 2006). However, the teaching environment, content and processes can all be modified, as follows:

- *Environment.* Children with attention deficits will be more productive in settings that are well organised, with clear procedures and predictable schedules. In classrooms, it can also be useful to seat children with ADHD in the least distracting location in the room (Lewis & Doorlag 2003).
- *Content modifications.* Children will need intensive instruction in problem-solving (Purdie et al. 2002) and self-restraint skills, such as using an inside voice, settling to activities, and taking turns (Merrell & Wolfe 1998, Rogers 2003), as well as remediation of their associated learning difficulties (e.g. language or reading impairments). At the same time, however, the children need ample opportunities to demonstrate their strengths to counteract this focus on their difficulties (Lewis & Doorlag 2003).

■ *Process adjustments.* Teaching and learning processes will need to be modified so that the children's attentional problems do not impede their ability to profit from instruction. They will need to be actively engaged in learning in contrast to passive listening, receive simplified instructions in short bursts, be allocated extra time to complete tasks, and be given assistance to structure activities and manage transitions. Fidget items can help them concentrate while sitting still.

Social and emotional interventions

The subgroup of children who display both ADHD *and* aggression have pervasive social difficulties, suffering impaired relationships with peers and family. Although their number of prosocial interactions is the same as for children without ADHD, their impaired social judgment leads to a ten-fold increase in physical aggression and a three-fold increase in verbal aggression (Goldstein 1995). Their low self-control is also associated with elevated levels of both victimisation and bullying by others and, in turn, peer rejection (Hay et al. 2004, Snyder et al. 2004).

If their aggression does not remit, their peer rejection becomes entrenched over time (Stormshak et al. 1999), while being rejected makes it more likely that they will remain aggressive (Snyder et al. 2004). Therefore, social interventions will need to focus on teaching self-monitoring and emotional self-control (particularly anger management), and adjusting dysfunctional thinking (Hinshaw 2006, Miranda & Presentación 2000). See Chapters 5 and 14 for ways to encourage prosocial skills.

Behavioural guidance

Educational adjustments are intended to make it *easier* for affected children to engage with learning; disciplinary methods must help them be more *willing* to do so by enhancing the children's relationships with adults. Despite the fact that these children's uncontrolled behaviours seem to imply that they *need* someone else to take charge of them, the children actually need to learn how to manage their own behaviour. Their cognitive impairments make this more difficult for them than for others, but they will never learn to manage themselves if adults do this task for them. Moreover, controlling methods with their delivery of rewards and punishments (star charts, time out, and the withdrawal of privileges) are unlikely even to teach these children to do as they are told.

As evidence of this, one study found that an extensive behaviourist treatment produced some improvements in children's functioning in the classroom, but no measurable improvement at home or on any test of academic skills (Barkley et al. 2000). In contrast, parents' use of a guidance approach improves the children's social skilfulness and reduces their antisocial and defiant behaviour (Hinshaw 2006). Therefore, I recommend the guidance methods described in Chapters 9 to 12 for teaching affected children how to regulate their own behaviour.

Dietary management

The research evidence for dietary restrictions is still scant, perhaps because all children were advised to eliminate the same food groups, when instead individuals can be sensitive to particular foods. (The foods most suspect were listed in Chapter 13 in the section on 'fussy eating'.) Food intolerances are more likely in children who have severe attention deficits and associated problems and who have family members with allergic conditions such as eczema, asthma or migraines (Goldstein 1995).

Elimination diets have been recommended, particularly to improve the emotional aspects of ADD and ADHD (Dengate 1997, 2004). However, these turn parents into helicopters, having to hover over their children to monitor what they eat. More successful in my clinical experience is bioresonance, which uses a computer to detect and then treat individuals' food intolerances and viral overloads (see the web address under 'Suggested further reading' at the end of the chapter).

Another potential dietary trigger is high insulin production. This causes affected children's blood sugar levels to drop too low. In response, blood (containing the fuel, sugar) is directed away from non-essential areas of the brain: namely, the pre-frontal lobes (Blum & Mercugliano 1997). The symptoms of ADD/ADHD then surface. This potential cause is particularly relevant for children aged under 10, as their brains use twice as much glucose as adults' (Glaser 2000). Low blood glucose levels are most likely in children who have a family member with diabetes or weight control difficulties, who crave carbohydrates, or whose symptoms appear around 2 hours after the last meal. Blood tests for glucose tolerance and serum insulin levels can flag hyperinsulinaemia as a potential cause.

Treatment can involve a low-carbohydrate diet, or a diet in which every meal contains at least half protein and not more than half carbohydrates. Naturally, medical advice would be essential before parents were to implement any dietary restrictions for their children. Although medical evidence is still accumulating, many practitioners consider that at least some children who have been diagnosed with ADHD can benefit from dietary modifications, and that these children would suffer unnecessarily if we withheld dietary management while awaiting unequivocal evidence.

Support parents

Parents may need your guidance to obtain accurate information about the attention deficits so that they can be effective decision makers and advocates for their child (Glanzman & Blum 2007). Their reduced confidence can also mean that they need emotional support. If they also have an attention deficit or are stressed by their child's demanding behaviours, they may discipline their children in ways that appear to be exacerbating their behavioural difficulties.

Alternatively, some parents report that their child has ADHD-like behaviour at home but you see none of it in your setting. This, however, is not evidence that the parents are incompetent or exaggerating. Children's behaviour does fluctuate across settings. Also, many children behave less well for their parents in the confidence that their parents will love them anyway.

Therefore, resist the temptation to doubt parents. Exchange information with them about what works and does not work for each of you. If they want more information and like to read, suggest some books that might give them some additional disciplinary strategies. Ask their permission to speak directly to their child's medical and developmental specialists, so that you are better equipped to understand their child's condition and treatment regime.

Medication

For children aged over 5 years and those with moderate to severe symptoms, medication still appears to have more benefits than any other form of treatment, although it produces no permanent improvements (Anastopoulos & Barkley 1992, Barkley 1988, Fox & Rieder

1993, Glanzman & Blum 2007, Goldstein 1995, Hinshaw 2006, Purdie et al. 2002). It is clear that some practitioners overprescribe medication, with one study finding that more than half who received medication did not meet the criteria for diagnosis; in contrast, however, other research has found that only 12% of those with the conditions receive medication and, thus, relief from their symptoms (Glanzman & Blum 2007).

While around 70 to 90% of those who are accurately diagnosed respond to medication (Glanzman & Blum 2007), the debate continues about which children benefit most from drug treatment, and at which doses (Levy 1993). Almost 40% experience significant side effects spanning fatigue, confusion, insomnia, appetite suppression (resulting in slowed growth), nausea, headaches, tremors and tics (Goldstein & Goldstein 1995, Levy 1993, Moline & Frankenberger 2001, Purdie et al. 2002), particularly at higher doses (Fox & Rieder 1993). Sustained-release methylphenidate (whose brand name is Concerta) is designed to avoid many of these side effects and, being a once-daily dose, also averts both the detrimental effects of missed doses and the social stigma of having to take medication. However, its therapeutic effects are more variable (Stein et al. 2002).

There is some preliminary evidence that children's inattentiveness responds better to medication than do their hyperactive symptoms (Kopecky et al. 2005), while the secondary problems such as aggression seem even less amenable to drug treatment (Hinshaw 2006). Moreover, while medication may improve some symptoms and young people report that it helps them to get along with their peers and parents, it does not completely ameliorate their restlessness, impatience, talkativeness or inattention, or improve their educational outcomes (Glanzman & Blum 2007, Moline & Frankenberger 2001, Purdie et al. 2002, Whalen et al. 2006). This means that educational interventions remain necessary, with or without accompanying medication.

Despite their effectiveness in particular cases, drugs should never be the first treatment option. On the other hand, the impact of severe ADHD on affected children and their families sometimes justifies the administration of drugs. The decision to use medication, then, will depend on:

- the severity of the condition
- whether other methods have been tried and have failed
- the child's age
- the child's and family's attitude to medication, and
- the ability of parents and caregivers or teachers to supervise a medication regime adequately (Goldstein & Goldstein 1995).

Medication does not have to continue indefinitely. Sometimes, children and their families benefit from giving themselves a few weeks' respite from the symptoms, during which time they can muster their resources to practise other forms of management.

OPPOSITIONAL DEFIANCE DISORDER (ODD)

Oppositional defiance disorder (ODD) is considered to be a mild conduct disorder (Pfiffner et al. 2005). It is mentioned here not because there is any underlying developmental cause of ODD, but simply because many children with ADHD also display oppositional behaviour that comes to be labelled as ODD.

The diagnostic criteria employed in the US and elsewhere include a pattern of negativistic, hostile and defiant behaviour that interferes with children's adaptive functioning for at least 6 months, spanning symptoms such as losing their temper, arguing with adults, defying requests and rules, being easily annoyed, angry and resentful, and acting out of spite or vindictiveness (American Psychiatric Association 1994, p. 102). According to these criteria, 3.9% of children will be diagnosed, whereas the alternative criteria used mainly in the UK allow more children (5.4%) to be classified (Rowe et al. 2005). Nevertheless, one community study identified a staggering 22.5% of 3-year-olds and 15% of 5-year-olds with the condition (Lavigne et al. 1996). Such high rates raise questions about the utility of a diagnostic label that includes so many children, particularly when they subsequently mature to display normal behaviour.

Unlike the attention-deficit disorders, no neurological impairments or learning problems have been found with ODD (van Goozen et al. 2004). The diagnosis is particularly worrying because it locates the problem within the child. Instead, fathers' (and, to a lesser extent mothers') antisocial behaviour or emotional difficulties increase the chances that their children will develop defiant behaviour; while, in the absence of parental pathology, negative or coercive discipline is the primary cause of children's defiance (Belsky et al. 1998, Pfiffner et al. 2005, Shaw et al. 2001).

In other words, ODD is a reactive behavioural difficulty—that is, the rebellious behaviours are a protest (albeit an extreme one) against disciplinary practices that violate the children's need for autonomy. In an effort to repress their antisocial behaviour, adults attempt to exert control over children, who then react with even more extreme resistance and rebellion. In other words, the more adults try to control these children, the worse their behaviour becomes. A guidance approach to discipline is the only way to escape this vicious cycle.

TRANSITION TO SCHOOL

School readiness is not just an attribute of children but, as listed in Box 15.4, comprises the family, educational and social resources that support their success at school (Piotrkowski et al. 2000). If we overlook these social supports and instead continue to define school readiness as a quality of the children only, we will unnecessarily hold some children back from starting school, a strategy that is often applied to boys. However, age of entry affects school adjustment only when combined with specific disadvantaging circumstances such as poverty (DeMeis & Stearns 1992). When considering delaying a child's school entry, parents and educators must query if another year at home or in an early childhood setting would be more productive for the child than attending school (Wesley & Buysse 2003).

Child attributes

Combined with children's learning styles, their intellectual maturity in general and metacognitive skills in particular play a central role in their readiness for and success at school (McWayne et al. 2004), accounting for 25% of their adjustment and success in the early years (La Paro & Pianta 2000). Their learning processes are more important than specific literacy and numeracy skills such as knowing the alphabet and being able to count (Piotrkowski et al. 2000). In my experience, one key learning process is children's ability to alternate or divide their attention—that is, to carry out one task while listening to further instructions as in, 'Once you've finished your drawing, put your book away and come sit on the mat'. In typically developing children, this skill starts to appear at

---

BOX 15.4 Resources supporting children's school readiness

Child attributes

- good physical health, including being well nourished and having the physical stamina to last a school day
- general cognitive skills such as literacy and numeracy
- effective communication skills, both to comprehend instructions and to communicate personal needs
- an enthusiastic and curious learning style, reflected in interest and engagement in the world
- learning-related skills: listening to and following instructions, working independently and persistence, and
- social and emotional competencies: the ability to regulate their own emotion and behaviour; interpersonal skills to participate cooperatively and interact prosocially with peers and teachers; and ability to separate from parents.

Family resources

- responsive parenting
- exposure to literacy-based activities (e.g. shared reading), and
- support for attention skills.

Educational resources

- affordable, high-quality childcare and preschool programs
- public libraries
- school transition programs
- warm relationships with teachers, and
- explicit instruction.

Neighbourhood resources

- safe playgrounds and streets, and
- social support for parents.

Source: McClelland & Morrison 2003, McClelland et al. 2000, McWayne et al. 2004, NICHD Early Child Care Research Network 2003a, 2003d, Piotrkowski et al. 2000, Wesley & Buysse 2003.

4½ to 5 years of age and, being the last attention skill to be achieved, signals that the children have also mastered the earlier abilities to control their arousal, focus, concentration and distractability.

Success at making the transition to school also depends on children's social and behavioural competencies (NICHD Early Child Care Research Network 2003d) as listed in Box 15.4. These account for around 10% of children's progress in the early school years (La Paro & Pianta 2000, McClelland & Morrison 2003, McClelland et al. 2000, Miles & Stipek 2006).

Third, children's ability to regulate their emotions within the context of group activities directly affects their success and productivity at school (Graziano et al. 2007). This skill may be particularly crucial for navigating school entry because the new learning environment and challenging academic tasks can arouse children's anxiety and frustration, which they must manage. In turn, teachers view well-regulated children more positively, which contributes to an improved teacher–child relationship that supports children's subsequent educational engagement and attainment (Graziano et al. 2007, Ladd et al. 1999).

Family resources

The resources that families can provide in the form of activities and responsive parenting help children to regulate both their emotions and learning processes. Parents can teach arousal regulation by soothing children when they are distressed, practise maintaining joint attention during conversation and play, redirect children's focus, and provide direct but responsive teaching that helps children sustain their attention (NICHD Early Child Care Research Network 2003a, 2005b).

The children who are least well equipped to adjust to school are those with stressful lives with insufficient resources to support their learning (Rimm-Kaufman et al. 2000, Schulting et al. 2005). In the face of family, neighbourhood and social stressors, these are the children and families who most need support from their schools and for whom transition practices are most effective at enhancing both student engagement and parent involvement (Schulting et al. 2005). Yet these children are the least likely to be given support for the transition, thus entrenching their early social disadvantage (Schulting et al. 2005).

For children with disabilities and their families, the transition to school can be a particular challenge. Parents might revisit their earlier grief at their child's disability and a renewed despair at the fact that the next placement will not meet the child's needs perfectly (Bentley-Williams & Butterfield 1996, Fowler et al. 1991). Because of their extra vulnerability, they might have developed more than the usual reliance on early childhood practitioners and are reluctant to lose your support. To assist them to move on to the next service, you can plan with them well in advance and gradually introduce both them and their child to the new setting. On the other hand, this phase should not be so drawn out that the child seems for prolonged periods not to belong either in the former or the new setting.

Educational resources

According to an extensive survey in the US, teachers reported that only half of school entrants navigate a successful entry to school, with over 30% experiencing some problems and 16% having serious difficulties making the transition (Rimm-Kaufman et al. 2000). The fact that *half* of all school entrants are experiencing difficulties raises the question of whether our expectations of children in schools are appropriate. Many early primary teachers report that the system requires of young children skills that are unattainable at that age (Wesley & Buysse 2003). This not only stresses them at school, but places downward pressure on early childhood education to enforce content and learning processes that are inappropriate at young ages.

The quality of instruction and level of emotional support provided to children are powerful predictors of children's adaptation to the school context. Even when individual children seem developmentally unready for school, their skilfulness improves in response to high-quality instruction and social support from their teachers (Hamre & Pianta 2005). Thus, perhaps the question should be not whether individual children are ready for school, but whether schools are appropriately providing for the needs of the young children they serve (La Paro & Pianta 2000).

Early childhood practitioners can be instrumental in easing children's transition to school by arranging school visits during the final weeks of preschool so that children and their parents can meet their new teacher and receive information from the school about its expectations.

CONCLUSION

When children have known disabilities such as a vision impairment, we would not instruct them to overcome their difficulties by demanding: 'Use your eyes!' Instead, we would adjust the environment to make it easier for them to function adaptively. Similarly, even when children have less explicable difficulties such as behavioural problems, rather than requiring *them* to change how they behave, we need to make adjustments so that it is easier for them to meet expectations.

When children's development is atypical, it is crucial to obtain an early assessment. Subsequent early intervention can prevent one problem from affecting other areas of their life, such as when their inability to speak or understand language causes social difficulties, or their atypical movement pattern leads to limb deformities. It is no kindness to parents to avoid raising your concerns with them, and it fails children by denying them timely assistance.

SUGGESTED FURTHER READING

ADHD

Green C, Chee K 2001 *Understanding ADHD: attention-deficit hyperactivity disorder in children*, 3rd edn. Doubleday, Sydney.
Bioresonance website: www.biocom-bioresonanz.de

Autism spectrum

Cumine V, Leach J, Stevenson G 1998 *Asperger syndrome: a practical guide for teachers*. David Fulton, London.
Gillberg C 2002 *A guide to Asperger syndrome*. Cambridge University Press, Cambridge, UK.

Disabilities

Allen KE, Cowdery GE 2005 *The exceptional child: inclusion in early childhood education*, 5th edn. Delmar, Albany, NY.
Kranowitz CS 1998 *The out-of-sync child: recognizing and coping with sensory integration dysfunction*. Perigee, New York.
Porter L (ed.) 2002 *Educating young children with additional needs*. Allen & Unwin, Sydney. Also published as *Educating young children with special needs*. Paul Chapman, London; Sage, Thousand Oaks, CA.
Sandall SR, Schwartz IS 2002 *Building blocks for teaching preschoolers with special needs*. Paul H Brookes, Baltimore, MD.

Giftedness

Harrison C 2003 *Giftedness in early childhood*, 3rd edn. Gerric, Sydney.
Porter L 2005 *Gifted young children: a guide for teachers and parents*, 2nd edn. Allen & Unwin, Sydney; Open University Press, Buckingham, UK.

part V

Supporting adults

'Positive and healthy organizational climates are characterized by high energy, openness, trust, a collective sense of efficacy, and a shared vision.'

JORDE-BLOOM (1988, p. 5)

The adults in childcare or preschool centres are like the hub of a wheel. You form the core, with your relationships with children, parents, the wider community, and your governing bodies being the spokes. Each spoke strengthens the wheel. But it is the core that shapes all the other aspects of the setting—its atmosphere, warmth of relationships, and the quality of the program.

The care and education of young children is a mutual concern of both their parents and early childhood practitioners. In order to feel empowered to fulfil their respective roles, both partners to this relationship will need support and resources. Therefore, in this section, I examine some of the issues that affect your ability to experience satisfaction in your work and to discharge your responsibilities in the best way you know how. Your role in caring for and educating young children is a demanding and complex one and, whenever demands are high, supports necessarily must be high also. Among other things, this involves recruiting the support of parents, which is more likely when you can appreciate their perspective and harness their expertise in caring for their children. The final chapter on writing a discipline policy is aimed at formalising some of these supports through a process of collaboration with colleagues and parents to define practices that will be effective, ethical and widely endorsed by all.

chapter 16

Nurturing staff

'The teachers of our children deserve the same quality of treatment that we expect them to offer our children.'

HILLIARD (1985, p. 22)

Children—particularly the very young—are highly sensitive to the morale of the people around them (Smith 1990). Therefore, providing staff with conducive working conditions helps not only them, but also directly affects the children in their care (Doherty-Derkowski 1995, Smith 1990). A supportive work environment enables adults to be more affectionate, less distant and less controlling with the children (Lambert 1994, Lewis 1997, Mill & Romano-White 1999). The particular features that promote staff satisfaction are given in Box 16.1.

MANAGEABLE DEMANDS

When they are feeling exploited, frustrated or angry, staff are less likely to think clearly, decide wisely or act strategically to solve problems (Strain & Joseph 2004). Therefore, the first means to promote high-quality care of children is to provide support to their teachers and caregivers.

Adult–child ratios

Staffing levels (adult–child ratios) are considered crucial in determining the quality of care which children receive, especially for infants and toddlers (Butterworth 1991, Gotts 1988, Katz 1992, 1995, Phillips & Howes 1987, Scarr et al. 1994, Wangmann 1992). However, the link is not as straightforward as might be imagined. In many human services, the most competent staff are typically allocated the most children and more complex difficulties (Mill & Romano-White 1999). The special skills of the most able

---

BOX 16.1 Features that foster staff satisfaction

Manageable demands
- role clarity
- reasonable workload and physical demands
- avoidance of stimulus overload (e.g. by providing breaks)
- provision of planning (non-contact) time, and
- balancing multiple roles.

Workers' personal resources
- high self-efficacy
- avoidance of perfectionism, overstriving or overcommitment
- recognition of one's own skills
- high levels of training, and
- reflection on practice.

Workplace support
- efficient administration and management so that staff can perform their duties unencumbered by bureaucratic duties
- effective leadership
- good working conditions: reasonable pay, adequate staffing levels, opportunities for advancement, job security
- supervision and mentoring
- trusting relationships with colleagues, parents and children
- a sense of professionalism and respect conveyed to workers
- worker control (decision latitude) over their work
- clear policies and procedures (e.g. for responding to behavioural disruptions)
- flexibility to enable staff to attend to personal or family responsibilities, and
- opportunities for professional development.

Source: Curbow et al. 2000, Noble & Macfarlane 2005.

---

staff mean that their larger groups do not necessarily experience declining quality. While this is a testament to their skills and many will thrive on the challenge, it is nevertheless important to avoid overloading capable workers lest they become overwhelmed.

Avoid overload

The sheer complexity of working with groups of children is an everyday challenge. The work is *multidimensional*, which is to say that many different people with different interests and abilities are sharing the same space; many things are happening *simultaneously*; and events can unfold rapidly and unpredictably, demanding *immediate* responses (Doyle 1986). Meanwhile, all your responses are *public*, being witnessed by other children, colleagues and any visitors to the centre. This has two effects: first, that one child's disruptive behaviour can become contagious (i.e. other children might join in) and, second, that any action that you take tells onlookers (both adults and children) about your skills and about how safe they are in this setting. Given that these demands are inevitable, some practical measures to avoid staff overload include the following:

- Minimise unnecessary tasks or streamline those that are essential.
- Ensure that staff members' breaks are provided in a pleasant area and give them long enough breaks to marshal their energies.
- Provide ample planning and preparation time.

Manage staff turnover

One sign of unconducive working conditions is high staff turnover. This is always higher in low-wage industries, of which centre-based care is a clear example, with figures for the US attesting that around 30% of staff leave their jobs per year, which is four times the turnover in primary (elementary) schools (Whitebook & Sakai 2003). This has numerous detrimental effects, including:

- It disrupts relationships between staff and children.
- The departure of a colleague unsettles surrounding staff members, increasing the likelihood that they too will resign.
- As a less experienced and less qualified replacement is likely to be hired, this reduces the experience of the staff team, and of the sector overall when departing staff leave the field altogether.
- Workloads increase as the centre is short-staffed while a replacement worker is being found and when an inexperienced worker is being inducted (Whitebook & Sakai 2003).

Staff turnover is less in centres where wages are higher, when the director remains stable and when caregivers/teachers receive support in their role (Whitebook & Sakai 2003). Even so, given the disparity of working conditions between the childcare and education sectors, highly qualified staff are still likely to depart childcare to work in preschools or schools. Therefore, centre directors will need to manage the process of staff turnover to minimise its disruptiveness for the children and remaining staff (Whitebook & Sakai 2003).

ENRICH ADULTS' PERSONAL RESOURCES

In care and teaching professions, stressed adults become more concerned with ensuring their own survival than with meeting children's needs (Lewis 1997). As well, exhausted staff tend to blame their job dissatisfaction on the behaviour of individual children, from which stance it is only a small step to diagnosing what is 'wrong' with them, rather than looking at the environment to determine what might be provoking disruptions (Lambert 1994).

Promote adults' self-efficacy

Professional self-efficacy is the extent to which you feel able to influence your work circumstances and the children in your care (Friedman 2003). Adults with low professional efficacy are more likely to become overwhelmed by their work, stressed by disruptions (Martin et al. 1999), and more concerned with promoting order than with meeting the children's needs. In contrast, those with high self-efficacy not only become less stressed but, when faced with challenges, take action to resolve the problems rather than avoiding them or venting emotion inappropriately (Friedman 2003). Confident of their ability to generate solutions rather than feeling helpless, adults with high self-efficacy exhibit high levels of planning and organisation, are open to new ideas and willing to experiment with new approaches, implement a varied program, modify tasks to attract children's engagement and create a supportive climate to maintain their involvement (Caprara et al. 2006, Tollefson 2000).

Encourage positive attributions about children's behaviours

Your attributions (i.e. explanations of events) influence how you will respond to disruptive behaviour. First, when you blame children's disruptive behaviour on causes beyond their control (such as a disability or family adversity), you are likely to be sympathetic, warm and supportive, expecting less of the children given their circumstances. However, while positively motivated, this further entrenches the children's own views of themselves as incapable. When you subsequently expend little effort to ensure that the children are successful, they will not engage or progress, which would only confirm your low expectations of them (Tollefson 2000).

On the other hand, when you regard children as being deliberately disruptive, you are likely to become angry and, in turn, less willing to help, provide more negative feedback and administer more punitive discipline (Martin et al. 1999, Scott-Little & Holloway 1992, Stormont 2002, Tollefson 2000, Weiner 2000). The result is a downward spiral of adult coercion and child resistance, with their deteriorating relationship giving adults declining influence over the children's behaviour.

While neither excusing nor blaming children is ideal, neither can you blame ongoing behavioural difficulties on yourself, because self-criticism paralyses rather than energises. The conclusion, therefore, is that you need to focus on *strategies* rather than on finding a culprit. According to this way of thinking, the persistence of problems merely indicates the need to change strategy, rather than signalling a personal failure of the children, their parents, or yourself.

Activate problem solving

Whereas the quality of the setting affects the level of warmth caregivers show children, workers' anger largely results from their own negative thinking about their circumstances (Mill & Romano-White 1999). Although we would prefer not to experience anger, it signals that our present methods are not working and therefore need to be changed. This will call for problem solving, which entails reflection about the shortcomings of present methods and generation of alternative strategies. To guide this process, those involved can ask:

- What do I want to achieve here?
- Is what I am doing helping me to achieve that?
- If not, what else could I do?

The next step is to act in new ways and then evaluate the success of the new strategies. This process does not have to occur in isolation, but can benefit from collaboration with colleagues. Any group problem solving needs to be led in such a way that ideas are freely expressed and explored so that all members endorse the group's ultimate decision (Rodd 2006).

WORKPLACE SUPPORT

In addition to adult–child ratios and group sizes, caregiver training and wages are considered to influence the quality of care that children receive. This is due in part to the fact that access to professional development and high wages typically occurs within a conducive wider environment characterised by effective leadership, collegial support and access to outside specialists.

Staff training and development

Caregivers with more extensive training and child-focused beliefs tend to be less restrictive or controlling with children and provide more stimulating activities and a better organised environment (Abbott-Shim et al. 2000, Arnett 1989, Burchinal et al. 2000, 2002, Clarke-Stewart et al. 2002, Howes 1983a, 1997, Howes et al. 2003, Phillipsen et al. 1997). Training can be gained both in formal education or professional development. Successful staff development will renew workers' enthusiasm for their work, improve their confidence in their abilities, and allow them to continue to grow professionally (Greenman & Stonehouse 2007). Its most important outcome is to enfranchise practitioners to reflect on their practices, questioning their underlying values, beliefs and assumptions, which otherwise might be taken for granted (Roth 1989, Smyth 1989).

A naturalistic form of staff development is supervision. Rather than fulfilling an authoritarian function of control and surveillance, supervision instead aims to support both the personal and professional development of workers through reflective discussion, feedback and the provision of information and advice (Rodd 2006). New workers are particularly likely to feel overwhelmed by the responsibility of caring for young children, uncertain of how their ideas will be accepted by more experienced staff, and anxious about responding to children's inconsiderate or disruptive behaviour (Brand 1990, Fleet & Clyde 1993, Noble & Macfarlane 2005). Therefore, novices are likely to need supervisory support to be concrete, whereas those with more experience will benefit from a reciprocal exchange of observations and insights with other experienced staff, both within and outside their setting.

Other forms of staff development include amassing a library of books and other resources for caregivers to access, arranging staff exchanges with other centres, and giving staff access to seminars or conferences (Abbott-Shim 1990). Hired consultants are the most expensive option, but when their input can be especially tailored to your centre's needs, the training can be most effective.

Wages

Staff wages account for around 70% of a centre's operational expenses and therefore it is tempting to reduce costs by keeping wages low (Roseman 1999). However, wages are the most significant influence on the quality of care that children receive (Phillips et al. 2000, Phillipsen et al. 1997). Higher pay attracts better qualified teachers, reduces staff turnover and thus contributes to the stability of the staff team and continuity of care for the children (Whitebook & Sakai 2003). It is probably also a proxy for other positive aspects of the setting, such as respect for staff members' professionalism, which also contribute to staff satisfaction and morale (Phillips et al. 2000).

Effective leadership

Effective leadership sets the tone for the workplace, contributing significantly to the establishment and maintenance of a coherent and committed staff team. Leadership is a purposeful activity intended to influence others to contribute to an agreed outcome (Rodd 2006). To that end, leaders need to be able to:

- enthuse staff to share a common vision of their purpose by enunciating an inspirational but achievable vision with clear goals and objectives
- develop open communication that listens to team members' ideas for innovations
- establish a respectful team culture
- trust staff members' decision making and creativity so that their professional autonomy can blossom into taking increased ownership of their work, and
- respond to children's and parents' changing needs (Billman 1995, Broinowski & Dau 2004, Nupponen 2006, Rodd 2006).

Leadership involves a vision for the future. As such, it is more than routine administration and management, which is concerned with maintenance and continuity in the present (Ebbeck & Waniganayake 2003, Rodd 2006). While both these functions are important, they do not constitute leadership as such. Efficient administration ensures that bureaucratic functions do not impair the work of those caring for the children by administering the centre's finances, maintaining appropriate records and ensuring compliance with regulations. These tasks provide the framework within which all other functions can be performed. Efficient managers plan, analyse needs and problems, organise, and evaluate the smooth functioning of the service. In contrast, the best leaders are proactive rather than reactive (Nupponen 2006). Their focus is the long-term enhancement of the centre's functioning by giving direction, inspiring new approaches, building teamwork, setting an example and motivating and managing change (Rodd 2006).

The most effective leaders are democratic motivators, who balance the need for task attainment with a concern for the individuals who make that happen (Nupponen 2006, Rodd 2006). Just as is the case with children, democratic leaders of adults do not dominate or exercise power over others, but instead act *with* them, gaining their authority from their expertise. Their competence earns team members' respect and loyalty and increases the team members' willingness to follow their leader's direction.

Collegial support

Collegiality is the extent to which staff support and trust each other and are friendly and caring towards each other (Jorde-Bloom 1988). In achieving this level of support, teams commonly progress through the following series of stages (Rodd 2006, pp. 155–60):

- *Task orientation.* In this phase, team members' main goal is to achieve what needs to be done.
- *Conflict.* This is when allegiances formed in the early phases to meet members' belonging needs now generate cliques of opinion about the administration, management and leadership of the setting. If this conflict is not resolved, high dissatisfaction and staff turnover can result.
- *Cooperation.* Under effective leadership the group starts to achieve cohesion and reach consensus and is willing to experiment with new practices now that all members are comfortable with their competence at basic tasks.

- *Collaboration*. This is when each member of staff contributes to the overall functioning of the setting. With emotional, practical and professional support from colleagues and a willingness to grow and learn, workers have moved from 'survival mode' to a consolidation or mastery stage in which they develop confidence and autonomy as professionals (Brand 1990, Clyde 1988, Fleet & Clyde 1993).

One occasion when staff will need planned support is when they are confronting a particularly chronic or challenging behavioural difficulty. In these instances, team discussions will need to plan how to supply both practical and moral support. Practical assistance during severe disruptions can entail having another member of staff step in for one who has become overwhelmed, perhaps releasing that adult for an unscheduled break or, as a last resort, moving the child to a different group for a short period. In the immediate aftermath of a disciplinary disturbance, colleagues can help the caregiver or teacher who dealt with it to *release* the emotion, *reflect* on what happened and why, and *rebuild* by planning how to deal with such incidents in future (Gamman 2003).

Subsequent staff meetings can consider longer term solutions. As mentioned in Chapter 12, this will require that the adults focus on what is working, rather than what is not. The fact that children's disruptions do not occur 100% of the time signals that someone is doing something to prevent occurrences or reduce the severity of incidents. Thus, the task will be to identify and expand on these solutions that are already partially in place, not to generate entirely new responses. Subsequently, although key staff members may be given the main task of enacting these solutions, all will nevertheless need to be familiar with the planned strategies, as they may need to intervene if they happen to be on the scene during an incident. To increase the likelihood of success, the team might have to organise enhanced adult–child ratios and adjusted staffing schedules until the child's behaviour settles and the extra demands on staff have abated.

Accounting for only 1 to 4% of the workforce and declining (Farquhar 1999), male staff members feel more isolated, experience higher expectations, and are regarded with greater suspicion than their female counterparts (Cooney & Bittner 2001, Sumsion 2005). Although there is no evidence that the employment of male caregivers challenges children's sex-role stereotypes, provides less sexist role models, offers greater responsiveness to boys' needs (Lyons et al. 2005, MacNaughton & Newman 2001, Sumsion 2005) or encourages increased involvement of fathers, men are as capable of nurturing young children as are females and have a right to enter a field where they can gain personal satisfaction. Therefore, particularly in a market with labour shortages, men are a welcome resource for the early childhood sector. In addition to providing them with the same supports as offered to all staff, to facilitate the retention of sole male employees, female staff will need to respect men's involvement, neither exalting them nor minimising the discrimination they experience (Farquhar 1999). Directors may also be able to support them to form a network with males in other venues.

ACCESS TO OUTSIDE EXPERTISE

When children's behaviours are not responding to present methods, outside experts need to be consulted. The first of these experts will be parents. Children's behaviour is likely to be similar across settings, which means that parents will have seen and dealt with comparable behaviour at home and can advise you about what works for them.

A second source of ideas is, with parental permission, to consult specialists already involved with individual children, or to instigate new referrals. To that end, it can be useful to be aware of the paediatric specialists in a range of fields, how parents can contact these, and the costs and waiting periods involved. Your parent group can be a useful fund of knowledge here. By asking them which practitioners they have used and can recommend, you can build up a list of practitioners in various fields (paediatricians, podiatrists, physiotherapists, chiropractors, psychologists, paediatric dentists, speech pathologists, naturopaths, and so on) whom you could recommend to parents when a need arises.

CONCLUSION

Teachers' child-focused beliefs can dissipate in the face of contextual constraints that limit the support available to them, with the result that they become less effective, less satisfied with their work and, in turn, more likely to leave their job or the field altogether (Noble & Macfarlane 2005). In short, they can be obliged to act in ways that violate their principles (Vartuli 1999). *This*—not the number of hours you put in—*is hard work*.

In contrast, caregivers who receive wages that fulfil their basic needs and whose social, educational and spiritual needs are met through their work are likely to be happy, stable employees who offer children a high quality of care (Roseman 1999). When staff are treated with respect and valued for their contributions, they are likely to treat children similarly, relate to them with interest and warmth, guide rather than control them, respond to them individually rather than as a group, and encourage them to be active in their learning.

SUGGESTED FURTHER READING

Broinowski I, Dau E 2004 *Managing children's services*. Tertiary Press, Melbourne.
Ebbeck M, Waniganayake M 2003 *Early childhood professionals: leading today and tomorrow*. MacLennan & Petty, Sydney.
Rodd J 2006 *Leadership in early childhood*, 3rd edn. Allen & Unwin, Sydney.

chapter 17

Collaborating with parents

'When a teacher talks to parents about their children, he [or she] inevitably intrudes on family dreams … What the teacher says about the child touches on deep feelings and hidden fantasies. A concerned teacher is aware of the impact of his [or her] words. He [or she] consciously avoids comments that may casually kill dreams.'

GINOTT (1972, pp. 277–8)

Although few early childhood professionals receive any specific training for collaborating with parents, those with the expertise to provide high-quality programs tend to be more open to collaboration, in all likelihood because they feel more confident about having others scrutinise their work (Abbott-Shim et al. 2000, Castro et al. 2004, Ghazvini & Readdick 1994). In high-quality care settings, staff and parents communicate frequently about children, which advances the children's development and furthers their emotional wellbeing. By harnessing parents' intimate knowledge of their child, you gain information that helps you to provide a better service to their child and family and are more likely to feel assured of parents' support for your efforts. The result of their enhanced knowledge of individual children and the climate of trust between parents and caregiver-teachers is that both are more sensitive and responsive towards children, both at home and in the care setting (Owen et al. 2000).

TRENDS IN RELATIONSHIPS WITH PARENTS

Parents have imperfect information on which to base their selection of care arrangements for their child, while many face practical constraints such as inflexible working schedules, low income or limited availability of care. Therefore, many have to choose care arrangements based on convenience and cost rather than their values (Cryer & Burchinal 1997, Cryer et al. 2002, Early & Burchinal 2001, Peyton et al. 2001). This makes parents vulnerable. Even when confident that they can select a high-quality placement, they are painfully aware that they cannot anticipate problems that might arise after they have enrolled their child (Larner & Phillips 1994). Staff changes, the unfolding needs of a growing child, and other unforeseen changes can neither be anticipated nor guarded against. Added to this, first-time parents in particular may doubt their own skills and instead defer to professionals' judgment about their children's needs. Furthermore, when children have behavioural or other difficulties, the stigma of having a troublesome child detracts from parents' power to advocate for their child and isolates them from the wider parent body (Fylling & Sandvin 1999).

Consequently, partnerships between parents and professionals are based on concealed power differences, with professionals having higher power and status. Particularly when families are socially disadvantaged, this can be translated into regarding parents as the *source of children's problems* (Fylling & Sandvin 1999). Sometimes this view is softened into a perception of them as *clients*, or *joint victims* of their circumstances. This, however, tends to define them as somewhat fragile and in need of 'empowerment', when in reality you cannot give people skills that they are incapable of performing, and therefore all they need is enfranchisement to use the skills they already have (Murphy 2006).

Another view sees parents as *passive recipients* of advice. Within this framework, professionals are considered to have expertise that exceeds parents' (rather than expertise that differs from or complements parents') and parents are expected not to question professionals' judgment.

A more active role for parents has often been termed 'involvement' and entails supporting their child's program by volunteering at the centre, fundraising, participating in parent–teacher conversations and meetings, and contributing to the management of the centre. This *associative* relationship between parents and educators is more reciprocal than a one-way flow of information, although parents' roles still tend to be defined mainly by educators, with minimal input or decision making by the parents themselves (Fylling & Sandvin 1999).

It is clear that a partnership with parents encompasses more than active parental involvement. True *collaboration* is a process of direct and voluntary interaction between parties of equal status engaged in shared decision making towards a common goal (Friend & Cook 2007). It entails both equal status and parity, which refers to a valuing and blending of each partner's ideas and expertise (Christenson 2004). This does not require parents' participation on a day-to-day basis, but instead is a philosophical stance of openness to parents that implies a shared responsibility for the care and education of their children.

However, even this form of collaboration can be tinged with the sense that professionals are 'giving' parents equality, rather than that equality is their entitlement (Roffey 2002). Thus, the ideas underpinning this chapter proceed one step beyond reciprocity by recognising that parents are the experts in their children's and family's needs and have experience at resolving their issues. They employ you for your expertise as an educator, much as they might employ a doctor for advice on medical matters. They pay your salary. Therefore, children's experiences are to be steered by their parents, rather than directed by teachers.

Although this stance may feel as though your authority is threatened, from an egalitarian point of view, your authority does not derive from your power but from your expertise.

IMPEDIMENTS TO COLLABORATION

Early childhood education explicitly encourages collaboration with parents, with the result that parents generally report feeling welcome in their children's care or preschool centres (Rimm-Kaufman & Pianta 1999). However, invitations alone will not guarantee that parents will attend, as they experience many impediments to becoming involved. The most significant of these is the competing demands posed by their employment status, having a young baby, and moving home (Castro et al. 2004, Lamb-Parker et al. 2001). Next, family stress, impoverishment and single parenting (Grolnick et al. 1997, McWayne et al. 2004), and purely practical problems with the likes of transport, babysitters and shift work, all limit the flexibility and resources available to support parents' involvement. Nevertheless, these impediments may limit only their presence, not their emotional interest and personal involvement in their child's education and care (Grolnick et al. 1997).

Personal qualities of parents may be less crucial but nevertheless still significant. The most vital one is their sense of self-efficacy—that is, their belief in their ability to solve their child's problems (Grolnick et al. 1997). Some will lack self-assurance, while others will believe that their child's difficulties are a reflection of some failing on their part and consequently are reluctant to expose themselves to any scrutiny.

A COLLABORATIVE STYLE

To overcome these impediments to collaboration and engage positively with early childhood professionals, parents require, first, that the program you provide for their child is of a high quality and, second, that you treat them with respect, warmth, positiveness and sensitivity. With these qualities in evidence, parents will be able to trust in your dependability and discretion (Blue-Banning et al. 2004).

Respect

Respect means honouring the person. Naturally, most of us find it easiest to accept others who share our values but, while you may not agree with all parents, you can respect their tenacity at surviving crises and enduring their challenging circumstances (Rosenthal & Sawyers 1996). This validation of parents is underpinned by the awareness that people do the best they can in the circumstances that confront them. Even parents' detrimental disciplining practices, for example, will be aimed at keeping their children safe or teaching them how to behave (Gowen & Nebrig 2002).

Warmth

Parents want an emotionally rich relationship with their child's teachers or caregivers, rather than formal and distant interactions. This is not the same, however, as being their friends. First, you are paid to work with their children and your relationship will usually end when their child leaves your care. Second, friendship has no agenda, whereas your relationship with parents has a particular purpose. Third, friendships have no boundaries (Stonehouse & Gonzalez-Mena 2004), whereas you will need to maintain limits on your professional responsibilities in order to prevent parents' dependence and to safeguard your own wellbeing.

Positiveness

Positiveness involves thinking the best about children's and families' strengths, your own skills and the possibilities for children. At the same time, this must be balanced with honesty. While honesty without tact is plain cruelty, neither is it a kindness to parents to withhold information about their child's difficulties out of a misguided wish to shield them or to protect yourself from a difficult task.

Sensitivity

When collaborating with families, it is important to be sensitive, first, to their circumstances, as these will affect what energies they have available to support their child's education or care. Second, you need to be receptive to their feelings about using childcare. Most will feel positively about your nurturing relationship with their child and will be satisfied with the quality of care that their child receives but, at the same time, many feel ambivalent about the restricted care options that are available to them and would prefer other forms of care if these were accessible and affordable (Galinsky 1989, 1990). Even when completely confident about their choice of care setting, many parents still feel conflict, guilt and sadness at separating from their child (Rolfe et al. 1991). Although a highly personal adjustment process, their feelings are more readily resolved when they feel safe about the quality of care their child is receiving (Larner & Phillips 1994).

A third aspect of sensitivity is listening to parents' aspirations for their son or daughter. Even for toddlers, parents want high-quality programs that advance their children's education (Cryer & Burchinal 1997, Cryer et al. 2002). At the same time, they want their children to be happy and to that end value your acting in ways that protect, nurture and encourage their child (Roffey 2002).

On the other hand, although sensitivity and empathy towards families are clearly beneficial, you must avoid feeling sympathy for those experiencing stressful circumstances. Pity does not give families confidence in their own ability to overcome adversity and can overwhelm you with 'compassion fatigue' and result in burn out.

Responsiveness

Having been sensitive to parents' and children's needs, responsiveness involves providing, arranging for or recommending services that can help them to meet these. Responsiveness can also mean not imposing services that parents do not want. But, like the other qualities, responsiveness can also be overdone. Being too available can unwittingly undermine parents, creating dependence and reducing their confidence in their ability to solve their own problems, while contributing to unmanageable demands on you.

COLLABORATIVE PRACTICES

Building meaningful connections with parents begins with establishing an inviting climate or family ethos (Christenson 2004, Overstreet et al. 2005, Raffaele & Knoff 1999).

Your environment can signal this by providing spaces that welcome parents into the centre (MacNaughton 2004) and, where possible, a parent lounge where they can form networks with each other. As one commonly excluded group, special effort may be required to attract fathers into the centre, particularly those who do not live with their children.

Maintain routine communication

Regular communication with parents about their child's activities and developmental progress, and providing ideas for supporting their child's learning, can cement cooperation between parents and teachers (Raffaele & Knoff 1999). There are many occasions when you can exchange positive information with parents, including orientation visits before their child starts at the centre, during everyday informal contacts, in brochures about centre policies and procedures, at meetings, in newsletters, and on posters or bulletin boards explaining the rationale of the various activities in which children participate at each location. Of these, everyday conversations seem to be the most beneficial for parents, whereas the more formal, written forms of communication tend to be least. A stack of paperwork might keep them informed, but does little to generate a spirit of collaboration (Dowling 2005).

Against such a backdrop of ongoing positive communication, problem solving with parents will be more successful. At these times, as mentioned in Chapter 9, communication with parents will require the same three skills that are necessary for working with children—namely, listening when parents are expressing a problem, being assertive when an issue negatively affects you or other children in your care, and solving problems collaboratively when both you and a child's parents are being inconvenienced. While these communication skills will be an essential ingredient to collaboration, on their own they will not be enough to secure a truly collaborative relationship if practitioners define giving parents a voice as a threat to their professional power (Hughes & MacNaughton 2002).

Foster parents' self-efficacy

The aim of parent collaboration is to foster self-efficacy in parents so that they can function effectively as the hub or key decision makers in their families. In order to do so, parents need to believe that they can advocate for their child and influence their child's development and behaviour. This self-efficacy requires recognition of their skills, information about their choices, a sense of control over their options, encouragement to contribute, and support (both formal and informal) for their family leadership role (Turnbull et al. 2006). Of this list, having information is fundamental to parents' self-efficacy. When providing this to parents, some will be comfortable receiving knowledge from books and articles, which you can amass in a parent resource library, while others will prefer verbal communication (Jacobson & Engelbrecht 2000).

A service hub

An emerging emphasis in early childhood services is that, as well as directly meeting children's needs, childhood services have a role in supporting parents and the wider community. To that end, your setting can be a hub of family and community services. This will not necessarily entail attracting more resources, but perhaps inviting community health professionals to deliver some of their services within your centre (e.g. child health checks or parenting sessions held in your building) so that services can be integrated and parents become accustomed to being involved with their child's care or educational setting.

COLLABORATIVE PROBLEM SOLVING

When children's behaviour is disrupting others, you will need to inform their parents. While this is their right, you must balance supplying enough information with providing a surfeit, because if all that parents receive from you is a daily barrage of complaints about their child, they will become defensive (Roffey 2002). Your subsequent problem solving will be based on recognition that you share a common interest in their child's wellbeing and, with respect to behavioural difficulties, you both want relief from the problem. With this as your starting point, three principles inform your interactions with parents over their child's disruptive behaviour.

First, it will be vital to communicate the clear expectation that, as the problem occurs in your setting, you are responsible for finding its solution. Correspondingly, you do not want parents to punish their child at home for incidents that occur in your care. (You would not punish a child in your setting for something that happened at home.)

Second, you must recognise that all parents want to be proud of their children, to give them educational and other opportunities that they themselves might not have had and to have a good relationship with their children (Berg & Steiner 2003). They want to have hope for their children. When collaborating with parents, then, it is crucial that you nourish their pride in their children.

Finally, it is important to avoid any implication of blame of parents or their child. It is self-evident that you will be working most closely with parents at times when there is a problem to be solved, rather than when all is going well. At such times of stress, it could be easy to fall into a trap of judging parents or assuming that their personal or parenting deficiencies are the cause of their child's difficulties. However, the source of the stress can be beyond the family's influence—as with poverty—or even be a product of the problem itself. Thus, the final key ingredient of collaborating with parents is to bear in mind that the child (or family) is not the problem: *the problem is the problem* (Winslade & Monk 1999).

Preparation

Problem-solving meetings must be conducted in a private space, without distractions or having to compete with program time (Hughes & MacNaughton 2002, MacNaughton 2004). You will need to allocate enough time to make parents feel comfortable and to discuss your concerns and listen to their reactions. These practical issues aside, a fundamental aspect of preparation for a conference with parents is to know their child well. Parents will need you to give examples of the child's concerning behaviours, but to frame these non-judgmentally.

Negotiate who to involve

Throughout this chapter, I use the term *parent* to encompass any caregivers who are significant in children's lives, regardless of whether these adults are the children's biological parents. In many families, grandparents or other extended family members have a crucial role, either as an elder or as a major or supplementary care provider for children. In light of this, discover ahead of time who is important to include in any meeting aimed at resolving children's behavioural difficulties.

Once the children are verbal, consider including them so that they can advise the adults about the thinking that leads to their disruptive actions and perhaps advise adults about how they could respond. Given their young age, we often exclude children but, in so doing, deny ourselves this vital source of information.

Engage parents' expertise

Children behave more negatively at home than in other settings (Ahnert et al. 2000). This means that parents will have experience and expertise with responding to their child's behaviour, which you can harness in your efforts to solve disruptions in your setting. They also see their child in a wide variety of contexts and over a long time period and therefore have intimate knowledge of their child's emotional wellbeing and characteristic behaviours. This expertise can inform solutions.

As well as being a direct source of information, when collaborating with them to solve their child's behavioural difficulties, parents can also fulfil the following functions (Freeman et al. 1997):

- Parents can give examples and enlarge on stories that enrich the descriptions of their child's problem and of exceptions to it.
- They can brainstorm ideas and solutions.
- They can become co-conspirators or part of the child's 'team', helping their child to outwit, combat or oppose the problem.
- They form an audience that can highlight and celebrate their child's mastery over the problem.

Phase 1: Define the problem

The first in a sequence of solution-focused steps is to define children's behavioural difficulties in ways that imply that these can change, rather than suggesting hopelessness. Some parents, for example, might believe that their child is genetically tainted (e.g. by a violent father, or a family history of mental illness). While it is important to honour such explanations, in a later phase, questioning will need to transform such static views into understandings that suggest the potential for improvement.

Phase 2: Articulate goals collaboratively

The family knows what they want their child to achieve and how they want their child to behave. One way to capture this is to ask the miracle question: If a miracle happened overnight and this problem were fixed, what would that look like? Their answer will encapsulate their goals. Another possibility is, using a scale of one to ten, the adults rate the child's present behaviour and nominate a figure that would indicate adequate change.

Phase 3: Explore present solutions

With any problem, there will always be times when it does not occur or is less severe than usual. As noted in Chapter 12, these times are called *exceptions*. Someone does something to bring these about. To discover what that is, you can ask who does what at the time the exceptions occur. In recognition that parents have expertise at solving problems, your role during this discussion is not to know more than they do, but to listen so you can discern and then highlight what they are already doing that works, if not for this problem then for a different one.

If parents are so paralysed by their child's or their own problems that they cannot notice exceptions or their role in enabling these, future-oriented questions can help. You might ask them to picture a time a few months hence when this problem is resolved and to imagine what they will have done in the interim to achieve this. How did they solve it? What has the child been doing differently to achieve this imagined success? What have the parents or other adults or peers been doing that contributed to the improvement? If even these future-oriented questions do not assist them to recognise their ability to attain their goals, you can externalise the problem (see Ch 12). This allows the problem to be the villain, rather than the child.

Phase 4: Expand on solutions

In this phase, you will expand on or adjust the methods that parents and others have been using to produce exceptions. You might decide to add a new element, try something that the child suggests, or do something new that those involved might previously have considered but not yet implemented (Selekman 1997).

As a group, you will select a solution in light of the needs of individual children and the group overall and the constraints in your setting. Your solution must also be in tune with your professional judgment about best practice. For example, if parents suggest smacking their child, which will conflict with your beliefs or aims, you can reflect their desire to fix the problem and ask what else they could suggest that would meet that same goal.

When parents feel confident that they can bring about improvements in their child's behaviour, their task will simply be to do more of what has been working so far. In contrast, for those who feel powerless, their first task can be to change nothing, but for the next week or so to *notice* when their child is behaving well and what they are doing at the time to bring that about.

Phase 5: Notice progress

At a subsequent meeting, you will ask what has changed since your previous conversation. In response, those involved could report that there has been some improvement, no change, a deterioration in the child's behaviour, or different members could have mixed opinions. For each of these four scenarios, Selekman (1997) advises the following:

- When parents report *improvements*, ask about and highlight what each person has done to bring those about. You can then all agree to continue using more of these successful strategies.
- When there appears to all those involved to have been *no change* in the child's behaviour, you could suggest that maybe the child is finding adults too predictable. Therefore, you all need to do something different to surprise the child. Despite not knowing in advance how it might help, you could try doing the opposite of what has been tried so far (Selekman 1997).
- When the problem appears *worse* than before, you will need to listen to the parents' despondency without blaming anyone or permitting their desperation to become

contagious (Freeman et al. 1997). Empathising with their despair will uncover their underlying love and worry for their child. To counterbalance their discouragement, you can highlight their resiliency by asking how come they have not given up, what keeps them hanging in there and trying, or asking how they have prevented the problem from becoming worse than it is.

- When progress reports are *mixed*, with some individuals reporting improvement while others are still pessimistic, acknowledge the caution of the sceptics, then highlight the improvements.

Refer on

If a child's behaviour remains of serious concern and you feel the need for advice from an outside specialist, or if parents are seeking some counselling, recommend them to specialists. To assist them to access these, find out in advance about available services, including details of waiting time, costs and contact telephone numbers.

CROSS-CULTURAL COLLABORATION

While it will never be possible to walk in another person's shoes and understand how others experience the social oppression that often accompanies their cultural membership, collaborative problem solving with parents from a minority culture will need to be grounded in your understanding of the impact of the dominant culture on others (Ingraham 2000, Ramirez et al. 1998).

Parents' cultural values can influence their aspirations for their child, their expectations of their own role in solving the problem, their expectations of your role, perceptions of your status, and non-verbal communication styles. You will need to ask about these aspects, which of course requires that parents are confident of their English skills or have access to interpreters.

A solution-focused approach as outlined here is ideal for working cross-culturally because, in having parents generate their own definitions of problems, determine their own goals and design interventions based on their own past successes, necessarily these will match their perspectives (cultural and otherwise). In turn, this congruence with their values will contribute to trust between you and to their openness to solutions.

RESPONDING TO PARENTS' COMPLAINTS

So far this chapter has dealt with how to enlist parents' advice for solving their child's behavioural difficulties. A second occasion when you need to collaborate with parents is when they have approached you with a complaint about an incident in your care. Given that you are accountable to parents, you must meet their concerns and questions with courtesy. Even 'difficult' parents are not being demanding just to make you jump through hoops: they both *need* and have a *right* to ask questions.

Any expression of strong emotions of blame, anger or hopelessness is a sign that they care deeply about their child. Although strong emotions can be intimidating, it will help not to take their behaviour personally, but to remember that it is being triggered by their situation (not by you) and that, from their perspective, parents feel that they have a valid reason for their feelings and behaviour. All mammals become feral when their young are under threat. Thus, you will need to listen to and acknowledge their frustration or anger.

Nevertheless, if they become belligerent, uncooperative, abusive or otherwise disrespectful, offensive or overpowering, you will need them to moderate how they are talking to you. Beginning by agreeing that you share a common interest—namely, providing the best possible care for their child—you can then direct them to what they want to accomplish (Jones & Jones 2004). For example: 'I agree that Simon and all the children deserve to be safe here and you have every right to be angry that he was bitten. I would like your ideas about what you would like us to do to prevent it happening again.'

Such conversations are best not held 'on the run', in public, while you are attempting to oversee the children's program, or while parents are angry. In these cases, listen briefly, but then set up an appointment time to talk it through more fully. A postponement will give you time to gather the information you need about the incident and will give parents time to calm down so they will be more receptive to reason.

In most instances, listening to the feeling behind parents' manner will effectively avoid a confrontation. However, you will also need a policy with specific procedures for protecting staff should parents ever become physically threatening.

COMPLAINTS FROM THIRD PARTIES

Parents whose children are being victimised repeatedly by another child have grounds for protest about this. Even when their own child is not a direct recipient of aggressive behaviour, they can still have legitimate concerns about how much time a disruptive child is detracting from the care that is available to their child and how their child, as an onlooker, may be intimidated by repeated aggression directed at peers.

The politics of behaviour management are actually more complex than the practice itself. Given the imperative to maintain confidentiality and dissuade gossip, the issue of how much you should disclose to other parents about the behaviour of a particular child is delicate and needs to be decided on a case-by-case basis. Giving the wider parent group too much information could be construed as a tacit invitation for protests. Conversely, if you do not discuss the issue, some parents might feel that you are not receptive to their concerns.

Obviously, this dilemma will be solved once the child's behaviour improves. Parents' understanding and endorsement of your disciplinary policy will be crucial in the meantime, so that you are confident of their support for your disciplinary measures.

CONCLUSION

Collaboration with parents over behavioural issues will not occur by chance. You will need to plan for it. A solution-focused approach is particularly valuable for collaborative problem solving, as it does not set you up as the expert and does not require specialist counselling skills other than being curious, listening and questioning. By formulating goals jointly with parents, you will not attempt to reform the family or ensure that parents use the same behavioural guidance approach as yourself. While ideal, such consistency is not essential, because children are wise enough to discern the various expectations of differing adults and adjust their behaviour accordingly.

SUGGESTED FURTHER READING

Communication skills

Bolton R 1987 *People skills*. Simon & Schuster, Sydney.

Rosenberg MB 2003 *Nonviolent communication: a language of life*, 2nd edn. Puddle Dancer Press, Encinitas, CA.

Collaboration

Friend M, Cook L 2007 *Interactions: collaboration skills for school professionals*, 5th edn. Pearson Allyn & Bacon, Boston, MA.

Porter L 2008 *Teacher-parent collaboration: early childhood to adolescence*. ACER, Melbourne.

Stonehouse A, Gonzalez-Mena J 2004 *Making links: a collaborative approach to planning and practice in early childhood services*. Pademelon, Sydney.

Formulating a discipline policy

'Busy people typically do not engage in reflection. They rarely treat themselves to reflective experiences, unless they are given some time, some structure, and the expectations to do so ... Through reflection, we develop context-specific theories that further our own understanding of our work and generate knowledge to inform future practice.'

KILLION & TODNEM (1991, p. 14)

BENEFITS OF FORMAL POLICIES

In general, policies are statements about what services you will offer and how you will deliver them. Although formulating policies is time consuming, the resulting statements can enshrine reasonable work demands, clarify teachers' roles and responsibilities, improve coordination and communication across the centre, and harness support for staff from management and parents (Hart et al. 2000, Rutter 1983). Writing a policy has the following additional advantages:

■ The process of formulation is an opportunity to involve parents and staff collaboratively (Stonehouse 1991) and gives them a forum to communicate their sense of shared purpose (Mathieson & Price 2002).

■ It offers caregivers/teachers and parents clear expectations of their roles, rights and responsibilities (Stonehouse 1991).

- The process of reviewing practice allows problems and grievances to be aired (Strain & Joseph 2004). This will be healthy as long as it shifts onto focusing on solutions and does not degenerate into gossip about particular children and families.
- The process of formulating a policy allows you to plan in advance how to respond to disruptiveness, rather than having to make hasty reactive decisions.
- A policy can be the basis for planning staff development (Mathieson & Price 2002).
- A policy clarifies how staff can obtain support to deal with demanding behaviours.
- Written documentation helps to familiarise new staff and parents with the philosophy and workings of the centre.
- Written policies assist with evaluation and accountability, enshrining safeguards for parents, children and staff (Farmer 1995, Stonehouse 1991).
- Consultation with parents increases the likelihood that they will understand and support your practices.

By far the most important advantage, however, comes not from the policy document itself, but from the process of developing it. This gives staff and parents the opportunity to clarify their views (Stonehouse 1991). Therefore, you cannot simply adopt the policy of another centre or preschool, as a policy acquires its power from the process of clarifying the assumptions that underpin practices. This process helps ensure that any subsequent changes in practice become embedded in the culture of the setting.

PRE-PLANNING

As illustrated in Figure 18.1, a first step of drafting a discipline policy will be to motivate staff to review its present policy and practices. This will entail helping team members to identify the need for change by recognising the shortcomings of present practices, without assigning blame for these and thus inviting resistance or defensiveness, but instead exciting a sense of anticipation at the possibility that innovations will produce improvements (Ebbeck & Waniganayake 2003, Rodd 2006). Staff members' commitment to change will depend on the quality of the information they can access, their sense of control (self-efficacy) over the changes, confidence so that they can ride out the early stages of uncertainty, and the level of support they receive (Ebbeck & Waniganayake 2003).

Next, an appointed staff member or small team will collate your present policy and others that affect it. Then, you will gather resources to inform you of your options, or locate some professional development training on discipline. The final step will be to discuss with staff and parents their views of present practices and suggested adaptations in order to meet their objectives for children's behaviour.

This information will be collated and discussed in a series of meetings on each of the elements of policy: philosophy, values, goals, theory, and preventive and interventive practices. During these discussions, you will need to consider how to incorporate differences in individuals' views and whether you expect majority consensus or require 100% endorsement by all staff. In instances where staff can use their own style without affecting the overall program, there can be some latitude in opinion, but where the tone of the setting is impeded by inappropriate practices, differences in style will somehow need to be resolved.

At this stage, you will also need to give some thought to how you can sustain changes evoked by the new policy. Staff can feel awkward when employing new methods and

FIGURE 18.1 Process of policy review

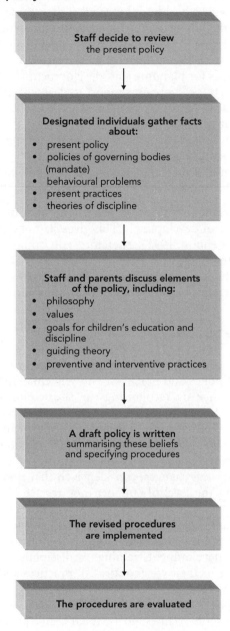

Staff decide to review
the present policy

Designated individuals gather facts
about:
- present policy
- policies of governing bodies
(mandate)
- behavioural problems
- present practices
- theories of discipline

Staff and parents discuss elements
of the policy, including:
- philosophy
- values
- goals for children's education and
discipline
- guiding theory
- preventive and interventive practices

A draft policy is written
summarising these beliefs
and specifying procedures

The revised procedures
are implemented

The procedures are evaluated

therefore will need support until they become familiar and more comfortable with new approaches and their sense of competency is restored (Rodd 2006).

COMPONENTS OF A POLICY

Discipline is a process for helping children to learn and to gain personal skills. It is not an end in itself. Therefore, a policy statement about discipline must include far more than statements about how staff will intervene with disruptive behaviour. It will specify the influences on your practices—namely, your theoretical knowledge of both education and discipline—and identify the constraints imposed by your mandate and features of your setting. In light of these, your discipline policy will document preventive and interventive practices that align with your beliefs, values and goals.

Mandate

Any policy that you generate will need to be framed within guidelines such as the code of ethical conduct for early childhood professionals (see Early Childhood Australia 2006, National Association for the Education of Young Children 1989, and, for Australia, the Quality Improvement and Accreditation Guidelines (National Childcare Accreditation Council 1993)). In addition, your funding body might have its own sets of policies that your centre is expected to observe. Typically, however, these general statements offer broad guidelines only, usually leaving day-to-day decisions about implementation to individual centres. This is as it should be, as educators are more effective when they can exercise some professional discretion (Lewis 1997).

Philosophical beliefs

This section of your policy needs to make explicit the following beliefs:

- What is your view of children and of their mistakes? Is this view different for developmental versus behavioural errors? If so, is that justified, and what does it imply for practice?
- Where do you locate individuals' control? If you believe that children are controlled internally, this will imply practices that adhere to a guidance approach. If you believe that children can and should be controlled externally, this will imply a controlling approach with its use of rewards and punishments.
- What do you assume causes disruptive behaviour? What do you think of the view that much of the disruptive behaviour displayed by young children is a reaction against external controls? What does your view on this issue imply for practice?

Once you have answered these questions, if your responses reflect a guidance view of the world, you will need to check that your practices section does not contradict this by detailing controlling methods (Lewis 1997, Porter 1999).

Values

A discipline policy will need to take account of staff members' personal and professional values. Although staff cannot be expected to reach consensus on these, individuals' values contribute to their goals, about which some agreement will be necessary.

Goals

In light of caregivers/teachers' professional values, your disciplinary policy must specify your educational goals for children's intellectual, social, emotional, physical and cultural growth. These might include those aims listed in Chapter 3.

Your second cluster of goals will be disciplinary. In general, your overall aim will probably be to create a well-disciplined environment in which you can work and children can learn. Beyond this, your specific behavioural goals will be either to secure children's compliance or to teach considerate behaviour (see Ch 1). The first of these gives rise to controlling practices and may contradict the educational goals that you endorse, while aiming for considerate behaviour requires the use of guidance practices and is more likely to align with your educational beliefs and goals.

Theory

The first part of your theory section will detail your educational theory. You can select from a top-down or teacher-directed model of education versus a constructivist, child-centred model. The next section will give a brief overview of the theory of discipline that you endorse. Your choice broadly will be between a behaviourist view of the world, which uses rewards and punishments to control children's behaviours, versus a guidance approach, which uses acknowledgment (informative feedback) and teaches emotional self-control. Given that your theory of discipline cannot contradict your educational beliefs, you will need to ensure that these two aspects of theory are consistent with each other.

Enabling and constraining aspects of your setting

Practitioners will need support to implement disciplinary methods. Therefore, you will need to conduct an audit to determine if the necessary resources and supports are indeed available. When constraints are unavoidable—such as a non-conducive physical environment, large group size or a socially disadvantaged community—you will need to plan ways to surmount these.

Practice

The next section of your policy will describe what practices are to be used and by whom. These procedures will focus on how you will organise your program so that most behavioural difficulties are prevented and those that do occur receive a constructive response (Cowin et al. 1990). As prevention is far more powerful than intervention, that aspect will be the largest part of your practices section.

Monitoring and assessment methods

As a universal preventive measure, you will need to plan procedures to monitor children's behaviour so that you will know when problems are arising and can respond promptly (Rutter & Maughan 2002). Secondary prevention will entail assessing individual children's learning needs and behaviour in order to judge if they need a more targeted intervention.

Recognition of considerate behaviour

In this section, you will need to determine your collective view about the use of informative versus judgmental feedback (i.e. acknowledgment versus praise) for children's achievements and prosocial behaviour.

Layered responses to disruptions

As depicted in Figure II.1 (on p. 34), your policy must incorporate three levels of responses to disciplinary issues: universal prevention, supportive interventions, and solutions, in that order of magnitude. *Primary* or *universal prevention* strategies are supportive measures aimed at preventing disruptions by meeting children's needs, as detailed in Part II of this book. Your primary measures can also widen their focus to supporting parents and the wider community.

Your secondary or *supportive* interventions aimed at avoiding future disruptions include supporting children to practise assertiveness and emotional self-control, as described in Part III. Secondary prevention will also entail gathering comprehensive assessments for children whose behavioural difficulties could be the expression of learning problems. This may require recommending to parents that they consult relevant specialists.

The third level of practice comprises short-term and long-term *solutions* to ongoing difficulties, as given in Chapters 12 to 15. Given an emphasis on prevention, this section of your policy should be the smallest. Nevertheless, it must be explicit because vague recommendations for staff (such as that they use 'positive measures' in response to disruptive behaviour) can mean different things to different people and generate confusion and ineffective practice.

Parental participation

The policy will need to declare an intention to seek parents' advice and support with any behavioural issues that arise with their children.

Collegial support

Next, your policy needs to state the practical measures that staff will use to support each other in their problem solving, to deal with a severe disturbance, to cope with its aftermath and to plan long-term solutions to chronically disruptive behaviour (Gamman 2003).

Use of consultants

Your policy should include a statement about the use of consultants: when, how and to whom you could recommend parents for child assessment and family support. To that end, it can be useful to collate a list of relevant private practitioners and social service agencies.

Special issues

Your discipline policy will need to refer to specific issues such as catering for children with additional learning needs, equity issues, and child protection and abuse.

EVALUATION OF THE POLICY

The final section of your policy will detail how, when and who will evaluate the effects of its procedures. Once the practices have been in place for enough time to allow them to take effect, individual staff could keep a tally over a brief period of the number and type of disruptions they have responded to, and which interventions they used. Less formal means include discussions in staff meetings and impressions of workers' morale, stress levels or work satisfaction.

To guide your reflection, you could consider the following questions, negative answers to which will indicate a need to change practices (Borland 2003, Cowin et al. 1990, Sharp & Thompson 1994):

- Is your discipline plan and its practices consistent with your philosophy, values, goals and theory?
- Are your recommendations realistic? Do they reflect actual practice, or are they a 'wish list'?
- Are the procedures being enacted as originally devised?
- Are the practices achieving what you set out to accomplish?
- Are there other important, unanticipated outcomes?
- Are there children for whom the procedures are more or less successful than others?
- What additional resources (including materials and personnel) are needed to make practices more effective? Are these available?

As well as assessing these outcomes, you will need to evaluate the effectiveness of inputs—such as the resources being used, the efficient use of teachers' time and the involvement of parents (Davis & Rimm 2004). Conducting a critique of practices does not imply criticism or disapproval, but an effort to make practices and their underlying beliefs visible and open to scrutiny in order to question convention and instead discover what is possible (Kilderry 2004).

CONCLUSION

Above all, the policy that you arrive at has to be a living document—one that is relevant, owned, communicated, practised and regularly reviewed (Drifte 2004, Roffey 2004). It will need to be adjusted to reflect changes in your centre brought about by evolving social circumstances, staff turnover and the enrolment of new children and families (Mathieson & Price 2002). Although the process of planning and evaluating practices might appear burdensome, it can be professionally fulfilling and confidence building to have the opportunity to reflect on your practice and to demonstrate its positive outcomes.

SUGGESTED FURTHER READING

Farmer S 1995 *Policy development in early childhood services*. Community Child Care Cooperative Ltd, Sydney.

references

Abbott-Shim MS 1990 In-service training: a means to quality care. *Young Children* 45(2):14–18.

Abbott-Shim M, Lambert R, McCarty F 2000 Structural model of Head Start classroom quality. *Early Childhood Research Quarterly* 15(1):115–34.

Aboud FE 2003 The formation of in-group favoritism and out-group prejudice in young children: are they distinct attitudes? *Developmental Psychology* 39(1):48–60.

Ackerman BP, Brown ED, D'Eramo KS, Izard CE 2002 Maternal relationship instability and the school behavior of children from disadvantaged families. *Developmental Psychology* 38(5):694–704.

Ackerman BP, Brown ED, Izard CE 2004 The relations between persistent poverty and contextual risk and children's behavior in elementary school. *Developmental Psychology* 40(3):367–77.

Ackerman BP, Kogos J, Youngstrom E, Schoff K, Izard C 1999 Family instability and the problem behaviors of children from economically disadvantaged families. *Developmental Psychology* 35(1):258–68.

Adler RB, Rosenfeld LB, Proctor RF II 2004 *Interplay: the process of interpersonal communication*, 9th edn. Oxford University Press, New York.

Afifi TO, Brownridge DA, Cox BJ, Sareen J 2006 Physical punishment, childhood abuse and psychiatric disorders. *Child Abuse and Neglect* 30(10):1093–103.

Aguilar B, Sroufe A, Egeland B, Carlson E 2000 Distinguishing the early-onset/persistent and adolescent-onset antisocial behavior types: from birth to 16 years. *Development and Psychopathology* 12(2):109–32.

Aguillard AE, Pierce SH, Benedict JH, Burts DC 2005 Barriers to the implementation of continuity-of-care practices in child care centers. *Early Childhood Research Quarterly* 20(3):329–44.

Ahnert L, Gunnar MR, Lamb ME, Barthel M 2004 Transition to child care: associations with infant–mother attachment, infant negative emotion, and cortisol elevations. *Child Development* 75(3):639–50.

Ahnert L, Pinquart M, Lamb ME 2006 Security of children's relationships with nonparental care providers: a meta-analysis. *Child Development* 74(3):664–79.

Ahnert L, Rickert H, Lamb ME 2000 Shared caregiving: comparisons between home and child-care settings. *Developmental Psychology* 36(3):339–51.

Ajmal Y 2001 Introducing solution-focused thinking. In Y Ajmal and I Rees (eds), *Solutions in schools*. BT Press, London, pp. 10–29.

Alberto PA, Troutman AC 2003 *Applied behavior analysis for teachers*, 6th edn. Merrill Prentice Hall, Upper Saddle River, NJ.

Algozzine B, Kay P (eds) 2002 *Preventing problem behaviors: a handbook of successful prevention strategies*. Corwin Press, Thousand Oaks, CA.

Alink LRA, Mesman J, Koot HM, van Zeijl J, Stolk MN, Juffer F, Bakermans-Kranenburg MJ, van Ijzedoorn MH 2006 The early childhood aggression curve: development of physical aggression in 10- to 5-month old children. *Child Development* 77(4):954–66.

Alsaker FD, Valkanover S 2001 Early diagnosis and prevention of victimization in kindergarten. In J Juvonen and S Graham (eds), *Peer harassment in school: the plight of the vulnerable and victimized.* Guilford, New York, pp. 175–95.

Amatea ES 1989 *Brief strategic interventions for school behavior problems.* Jossey Bass, San Francisco, CA.

Amato PR, Fowler F 2002 Parenting practices, child adjustment, and family diversity. *Journal of Marriage and Family* 64(3):703–16.

American Psychiatric Association 1994 *Diagnostic and statistical manual of mental disorders*, 4th edn. American Psychiatric Association, Washington, DC.

Anan RM, Barnett D 1999 Perceived social support mediates between prior attachment and subsequent adjustment: a study of urban African American children. *Developmental Psychology* 35(5):1210–22.

Anastopoulos AD, Barkley RA 1992 Attention deficit-hyperactivity disorder. In CE Walker and MC Roberts (eds), *Handbook of clinical child psychology*, 2nd edn. John Wiley & Sons, New York, pp. 413–30.

Andersson B-E 1989 Effects of public day-care—a longitudinal study. *Child Development* 60(4):857–66.

—— 1992 Effects of day care on cognitive and socioemotional competence of thirteen-year-old Swedish schoolchildren. *Child Development* 63(1):20–36.

Arnett J 1989 Caregivers in day care centers: does training matter? *Journal of Applied Developmental Psychology* 10:541–52.

Arnold DH 1997 Co-occurrence of externalizing behavior problems and emergent academic difficulties in young high-risk boys: a preliminary evaluation of patterns and mechanisms. *Journal of Applied Developmental Psychology* 18(3):317–30.

Arnold DH, Homrok S, Ortiz C, Stowe RM 1999 Direct observation of peer rejection acts and their temporal relation with aggressive acts. *Early Childhood Research Quarterly* 14(2):183–96.

Arnold DH, McWilliams L, Arnold EH 1998 Teacher discipline and child misbehavior in day care: untangling causality with correlational data. *Developmental Psychology* 34(2):276–87.

Arnold LE 1996 Sex differences in ADHD: conference summary. *Journal of Abnormal Child Psychology* 24(5):555–69.

Arthur M, Gordon C, Butterfield N 2003 *Classroom management: creating positive learning environments.* Thomson, Melbourne.

Asher SR 1983 Social competence and peer status: recent advances and future directions. *Child Development* 54:1427–34.

Asher SR, Parker JG 1989 Significance of peer relationship problems in childhood. In BH Schneider, G Attili, J Nadel and RP Weissberg (eds), *Social competence in developmental perspective.* Kluwer Academic Publishers, Dordrecht, pp. 5–23.

Asher SR, Renshaw PD 1981 Children without friends: social knowledge and social skill training. In SR Asher and JM Gottman (eds), *The development of children's friendships.* Cambridge University Press, Cambridge, UK, pp. 273–96.

Ashiabi GS 2000 Promoting the emotional development of preschoolers. *Early Childhood Education Journal* 28(2):79–84.

Ashton J 2004 Life after the shock! The impact on families of caring for young children with chronic illness. *Australian Journal of Early Childhood* 29(1):22–6.

Ashton J, Bailey J 2004 Slipping through the policy cracks: children with chronic illness in early childhood settings. *Australian Journal of Early Childhood* 29(1):50–8.

Assor A, Kaplan H, Roth G 2002 Choice is good, but relevance is excellent: autonomy-enhancing and suppressing teacher behaviours predicting students' engagement in schoolwork. *British Journal of Educational Psychology* 72(2):261–78.

Attwood T 2004 Strategies to reduce the bullying of young children with Asperger syndrome. *Australian Journal of Early Childhood* 29(3):15–23.

Atwater JB, Morris EK 1988 Teachers' instructions and children's compliance in preschool classrooms: a descriptive analysis. *Journal of Applied Behavior Analysis* 21(2):157–67.

Aucoin KJ, Frick PJ, Bodin SD 2006 Corporal punishment and child adjustment. *Journal of Applied Developmental Psychology* 27(6):527–41.

Auerbach JG, Landau R, Berger A, Arbelle S, Faroy M, Karplus M 2005 Neonatal behavior of infants at familial risk for ADHD. *Infant Behavior and Development* 28(2):220–34.

Aunola, K, Nurmi, J-E 2004 Maternal affection moderates the impact of psychological control on a child's mathematical performance. *Developmental Psychology* 40(6):965–78.

—— 2005 The role of parenting styles in children's problem behavior. *Child Development* 76(6):1144–59.

Australian Early Childhood Association 1991 Australian Early Childhood Association code of ethics. *Australian Journal of Early Childhood* 16(1):3–6.

Bailey DB Jr 2002 Are critical periods critical for early childhood education? The role of timing in early childhood pedagogy. *Early Childhood Research Quarterly* 17(3):281–94.

Baillargeon RH, Normand CL, Séguin JR, Zoccolillo M, Japel C, Pérusse D, Wu H-X, Boivin M, Tremblay RE 2007 The evolution of problem and social competence behaviors during toddlerhood: a prospective population-based cohort survey. *Infant Mental Health Journal* 28(1):12–38.

Baker BL, Blacher J, Crnic KA, Edelbrock C 2002 Behavior problems and parenting stress in families of three-year-old children with and without developmental delays. *American Journal on Mental Retardation* 107(6):433–44.

Baker BL, McIntyre LL, Blacher J, Crnic K, Edelbrock C, Low C 2003 Pre-school children with and without developmental delay: behaviour problems and parenting stress over time. *Journal of Intellectual Disability Research* 47(4–5):217–30.

Baker JA 2006 Contributions of teacher–child relationships to positive school adjustment during elementary school. *Journal of School Psychology* 44(3):211–29.

Bakermans-Kranenburg MJ, van Ijzendoorn MH, Kroonenberg PM 2004 Differences in attachment security between African-American and white children: ethnicity or socio-economic status? *Infant Behavior and Development* 27(3):417–33.

Balson M 1992 *Understanding classroom behaviour*, 3rd edn. ACER, Melbourne.

Banks R 2005 Solution-focused group therapy. In TS Nelson (ed.), *Education and training in solution-focused brief therapy*. Haworth Press, New York, pp. 17–21.

Barber BK 1996 Parental psychological control: revisiting a neglected construct. *Child Development* 67(6):3296–319.

Barbour AC 1999 The impact of playground design on the play behaviors of children with differing levels of physical competence. *Early Childhood Research Quarterly* 14(1):75–98.

Barkley RA 1988 Attention deficit disorder with hyperactivity. In EJ Mash and LG Terdal (eds), *Behavioral assessment of childhood disorders*, 2nd edn. Guilford, New York, pp. 69–104.

Barkley RA, Shelton TL, Crosswait C, Moorehouse M, Fletcher K, Barrett S, Jenkins L, Metevia L 2000. Multi-method psycho-educational intervention for preschool children with disruptive behavior: preliminary results at post-treatment. *Journal of Child Psychology and Psychiatry* 41(3):319–32.

Baumeister RF, Leary MF 1995 The need to belong: desire for interpersonal attachments as a fundamental human motivation. *Psychological Bulletin* 117(3):497–529.

Bauminger N, Kasari C 2000 Loneliness and friendship in high-functioning children with autism. *Child Development* 71(2):447–56.

Baumrind D 1967 Child care practices anteceding three patterns of preschool behavior. *Genetic Psychology Monographs* 75:43–88.

—— 1971 Current patterns of parental authority. *Developmental Psychology Monograph* 4(1):1–103.

Bayer JK, Sanson AV, Hemphill SA 2006 Parent influences on early childhood internalizing difficulties. *Journal of Applied Developmental Psychology* 27(6):542–59.

Bear GG, Manning MA, Izard CE 2003 Responsible behavior: the importance of social cognition and emotion. *School Psychology Quarterly* 18(2):140–57.

Beitchman JH, Wilson B, Johnson CJ, Atkinson L, Young A, Adlaf E, Escobar M, Douglas L 2001 Fourteen-year follow-up of speech/language-impaired and control children: psychiatric outcome. *Journal of the American Academy of Child and Adolescent Psychiatry* 40(1):75–82.

Belsky J, Hsieh K-H, Crnic K 1998 Mothering, fathering, and infant negativity as antecedents of boys' externalizing problems and inhibition at age 3 years: differential susceptibility to rearing experience? *Development and Psychopathology* 10(2):301–19.

Benasich AA, Curtiss S, Tallal P 1993 Language, learning, and behavioral disturbances in childhood: a longitudinal perspective. *Journal of the American Academy of Child and Adolescent Psychiatry* 32(3):585–94.

Bender HL, Allen JP, McElhaney KB, Antonishak J, Moore CM, Kelly HO, Davs SM 2007 Use of harsh physical discipline and developmental outcomes in adolescence. *Development and Psychopathology* 19(1):227–42.

Bendersky M, Lewis M 2000 Prenatal cocaine exposure and neonatal condition. *Infant Behavior and Development* 22(3):353–66.

Bentley-Williams R, Butterfield N 1996 Transition from early intervention to school: a family focussed view of the issues involved. *Australasian Journal of Special Education* 20(2):17–28.

Berg IK, Steiner S 2003 *Children's solution work*. Norton, New York.

Bergen D 1994 Should teachers permit or discourage violent play themes? *Childhood Education* 70(5):300–1.

Berk LE, Landau S 1993 Private speech of learning disabled and normally achieving children in classroom academic and laboratory contexts. *Child Development* 64(2):556–71.

Berk LE, Potts MK 1991 Development and functional significance of private speech among attention-deficit hyperactivity disordered and normal boys. *Journal of Abnormal Child Psychology* 19(3):357–77.

Berndt TJ 2004 Children's friendships: shifts over a half-century in perspectives on their development and effects. *Merrill-Palmer Quarterly* 50(3):206–23.

Bessell AG 2001 Children surviving cancer: psychosocial adjustment, quality of life, and school experiences. *Exceptional Children* 67(3):345–59.

Bevill AR, Gast DL 1998 Social safety for young children: a review of the literature on safety skills instruction. *Topics in Early Childhood Special Education* 18(4):222–34.

Bibou-Nakou I, Kiosseoglou G, Stogiannidou A 2000 Elementary teachers' perceptions regarding school behavior problems: implications for school psychological services. *Psychology in the Schools* 37(2):123–34.

Biddulph S 1998 *The secret of happy children*, 3rd edn. HarperCollins, Sydney; Free Spirit Press, Minneapolis, MN.

—— 2003 *Raising boys*, 2nd edn. Finch, Sydney.

Billman J 1995 Child care program directors: what skills do they need? Results of a statewide survey. *Early Childhood Education Journal* 23(2):63–70.

Birch LL, Johnson SL, Fisher JA 1995 Children's eating: the development of food-acceptance patterns. *Young Children* 50(2):71–8.

Birch SH, Ladd GW 1997 The teacher–child relationship and children's early school adjustment. *Journal of School Psychology* 35(1):61–79.

—— 1998 Children's interpersonal behaviors and the teacher–child relationship. *Developmental Psychology* 34(5):934–46.

Birns B 1999 Attachment theory revisited: challenging conceptual and methodological sacred cows. *Feminism and Psychology* 9(1):10–21.

Black B, Uhde TW 1995 Psychiatric characteristics of children with selective mutism: a pilot study. *Journal of the American Academy of Child and Adolescent Psychiatry* 34(7):847–56.

Blankemeyer M, Flannery DJ, Vazsonyi AT 2002 The role of aggression and social competence in children's perceptions of the child–teacher relationship. *Psychology in the Schools* 39(3):293–304.

Blue-Banning M, Summers JA, Frankland HC, Nelson LL, Beegle G 2004 Dimensions of family and professional partnerships: constructive guidelines for collaboration. *Exceptional Children* 70(2):167–84.

Blum NJ, Mercugliano M 1997 Attention-deficit/hyperactivity disorder. In ML Batshaw (ed.), *Children with disabilities*, 4th edn. MacLennan & Petty, Sydney, pp. 449–70.

Bogat GA, DeJonghe E, Levendosky AA, Davidson WS, von Eye A 2006 Trauma symptoms among infants exposed to intimate partner violence. *Child Abuse and Neglect* 30(2):109–25.

Bohlin G, Hagekull B, Andersson K 2005 Behavioral inhibition as a precursor of peer social competence in early school age: the interplay with attachment and nonparental care. *Merrill-Palmer Quarterly* 51(1):1–19.

Bohlin G, Hagekull B, Rydell A-M 2000 Attachment and social functioning: a longitudinal study from infancy to middle childhood. *Social Development* 9(1):24–39.

Bolger KE, Patterson CJ 2001 Developmental pathways from child maltreatment to peer rejection. *Child Development* 72(2):549–68.

Bolton R 1987 *People skills*. Simon & Schuster, Sydney.

Bonner BL, Kaufman KL, Harbeck C, Brassard MR 1992 Child maltreatment. In CE Walker and MC Roberts (eds), *Handbook of clinical child psychology*, 2nd edn. John Wiley & Sons, New York, pp. 967–1008.

Booth CL, Rose-Krasnor L, McKinnon J-A, Rubin KH 1994 Predicting social adjustment in middle childhood: the role of preschool attachment security and maternal style. *Social Development* 3(3):189–204.

Borland JH 2003 Evaluating gifted programs: a broader perspective. In N Colangelo and GA Davis (eds), *Handbook of gifted education*, 3rd edn. Allyn & Bacon, Boston, MA, pp. 293–307.

Bornstein MH, Putnick DL, Suwalsky JTD, Gini M 2006 Maternal chronological age, prenatal and perinatal history, social support, and parenting of infants. *Child Development* 77(4):875–92.

Bouffard T, Marcoux M-F, Vezeau C, Bordeleau L 2003 Changes in self-perceptions of competence and intrinsic motivation among elementary schoolchildren. *British Journal of Educational Psychology* 73(2):171–86.

Bradley RH, Corwyn RF, Burchinal M, McAdoo HP, Coll CG 2001 The home environments of children in the United States part II: relations with behavioral development through age thirteen. *Child Development* 72(6):1868–86.

Brand SF 1990 Undergraduates and beginning preschool teachers working with young children: educational and developmental issues. *Young Children* 45(2):19–24.

Brendgen M, Dionne G, Girard A, Boivin M, Vitaro F, Pérusse D 2005 Examining genetic and environmental effects on social aggression: a study of 6-year-old twins. *Child Development* 76(4):930–46.

Brenner V, Fox RA 1999 An empirically derived classification of parenting practices. *Journal of Genetic Psychology* 160(3):343–56.

Briggs F 1993 *Why my child? Supporting the families of victims of child sexual abuse*. Allen & Unwin, Sydney.

Briggs F, McVeity M 2000 *Teaching children to protect themselves*. Allen & Unwin, Sydney.

Broidy LM, Nagin DS, Tremblay RE, Bates JE, Brame B, Dodge KA, Fergusson D, Horwood JL, Loeber R, Laird R, Lynam DR, Moffitt TE, Pettit GS, Vitaro F 2003 Developmental trajectories of childhood disruptive behaviors and adolescent delinquency: a six-site, cross-national study. *Developmental Psychology* 39(2):222–45.

Broinowski I, Dau E 2004 *Managing children's services*. Tertiary Press, Melbourne.

Bromberg DS, Johnson BT 2001 Sexual interest in children, child sexual abuse, and psychological sequelae for children. *Psychology in the Schools* 38(4):343–55.

Brophy M, Taylor E, Hughes C 2002 To go or not to go: inhibitory control in 'hard to manage' children. *Infant and Child Development* 11(2):125–40.

Brown CS, Bigler RS 2005 Children's perceptions of discrimination: a developmental model. *Child Development* 76(3):533–53.

Brown ER 1996 Effects of resource availability on children's behavior and conflict management. *Early Education and Development* 7(2):149–64.

Brown PM, Remine MD, Prescott SJ, Rickards FW 2000 Social interactions of preschoolers with and without impaired hearing in integrated kindergarten. *Journal of Early Intervention* 23(3):200–11.

Brown WH, Odom SL, Li S, Zercher C 1999 Ecobehavioral assessment in early childhood programs: a portrait of preschool inclusion. *Journal of Special Education* 33(3):138–53.

Brownell CA, Ramani GB, Zerwas S 2006 Becoming a social partner with peers: cooperation and social understanding in one- and two-year-olds. *Child Development* 77(4):803–21.

Bryant D, Vizzard LH, Willoughby M, Kupersmidt J 1999 A review of interventions for preschoolers with aggressive and disruptive behavior. *Early Education and Development* 10(1):47–68.

Buckingham D 2000 *After the death of childhood: growing up in the age of electronic media*. Polity Press, Cambridge, UK.

Bugental DB, Happaney K 2004 Predicting infant maltreatment in low-income families: the interactive effects of maternal attributions and child status at birth. *Developmental Psychology* 40(2):234–43.

Buhs ES, Ladd GW 2001 Peer rejection as an antecedent of young children's social adjustment: an examination of mediating processes. *Developmental Psychology* 37(4):550–60.

Bukowski WM 2003 What does it mean to say that aggressive children are competent or incompetent? *Merrill-Palmer Quarterly* 49(3):390–400.

Burack JA, Flanagan T, Peled T, Sutton HM, Zygmuntowicz C, Manly JT 2006 Social perspective-taking skills in maltreated children and adolescents. *Developmental Psychology* 42(2):207–17.

Burchinal MR, Cryer D 2003 Diversity, child care quality, and developmental outcomes. *Early Childhood Research Quarterly* 18(4):401–26.

Burchinal MR, Howes C, Kontos S 2002 Structural predictors of child care quality in child care homes. *Early Childhood Research Quarterly* 17(1):87–105.

Burchinal MR, Roberts JE, Nabors LA, Bryant DM 1996 Quality of center child care and infant cognitive and language development. *Child Development* 67(2):606–20.

Burchinal MR, Roberts JE, Riggins R Jr, Zeisel SA, Neebe E, Bryant D 2000 Relating quality of center-based child care to early cognitive and language development longitudinally. *Child Development* 71(2):339–57.

Burgess KB, Wojslawowicz JC, Rubin KH, Rose-Krasnor L, Booth-LaForce C 2006 Social information processing and coping strategies of shy/withdrawn and aggressive children: does friendship matter? *Child Development* 77(2):371–83.

Burhans KK, Dweck CS 1995 Helplessness in early childhood: the role of contingent worth. *Child Development* 66(6):1719–38.

Burnip B 2002a Communication skills. In L Porter (ed.), *Educating young children with additional needs*. Allen & Unwin, Sydney, pp. 154–73

—— 2002b Communication skills. In L Porter (ed.), *Educating young children with special needs*. Paul Chapman, London; Sage, Thousand Oaks, CA, pp. 154–73.

Burnip L 2002a Hearing. In L Porter (ed.), *Educating young children with additional needs.* Allen & Unwin, Sydney, pp. 140–53.

—— 2002b Hearing. In L Porter (ed.), *Educating young children with special needs.* Paul Chapman, London; Sage, Thousand Oaks, CA, pp. 140–53.

Bussey K 1999 Children's categorization and evaluation of different types of lies and truths. *Child Development* 70(6):1338–47.

Butterworth D 1991 The challenge of day care: liberation or constraint? *Australian Journal of Early Childhood* 16(2):20–3.

Calkins SD, Johnson MC 1998 Toddler regulation of distress to frustrating events: temperamental and maternal correlates. *Infant Behavior and Development* 21(3):379–95.

Camodeca M, Goossens FA 2005 Aggression, social cognitions, anger and sadness in bullies and victims. *Journal of Child Psychology and Psychiatry* 46(2):186–97.

Campbell SB 1995 Behavior problems in preschool children: a review of recent research. *Journal of Child Psychology and Psychiatry* 36(1):113–49.

Campbell SB, Ewing LJ 1990 Follow-up of hard-to-manage preschoolers: adjustment at age 9 and predictors of continuing symptoms. *Journal of Child Psychology and Psychiatry* 31(6):871–89.

Campbell SB, March CL, Pierce EW, Ewing LJ, Szumowski EK 1991a Hard-to-manage preschool boys: family context and the stability of externalizing behavior. *Journal of Abnormal Child Psychology* 19(3):301–18.

Campbell SB, Pierce EW, March CL, Ewing LJ 1991b Noncompliant behavior, overactivity, and family stress as predictors of negative maternal control with preschool children. *Development and Psychopathology* 3:175–90.

Campbell SB, Shaw DS, Gilliom M 2000 Early externalizing behavior problems: toddlers and preschoolers at risk for later maladjustment. *Development and Psychopathology* 12(3):467–88.

Canter L, Canter M 2001 *Assertive discipline: positive behavior management for today's classroom.* Canter & Associates, Los Angeles, CA.

Caprara GV, Barbaranelli C, Steca P, Malone PS 2006 Teachers' self-efficacy beliefs as determinants of job satisfaction and students' academic achievement: a study at the school level. *Journal of School Psychology* 44(6):473–90.

Carey M 1999 Escaping the effects of violence: therapeutic gatherings with mothers and their children. In A Morgan (ed.), *Once upon a time … Narrative therapy with children and their families.* Dulwich Centre Publications, Adelaide, pp. 109–24.

Carey M, Russell S 2003 Re-authoring: some answers to commonly asked questions. *The International Journal of Narrative Therapy and Community Work* 3:60–71.

Carr EG 1997 Invited commentary: the evolution of applied behavior analysis into positive behavior support. *Journal of the Association for Persons with Severe Handicaps* 22(4):208–9.

Carrey NJ, Butter HJ, Persinger MA, Bialik RJ 1995 Physiological and cognitive correlates of child abuse. *Journal of the American Academy of Child and Adolescent Psychiatry* 34(8):1067–75.

Carson JL, Parke RD 1996 Reciprocal negative affect in parent–child interactions and children's peer competency. *Child Development* 67(5):2217–26.

Cartwright-Hatton S, Hodges L, Porter J 2003 Social anxiety in childhood: the relationship with self and observer rated social skills. *Journal of Child Psychology and Psychiatry* 44(5):737–42.

Caruso JJ 1991 Supervisors in early childhood programs: an emerging profile. *Young Children* 46(6):20–6.

Carver PR, Egan SK, Perry DG 2004 Children who question their heterosexuality. *Developmental Psychology* 40(1):43–53.

Casas JF, Weigel SM, Crick NR, Ostrov JM, Woods KE, Yeh EAJ, Huddleston-Casas CA 2006 Early parenting and children's relational and physical aggression in the preschool and home contexts. *Journal of Applied Developmental Psychology* 27(3):209–27.

Cassidy DJ, Hestenes LL, Hegde A, Hestenes S, Mims S 2005 Measurement of quality in preschool child care classrooms: an exploratory and confirmatory factor analysis of the early childhood environment rating scale—revised. *Early Childhood Research Quarterly* 20(3):345–60.

Castro CC, Bryant DM, Peisner-Feinberg ES, Skinner ML 2004 Parent involvement in Head Start programs: the role of parent, teacher and classroom characteristics. *Early Childhood Research Quarterly* 19(3):413–30.

Caughey C 1991 Becoming the child's ally—observations in a classroom for children who have been abused. *Young Children* 46(4):22–8.

Caulfield MB, Fischel JE, DeBaryshe BD, Whitehurst GJ 1989 Behavioral correlates of developmental expressive language disorder. *Journal of Abnormal Child Psychology* 17(2):187–201.

Chang L 2004 The role of classroom norms in contextualizing the relations of children's social behaviors to peer acceptance. *Developmental Psychology* 40(5):691–702.

Chapman JW, Lambourne R, Silva PA 1990 Some antecedents of academic self-concept: a longitudinal study. *British Journal of Educational Psychology* 60(1):142–52.

Charman T, Taylor E, Drew A, Cockerill H, Brown J-A, Baird G 2005 Outcome at 7 years of children diagnosed with autism at age 2: predictive validity of assessments conducted at 2 and 3 years of age and pattern of symptom change over time. *Journal of Child Psychology and Psychiatry* 46(95):500–13.

Chen X, Dong Q, Zhou H 1997 Authoritative and authoritarian parenting practices and social and school performance in Chinese children. *International Journal of Behavioral Development* 21(4):855–73.

Chen X, Li D, Li Z, Li B, Liu M 2000 Sociable and prosocial dimensions of social competence in Chinese children: common and unique contributions to social, academic, and psychological adjustment. *Developmental Psychology* 36(3):302–14.

Chew AL 1998 *A primer on Adlerian psychology: behavior management techniques for young children.* Humanics, Lake Worth, FL.

Chick KA, Heilman-Houser RA, Hunter MW 2002 The impact of child care on gender role development and gender stereotypes. *Early Childhood Education Journal* 29(3):149–54.

Christenson SL 2004 The family–school partnership: an opportunity to promote the learning competence of all students. *School Psychology Review* 33(1):83–104.

Cillessen AHN, Mayeux L 2004 From censure to reinforcement: developmental changes in the association between aggression and social status. *Child Development* 75(1):147–63.

Clark C, Prior M, Kinsella G 2002 The relationship between executive function abilities, adaptive behaviour, and academic achievement in children with externalizing behaviour problems. *Journal of Child Psychology and Psychiatry* 43(6):785–96.

Clark KE, Ladd GW 2000 Connectedness and autonomy support in parent–child relationships: links to children's socioemotional orientation and peer relationships. *Developmental Psychology* 36(4):485–98.

Clarke-Stewart A, Vandell DL, Burchinal M, O'Brien M, McCartney K 2002 Do regulable features of child-care homes affect children's development? *Early Childhood Research Quarterly* 17(1):52–86.

Clyde M 1988 Staff burnout—the ultimate reward? In A Stonehouse (ed.), *Trusting toddlers: programming for one to three year olds in child care centres.* Australian Early Childhood Association, Canberra, pp. 170–7.

Coie JD, Cillessen AHN, Dodge KA, Hubbard JA, Schwartz D, Lemerise EA, Bateman H 1999 It takes two to fight: a test of relational factors and a method for assessing aggressive dyads. *Developmental Psychology* 35(5):1179–88.

Colder CR, Lochman JE, Wells KC 1997 The moderating effects of children's fear and activity level on relations between parenting practices and childhood symptomatology. *Journal of Abnormal Child Psychology* 25(3):251–63.

Coldwell J, Pike A, Dunn J 2006 Household chaos—links with parenting and child behaviour. *Journal of Child Psychology and Psychiatry* 47(11):1116–22.

Cole DA, Maxwell SE, Martin JM, Peeke LG, Seroczynski AD, Tram JM, Hoffman KB, Ruiz MD, Jacquez F, Maschman T 2001 The development of multiple domains of child and adolescent self-concept: a cohort sequential longitudinal design. *Child Development* 72(6):1723–46.

Collins WA, Maccoby EE, Steinberg L, Hetherington EM, Bornstein MH 2000 Contemporary research on parenting: the case for nature *and* nurture. *American Psychologist* 55(2):218–32.

Compas BE 1987 Coping with stress during childhood and adolescence. *Psychological Bulletin* 101(3):393–403.

Conlon A 1992 Giving Mrs Jones a hand: making group storytime more pleasurable and meaningful for young children. *Young Children* 47(3):14–18.

Connell S, Sanders MR, Markie-Dadds C 1997 Self-directed behavioral family intervention for parents of oppositional children in rural and remote areas. *Behavior Modification* 21(4):379–408.

Conrad P 2006 *Identifying hyperactive children: the medicalization of deviant behavior*, expired edn. Ashgate, Aldershot, UK.

Coolahan K, McWayne C, Fantuzzo J, Grim S 2002 Validation of a multidimensional assessment of parenting styles for low-income African-American families with preschool children. *Early Childhood Research Quarterly* 17(3):356–73.

Cooney MH, Bittner MT 2001 Men in early childhood education: their emergent issues. *Early Childhood Education Journal* 29(2):77–82.

Coplan RJ, Gavinski-Molina M-H, Lagacé-Séguin DG, Wichmann C 2001 When girls versus boys play alone: nonsocial play and adjustment in kindergarten. *Developmental Psychology* 37(4):464–74.

Coplan RJ, Prakash K 2003 Spending time with teacher: characteristics of preschoolers who frequently elicit versus initiate interactions with teachers. *Early Childhood Research Quarterly* 18(1):143–58.

Coplan RJ, Prakash K, O'Neil K, Armer M 2004 Do you 'want' to play? Distinguishing between conflicted shyness and social disinterest in early childhood. *Developmental Psychology* 40(2):244–58.

Cordova DI, Lepper MR 1996 Intrinsic motivation and the process of learning: beneficial effects of contextualization, personalization, and choice. *Journal of Educational Psychology* 88(4):715–30.

Corey G 1996 *Theory and practice of counseling and psychotherapy*, 5th edn. Brooks/Cole, Monterey, CA.

Cornell DG, Delcourt MAB, Bland LC, Goldberg MD, Oram G 1994 Low incidence of behavior problems among elementary school students in gifted programs. *Journal for the Education of the Gifted* 18(1):4–19.

Cornish AM, McMahon CA, Ungerer JA, Barnett B, Kowalenko N, Tennant C 2005 Postnatal depression and infant cognitive and motor development in the second postnatal year: the impact of depression chronicity and infant gender. *Infant Behavior and Development* 28(4):407–17.

Côté SM, Vaillancourt T, LeBlanc JC, Nagin DS, Tremblay RE 2006 The development of physical aggression from toddlerhood to pre-adolescence: a nation wide longitudinal study of Canadian children. *Journal of Abnormal Child Psychology* 34(1):68–82.

Covaleskie JF 1992 Discipline and morality: beyond rules and consequences. *The Educational Forum* 56(2):173–83.

Covington MV, Müeller KJ 2001 Intrinsic versus extrinsic motivation: an approach/avoidance reformulation. *Educational Psychology Review* 13(2):157–76.

Cowin M, Freeman L, Farmer A, James M, Drent A, Arthur R 1990 *Positive school discipline: a practical guide to developing policy*, revised edn. Narbethong Publications, Melbourne.

Crary E 1992 Talking about differences children notice. In B Neugebauer (ed.), *Alike and different: exploring our humanity with young children*, revised edn. National Association for the Education of Young Children, Washington, DC, pp. 11–15.

Crick NR, Casas JF, Ku H-C 1999 Relational and physical forms of peer victimization in preschool. *Developmental Psychology* 35(2):376–85.

Crick NR, Grotpeter JK, Bigbee MA 2002 Relationally and physically aggressive children's intent attributions and feelings of distress for relational and instrumental peer provocations. *Child Development* 73(4):1134–42.

Crick NR, Nelson DA, Morales JR, Cullerton-Sen C, Casas JF, Hickman SE 2001 Relational victimization in childhood and adolescence: I hurt you through the grapevine. In J Juvonen and S Graham (eds), *Peer harassment in school: the plight of the vulnerable and victimized*. Guilford, New York, pp. 196–214.

Criss MM, Pettit GS, Bates JE, Dodge KA, Lapp AL 2002 Family adversity, positive peer relationships, and children's externalizing behavior: a longitudinal perspective on risk and resilience. *Child Development* 73(4):1220–37.

Crockenberg S, Litman C 1990 Autonomy as competence in 2-year-olds: maternal correlates of child defiance, compliance, and self-assertion. *Developmental Psychology* 26(6):961–71.

Cryer D, Burchinal M 1997 Parents as child care consumers. *Early Childhood Research Quarterly* 12(1):35–58.

Cryer D, Hurwitz S, Wolery M 2000 Continuity of caregiver for infants and toddlers in center-based child care: report on a survey of center practices. *Early Childhood Research Quarterly* 15(4):497–514.

Cryer D, Tietze W, Burchinal M, Leal T, Palacios J 1999 Predicting process quality from structural quality in preschool programs: a cross-country comparison. *Early Childhood Research Quarterly* 14(3):339–61.

Cryer D, Tietze W, Wessels H 2002 Parents' perceptions of their children's child care: a cross-national comparison. *Early Childhood Research Quarterly* 17(2):259–77.

Cryer D, Wagner-Moore L, Burchinal M, Yazejian N, Hurwitz S, Wolery M 2005 Effects of transitions to new child care classes on infant/toddler distress and behavior. *Early Childhood Research Quarterly* 20(1):37–56.

Cumine V, Leach J, Stevenson G 1998 *Asperger syndrome: a practical guide for teachers*. David Fulton, London.

Cummings EM 1998 Stress and coping approaches and research: the impact of marital conflict on children. In BBR Rossman and MS Rosenberg (eds), *Multiple victimization of children: conceptual, developmental, research, and treatment issues*. Haworth Press, London, pp. 31–50.

Cummings EM, Goeke-Morey MC, Papp LM 2003 Children's responses to everyday marital conflict tactics in the home. *Child Development* 74(6):1918–29.

Cummings EM, Schermerhorn AC, Davies PT, Goeke-Morey MC, Cummings JS 2006 Interparental discord and child adjustment: prospective investigations of emotional security as an explanatory mechanism. *Child Development* 77(1):132–52.

Cunningham CE, McHolm A, Boyle MH, Patel S 2004 Behavioral and emotional adjustment, family functioning, academic performance, and social relationship in children with selective mutism. *Journal of Child Psychology and Psychiatry* 45(8):1363–72.

Cupit CG 1989 *Socialising the superheroes*. Australian Early Childhood Association, Canberra.

Curbow B, Spratt K, Ungaretti A, McDonnell K, Breckler S 2000 Development of the child care worker job stress inventory. *Early Childhood Research Quarterly* 15(4):515–36.

Curry NE, Johnson CN 1990 *Beyond self-esteem: developing a genuine sense of human value*. National Association for the Education of Young Children, Washington, DC.

Dahlberg G, Moss P, Pence A 1999 *Beyond quality in early childhood education and care: postmodern perspectives*. Routledge Falmer, London.

Dallaire DH, Weinraub M 2005 The stability of parenting behaviors over the first 6 years of life. *Early Childhood Research Quarterly* 20(2):201–19.

Davidov M, Grusec JE 2006 Untangling the links of parental responsiveness to distress and warmth to child outcomes. *Child Development* 77(1):44–58.

Davis GA, Rimm SB 2004 *Education of the gifted and talented*, 5th edn. Pearson Allyn & Bacon, Boston, MA.

Davis TE, Osborn CJ 2000 *The solution-focused school counselor: shaping professional practice*. Brunner-Routledge, New York.

Dawkins M 1991 Hey dudes, what's the rap? A plea for leniency towards superhero play. *Australian Journal of Early Childhood* 16(2):3–8.

de Castro BO, Veerman JW, Koops W, Bosch JD, Monshouwer HJ 2002 Hostile attribution of intent and aggressive behavior: a meta-analysis. *Child Development* 73(3):916–34.

De Jong P, Berg IK 2002 *Interviewing for solutions*, 2nd edn. Brooks/Cole Thomson, Pacific Grove, CA.

de Kruif REL, McWilliam RA, Ridley SM, Wakely MB 2000 Classification of teachers' interaction behaviors in early childhood classrooms. *Early Childhood Research Quarterly* 15(2):247–68.

De Schipper JC, Tavecchio LWC, van Ijzendoorn MH, Van Zeijl J 2004 Goodness-of-fit in center day care: relations of temperament, stability, and quality of care with the child's adjustment. *Early Childhood Research Quarterly* 19(4):257–72.

de Shazer S 1988 *Clues: investigating solutions in brief therapy*. Norton, New York.

—— 1993 Creative misunderstanding: there is no escape from language. In S Gilligan and R Price (eds), *Therapeutic conversations*. WW Norton, New York, pp. 81–135.

de Shazer S, Berg IK, Lipchik E, Nunnally E, Molnar A, Gingerich W, Weiner-Davis M 1986 Brief therapy: focused solution development. *Family Process* 25(2):207–22.

de Wied M, Goudena PP, Matthys W 2005 Empathy in boys with disruptive behavior disorders. *Journal of Child Psychology and Psychiatry* 46(8):867–80.

Dearing E 2004 The developmental implications of restrictive and supportive parenting across neighborhoods and ethnicities: exceptions are the rule. *Journal of Applied Developmental Psychology* 25(5):555–75.

Dearing E, McCartney K, Taylor BA 2006 Within-child associations between family income and externalizing and internalizing problems. *Developmental Psychology* 42(2):237–52.

Deater-Deckard K 2001 Annotation: recent research examining the role of peer relationships in the development of psychopathology. *Journal of Child Psychology and Psychiatry* 42(5):565–79.

Deater-Deckard K, Dodge KA 1997 Externalizing behavior problems and discipline revisited: nonlinear effects and variation by culture, context, and gender. *Psychological Inquiry* 8(3):161–75.

Deci EL, Driver RE, Hotchkiss L, Robbins RJ, Wilson IM 1993 The relations of mothers' controlling vocalizations to children's intrinsic motivation. *Journal of Experimental Child Psychology* 55(2):151–62.

Deci EL, Eghrari H, Patrick BC, Leone DR 1994 Facilitating internalization: the self-determination theory perspective. *Journal of Personality* 62:119–42.

Deci EL, Koestner R, Ryan RM 1999 A meta-analytic review of experiments examining the effects of extrinsic rewards on intrinsic motivation. *Psychological Bulletin* 125(6):627–68.

—— 2001 Extrinsic rewards and intrinsic motivation in education: reconsidered once again. *Review of Educational Research* 71(1):1–27.

Deci EL, Ryan RM 2000 The 'what' and 'why' of goal pursuits: human needs and the self-determination of behavior. *Psychological Inquiry* 11(4):227–68.

Deci EL, Vallerand RJ, Pelletier LG, Ryan RM 1991 Motivation and education: the self-determination perspective. *Educational Psychologist* 26(3, 4):325–46.

Decker DM, Dona DP, Christenson SL 2007 Behaviorally at-risk African American students: the importance of student–teacher relationships for student outcomes. *Journal of School Psychology* 45(1):83–109.

Dekovic M, Janssens JMAM, Van As NMC 2003 Family predictors of antisocial behavior in adolescence. *Family Process* 42(2):223–35.

DeMeis JL, Stearns ES 1992 Relationship of school entrance age to academic and social performance. *Journal of Educational Research* 86(1):20–7.

DeMulder EK, Denham S, Schmidt M, Mitchell J 2000 Q-sort assessment of attachment security during the preschool years: links from home to school. *Developmental Psychology* 36(2):274–82.

Dengate S 1997 Dietary management of attention deficit disorder. *Australian Journal of Early Childhood* 22(4):29–33.

—— 2004 *Fed up with ADHD*. Random House, Sydney.

Denham SA, Blair KA, DeMulder E, Levitas J, Sawyer K, Auerbach-Major S, Queenan P 2003 Preschool emotional competence: pathway to social competence? *Child Development* 74(1):238–56.

Denham SA, Caverly S, Schmidt M, Blair K, DeMulder E, Caal S, Hamada H, Mason T 2002 Preschool understanding of emotions: contributions to classroom anger and aggression. *Journal of Child Psychology and Psychiatry* 43(7):901–16.

Denham SA, Workman E, Cole PM, Weissbrod C, Kendziora KT, Zahn-Waxler C 2000 Prediction of externalizing behavior problems from early to middle childhood: the role of parental socialization and emotion expression. *Development and Psychopathology* 12(1):23–45.

DesRosiers F, Vrsalovic WT, Knauf DE, Vargas M, Busch-Rossnagel NA 1999 Assessing the multiple dimensions of the self-concept of young children: a focus on Latinos. *Merrill-Palmer Quarterly* 45(4):543–66.

Devore S, Hanley-Maxwell C 2000 'I wanted to see if we could make it work': perspectives on inclusive childcare. *Exceptional Children* 66(2):241–55.

Deynoot-Schaub MG, Riksen-Walraven JM 2006 Peer interaction in child care centres at 15 and 23 months: stability and links with children's socio-emotional adjustment. *Infant Behavior and Development* 29(2):276–88.

Diaz RM, Berk LE 1995 A Vygotskian critique of self-instructional training. *Development and Psychopathology* 7(2):369–92.

DiCintio MJ, Gee S 1999 Control is the key: unlocking the motivation of at-risk students. *Psychology in the Schools* 36(3):231–7.

Diego MA, Field T, Hernandez-Reif M 2005 Prepartum, postpartum and chronic depression effects on neonatal behavior. *Infant Behavior and Development* 28(2):155–64.

Diener ML, Mangelsdorf SC 1999 Behavioral strategies for emotion regulation in toddlers: associations with maternal involvement and emotional expressions. *Infant Behavior and Development* 22(4):569–83.

Diener ML, Nievar MA, Wright C 2003 Attachment security among mothers and their young children living in poverty: associations with maternal, child, and contextual factors. *Merrill-Palmer Quarterly* 49(2):154–82.

Dinkmeyer D, Dreikurs R 1963 *Encouraging children to learn: the encouragement process*. Prentice Hall, Englewood Cliffs, NJ.

Dinkmeyer D, McKay G 1989 *Systematic training for effective parenting*, 3rd edn. American Guidance Service, Circle Pines, MN.

Dinkmeyer D, McKay G, Dinkmeyer D 1980 *Systematic training for effective teaching*. American Guidance Service, Circle Pines, MN.

Dinkmeyer D Sr, McKay GD, Dinkmeyer JS, Dinkmeyer D Jr, McKay JL 1997 *Parenting young children: systematic training for effective parenting (STEP) of children under six.* American Guidance Service, Circle Pines, MN.

Dionne G, Tremblay R, Boivin M, Laplante D, Pérusse D 2003 Physical aggression and expressive vocabulary in 19-month-old twins. *Developmental Psychology* 39(2):261–73.

Dissanayake C 2004 Change in behavioural symptoms in children with high-functioning autism and Asperger syndrome: evidence of one disorder? *Australian Journal of Early Childhood* 29(3):48–57.

Dixon L, Browne K, Hamilton-Giachritsis C 2005a Risk factors of parents abused as children: a mediational analysis of the intergenerational continuity of child maltreatment (Part I). *Journal of Child Psychology and Psychiatry* 46(1):47–57.

Dixon L, Hamilton-Giachritsis C, Browne K 2005b Attributions and behaviours of parents abused as children: a mediational analysis of the intergenerational continuity of child maltreatment (Part II). *Journal of Child Psychology and Psychiatry* 46(1):58–68.

Dockett S 2004 'Everyone was really happy to see me': the importance of friendships in the return to school of children with chronic illness. *Australian Journal of Early Childhood* 29(1):27–32.

Doctoroff GL, Greer JA, Arnold DH 2006 The relationship between social behavior and emergent literacy among preschool boys and girls. *Journal of Applied Developmental Psychology* 27(1):1–13.

Doctoroff S 2001 Adapting the physical environment to meet the needs of *all* young children for play. *Early Childhood Education Journal* 29(2):105–9.

Dodge KA 1983 Behavioral antecedents of peer social status. *Child Development* 54:1386–99.

Dodge KA, Lansford JE, Burks VS, Bates JE, Pettit GS, Fontaine R, Price JM 2003 Peer rejection and social information-processing factors in the development of aggressive behavior problems in children. *Child Development* 74(2):374–93.

Doherty-Derkowski G 1995 *Quality matters: excellence in early childhood programs.* Addison-Wesley, Don Mills, Ontario.

Domitrovich CE, Bierman KL 2001 Parenting practices and child social adjustment: multiple pathways of influence. *Merrill-Palmer Quarterly* 47(2):235–63.

Donohue KM, Perry KE, Weinstein RS 2003 Teachers' classroom practices and children's rejection by their peers. *Journal of Applied Developmental Psychology* 24(1):91–118.

Donovan WL, Leavitt LA, Walsh RO 2000 Maternal illusory control predicts socialization strategies and toddler compliance. *Developmental Psychology* 36(3):402–11.

Dornbusch SM, Ritter PL, Liederman PH, Roberts DF, Fraleigh MJ 1987 The relation of parenting style to adolescent school performance. *Child Development* 58(5):1244–57.

Dowling M 2005 *Young children's personal, social and emotional development,* 2nd edn. Paul Chapman, London.

Doyle W 1986 Classroom organization and management. In MC Wittrock (ed.), *Handbook of research on teaching,* 3rd edn. Macmillan, New York, pp. 392–431.

Dreikurs R, Cassel P 1990 *Discipline without tears,* 2nd edn. Dutton, New York.

Drifte C 2004 *Encouraging positive behaviour in the early years: a practical guide.* Paul Chapman, London.

Dummit ES III, Klein RG, Tancer NK, Asche B, Martin J, Fairbanks JA 1997 Systematic assessment of 50 children with selective mutism. *Journal of the American Academy of Child and Adolescent Psychiatry* 36(5):653–60.

Dunlap G, dePerczel M, Clarke S, Wilson D, Wrights S, White R, Gomez A 1994 Choice making to promote adaptive behavior for students with emotional and behavioral challenges. *Journal of Applied Behavior Analysis* 27(3):505–18.

Durrant M 1995 *Creative strategies for school problems.* Eastwood Family Therapy Centre, Sydney; Norton, New York.

Dweck CS, Leggett EL 1988 A social-cognitive approach to motivation and personality. *Psychological Review* 95(2):256–73.

Dykman BM 1998 Integrating cognitive and motivational factors in depression: initial tests of a goal-orientation approach. *Journal of Personality and Social Psychology* 74(1):139–58.

Dyson LL 2005 Kindergarten children's understanding of and attitudes toward people with disabilities. *Topics in Early Childhood Special Education* 25(2):95–105.

Eamon MK 2001 Antecedents and socioemotional consequences of physical punishment on children in two-parent families. *Child Abuse and Neglect* 6(6):787–802.

Early Childhood Australia 2006 *Early Childhood Australia's code of ethics.* Early Childhood Australia, Canberra.

Early DM, Burchinal MR 2001 Early childhood care: relations with family characteristics and preferred care characteristics. *Early Childhood Research Quarterly* 16(4):475–97.

Ebbeck M, Waniganayake M 2003 *Early childhood professionals: leading today and tomorrow.* MacLennan & Petty, Sydney.

Egan SK, Monson TC, Perry DG 1998 Social-cognitive influences on change in aggression over time. *Developmental Psychology* 34(5):996–1006.

Egan SK, Perry DG 1998 Does low self-regard invite victimization? *Developmental Psychology* 34(2):299–309.

—— 2001 Gender identity: a multidimensional analysis with implications for psychosocial adjustment. *Developmental Psychology* 37(4):451–63.

Eisenberg N, Champion C, Ma Y 2004a Emotion-related regulation: an emerging construct. *Merrill-Palmer Quarterly* 50(3):236–59.

Eisenberg N, Cumberland A, Spinrad TL, Fabes RA, Shepard SA, Reiser M, Murphy BC, Losoya SH, Guthrie IK 2001 The relations of regulation and emotionality to children's externalizing and internalizing problem behavior. *Child Development* 72(4):1112–34.

Eisenberg N, Fabes RA, Shepard SA, Guthrie IK, Murphy BC, Reiser M 1999 Parental reactions to children's negative emotions: longitudinal relations to quality of children's social functioning. *Child Development* 70(2):513–34.

Eisenberg N, Guthrie IK, Fabes RA, Shepard SA, Losoya S, Murphy BC, Jones S, Poulin R, Reiser M 2000 Prediction of elementary school children's externalizing problem behaviors from attentional and behavioral regulation and negative emotionality. *Child Development* 71(5):1367–82.

Eisenberg N, Sadovsky A, Spinrad TL, Fabes RA, Losoya SH, Valiente C, Reiser M, Cumberland A, Shepard SA 2005 The relations of problem behavior status to children's negative emotionality, effortful control, and impulsivity: concurrent relations and prediction of change. *Developmental Psychology* 41(1):193–211.

Eisenberg N, Spinrad TL, Fabes RA, Reiser M, Cumberland A, Shepard SA, Valiente C, Losoya SH, Guthrie IK, Thompson M 2004b The relations of effortful control and impulsivity to children's resiliency and adjustment. *Child Development* 75(1):25–46.

Eisenberg N, Valiente C, Fabes RA, Smith CL, Reiser M, Shepard SA, Losoya SH, Guthrie IK, Murphy BC, Cumberland A 2003 The relations of effortful control and ego control to children's resiliency and social functioning. *Developmental Psychology* 39(4):761–76.

El-Sheikh M, Buckhalt J, Mize J, Acebo C 2006 Marital conflict and disruption of children's sleep. *Child Development* 77(1):31–43.

El-Sheikh M, Harger J 2001 Appraisals of marital conflict and children's adjustment, health, and physiological reactivity. *Developmental Psychology* 37(6):875–85.

Elkind D 2001 *The hurried child: growing up too fast too soon*, 3rd edn. Perseus Books, Cambridge, MA.

Elliott ES, Dweck CS 1988 Goals: an approach to motivation and achievement. *Journal of Personality and Social Psychology* 54(1):5–12.

Ellis A 1962 *Reason and emotion in psychotherapy.* Lyle Stuart, Secaucus, NJ.

—— 2005 Rational emotive behavior therapy. In RJ Corsini and D Wedding (eds), *Current psychotherapies*, 7th edn. Thomson Brooks/Cole, Belmont, CA, pp. 166–201.

Elswood R 1999 Really including diversity in early childhood classrooms. *Young Children* 54(4):62–6.

Ervin RA, Radford PM, Bertsch K, Piper AL, Ehrhardt KE, Poling A 2001 A descriptive analysis and critique of the empirical literature on school-based functional assessment. *School Psychology Review* 30(2):193–210.

Eslea M 1999 Attributional styles in boys with severe behaviour problems: a possible reason for lack of progress on a positive behaviour programme. *British Journal of Educational Psychology* 69(1):33–45.

Essa EL, Murray CI 1999 Sexual play: when should you be concerned? *Childhood Education* 75(4):231–4.

Evans GW, English K 2002 The environment of poverty: multiple stressor exposure, psychophysiological stress, and socioemotional adjustment. *Child Development* 73(4):1238–48.

Faber A, Mazlish E, Nyberg L, Templeton RA 1995 *How to talk so kids can learn at home and in school*. Fireside, New York.

Fabes RA, Eisenberg N, Jones S, Smith M, Guthrie I, Poulin R, Shepard S, Friedman J 1999 Regulation, emotionality, and preschoolers' socially competent peer interactions. *Child Development* 70(2):432–42.

Fabes RA, Hanish LD, Martin CL, Eisenberg N 2002 Young children's negative emotionality and social isolation: a latent growth curve analysis. *Merrill-Palmer Quarterly* 48(3):284–307.

Fabes RA, Leonard SA, Kupanoff K, Martin CL 2001 Parental coping with children's negative emotions: relations with children's emotional and social responding. *Child Development* 72(3):907–20.

Fabes RA, Martin CL, Hanish LD 2003 Young children's play qualities in same-, other-, and mixed-sex peer groups. *Child Development* 74(3):921–32.

—— 2004 The next 50 years: considering gender as a context for understanding young children's peer relationships. *Merrill-Palmer Quarterly* 50(3):260–73.

Farmer S 1995 *Policy development in early childhood services*. Community Child Care Cooperative Ltd, Sydney.

Farmer TW, Estell DB, Bishop JL, O'Neal KK, Cairns BD 2003 Rejected bullies or popular leaders? The social relations of aggressive subtypes of rural African American early adolescents. *Developmental Psychology* 39(6):992–1004.

Farquhar S-E 1999 Men in early childhood teaching. *New Zealand Council for Educational Research Early Childhood Folio* 4:29–32.

Farver JM 1996 Aggressive behavior in preschoolers' social networks: do birds of a feather flock together? *Early Childhood Research Quarterly* 11(3):333–50.

Feagans LV, Kipp E, Blood I 1994 The effects of otitis media on the attention skills of day-care-attending toddlers. *Developmental Psychology* 30(5):701–8.

Feiring C, Taska L, Lewis M 2002 Adjustment following sexual abuse discovery: the role of shame and attributional style. *Developmental Psychology* 38(1):79–92.

Feldhusen JF 1989 Synthesis of research on gifted youths. *Educational Leadership* 46(6):6–11.

Feldman R, Klein PS 2003 Toddlers' self-regulated compliance to mothers, caregivers, and fathers: implications for theories of socialization. *Developmental Psychology* 39(4):680–92.

Fergusson DM, Horwood LJ, Ridder EM 2005 Show me the child at seven: the consequences of conduct problems in childhood for psychosocial functioning in adulthood. *Journal of Child Psychology and Psychiatry* 46(8):837–49.

Fergusson DM, Lynskey MT 1997 Physical punishment/maltreatment during childhood and adjustment in young adulthood. *Child Abuse and Neglect* 21(7):617–30.

Field T 1991 Quality infant day-care and grade school behavior and performance. *Child Development* 62(4):863–70.

Field T, Diego MA, Dieter J, Hernandez-Reif M, Schanberg S, Kuhn C, Yando R, Bendell D 2001 Depressed withdrawn and intrusive mothers' effects on their fetuses and neonates. *Infant Behavior and Development* 24(1):27–39.

—— 2004 Prenatal depression effects on the fetus and the newborn. *Infant Behavior and Development* 27(2):216–29.

Field T, Diego M, Hernandez-Reif M, Schanberg S, Kuhn C 2003 Depressed mothers who are 'good interaction' partners versus those who are withdrawn or intrusive. *Infant Behavior and Development* 26(2):238–52.

Field T, Masi W, Goldstein S, Perry S, Parl S 1988 Infant day care facilitates preschool social behavior. *Early Childhood Research Quarterly* 3(4):341–59.

Fields M, Boesser C 2002 *Constructive guidance and discipline*, 3rd edn. Merrill Prentice Hall, Upper Saddle River, NJ.

Findlay LC, Girardi A, Coplan RJ 2006 Links between empathy, social behavior, and social understanding in early childhood. *Early Childhood Research Quarterly* 21(3):347–59.

Fisch R, Weakland JH, Segal L 1982 *The tactics of change: doing therapy briefly*. Jossey Bass, San Francisco, CA.

Fischer M, Barkley RA, Edelbrock CS, Smallish L 1990 The adolescent outcome of hyperactive children diagnosed by research criteria: II. Academic, attentional and neurological status. *Journal of Consulting and Clinical Psychology* 58(5):580–8.

Fischer M, Barkley RA, Fletcher KE, Smallish L 1993 The adolescent outcome of hyperactive children: predictors of psychiatric, academic, social and emotional adjustment. *Journal of the American Academy of Child and Adolescent Psychiatry* 32(2):324–32.

Fleer M 1998 'Me not a boy, me a person!' Deconstructing gendered interactional patterns in early childhood. *Australian Journal of Early Childhood* 23(1):22–8.

Fleet A, Clyde M 1993 *What's in a day? Working in early childhood*. Social Science Press, Wentworth Falls.

Flook L, Repetti RL, Ullman JB 2005 Classroom social experiences as predictors of academic performance. *Developmental Psychology* 41(2):319–27.

Flores E, Cicchetti D, Rogosch FA 2005 Predictors of resilience in maltreated and nonmaltreated Latino children. *Developmental Psychology* 41(2):338–51.

Ford MA, Sladeczek IE, Carlson J, Kratochwill TR 1998 Selective mutism: phenomenological characteristics. *School Psychology Quarterly* 13(3):192–227.

Forgatch MS, DeGarmo DS 1999 Parenting through change: an effective prevention program for single mothers. *Journal of Consulting and Clinical Psychology* 67(5):711–24.

Fowler SA, Schwartz I, Atwater J 1991 Perspectives on the transition from preschool to kindergarten for children with disabilities and their families. *Exceptional Children* 58(2):136–45.

Fox AM, Rieder MJ 1993 Risks and benefits of drugs used in the management of the hyperactive child. *Drug Safety* 9(1):38–50.

Frankel F, Myatt R 1996 Self-esteem, social competence and psychopathology in boys without friends. *Personality and Individual Differences* 20(3):401–7.

Fraser S, Gestwicki C 2002 *Authentic childhood: exploring Reggio Emilia in the classroom*. Delmar, Albany, NY.

Freeman J, Epston D, Lobovits D 1997 *Playful approaches to serious problems: narrative therapy with children and their families*. Norton, New York.

Frias-Armenta M 2002 Long-term effects of child punishment on Mexican women: a structural model. *Child Abuse and Neglect* 26(4):371–86.

Frick PJ, Cornell AH, Bodin SD, Dane HE, Barry CT, Loney BR 2003 Callous-unemotional traits and developmental pathways to severe conduct problems. *Developmental Psychology* 39(2):246–60.

Friedman IA 2003 Self-efficacy and burnout in teaching: the importance of interpersonal-relations efficacy. *Social Psychology of Education* 6(3):191–215.

Friend KB, Goodwin MS, Lipsitt LP 2004 Alcohol use and sudden infant death syndrome. *Developmental Review* 24(3):235–51.

Friend M, Cook L 2007 *Interactions: collaboration skills for school professionals*, 5th edn. Pearson Allyn & Bacon, Boston, MA.

Frith U 2004 Emanuel Miller lecture: confusions and controversies about Asperger syndrome. *Journal of Child Psychology and Psychiatry* 45(4):672–86.

Furrer C, Skinner E 2003 Sense of relatedness as a factor in children's academic engagement and performance. *Journal of Educational Psychology* 95(1):148–62.

Fylling I, Sandvin JT 1999 The role of parents in special education: the notion of partnership revised. *European Journal of Special Needs Education* 14(2):144–57.

Gagné F 2003 Transforming gifts into talents: the DMGT as a developmental theory. In N Colangelo and GA Davis (eds), *Handbook of gifted education*, 3rd edn. Allyn & Bacon, Boston, MA, pp. 60–74.

Galanaki E 2005 Solitude in the school: a neglected facet of children's development and education. *Childhood Education* 81(3):128–32.

Galinsky E 1989 A parent/teacher study: interesting results. *Young Children* 45(1):2–3.

—— 1990 Why are some parent/teacher partnerships clouded with difficulties? *Young Children* 45(5):2–3; 38–9.

Gallucci NT 1988 Emotional adjustment of gifted children. *Gifted Child Quarterly* 32(2):273–6.

Gamman R 2003 Sharing the load, supporting the staff: collaborative management of difficult behaviour in primary schools. *Emotional and Behavioural Difficulties* 8(3):217–29.

Gartrell D 1998 *A guidance approach for the encouraging classroom*. Delmar, New York.

—— 2003 *A guidance approach for the encouraging classroom*, 3rd edn. Delmar, New York.

Gartstein MA, Fagot BI 2003 Parental depression, parenting and family adjustment, and child effortful control: explaining externalizing behaviors for preschool children. *Journal of Applied Developmental Psychology* 24(2):143–77.

Gazelle H, Ladd GW 2003 Anxious solitude and peer exclusion: a diathesis-stress model of internalizing trajectories in childhood. *Child Development* 74(1):257–78.

Geary DC, Byrd-Craven J, Hoard MK, Vigil J, Numtee C 2003 Evolution and development of boys' social behavior. *Developmental Review* 23(4):444–70.

George C, Main M 1979 Social interactions of young abused children: approach, avoidance, and aggression. *Child Development* 50(2):306–18.

Gershoff ET 2002a Corporal punishment by parents and associated child behaviors and experiences: a meta-analytic and theoretical review. *Psychological Bulletin* 128(4):539–79.

—— 2002b Corporal punishment, physical abuse, and the burden of proof: reply to Baumrind, Larzelere, and Cowan (2002); Holden (2002); and Parke (2002). *Psychological Bulletin* 128(4):602–11.

Gest SD, Freeman NR, Domitrovich CE, Welsh JA 2004 Shared book reading and children's language comprehension skills: the moderating role of parental discipline practices. *Early Childhood Research Quarterly* 19(2):319–36.

Ghazvini AS, Readdick CA 1994 Parent–caregiver communication and quality of care in diverse child care settings. *Early Childhood Research Quarterly* 9(2):207–22.

Gilbert S 2000 *A field guide to boys and girls*. Quill, New York.

Gillberg C 2002 *A guide to Asperger syndrome*. Cambridge University Press, Cambridge, UK.

Gilliam WS, Zigler EF 2000 A critical meta-analysis of all evaluations of state-funded preschool from 1977 to 1998: implications for policy, service delivery and program evaluation. *Early Childhood Research Quarterly* 15(4):441–73.

Gilliom M, Shaw DS, Beck JE, Schonberg MA, Lukon JL 2002 Anger regulation in disadvantaged preschool boys: strategies, antecedents, and the development of self-control. *Developmental Psychology* 38(2):222–35.

Ginott HG 1972 *Teacher and child*. Macmillan, New York.

Ginott HG, Ginott A, Goddard HW 2003 *Between parent and child*, 2nd edn. Three Rivers Press, New York.

Ginsberg GS, Bronstein P 1993 Family factors related to children's intrinsic/extrinsic motivational orientation and academic performance. *Child Development* 64(5):1461–74.

Glanzman M, Blum N 2007 Attention deficits and hyperactivity. In ML Batshaw, L Pellegrino, NJ Roizen (eds.), *Children with disabilities*, 6th edn. Elsevier, Sydney; Brookes, Baltimore, MD, pp. 349–69.

Glaser D 2000 Child abuse and neglect and the brain: a review. *Journal of Child Psychology and Psychiatry* 41(1):97–116.

Glasser W 1988 *Choice theory in the classroom*, revised edn. HarperCollins, New York.

Gmitrova V, Gmitrov J 2003 The impact of teacher-directed and child-directed pretend play on cognitive competence in kindergarten children. *Early Childhood Education Journal* 30(4):241–6.

Goldstein M, Goldstein S 1995 Medications and behavior in the classroom. In S Goldstein (ed.), *Understanding and managing children's classroom behavior*. John Wiley & Sons, New York, pp. 181–219.

Goldstein S 1995 Attention deficit hyperactivity disorder. In S Goldstein (ed.), *Understanding and managing children's classroom behavior*. John Wiley & Sons, New York, pp. 56–78.

Goleman D 1995 *Emotional intelligence*. Bantam Books, New York.

Golombok S, Perry B, Burston A, Murray C, Mooney-Somers J, Stevens M, Golding J 2003 Children with lesbian parents: a community study. *Developmental Psychology* 39(1):20–33.

Gonzalez JE, Nelson JR, Gutkin TB, Saunders A, Galloway A, Shwery CS 2004 Rational emotive therapy with children and adolescents: a meta-analysis. *Journal of Emotional and Behavioral Disorders* 12(4):222–35.

Gonzalez-DeHass AR, Willems PP, Holbein MFD 2005 Examining the relationship between parental involvement and student motivation. *Educational Psychology Review* 17(2):99–123.

Goodnow JJ 1989 Setting priorities for research on group care of children. *Australian Journal of Early Childhood* 14(1):4–10.

Goodwin RD, Fergusson DM, Horwood LJ 2004 Early anxious/withdrawn behaviours predict later internalising disorders. *Journal of Child Psychology and Psychiatry* 45(4):874–83.

Gordon T 1970 *Parent effectiveness training*. Plume, New York.

—— 1974 *Teacher effectiveness training*. Peter H Wyden, New York.

—— 1991 *Teaching children self-discipline at home and at school*. Random House, Sydney.

Gormley WT Jr, Gayer T, Phillips D, Dawson B 2005 The effects of universal pre-K on cognitive development. *Developmental Psychology* 41(6):872–84.

Gottfried AE, Fleming JS, Gottfried AW 1994 Role of parental motivational practices in children's academic intrinsic motivation and achievement. *Journal of Educational Psychology* 86(1):104–13.

Gotts EE 1988 The right to quality child care. *Childhood Education* 64(5):268–75.

Gowen JW, Nebrig JB 2002 *Enhancing early emotional development: guiding parents of young children*. Paul H Brookes, Baltimore, MD.

Gray MR, Steinberg L 1999 Unpacking authoritative parenting: reassessing a multidimensional construct. *Journal of Marriage and the Family* 61(3):574–87.

Graziano PA, Reavis RD, Keane SP, Calkins SD 2007 The role of emotion regulation in children's early academic success. *Journal of School Psychology* 45(1):3–19.

Greco LA, Morris TL 2001 Treating childhood shyness and related behavior: empirically evaluated approaches to promote positive social interactions. *Clinical Child and Family Psychology Review* 4(4):299–318.

Green C, Chee K 2001 *Understanding ADHD: attention-deficit hyperactivity disorder in children*, 3rd edn. Doubleday, Sydney.

Green VA, Rechis R 2006 Children's competitive and cooperative interactions in limited resource situations: a literature review. *Journal of Applied Developmental Psychology* 27(1):42–59.

Greenberg P 1992 Why not academic preschool? Part 2: autocracy or democracy in the classroom? *Young Children* 47(3):54–64.

Greene RW, Biederman J, Faraone SV, Sienna M, Garcia-Jetton J 1997 Adolescent outcome of boys with attention-deficit/hyperactivity disorder and social disability: results from a 4-year longitudinal follow-up. *Journal of Consulting and Clinical Psychology* 65(5):758–67.

Greenman J, Stonehouse A 2007 *Prime times: a handbook for excellence in infant and toddler programs*, 2nd edn. Redleaf Press, St Paul, MN.

Grille R 2005 *Parenting for a peaceful world*. Longueville Media, Sydney.

Grolnick WS 2003 *The psychology of parental control: how well-meant parenting backfires*. Lawrence Erlbaum, Mahwah, NJ.

Grolnick WS, Benjet C, Kurowski CO, Apostoleris NH 1997 Predictors of parent involvement in children's schooling. *Journal of Educational Psychology* 89(3):538–48.

Grolnick WS, Bridges LJ, Connell JP 1996 Emotion regulation in two-year-olds: strategies and emotional expression in four contexts. *Child Development* 67(3):928–41.

Grolnick WS, Frodi A, Bridges LJ 1984 Maternal control style and the mastery motivation of one-year-olds. *Infant Mental Health Journal* 5:72–82.

Grolnick WS, Ryan RM 1989 Parent styles associated with children's self-regulation and competence in school. *Journal of Educational Psychology* 81(2):143–54.

Gronlund G 1992 Coping with Ninja turtle play in my kindergarten classroom. *Young Children* 48(1):21–5.

Groot AS, de Sonneville LMJ, Stins JF, Boomsma DI 2004 Familial influences on sustained attention and inhibition in preschoolers. *Journal of Child Psychology and Psychiatry* 45(2):306–14.

Grusec JE, Goodnow JJ 1994 Impact of parental discipline methods on the child's internalization of values: a reconceptualization of current points of view. *Developmental Psychology* 30(1):4–19.

Guralnick MJ 1994 Mothers' perceptions of the benefits and drawbacks of early childhood mainstreaming. *Journal of Early Intervention* 18(2):168–83.

Guralnick MJ, Groom JM 1987 The peer relations of mildly delayed and nonhandicapped preschool children in mainstreamed playgroups. *Child Development* 58(6):1556–72.

Guralnick MJ, Hammond MA, Connor RT, Neville B 2006 Stability, change, and correlates of the peer relationships of young children with mild developmental delays. *Child Development* 77(2):312–24.

Guralnick MJ, Neville B, Hammond MA, Connor RT 2007 The friendships of young children with developmental delays: a longitudinal analysis. *Journal of Applied Developmental Psychology* 28(1):64–79.

Halpern LF 2004 The relations of coping and family environment to preschoolers' problem behavior. *Journal of Applied Developmental Psychology* 25(4):399–421.

Hamilton CE 2000 Continuity and discontinuity of attachment from infancy to adolescence. *Child Development* 71(3):690–4.

Hamre BK, Pianta RC 2005 Can instructional and emotional support in the first-grade classroom make a difference for children at risk of school failure? *Child Development* 76(5):949–67.

Hanline MF 1993 Inclusion of preschoolers with profound disabilities: an analysis of children's interactions. *Journal of the Association for Persons with Severe Handicaps* 18(1):28–35.

Harker M 2001 How to build solutions at meetings. In Y Ajmal and I Rees (eds), *Solutions in schools*. BT Press, London, pp. 30–44.

Harper LV, McCluskey KS 2002 Caregiver and peer responses to children with language and motor disabilities in inclusive preschool programs. *Early Childhood Research Quarterly* 17(2):148–66.

—— 2003 Teacher–child and child–child interactions in inclusive preschool settings: do adults inhibit peer interactions? *Early Childhood Research Quarterly* 18(2):163–84.

Harris PL 1983 Children's understanding of the link between situation and emotion. *Journal of Experimental Child Psychology* 36(3):490–509.

Harrison J 2004 *Understanding children: foundations for quality*, 3rd edn. ACER, Melbourne.

Harrison LJ, Ungerer JA 2002 Maternal employment and infant–mother attachment security at 12 months postpartum. *Developmental Psychology* 38(5):758–73.

Harrist AW, Bradley KD 2003 'You can't say you can't play': intervening in the process of social exclusion in the kindergarten classroom. *Early Childhood Research Quarterly* 18(2):185–205.

Harskamp A 2002 Working with parents who harm their children. In S Roffey (ed.), *School behaviour and families*. David Fulton, London, pp. 77–92.

Hart CH, Burts DC, Durland MA, Charlesworth R, DeWolf M, Fleege PO 1998 Stress behaviors and activity type participation of preschoolers in more and less developmentally appropriate classrooms: SES and sex differences. *Journal of Research in Childhood Education* 12(2):176–96.

Hart CH, DeWolf DM, Wozniak P, Burts DC 1992 Maternal and paternal disciplinary styles: relations with preschoolers' playground behavioral orientations and peer status. *Child Development* 63(4):879–92.

Hart EL, Lahey BB, Loeber R, Applegate B, Frick PJ 1995 Developmental change in attention-deficit hyperactivity in boys: a four-year longitudinal study. *Journal of Abnormal Child Psychology* 23(6):729–49.

Hart PM, Wearing AJ, Conn M, Carter NL, Dingle RK 2000 Development of the School Organisational Health Questionnaire: a measure for assessing teacher morale and school organisational climate. *British Journal of Educational Psychology* 70(2):211–28.

Hart S, Hodson VK 2004 *The compassionate classroom: relationship based teaching and learning*. Puddle Dancer Press, Encinitas, CA.

Hartup WW 1979 Peer relations and social competence. In MW Kent and JE Rolf (eds), *Social competence in children*. University Press of New England, Hanover, NH, pp. 150–70.

—— 1989 Social relationships and their developmental significance. *American Psychologist* 44(2):120–6.

—— 1996 The company they keep: friendships and their developmental significance. *Child Development* 67(1):1–13.

Hartup WW, Moore SG 1990 Early peer relations: developmental significance and prognostic implications. *Early Childhood Research Quarterly* 5(1):1–17.

Haselager GJT, Cillessen AHN, van Lieshout CFM, Riksen-Walraven JMA, Hartup WW 2002 Heterogeneity among peer-rejected boys across middle childhood: developmental pathways of social behavior. *Developmental Psychology* 38(3):446–56.

Haslam DM, Pakenham KI, Smith A 2006 Social support and postpartum depressive symptomatology: the mediating role of maternal self-efficacy. *Infant Mental Health Journal* 27(3):276–91.

Hastings PD, Rubin KH 1999 Predicting mothers' beliefs about preschool-aged children's social behavior: evidence for maternal attitudes moderating child effects. *Child Development* 70(3):722–41.

Hastings PD, Zahn-Waxler C, Robinson J, Usher B, Bridges D 2000 The development of concern for others in children with behavior problems. *Developmental Psychology* 36(5):531–46.

Hauser-Cram P, Bronson MB, Upshur CC 1993 The effects of the classroom environment on the social and mastery behavior of preschool children with disabilities. *Early Childhood Research Quarterly* 8(4):479–97.

Hawley PH, Little TD 1999 On winning some and losing some: a social relations approach to social dominance in toddlers. *Merrill-Palmer Quarterly* 45(2):185–214.

Hay DF, Pawlby S, Angold A, Harold GT, Sharp D 2003 Pathways to violence in the children of mothers who were depressed postpartum. *Developmental Psychology* 39(6):1083–94.

Hay DF, Payne A, Chadwick A 2004 Peer relations in childhood. *Journal of Child Psychology and Psychiatry* 45(1):84–108.

Haynes-Seman C, Baumgarten D 1998 The victimization of young children. In BBR Rossman and MS Rosenberg (eds), *Multiple victimization of children: conceptual, developmental, research, and treatment issues.* Haworth Press, New York, pp. 67–86.

Henderson HA, Marshall PJ, Fox NA, Rubin KH 2004 Psychophysiological and behavioral evidence for varying forms and functions of nonsocial behavior in preschoolers. *Child Development* 75(1):251–63.

Henning-Stout M, James S, Macintosh S 2000 Reducing harassment of lesbian, gay, bisexual, transgender, and questioning youth in schools. *School Psychology Review* 29(2):180–91.

Henricsson L, Rydell A-M 2004 Elementary school children with behavior problems: teacher–child relations and self-perception: a prospective study. *Merrill-Palmer Quarterly* 50(2):111–38.

Heyman GD, Dweck CS, Cain KM 1992 Young children's vulnerability to self-blame and helplessness: relationship to beliefs about goodness. *Child Development* 63(2):401–15.

Hilliard AG 1985 What is quality care? In BM Caldwell and AG Hilliard III (eds.), *What is quality care?* National Association for the Education of Young Children, Washington, DC, pp. 17–32.

Hinshaw SP 2006 Attention-deficit/hyperactivity disorder: the search of viable treatments. In PC Kendall (ed.), *Child and adolescent therapy: cognitive-behavioral procedures*, 3rd edn. Guilford, New York, pp. 82–113.

Hitz R, Driscoll A 1988 Praise or encouragement? New insights into praise: implications for early childhood teachers. *Young Children* 43(5):6–13.

Hoffman-Plotkin D, Twentyman CT 1984 A multimodal assessment of behavioral and cognitive deficits in abused and neglected preschoolers. *Child Development* 55(3):794–802.

Holden GW 2002 Perspectives on the effects of corporal punishment: comment on Gershoff (2002) *Psychological Bulletin* 128(4):590–5.

Holland P 2004 *Picturing childhood: the myth of the child in popular imagery.* IB Tauris, London.

Honig AS 2002 *Secure relationships: nurturing infant/toddler attachment in early care settings.* National Association for the Education of Young Children, Washington, DC.

Howard VF, Williams BF, Lepper C 2005 *Very young children with special needs: a formative approach for today's children*, 3rd edn. Pearson Merrill Prentice Hall, Upper Saddle River, NJ.

Howes C 1983a Caregiver behavior in center and family day care. *Journal of Applied Developmental Psychology* 4:99–107.

—— 1983b Patterns of friendship. *Child Development* 54(4):1041–53.

—— 1987 Social competence with peers in young children: developmental sequences. *Developmental Review* 7(3):252–72.

—— 1997 Children's experiences in center-based child care as a function of teacher background and adult:child ratio. *Merrill-Palmer Quarterly* 43(3):404–25.

—— 2000 Social-emotional classroom climate in child care, child–teacher relationships and children's second grade peer relations. *Social Development* 9(2):191–204.

Howes C, James J, Ritchie S 2003 Pathways to effective teaching. *Early Childhood Research Quarterly* 18(1):104–20.

Howes C, Ritchie S 2002 *A matter of trust: connecting teachers and learners in the early childhood classroom.* Teachers College Press, New York.

Howes C, Rodning C, Galluzzo DC, Myers L 1988 Attachment and child care: relationships with mother and caregiver. *Early Childhood Research Quarterly* 3(4):403–16.

Howes C, Rubenstein JL 1985 Determinants of toddlers' experience in day care: age of entry and quality of setting. *Child Care Quarterly* 14(2):140–51.

Howlin P, Goode S, Hutton J, Rutter M 2004 Adult outcome for children with autism. *Journal of Child Psychology and Psychiatry* 45(2):212–29.

Hoza B, Waschbusch DA, Pelham WE, Molina BSG, Milich R 2000 Attention-deficit/hyperactivity disordered and control boys' responses to social success and failure. *Child Development* 71(2):432–46.

Hubbard JA 2001 Emotion expression processes in children's peer interaction: the role of peer rejection, aggression, and gender. *Child Development* 72(5):1426–38.

Hubbs-Tait L, Culp AM, Huey E, Culp R, Starost H-J, Hare C 2002 Relation of Head Start attendance to children's cognitive and social outcomes: moderation by family risk. *Early Childhood Research Quarterly* 17(4):539–58.

Huffman LR, Speer PW 2000 Academic performance among at-risk children: the role of developmentally appropriate practices. *Early Childhood Research Quarterly* 15(2):167–84.

Hughes C, Cutting AL, Dunn J 2001 Acting nasty in the face of failure? Longitudinal observations of 'hard-to-manage' children playing a rigged competitive game with a friend. *Journal of Abnormal Child Psychology* 29(5):405–16.

Hughes C, White A, Sharpen J, Dunn J 2000 Antisocial, angry, and unsympathetic: 'hard-to-manage' preschoolers' peer problems and possible cognitive influences. *Journal of Child Psychology and Psychiatry* 41(2):169–79.

Hughes P, MacNaughton G 2002 Preparing early childhood professionals to work with parents: the challenge of diversity and dissensus. *Australian Journal of Early Childhood* 28(2):14–20.

Hunter SC, Boyle JME 2004 Appraisal and coping strategy use in victims of school bullying. *British Journal of Educational Psychology* 74(1):83–107.

Huntley J 1999 A narrative approach to working with students who have 'learning difficulties'. In A Morgan (ed.), *Once upon a time … Narrative therapy with children and their families.* Dulwich Centre Publications, Adelaide, pp. 35–49.

Ingraham CL 2000 Consultation through a multicultural lens: multicultural and cross-cultural consultation in schools. *School Psychology Review* 29(3):320–43.

Ispa JM, Fine MA, Halgunseth LC, Harper S, Robinson J, Boyce L, Brooks-Gunn J, Brady-Smith C 2004 Maternal intrusiveness, maternal warmth, and mother–toddler relationship outcomes: variations across low-income ethnic and acculturation groups. *Child Development* 75(6):1613–31.

Ivory JJ, McCollum JA 1999 Effects of social and isolate toys on social play in an inclusive setting. *Journal of Special Education* 32(4):238–43.

Jacobs B 2005 The myth of ADHD: psychiatric oppression of children. In J Bessant, R Hill and R Watts (eds.), *Violations of trust: how social and welfare institutions fail children and young people.* Ashgate, Hampshire, UK, pp. 133–46.

Jacobson AL, Engelbrecht J 2000 Parenting education needs and preferences of parents of young children. *Early Childhood Education Journal* 28(2):139–47.

Jaffee SR, Caspi A, Moffitt TE, Polo-Tomas M, Price TS, Taylor A 2004 The limits of child effects: evidence for genetically mediated child effects on corporal punishment but not on physical maltreatment. *Developmental Psychology* 40(6):1047–58.

Jakubowski P, Lange A 1978 *The assertive option: your rights and responsibilities.* Research Press, Champaign, IL.

Jenkins J, Simpson A, Dunn J, Rasbash J, O'Connor TG 2005 Mutual influence of marital conflict and children's behavior problems: shared and nonshared family risks. *Child Development* 76(1):24–39.

Jennings KD, Abrew AJ 2004 Self-efficacy in 18-month-old toddlers of depressed and nondepressed mothers. *Journal of Applied Developmental Psychology* 25(2):133–47.

Joiner Jr TE, Metalsky GI, Katz J, Beach SRH 1999 Depression and excessive reassurance-seeking. *Psychological Inquiry* 10(4):269–78.

Johnson BM, Miltenberger RG, Egemo-Helm K, Jostad CM, Flessner C, Gatheridge B 2005 Evaluation of behavioral skills training for teaching abduction-prevention skills to young children. *Journal of Applied Behavior Analysis* 38(1):67–78.

Johnson C, Ironsmith M, Snow CW, Poteat GM 2000 Peer acceptance and social adjustment in preschool and kindergarten. *Early Childhood Education Journal* 27(4):207–12.

Johnson DW, Johnson RT 1991 *Learning together and alone*, 3rd edn. Allyn & Bacon, Boston, MA.

Johnston JM 1972 Punishment of human behavior. *American Psychologist* 27(11):1033–54.

Jones VF, Jones LS 2004 *Comprehensive classroom management: creating communities of support and solving problems*, 7th edn. Pearson Allyn & Bacon, Boston, MA.

Jordan NH 1993 Sexual abuse prevention programs in early childhood education: a caveat. *Young Children* 48(6):76–9.

Jordan R 2004 Meeting the needs of children with autistic spectrum disorders in the early years. *Australian Journal of Early Childhood* 29(3):1–7.

Jorde-Bloom P 1988 Teachers need 'TLC' too. *Young Children* 43(6):4–8.

Jules V 1991 Interaction dynamics of cooperative learning groups in Trinidad's secondary schools. *Adolescence* 26(104):931–49.

Kamii C 1985 Autonomy: the aim of education envisioned by Piaget. *Australian Journal of Early Childhood* 10(1):3–10.

Kamins ML, Dweck CS 1999 Person versus process praise and criticism: implications for contingent self-worth and coping. *Developmental Psychology* 35(3):835–47.

Kaplan JS, Carter J 1995 *Beyond behavior modification: a cognitive-behavioral approach to behavior management in the school*, 3rd edn. Pro-Ed, Austin, TX.

Karatekin C 2004 A test of integrity of the components of Baddeley's model of working memory in attention-deficit/hyperactivity disorder (ADHD). *Journal of Child Psychology and Psychiatry* 45(5):912–26.

Katsurada E, Sugawara AI 1998 The relationship between hostile attributional bias and aggressive behavior in preschoolers. *Early Childhood Research Quarterly* 13(4):623–36.

Katz LF, Woodin EM 2002 Hostility, hostile detachment, and conflict engagement in marriages: effects on child and family functioning. *Child Development* 73(2):636–52.

Katz LG 1992 Early childhood programs: multiple perspectives on quality. *Childhood Education* 69(2):66–71.

—— 1995 *Talks with teachers of young children*. Ablex, Norwood, NJ.

Katz LG, Chard SC 1989 *Engaging children's minds: the project approach*. Ablex, Norwood, NJ.

Katz LG, Evangelou D, Hartman JA 1990 *The case for mixed-age grouping in early education*. National Association for the Education of Young Children, Washington, DC.

Kaufmann D, Gesten E, Santa Lucia RC, Salcedo O, Rendina-Gobioff G, Gadd R 2000 The relationship between parenting style and children's adjustment: the parents' perspective. *Journal of Child and Family Studies* 9(2):231–45.

Kavussanu M, Harnisch DL 2000 Self-esteem in children: do goal orientations matter? *British Journal of Educational Psychology* 70(2):229–42.

Keane E 2004 Autism: the heart of the disorder? Sensory processing and social engagement—illustrations from autobiographical accounts and selected research findings. *Australian Journal of Early Childhood* 29(3):8–14.

Keiley MK, Bates JE, Dodge KE, Pettit GS 2000 A cross-domain growth analysis: externalizing and internalizing behaviors during eight years of childhood. *Journal of Abnormal Child Psychology* 28(2):161–79.

Kerns KA, Cole A, Andrews PB 1998 Attachment security, parent peer management practices, and peer relationships in preschoolers. *Merrill-Palmer Quarterly* 44(4):504–22.

Kerr BA, Cohn SJ 2001 *Smart boys: talent, manhood, and the search for meaning*. Great Potential Press, Scottsdale, AZ.

Kerr MM, Nelson CM 2006 *Strategies for addressing behavior problems in the classroom*, 5th edn. Pearson Merrill Prentice Hall, Upper Saddle River, NJ.

Kilderry A 2004 Critical pedagogy: a useful framework for thinking about early childhood curriculum. *Australian Journal of Early Childhood* 29(4):33–7.

Kilgore K, Snyder J, Lentz C 2000 The contribution of parental discipline, parenting monitoring, and school risk to early-onset conduct problems in African-American boys and girls. *Developmental Psychology* 36(6):835–45.

Killen M, Pisacane K, Lee-Kim J, Ardila-Rey A 2001 Fairness or stereotypes? Young children's priorities when evaluating group exclusion and inclusion. *Developmental Psychology* 37(5):587–96.

Killen M, Smetana JG 1999 Social interactions in preschool classrooms and the development of young children's conceptions of the personal. *Child Development* 70(2):486–501.

Killion JP, Todnem GR 1991 A process for personal theory building. *Educational Leadership* 48(6):14–16.

Kim J, Cicchetti D 2004 A longitudinal study of child maltreatment, mother–child relationship quality and maladjustment: the role of self-esteem and social competence. *Journal of Abnormal Child Psychology* 32(4):341–54.

—— 2006 Longitudinal trajectories of self-system processes and depressive symptoms among maltreated and nonmaltreated children. *Child Development* 77(3):624–39.

Kim JE, Hetherington EM, Reiss D 1999 Associations among family relationships, antisocial peers, and adolescents' externalizing behaviors: gender and family type differences. *Child Development* 70(5):1209–30.

Kim J-M, Mahoney G 2004 The effects of mother's style of interaction on children's engagement: implications for using responsive interventions with parents. *Topics in Early Childhood Special Education* 24(1):31–8.

Kistner JA, Ziegert DI, Castro R, Robertson B 2001 Helplessness in early childhood: prediction of symptoms associated with depression and negative self-worth. *Merrill-Palmer Quarterly* 47(3):336–54.

Klass CS 1999 *The child care provider: promoting young children's development.* Paul H Brookes, Baltimore, MD.

Klein PS 1992 Mediating the cognitive, social, and aesthetic development of precocious young children. In PS Klein and AJ Tannenbaum (eds), *To be young and gifted.* Ablex, Norwood, NJ, pp. 245–77.

Klimes-Dougan B, Kistner J 1990 Physically abused preschoolers' responses to peers' distress. *Developmental Psychology* 26(4):599–602.

Knight BA 1995 The influence of locus of control on gifted and talented students. *Gifted Education International* 11(1):31–3.

Ko SF, Cosden MA 2001 Do elementary school-based child abuse prevention programs work? A high school follow-up. *Psychology in the Schools* 38(1):57–66.

Kochanska G 2001 Emotional development in children with different attachment histories: the first three years. *Child Development* 72(2):474–90.

—— 2002a Committed compliance, moral self, and internalization: a mediational model. *Developmental Psychology* 38(3):339–51.

—— 2002b Mutually responsive orientation between mothers and their young children: a context for the early development of conscience. *Current Directions in Psychological Science* 11(6):191–5.

Kochanska G, Aksan N 2004 Conscience in childhood: past, present and future. *Merrill-Palmer Quarterly* 50(3):299–310.

Kochanska G, Aksan N, Carlson JJ 2005 Temperament, relationships, and young children's receptive cooperation with their parents. *Developmental Psychology* 41(4):648–60.

Kochanska G, Aksan N, Nichols KE 2003 Maternal power assertion in discipline and moral discourse contexts: commonalities, differences, and implications for children's moral conduct and cognition. *Developmental Psychology* 39(6):949–63.

Kochanska G, Coy KC, Murray KT 2001 The development of self-regulation in the first four years of life. *Child Development* 72(4):1091–111.

Kochanska G, Forman DR, Coy KC 1999 Implications of the mother–child relationship in infancy for socialization in the second year of life. *Infant Behavior and Development* 22(2):249–65.

Kochanska G, Murray KT, Harlan ET 2000 Effortful control in early childhood: continuity and change, antecedents, and implications for social development. *Developmental Psychology* 36(2):220–32.

Kochenderfer BJ, Ladd GW 1996 Peer victimization: cause or consequence of school maladjustment? *Child Development* 67(4):1305–17.

Kochenderfer-Ladd B, Ladd GW 2001 Variations in peer victimization: relations to children's maladjustment. In J Juvonen and S Graham (eds), *Peer harassment in school: the plight of the vulnerable and victimized*. Guilford, New York, pp. 25–48.

Koenig AL, Cicchetti D, Rogosch FA 2000 Child compliance/noncompliance and maternal contributors to internalization in maltreating and nonmaltreating dyads. *Child Development* 71(4):1018–32.

Kohler FW, Strain PS 1993 The early childhood social skills program. *Teaching Exceptional Children* 25(2):41–2.

Kohn A 1996 *Beyond discipline: from compliance to community*. Association for Supervision and Curriculum Development, Alexandria, VA.

—— 1999 *Punished by rewards: the trouble with gold stars, incentive plans, A's, praise and other bribes*, 2nd edn. Houghton Mifflin, Boston, MA.

—— 2000 *What to look for in a classroom … and other essays*. Jossey Bass, San Francisco, CA.

Kolvin I, Fundudis T 1981 Elective mute children: psychological development and background factors. *Journal of Child Psychology and Psychiatry* 22(3):219–32.

Kontos S 1999 Preschool teachers' talk, roles, and activity settings during free play. *Early Childhood Research Quarterly* 14(3):363–82.

Kontos S, Burchinal M, Howes C, Wisseh S, Galinsky E 2002 An eco-behavioral approach to examining the contextual effects of early childhood classrooms. *Early Childhood Research Quarterly* 17(2):239–58.

Kontos S, Keyes L 1999 An ecobehavioral analysis of early childhood classrooms. *Early Childhood Research Quarterly* 14(1):35–50.

Kontos S, Wilcox-Herzog A 1997a Influences on children's competence in early childhood classrooms. *Early Childhood Research Quarterly* 12(3):247–62.

—— 1997b Teachers' interactions with children: why are they so important? *Young Children* 52(2):4–12.

Kopecky H, Chang HT, Klorman R, Thatcher JE, Borgstedt AD 2005 Performance and private speech of children with attention-deficit/hyperactivity disorder while taking the tower of Hanoi test: effects of depth search, diagnostic subtype, and methlyphenidate. *Journal of Abnormal Child Psychology* 33(5):625–38.

Koren-Karie N, Oppenheim D, Smadar D, Sher E, Etzion-Carasso A 2002 Mothers' insightfulness regarding their infants' internal experience: relations with maternal sensitivity and infant attachment. *Developmental Psychology* 38(4):534–42.

Kostelnik MJ, Whiren AP, Soderman AK, Gregory K 2006 *Guiding children's social development: theory to practice*, 5th edn. Thomson Delmar, New York.

Kral R, Kowalski K 1989 After the miracle: the second stage in solution focused brief therapy. *Journal of Strategic and Systemic Therapies* 8(2):73–6.

Kranowitz CS 1998 *The out-of-sync child: recognizing and coping with sensory integration dysfunction*. Perigee, New York.

Kristensen H 2000 Selective mutism and comorbidity with developmental disorder/delay, anxiety disorder, and elimination disorder. *Journal of the American Academy of Child and Adolescent Psychiatry* 39(2):249–56.

Kugelmass JW, Ross-Bernstein J 2000 Explicit and implicit dimensions of adult–child interactions in a quality childcare center. *Early Childhood Education Journal* 28(1):19–27.

La Paro KM, Pianta RC 2000 Predicting children's competence in the early school years: a meta-analytic review. *Review of Educational Research* 70(4):443–84.

Ladd GW 2006 Peer rejection, aggressive or withdrawn behavior, and psychological maladjustment from ages 5 to 12: an examination of four predictive models. *Child Development* 77(4):822–46.

Ladd GW, Birch SH, Buhs ES 1999 Children's social and scholastic lives in kindergarten: related spheres of influence? *Child Development* 70(6):1373–400.

Ladd GW, Burgess KB 1999 Charting the relationship trajectories of aggressive, withdrawn, and aggressive/withdrawn children during early grade school. *Child Development* 70(4):910–29.

—— 2001 Do relational and protective factors moderate the linkages between childhood aggression and early psychological adjustment? *Child Development* 72(5):1579–601.

Ladd GW, Kochenderfer-Ladd B 1998 Parenting behaviors and parent–child relationships: correlates of peer victimization in kindergarten? *Developmental Psychology* 34(6):1450–8.

Ladd GW, Kochenderfer-Ladd BJ, Coleman CC 1996 Friendship quality as a predictor of young children's early school adjustment. *Child Development* 67(3):1103–18.

Ladd GW, Troop-Gordon W 2003 The role of chronic peer difficulties in the development of children's psychological adjustment problems. *Child Development* 74 (5):1344–67.

LaFontana KM, Cillessen AHN 2002 Children's perceptions of popular and unpopular peers: a multimethod assessment. *Developmental Psychology* 38(5):635–47.

Laible DJ, Thompson R 2002 Mother–toddler conflict in the toddler years: lessons in emotion, morality, and relationships. *Child Development* 73(4):1187–203.

Lamb-Parker F, Piotrkowski CS, Baker AJL, Kessler-Sklar S, Clark B, Peay L 2001 Understanding barriers to parent involvement in Head Start: a research-community partnership. *Early Childhood Research Quarterly* 16(1):35–51.

Lambert B 1994 Beating burnout: a multi-dimensional perspective. *AECA Resource Book Series*, 1(2). Australian Early Childhood Association, Canberra.

Lambert EB, Clyde M 2000 *Re-thinking early childhood theory and practice*. Social Science Press, Katoomba.

Landry SH, Smith KE, Swank PR, Assel MA, Vellet S 2001 Does early responsive parenting have a special importance for children's development or is consistency across early childhood necessary? *Developmental Psychology* 37(3):387–403.

Lansford JE, Deater-Deckard K, Dodge KA, Bates JE, Pettit GS 2004 Ethnic differences in the link between physical discipline and later adolescent externalizing behaviors. *Journal of Child Psychology and Psychiatry* 45(4):801–12.

Lansford JE, Dodge KA, Malone PS, Bacchini D, Zelli A, Chaudhary N, Manke B, Chang L, Oburu P, Palmérus K, Pastorelli C, Bombi AS, Tapanya S, Deater-Deckard K, Quinn N 2005 Physical discipline and children's adjustment: cultural normativeness as a moderator. *Child Development* 76(6):1234–46.

Larner M, Phillips D 1994 Defining and valuing quality as a parent. In P Moss and A Pence (eds), *Transforming nursery education*. Paul Chapman Publishing, London, pp. 43–60.

Larrivee B 2002 The potential perils of praise in a democratic interactive classroom. *Action in Teacher Education* 23(4):77–88.

—— 2005 *Authentic classroom management: creating a learning community and building reflective practice*, 2nd edn. Pearson Allyn & Bacon, Boston, MA.

Larzelere RE 2000 Child outcomes of nonabusive and customary physical punishment by parents: an updated literature review. *Clinical Child and Family Psychology Review* 3(4):199–221.

Lauritsen MB, Pedersen CB, Mortensen PB 2005 Effects of familial risk factors and place of birth on the risk of autism: a nationwide register-based study. *Journal of Child Psychology and Psychiatry* 46(9):963–71.

Lavigne JV, Gibbons RD, Christoffel KK, Arend R, Rosenbaum D, Binns H, Dawson N, Sobel H, Isaacs C 1996 Prevalence rates and correlates of psychiatric disorders among preschool children. *Journal of the American Academy of Child and Adolescent Psychiatry* 35(2):204–14.

Leary A, Katz LF 2005 Observations of aggressive children during peer provocation and with a best friend. *Developmental Psychology* 41(1):124–34.

Lee N 2001 *Childhood and society: growing up in an age of uncertainty*. Open University Press, Buckingham, UK.

Leekam S, Libby S, Wing L, Gould J, Gillberg C 2000 Comparison of ICD-10 and Gillberg's criteria for Asperger syndrome. *Autism* 4(1):11–28.

Lee-Thomas K, Sumsion J, Roberts S 2005 Teacher understandings of and commitment to gender equity in the early childhood setting. *Australian Journal of Early Childhood* 30(1):21–7.

Lengua LJ 2003 Associations among emotionality, self-regulation, adjustment problems, and positive adjustment in middle childhood. *Journal of Applied Developmental Psychology* 24(5):595–618.

Lerman DC, Vorndran CM 2002 On the status of knowledge for using punishment: implications for treating behavior disorders. *Journal of Applied Behavior Analysis* 35(4):431–64.

Letcher P, Toumbourou J, Sanson A, Prior M, Smart D, Oberklaid F 2004 Parenting style as a moderator of the effect of temperament on adolescent externalising and internalising behaviour problems. *Australian Educational and Developmental Psychologist* 20(1):5–34.

Leung C, Sanders MR, Leung S, Mak R, Lau J 2003 An outcome evaluation of the implementation of the Triple P—Positive Parenting Program in Hong Kong. *Family Process* 42(4):531–44.

Leung PWL, Kwan KSF 1998 Parenting styles, motivational orientations, and self-perceived academic competence: a mediational model. *Merrill-Palmer Quarterly* 44(1):1–19.

Levy F 1993 Side effects of stimulant use. *Journal of Paediatric Child Health* 29:250–4.

Lewis M, Feiring C, Rosenthal S 2000 Attachment over time. *Child Development* 71(3):707–20.

Lewis R 1997 *The discipline dilemma: control, management, influence*, 2nd edn. ACER, Melbourne.

Lewis R, Frydenberg E 2002 Concomitants of failure to cope: what we should teach adolescents about coping. *British Journal of Educational Psychology* 72(3):419–31.

Lewis RB, Doorlag DH 2003 *Teaching special education students in general education*, 6th edn. Prentice Hall, Upper Saddle River, NJ.

Linn MI, Goodman JF, Lender WL 2000 'Played out?' Passive behavior by children with Down syndrome during unstructured play. *Journal of Early Intervention* 23(4):264–78.

Little TD, Brauner J, Jones SM, Nock MK, Hawley PH 2003 Rethinking aggression: a typological examination of the functions of aggression. *Merrill-Palmer Quarterly* 49(3):343–69.

Lloyd L 1997 Multi-age classes: an option for all students? *Australasian Journal of Gifted Education* 6(1):46–54.

Lochman JE, Powell NR, Whidby JM, FitzGerald DP 2006 Aggressive children: cognitive-behavioral assessment and treatment. In PC Kendall (ed.), *Child and adolescent therapy: cognitive-behavioral procedures*, 3rd edn. Guilford, New York, pp. 33–81.

Loeber R, Hay D 1997 Key issues in the development of aggression and violence from childhood to early adulthood. *Annual Review of Psychology* 48:371–410.

Lonigan CJ, Bloomfield BG, Anthony JL, Bacon KD, Phillips BM, Samwel CS 1999 Relations among emergent literacy skills, behavior problems, and social competence in preschool children from low- and middle-income backgrounds. *Topics in Early Childhood Special Education* 19(1):40–53.

Love JM, Harrison L, Sagi-Schwartz A, van Ijzendoorn MH, Ross C, Ungerer JA, Raikes H, Brady-Smith C, Boller K, Brooks-Gunn J, Constantine J, Kisker EE, Paulsell D, Chazan-Cohen R 2003 Child care quality matters: how conclusions may vary with context. *Child Development* 74(4):1021–33.

Lundy BL, Jones NA, Field T, Nearing G, Davalos M, Pietro PA, Schanberg S, Kuhn C 1999 Prenatal depression effects on neonates. *Infant Behavior and Development* 22(1):119–29.

Luthar SS, Cicchetti D, Becker B 2000 The construct of resilience: a critical evaluation and guidelines for future work. *Child Development* 71(3):543–62.

Lutz MN, Fantuzzo J, McDermott P 2002 Multidimensional assessment of emotional and behavioral adjustment problems of low-income preschool children: development and initial validation. *Early Childhood Research Quarterly* 17(3):338–55.

Lyons M, Quinn A, Sumsion J 2005 Gender, the labour market, the workplace and policy in children's services: parent, staff and student attitudes. *Australian Journal of Early Childhood* 30(1):6–13.

Lytton H 1997 Physical punishment is a problem, whether conduct disorder is endogenous or not. *Psychological Inquiry* 8(3):211–14.

MacCallum F, Golombok S 2004 Children raised in fatherless families from infancy: a follow-up of children of lesbian and single heterosexual mothers at early adolescence. *Journal of Child Psychology and Psychiatry* 45(8):1407–19.

Macintosh KE, Dissanayake C 2004 Annotation: the similarities and differences between autistic disorder and Asperger's disorder: a review of the empirical evidence. *Journal of Child Psychology and Psychiatry* 45(3):421–34.

MacKinnon-Lewis C, Rabiner D, Starnes R 1999 Predicting boys' social acceptance and aggression: the role of mother–child interactions and boys' beliefs about peers. *Developmental Psychology* 35(3):632–9.

MacMillan HE, Boyle MH, Wong MY-Y, Duku EK, Fleming JE, Walsh CA 1999 Slapping and spanking in childhood and its association with lifetime prevalence of psychiatric disorders in a general population sample. *Canadian Medical Association Journal* 161(7):805–9.

Macmillan R, McMorris BJ, Kruttschnitt C 2004 Linked lives: stability and change in maternal circumstances and trajectories of antisocial behavior in children. *Child Development* 75(1):205–30.

MacNaughton G 2003 *Shaping early childhood learners, curriculum and contexts.* Open University Press, Maidenhead, UK.

—— 2004 Children, staff and parents: building respectful relationships in New Zealand and Australian early childhood contexts—the Australian context. *Australian Journal of Early Childhood* 29(1):1–7.

MacNaughton G, Newman B 2001 Masculinities and men in early childhood: reconceptualising our theory and our practice. In E Dau (ed.), *The anti-bias approach in early childhood*, 2nd edn. Pearson Education, Sydney, pp. 145–57.

McCabe PC 2005 Social and behavioral correlates of preschoolers with specific language impairment. *Psychology in the Schools* 42(4):373–87.

McCarthy M 1987 Chronic illness and hospitalization. In JT Neisworth and SJ Bagnato (eds), *The young exceptional child: early development and education.* Macmillan, New York, pp. 231–59.

McCaslin M, Good TL 1992 Compliant cognition: the misalliance of management and instructional goals in current school reform. *Educational Researcher* 21(3):4–17.

McClelland MM, Morrison FJ 2003 The emergence of learning-related social skills in preschool children. *Early Childhood Research Quarterly* 18(2):206–24.

McClelland MM, Morrison FJ, Holmes DL 2000 Children at risk for early academic problems: the role of learning-related social skills. *Early Childhood Research Quarterly* 15(3):307–29.

McClun LA, Merrell KA 1998 Relationship of perceived parenting styles, locus of control orientation, and self-concept among junior high age students. *Psychology in the Schools* 35(4):381–90.

McCoach DB, Siegle D 2003 The structure and function of academic self-concept in gifted and general education students. *Roeper Review* 25(2):61–5.

McCollum JA, Bair H 1994 Research in parent–child interaction. Guidance to developmentally appropriate practice for young children with disabilities. In BL Mallory and RS New (eds),

Diversity and developmental appropriate practices: challenges for early childhood education. Teachers College Press, New York, pp. 84–106.

McCord J 1997 On discipline. *Psychological Inquiry* 8(3):215–17.

McDowell DJ, Parke RD, Wang SJ 2003 Differences between mothers' and fathers' advice-giving style and content: relations with social competence and psychological functioning in middle childhood. *Merrill-Palmer Quarterly* 49(1):55–76.

McFadyen-Ketchum SA, Bates JE, Dodge KA, Pettit GS 1996 Patterns of change in early childhood aggressive-disruptive behavior: gender differences in predictions from early coercive and affectionate mother–child interactions. *Child Development* 67(5):2417–33.

McGee R, Partridge F, Williams S, Silva PA 1991 A twelve-year follow-up of preschool hyperactive children. *Journal of the American Academy of Child and Adolescent Psychiatry* 30(2):224–32.

McGee R, Prior M, Williams S, Smart D, Sanson A 2002 The long-term significance of teacher-rated hyperactivity and reading ability in childhood: findings from two longitudinal studies. *Journal of Child Psychology and Psychiatry* 43(8):1004–17.

McGroder SM 2000 Parenting among low-income, African American single mothers with preschool-age children: patterns, predictors, and developmental correlates. *Child Development* 71(3):752–71.

McLeod W 1989 Minor miracles or logical processes? Therapeutic interventions and techniques. *Journal of Family Therapy* 11(3):257–80.

McLoughlin JA, Lewis RB 2005 *Assessing students with special needs*, 6th edn. Pearson Merrill Prentice Hall, Upper Saddle River, NJ.

McWayne CM, Fantuzzo JW, McDermott PA 2004 Preschool competency in context: an investigation of the unique contribution of child competences to early academic success. *Developmental Psychology* 40(4):633–45.

Maag JW 2001 Rewarded by punishment: reflections on the disuse of positive reinforcement in schools. *Exceptional Children* 67(2):173–86.

Maccoby EE, Lewis CC 2003 Less day care or different day care? *Child Development* 74(4):1069–75.

Maccoby EE, Martin JA 1983 Socialization in the context of the family: parent–child interaction. In PH Mussen and EM Hetherington (eds), *Handbook of child psychology vol IV: socialization, personality and social development*, 4th edn. Wiley, New York, pp. 1–101.

Maguen S, Floyd FJ, Bakeman R, Armistead L 2002 Developmental milestones and disclosure of sexual orientation among gay, lesbian, and bisexual youths. *Journal of Applied Developmental Psychology* 23(2):219–33.

Mapp SC 2006 The effects of sexual abuse as a child on the risk of mothers physically abusing their children: a path analysis using systems theory. *Child Abuse and Neglect* 30(11):1293–310.

Marchand JF, Schedler S, Wagstaff DA 2004 The role of parents' attachment orientations, depressive symptoms, and conflict behaviors in children's externalizing and internalizing behavior problems. *Early Childhood Research Quarterly* 19(3):449–62.

Marchant M, Young KR, West RP 2004 The effects of parental teaching on compliance behavior of children. *Psychology in the Schools* 41(3):337–50.

Marsh HW, Craven RG, Debus R 1999 Separation of competency and affect components of multiple dimensions of academic self-concept: a developmental perspective. *Merrill-Palmer Quarterly* 45(4):567–601.

Marsh HW, Craven RG, Martin AJ 2006 What is the nature of self-esteem?: unidimensional and multidimensional perspectives. In MH Kernis (ed), *Self-esteem: issues and answers: a sourcebook of current perspectives*. Psychology Press, New York, pp. 16–24.

Marsh HW, Ellis LA, Craven RG 2002 How do preschool children feel about themselves? Unraveling measurement and multidimensional self-concept structure. *Developmental Psychology* 38(3):376–93.

Martel MM, Nigg JT 2006 Child ADHD and personality/temperament traits of reactive and effortful control, resiliency, and emotionality. *Journal of Child Psychology and Psychiatry* 47(11):1175–83.

Martin AJ, Linfoot K, Stephenson J 1999 How teachers respond to concerns about misbehavior in their classroom. *Psychology in the Schools* 36(4):347–58.

Martin G, Pear J 2007 *Behavior modification: what it is and how to do it*, 8th edn. Prentice Hall, Upper Saddle River, NJ.

Maslow AH 1968 *Toward a psychology of being*, 2nd edn. Van Nostrand, Princeton, NJ.

Mason DA, Burns RB 1996 'Simply no worse and simply no better' may simply be wrong: a critique of Veenman's conclusion about multigrade classes. *Review of Educational Research* 66(3):307–22.

Massey SL 2004 Teacher–child conversation in the preschool classroom. *Early Childhood Education Journal* 31(4):227–31.

Maszk P, Eisenberg N, Guthrie IK 1999 Relations of children's social status to their emotionality and regulation: a short-term longitudinal study. *Merrill-Palmer Quarterly* 45(3):468–92.

Mathieson K, Price M 2002 *Better behaviour in classrooms: a framework for inclusive behaviour management*. Routledge/Falmer, London.

Mattanah JF 2001 Parental psychological autonomy and children's academic competence and behavioral adjustment in late childhood: more than just limit-setting and warmth. *Merrill-Palmer Quarterly* 47(3):355–76.

Maughan A, Cicchetti D 2002 Impact of child maltreatment and interadult violence on children's emotion regulation and socioemotional adjustment. *Child Development* 73(5):1525–42.

Maxwell KL, McWilliam RA, Hemmeter ML, Ault MJ, Schuster JW 2001 Predictors of developmentally appropriate classroom practices in kindergarten through third grade. *Early Childhood Research Quarterly* 16(4):431–52.

May L 2005 *Transgenders and intersexuals: everything you ever wanted to know but couldn't think of the question*. East Street Publications, Adelaide.

Meehan BT, Hughes JN, Cavell TA 2003 Teacher–student relationships as compensatory resources for aggressive children. *Child Development* 74(4):1145–57.

Mercurio CM 2003 Guiding boys in the early years to lead healthy emotional lives. *Early Childhood Education Journal* 30(4):255–8.

Merrell KW, Wolfe TM 1998 The relationship of teacher-rated social skills deficits and ADHD characteristics among kindergarten-age children. *Psychology in the Schools* 35(2):101–9.

Metzner JL, Ryan GD 1995 Sexual abuse perpetration. In GP Sholevar (ed.), *Conduct disorders in children and adolescents*. American Psychiatric Press, Washington, DC, pp. 119–42.

Meyers SA 1999 Mothering in context: ecological determinants of parent behavior. *Merrill-Palmer Quarterly* 45(2):332–57.

Mikkelsen EJ 1997 Responding to allegations of sexual abuse in child care and early childhood education programs. *Young Children* 52(3):47–51.

Miles SB, Stipek D 2006 Contemporaneous and longitudinal associations between social behavior and literacy achievement in a sample of low-income elementary school children. *Child Development* 77(1):103–17.

Milgram N, Toubiana Y 1999 Academic anxiety, academic procrastination, and parents' involvement in students and their parents. *British Journal of Educational Psychology* 69(3):345–61.

Milgram S 1963 Behavioral study of obedience. *Journal of Abnormal and Social Psychology* 67(4):371–8.

Mill D, Romano-White D 1999 Correlates of affectionate and angry behavior in child care educators of preschool-aged children. *Early Childhood Research Quarterly* 14(2):155–78.

Miller A 2003 *Teachers, parents and classroom behaviour: a psychosocial approach*. Open University Press, Maidenhead, UK.

Miller GE, Brehm K, Whitehouse S 1998 Reconceptualizing school-based prevention for antisocial behavior within a resiliency framework. *School Psychology Review* 27(3):364–79.

Miller-Lewis LR, Baghurst PA, Sawyer MG, Prior MR, Clark JJ, Arney FM, Carbone JA 2006 Early childhood externalizing behaviour problems: child, parenting, and family-related predictors over time. *Journal of Abnormal Child Psychology* 34(6):891–906.

Mintz J 2003 *No homework and recess all day: how to have freedom and democracy in education.* Bravura, New York.

Miranda A, Presentación MJ 2000 Efficacy of cognitive-behavioral therapy in the treatment of children with ADHD, with and without aggressiveness. *Psychology in the Schools* 37(2):169–82.

Mitchell G 1993 *Help! What do I do about …?* Scholastic, New York.

Mize J 1995 Coaching preschool children in social skills: a cognitive-social learning curriculum. In G Cartledge and JF Milburn (eds), *Teaching social skills to children and youth: innovative approaches*, 3rd edn. Pergamon, New York, pp. 237–61.

Mohay H, Reid E 2006 The inclusion of children with a disability in child care: the influence of experience, training and attitudes of childcare staff. *Australian Journal of Early Childhood* 31(1):35–42.

Moline S, Frankenberger W 2001 Use of stimulant medication for treatment of attention-deficit/hyperactivity disorder: a survey of middle and high school students' attitudes. *Psychology in the Schools* 38(6):569–84.

Molnar A, de Shazer S 1987 Solution-focused therapy: toward the identification of therapeutic tasks. *Journal of Marital and Family Therapy* 13(4):349–58.

Molnar A, Lindquist B 1989 *Changing problem behavior in schools.* Jossey Bass, San Francisco, CA.

Montgomery H 2003 Childhood in time and place. In M Woodhead and H Montgomery (eds), *Understanding childhood: an interdisciplinary approach.* Open University Press, Milton Keynes, UK, pp. 45–83.

Monuteaux MC, Blacker D, Biederman J, Fitzmaurice G, Buka SL 2006 Maternal smoking during pregnancy and offspring overt and covert conduct problems: a longitudinal study. *Journal of Child Psychology and Psychiatry* 47(9):883–90.

Morgan A 2000 *What is narrative therapy? An easy-to-read introduction.* Dulwich Centre Publications, Adelaide.

Morris A 2005 Too attached to attachment theory? Paper presented to 'Theorising and representating maternal subjectivities', 29 September–1 October 2005, Brisbane.

Moss E 1992 Early interactions and metacognitive development of gifted preschoolers. In PS Klein and AJ Tannenbaum (eds), *To be young and gifted.* Ablex, Norwood, NJ, pp. 278–318.

Moss E, Cyr C, Bureau J-F, Tarabulsy GM, Dubois-Comtois K 2005 Stability of attachment during the preschool period. *Developmental Psychology* 41(5):773–83.

Moss E, Cyr C, Dubois-Comtois K 2004 Attachment at early school age and developmental risk: examining family contexts and behavior problems of controlling-caregiving, controlling-punitive, and behaviorally disorganized children. *Developmental Psychology* 40(4):519–32.

Moss E, St-Laurent D 2001 Attachment at school age and academic performance. *Developmental Psychology* 37(6):863–74.

Mosteller F, Light RJ, Sachs JA 1996 Sustained inquiry in education: lessons from skill grouping and class size. *Harvard Educational Review* 66(4):797–842.

Mruk CJ 1999 *Self-esteem: research, theory and practice*, 2nd edn. Free Association Books, London.

—— 2006 Defining self-esteem: an often overlooked issue with crucial implications. In MH Kernis (ed), *Self-esteem: issues and answers: a sourcebook of current perspectives.* Psychology Press, New York, pp. 10–15.

Mueller CM, Dweck CS 1998 Praise for intelligence can undermine children's motivation and performance. *Journal of Personality and Social Psychology* 75(1):33–52.

Muijs RD 1997 Symposium: self perception and performance: predictors of academic achievement and academic self-concept: a longitudinal perspective. *British Journal of Educational Psychology* 67(3):263–77.

Mullen PE, Martin JL, Anderson JC, Romans SE, Herbison GP 1996 The long-term impact of the physical, emotional, and sexual abuse of children: a community study. *Child Abuse and Neglect* 20(1):7–21.

Murdock TB, Bolch MB 2005 Risk and protective factors for poor school adjustment in lesbian, gay, and bisexual (LGB) high school youth: variable and person-centered analyses. *Psychology in the Schools* 42(2):159–72.

Murphy BC, Eisenberg N, Fabes RA, Shepard S, Guthrie IK 1999 Consistency and change in children's emotionality and regulation: a longitudinal study. *Merrill-Palmer Quarterly* 45(3):413–44.

Murphy JJ 2006 *Solution-focused counseling in middle and high schools.* Pearson Merrill Prentice Hall, Upper Saddle River, NJ.

Murphy JJ, Duncan BL 1997 *Brief intervention for school problems: collaborating for practical solutions.* Guilford, New York.

Murray C, Greenberg MT 2000 Children's relationships with teachers and bonds with school: An investigation of patterns and correlates in middle childhood. *Journal of School Psychology* 38(5):423–45.

Myers CL, Holland KL 2000 Classroom behavioral interventions: do teachers consider the function of the behavior? *Psychology in the Schools* 37(3):271–80.

Myers DG 2005 *Social psychology*, 8th edn. McGraw-Hill, Boston, MA.

Nagin D, Tremblay RE 1999 Trajectories of boys' physical aggression, opposition, and hyperactivity on the path to physically violent and nonviolent juvenile delinquency. *Child Development* 70(5):1181–96.

National Association for the Education of Young Children 1989 Code of ethical conduct. *Young Children* 45(1):25–9.

NAEYC (National Association for the Education of Young Children), NAECS/SDE (National Association of Early Childhood Specialists in State Departments of Education) 1991 Guidelines for appropriate curriculum content and assessment in programs serving children ages 3 through 8. *Young Children* 46(3):21–38.

National Childcare Accreditation Council 1993 *Putting children first: quality improvement and accreditation system handbook.* Author, Sydney.

National Institute of Child Health and Human Development (NICHD) Early Child Care Research Network 1999 Chronicity of maternal depressive symptoms, maternal sensitivity, and child functioning at 36 months. *Developmental Psychology* 35(5):1297–310.

—— 2000 The relation of child care to cognitive and language development. *Child Development* 71(4):960–80.

—— 2001a Child care and children's peer interaction at 24 and 36 months: the NICHD study of early child care. *Child Development* 72(5):1478–500.

—— 2001b Child-care and family predictors of preschool attachment and stability from infancy. *Developmental Psychology* 37(6):847–62.

—— 2003a Do children's attention processes mediate the link between family predictors and school readiness? *Developmental Psychology* 39(3):581–93.

—— 2003b Does amount of time spent in child care predict socioemotional adjustment during the transition to kindergarten? *Child Development* 74(4):976–1005.

—— 2003c Does quality of child care affect child outcomes at age 4½? *Developmental Psychology* 39(3):451–69.

—— 2003d Social functioning in first grade: associations with earlier home and child care predictors and with current classroom experiences. *Child Development* 74(6):1639–62.

—— 2005a Duration and developmental timing of poverty and children's cognitive and social development from birth through third grade. *Child Development* 76(4):795–810.

—— 2005b Predicting individual differences in attention, memory, and planning in first graders from experiences at home, child care, and school. *Developmental Psychology* 41(1):99–114.

—— 2006 Infant–mother attachment classification: risk and protection in relation to changing maternal caregiving quality. *Developmental Psychology* 42(1):38–58.

National Institute of Child Health and Human Development (NICHD) Early Child Care Research Network, Duncan GJ 2003 Modeling the impacts of child care quality on children's preschool cognitive development. *Child Development* 74(5):1454–75.

Nelsen J, Lott L, Glenn HS 2000 *Positive discipline in the classroom*, 3rd edn. Prima Publishing, Roseville, CA.

Nelson DA, Hart CH, Yang C, Olson JA, Jin S 2006 Aversive parenting in China: associations with child physical and relational aggression. *Child Development* 77(3):554–72.

Nelson JJ, Rubin KH, Fox NA 2005 Social withdrawal, observed peer acceptance, and the development of self-perceptions in children ages 4 to 7 years. *Early Childhood Research Quarterly* 20(2):185–200.

Nelson JR, Roberts ML, Mathur SR, Rutherford RB Jr 1999 Has public policy exceeded our knowledge base? A review of the functional behavioral assessment literature. *Behavioral Disorders* 24(2):169–79.

Nesdale D, Griffith J, Durkin K, Maass A 2005 Empathy, group norms and children's ethnic attitudes. *Journal of Applied Developmental Psychology* 26(6):623–37.

Nix RL, Pinderhughes EE, Dodge KA, Bates JE, Pettit GS, McFadyen-Ketchum SA 1999 The relation between mothers' hostile attribution tendencies and children's externalizing behavior problems: the mediating role of mothers' harsh discipline. *Child Development* 70(4):896–909.

Noble K, Macfarlane K 2005 Romance or reality: examining burnout in early childhood teachers. *Australian Journal of Early Childhood* 30(3):53–8.

Nupponen H 2006 Leadership concepts and theories: reflections for practice for early childhood directors. *Australian Journal of Early Childhood* 31(1):43–50.

O'Brien EJ, Bartoletti M, Leitzel JD, O'Brien JP 2006 Global self-esteem: divergent and convergent validity issues. In MH Kernis (ed.), *Self-esteem: issues and answers: a sourcebook of current perspectives*. Psychology Press, New York, pp. 26–35.

O'Brien M, Roy C, Jacobs A, Macaluso M, Peyton V 1999 Conflict in the dyadic play of 3-year-old children. *Early Education and Development* 10(3):289–313.

O'Connor TG 2002 Annotation: the 'effects' of parenting reconsidered: findings, challenges, and applications. *Journal of Child Psychology and Psychiatry* 43(5):555–72.

O'Leary SG, Slep AMS, Reid MJ 1999 A longitudinal study of mothers' overreactive discipline and toddlers' externalizing behavior. *Journal of Abnormal Child Psychology* 27(5):331–41.

Odom SL, McConnell SR, McEvoy MA, Peterson C, Ostrosky M, Chandler LK, Spicuzza RJ, Skellenger A, Creighton M, Favazza PC 1999 Relative effects of interventions supporting the social competence of young children with disabilities. *Topics in Early Childhood Special Education* 19(2):75–91.

Olson SL, Bates JE, Sandy JM, Schilling EM 2002 Early developmental precursors of impulsive and inattentive behavior: from infancy to middle childhood. *Journal of Child Psychology and Psychiatry* 43(4):435–47.

Okagaki L, Diamond KE, Kontos SJ, Hestenes LL 1998 Correlates of young children's interactions with classmates with disabilities. *Early Childhood Research Quarterly* 13(1):67–86.

Osterman KF 2000 Students' need for belonging in the school community. *Review of Educational Research* 70(3):323–67.

Ostrov JM, Crick NR, Stauffacher K 2006 Relational aggression in sibling and peer relationships during early childhood. *Journal of Applied Developmental Psychology* 27(3):241–53.

Ostrov JM, Woods KE, Jansen EA, Casas JF, Crick NR 2004 An observational study of delivered and received aggression, gender, and social–psychological adjustment in preschool: 'This white crayon doesn't work …' *Early Childhood Research Quarterly* 19(2):355–71.

Overstreet S, Devine J, Bevans K, Efreom Y 2005 Predicting parental involvement in children's schooling within an economically disadvantaged African American sample. *Psychology in the Schools* 42(1):101–11.

Owen MT, Ware AM, Barfoot B 2000 Caregiver–mother partnership behavior and the quality of caregiver–child and mother–child interactions. *Early Childhood Research Quarterly* 15(3):413–28.

Ozonoff S, South M, Miller JN 2000 DSM-IV-defined Asperger syndrome: cognitive, behavioral and early history differentiation from high-functioning autism. *Autism* 4(1):29–46.

Paley VG 1992 *You can't say you can't play*. Harvard University Press, Cambridge, MA.

Papadopoulos TC, Panayiotou G, Spanoudis G, Natsopoulos D 2005 Evidence of poor planning in children with attention deficits. *Journal of Abnormal Child Psychology* 33(5):611–23.

Papero AL 2005 Is early, high-quality daycare an asset for children of low-income, depressed mothers? *Developmental Review* 25(2):181–211.

Paradise JL, Rockette HE, Colborn DK, Bernard BS, Smith CG, Kurs-Lasky M, Janosky JE 1997 Otitis media in 2253 Pittsburgh-area infants: prevalence and risk factors during the first two years of life. *Pediatrics* 99(3):318–33.

Parke RD, Coltrane S, Duffy S, Buriel R, Dennis J, Powers J, French S, Widaman KF 2004 Economic stress, parenting, and child adjustment in Mexican American and European American families. *Child Development* 75(6):1632–56.

Parker FL, Boak AY, Griffin KW, Ripple C, Peay L 1999 Parent–child relationship, home learning environment, and school readiness. *School Psychology Review* 28(3):413–25.

Parpal M, Maccoby EE 1985 Maternal responsiveness and subsequent child compliance. *Child Development* 56(5):1326–34.

Pauli-Pott U, Haverkock A, Pott W, Beckmann D 2007 Negative emotionality, attachment quality, and behavior problems in early childhood. *Infant Mental Health Journal* 28(1):39–53.

Paulson SE, Marchant GJ, Rothlisberg BA 1998 Early adolescents' perceptions of patterns of parenting, teaching, and school atmosphere: implications for achievement. *Journal of Early Adolescence* 18(1):5–26.

Payne M 2000 *Narrative therapy: an introduction for counsellors*. Sage, London.

Peisner-Feinberg ES, Burchinal MR 1997 Relations between preschool children's child-care experiences and concurrent development: the cost, quality, and outcomes study. *Merrill-Palmer Quarterly* 43(3):451–77.

Peisner-Feinberg ES, Burchinal MR, Clifford RM, Culkin ML, Howes C, Kagan SL, Yazejian N 2001 The relation of preschool child-care quality to children's cognitive and social developmental trajectories through second grade. *Child Development* 72(5):1534–53.

Perkins DN, Jay E, Tishman S 1993 Beyond abilities: a dispositional theory of thinking. *Merrill-Palmer Quarterly* 39(1):1–21.

Perry D, Bussey K 1984 *Social development*. Prentice Hall, Englewood Cliffs, NJ.

Peterson JL, Zill N 1986 Marital disruption, parent–child relationships, and behavior problems in children. *Journal of Marriage and the Family* 48(2):295–307.

Peterson JS, Rischar H 2000 Gifted and gay: a study of the adolescent experience. *Gifted Child Quarterly* 44(4):231–46.

Petterson SM, Albers AB 2001 Effects of poverty and maternal depression on early child development. *Child Development* 72(6):1794–813.

Peyton V, Jacobs A, O'Brien M, Roy C 2001 Reasons for choosing child care: associations with family factors, quality, and satisfaction. *Early Childhood Research Quarterly* 16(2):191–208.

Pfiffner LJ, McBurnett K, Rathouz PJ, Judice S 2005 Family correlates of oppositional and conduct disorders in children with attention deficit/hyperactiviy disorder. *Journal of Abnormal Child Psychology* 33(5):551–63.

Pfiffner LJ, O'Leary SG 1989 Effects of maternal discipline and nurturance on toddlers' behavior and affect. *Journal of Abnormal Child Psychology* 17(5):527–40.

Phelan TW 2003 *1-2-3-magic: effective discipline for children 2–12,* 3rd edn. ParentMagic Inc, Glen Ellyn, IL.

Phillips DA, Howes C 1987 Indicators of quality child care: review of research. In D Phillips (ed.), *Quality in child care: what does research tell us?* National Association for the Education of Young Children, Washington, DC, pp. 1–19.

Phillips DA, McCartney K, Scarr S 1987 Child-care quality and children's social development. *Developmental Psychology* 23(4):537–43.

Phillips D, Mekos D, Scarr S, McCartney K, Abbott-Shim M 2000 Within and beyond the classroom door: assessing quality in child care centers. *Early Childhood Research Quarterly* 15(4):475–96.

Phillipsen LC, Burchinal MR, Howes C, Cryer D 1997 The prediction of process quality from structural features of child care. *Early Childhood Research Quarterly* 12(3):281–303.

Pianta RC, Stuhlman MW 2004 Teacher–child relationships and children's success in the first years of school. *School Psychology Review* 33(3):444–58.

Pintrich PR 2000 Multiple goals, multiple pathways: the role of goal orientation in learning and achievement. *Journal of Educational Psychology* 92(3):544–55.

Piotrkowski C, Botsko M, Matthews E 2000 Parents' and teachers' beliefs about children's school readiness in a high-need community. *Early Childhood Research Quarterly* 15(4):537–58.

Plomin R, Price TS, Eley TC, Dale PS, Stevenson J 2002 Associations between behavior problems and verbal and nonverbal cognitive abilities and disabilities in early childhood. *Journal of Child Psychology and Psychiatry* 43(5):619–33.

Pollak SD, Vardi S, Bechner AMP, Curtin JJ 2005 Physically abused children's regulation of attention in response to hostility. *Child Development* 76(5):968–77.

Pope AW, McHale SM, Craighead EW 1988 *Self-esteem enhancement with children and adolescents.* Pergamon, New York.

Porter L 1999 Behaviour management practices in child care centres. Unpublished doctoral thesis. University of South Australia, Adelaide.

Posada G, Jacobs A, Carbonell OA, Alzate G, Bustamante MR, Arenas A 1999 Maternal care and attachment security in ordinary and emergency contexts. *Developmental Psychology* 35(6):1379–88.

Posserud M-B, Lundervold AJ, Gillberg C 2006 Autistic features in a total population of 7–9-year-old children assessed by the ASSQ (Autism Spectrum Screening Questionnaire). *Journal of Child Psychology and Psychiatry* 47(2):167–75.

Poulin F, Boivin M 2000 The role of proactive and reactive aggression in the formation and development of boys' friendships. *Developmental Psychology* 36(2):233–40.

Prince DL, Howard EM 2002 Children and their basic needs. *Early Childhood Education Journal* 30(1):27–31.

Prinstein MJ, Cillessen AHN 2003 Forms and functions of adolescent peer aggression associated with high peer status. *Merrill-Palmer Quarterly* 49(3):310–42.

Propper C, Moore GA 2006 The influence of parenting on infant emotionality: a multi-level psychobiological perspective. *Developmental Review* 26(4):427–60.

Pugh G, Selleck DR 1996 Listening to and communicating with young children. In R Davie, G Upton and V Varma (eds), *The voice of the child: a handbook for professionals.* Falmer Press, London, pp. 120–36.

Purdie N, Hattie J, Carroll A 2002 A review of research on interventions for attention deficit hyperactivity disorder: what works best? *Review of Educational Research* 72(1):61–99.

Purvis KL, Tannock R 1997 Language abilities in children with attention deficit hyperactivity disorder, reading disabilities, and normal controls. *Journal of Abnormal Child Psychology* 25(2):133–44.

Putallaz M, Gottman JM 1981 An interactional model of children's entry into peer groups. *Child Development* 52(3):986–94.

Putallaz M, Wasserman A 1990 Children's entry behavior. In SR Asher and JD Coie (eds), *Peer rejection in childhood*. Cambridge University Press, Cambridge, UK, pp. 60–89.

Qi CH, Kaiser AP 2003 Behavior problems of preschool children from low-income families. *Topics in Early Childhood Special Education* 23(4):188–216.

Rabiner D, Coie JD, Conduct Problems Prevention Research Group 2000 Early attention problems and children's reading achievement: a longitudinal investigation. *Journal of the American Academy of Child and Adolescent Psychiatry* 39(7):859–67.

Raffaele LM, Knoff HM 1999 Improving home–school collaboration with disadvantaged families: organizational principles, perspectives, and approaches. *School Psychology Review* 28(3):448–66.

Raggi VL, Chronis AM 2006 Interventions to address the academic impairment of children and adolescents with ADHD. *Clinical Child and Family Psychology Review* 9(2):85–110.

Ramirez SZ, Lepage KM, Kratochwill TR, Duffy JL 1998 Multicultural issues in school-based consultation: conceptual and research considerations. *Journal of School Psychology* 36(4):479–509.

Raskin NJ, Rogers CR 2005 Person-centered therapy. In RJ Corsini and D Wedding (eds), *Current psychotherapies*, 7th edn. Thomson Brooks/Cole, Belmont, CA, pp. 130–65.

Raval V, Goldberg S, Atkinson L, Benoit D, Myhal N, Poulton L, Zwiers M 2001 Maternal attachment, maternal responsiveness and infant attachment. *Infant Behavior and Development* 24(3):281–304.

Raviv T, Kessenich M, Morrison FJ 2004 A mediational model of the association between socioeconomic status and three-year-old language abilities: the role of parenting factors. *Early Childhood Research Quarterly* 19(4):528–47.

Reid NA 2004 Evaluation of programs. In D McAlpine and R Moltzen (eds), *Gifted and talented: New Zealand perspectives*. Kanuka Grove Press, Palmerston North, pp. 425–39.

Reinke WM, Herman KC 2002 Creating school environments that deter antisocial behaviors in youth. *Psychology in the Schools* 39(5):549–59.

Reynolds AJ, Ou S-R, Topitzes JW 2004 Paths of effects of early childhood intervention on educational attainment and delinquency: a confirmatory analysis of Chicago Child–Parent Centers. *Child Development* 75(5):1299–328.

Reynolds MA, Holdgrafer G 1998 Social-communicative interactions of preschool children with developmental delays in integrated settings: an exploratory study. *Topics in Early Childhood Special Education* 18(4):235–42.

Rhodes J 1993 The use of solution-focused brief therapy in schools. *Educational Psychology in Practice* 9(1):27–34.

Rigby K 2006 What international research tells us about bullying. In H McGrath and T Noble (eds), *Bullying solutions: evidence-based approaches to bullying in Australian schools*. Pearson Longman, Sydney, pp. 3–15.

Riggs NR, Jahromi LB, Razza RP, Dillworth-Bart JE, Mueller U 2006 Executive function and the promotion of social-emotional competence. *Journal of Applied Developmental Psychology* 27(4):300–9.

Rimm-Kaufman SE, Early DM, Cox MJ, Saluja G, Pianta RC, Bradley RH, Payne C 2002 Early behavioral attributes and teachers' sensitivity as predictors of competent behavior in the kindergarten classroom. *Journal of Applied Developmental Psychology* 23(3):451–70.

Rimm-Kaufman SE, Pianta RC 1999 Patterns of family–school contact in preschool and kindergarten. *School Psychology Review* 28(3):426–38.

Rimm-Kaufman SE, Pianta RC, Cox MJ 2000 Teachers' judgments of problems in the transition to kindergarten. *Early Childhood Research Quarterly* 15(2):147–66.

Ripley K, Yuill N 2005 Patterns of language impairment and behaviours in boys excluded from school. *British Journal of Educational Psychology* 75(1):37–50.

Ritchhart R 2001 From IQ to IC: a dispositional view of intelligence. *Roeper Review* 23(3):143–50.

Rivers S 2001 The bullying of sexual minorities at school: its nature and long-term correlates. *Educational and Child Psychology* 18(1):32–46.

Robbins J 1997 Separation anxiety: a study on commencement at preschool. *Australian Journal of Early Childhood* 22(1):12–17.

Roberts JE, Burchinal MR, Bailey DB 1994 Communication among preschoolers with and without disabilities in same-age and mixed-age classes. *American Journal on Mental Retardation* 99(3):231–49.

Roberts JE, Burchinal MR, Zeisel SA, Neebe EC, Hooper SR, Roush J, Bryant D, Mundy M, Henderson FW 1998 Otitis media, the caregiving environment, and language and cognitive outcomes at 2 years. *Pediatrics* 102(2):346–53.

Robertson JS 2000 Is attribution training a worthwhile classroom intervention for K–12 students with learning difficulties? *Educational Psychology Review* 12(1):111–34.

Robinson CW, Sloutsky VM 2004 Auditory dominance and its change in the course of development. *Child Development* 75(5):1387–401.

Robinson KH 2002 Making the invisible visible: gay and lesbian issues in early childhood education. *Contemporary Issues in Early Childhood* 3(3):415–34.

—— 2005 'Queerying' gender: heteronormativity in early childhood education. *Australian Journal of Early Childhood* 30(2):19–28.

Robinson KH, Jones Díaz C 2006 *Diversity and difference in early childhood education: issues for theory and practice*. Open University Press, Maidenhead, UK.

Robson S 1996 The physical environment. In S Robson and S Smedley (eds), *Education in early childhood: first things first*. David Fulton, London, pp. 153–71.

Rodd J 2006 *Leadership in early childhood*, 3rd edn. Allen & Unwin, Sydney.

Rodkin PC, Farmer TW, Pearl R, Van Acker R 2000 Heterogeneity of popular boys: antisocial and prosocial configurations. *Developmental Psychology* 36(1):14–24.

Rodriguez A, Bohlin G 2005 Are maternal smoking and stress during pregnancy related to ADHD symptoms in children? *Journal of Child Psychology and Psychiatry* 46(3):246–54.

Roffey S 2002 *School behaviour and families: frameworks for working together*. David Fulton, London.

—— 2004 *The new teacher's survival guide to behaviour*. Paul Chapman, London.

Roffey S, O'Reirdan T 2001 *Young children and classroom behaviour: needs, perspectives and strategies*. David Fulton, London.

—— 2003 *Plans for better behaviour in primary school: management and intervention*. David Fulton, London.

Rogers B 2003 *Behaviour recovery: practical programs for challenging behaviour*, 2nd edn. ACER, Melbourne.

Rogers CR, Freiberg H 1994 *Freedom to learn*, 3rd edn. Merrill, New York.

Rogers SJ, Ozonoff S 2005 Annotation: what do we know about sensory dysfunction in autism? A critical review of the empirical evidence. *Journal of Child Psychology and Psychiatry* 46(12):1255–68.

Rolfe S, Lloyd-Smith J, Richards L 1991 Understanding the effects of infant care: the case of qualitative study of mothers' experiences. *Australian Journal of Early Childhood* 16(2):24–32.

Romano E, Tremblay RE, Boulerice B, Swisher R 2005 Multilevel correlates of childhood physical aggression and prosocial behavior. *Journal of Abnormal Child Psychology* 33(5):565–78.

Rose AJ, Swenson LP, Waller EM 2004 Overt and relational aggression and perceived popularity: developmental differences in concurrent and prospective relations. *Developmental Psychology* 40(3):378–87.

Rose SR 1983 Promoting social competence in children: a classroom approach to social and cognitive skill training. In CW LeCroy (ed.), *Social skills training for children and youth*. Haworth Press, New York, pp. 43–59.

Roseman MJ 1999 Quality child care: at whose expense? *Early Childhood Education Journal* 27(1):5–11.

Rosenberg MB 2003 *Nonviolent communication: a language of life*, 2nd edn. Puddle Dancer Press, Encinitas, CA.

Rosenthal DM, Sawyers JY 1996 Building successful home/school partnerships: strategies for parent support and involvement. *Childhood Education* 72(4):194–200.

Rossman BBR, Hughes HM, Hanson KL 1998 The victimization of school-age children. In BBR Rossman and MS Rosenberg (eds), *Multiple victimization of children: conceptual, developmental, research, and treatment issues*. Haworth Press, New York, pp. 87–106.

Roth RA 1989 Preparing the reflective practitioner: transforming the apprentice through the dialectic. *Journal of Teacher Education* 40(2):31–5.

Rothbaum F, Grauer A, Rubin DJ 1997 Becoming sexual: differences between child and adult sexuality. *Young Children* 52(6):22–8.

Rowe R, Maughan B, Costello EJ, Angold A 2005 Defining oppositional defiant disorder. *Journal of Child Psychology and Psychiatry* 46(12):1309–16.

Rubenstein JL, Howes C, Boyle P 1981 A two-year follow-up of infants in community-based day care. *Journal of Child Psychology and Psychiatry* 22(3):209–18.

Rubin KH 1998 Social and emotional development from a cultural perspective. *Developmental Psychology* 34(4):611–15.

Rubin KH, Burgess KB, Dwyer KM, Hastings PD 2003 Predicting preschoolers' externalizing behaviors from toddler temperament, conflict, and maternal negativity. *Developmental Psychology* 39(1):164–76.

Rubin KH, Burgess KB, Hastings PD 2002 Stability and social-behavioral consequences of toddlers' inhibited temperament and parenting behaviors. *Child Development* 73(2):483–95.

Rubin KH, Coplan RJ 2004 Paying attention to and not neglecting social withdrawal and social isolation. *Merrill-Palmer Quarterly* 50(4):506–34.

Rubin KH, Wojslawowicz JC, Rose-Krasnor L, Booth-LaForce C, Burgess KB 2006 The best friendships of shy-withdrawn children: prevalence, stability, and relationship quality. *Journal of Abnormal Child Psychology* 34(2):143–57.

Rubin Z 1980 *Children's friendships*. Harvard University Press, Boston, MA.

Russell A, Petit GS, Mize J 1998 Horizontal qualities in parent–child relationships: parallels with and possible consequences for children's peer relationships. *Developmental Review* 18(3):313–52.

Rutter M 1983 School effects on pupil progress: research findings and policy implications. *Child Development* 54(1):1–29.

—— 1985 Resilience in the face of adversity: protective factors and resistance to psychiatric disorder. *British Journal of Psychiatry* 147:598–611.

—— 1999 Resilience concepts and findings: implications for family therapy. *Journal of Family Therapy* 21(2):119–44.

Rutter M, Maughan B 2002 School effectiveness findings 1979–2002. *Journal of School Psychology* 40(6):451–75.

Ryan RM, Deci EL 1996 When paradigms clash: comments on Cameron and Pierce's claim that rewards do not undermine intrinsic motivation. *Review of Educational Research* 66(1):33–8.

—— 2000 Self-determination theory and the facilitation of intrinsic motivation, social development, and well-being. *American Psychologist* 55(1):68–78.

Saifer S, Clark S 2005 *Practical solutions to practically every problem: the early childhood teacher's manual*, 2nd edn. Pademelon, Sydney.

Salmivalli C, Ojanen T, Haanpää J, Peets H 2005 'I'm OK but you're not' and other peer-relational schemas: explaining individual differences in children's social goals. *Developmental Psychology* 41(2):363–75.

Sanders MR 1999 Triple P—Positive Parenting Program: towards an empirically validated multilevel parenting and support strategy for the prevention of behaviour and emotional problems in children. *Clinical Child and Family Psychology Review* 2(2):71–90.

Sanders MR, Marakie-Dadds C, Tully LA, Bor W 2000 The Triple P—Positive Parenting Program: a comparison of enhanced, standard, and self-directed behavioral family intervention for children with early onset conduct problems. *Journal of Consulting and Clinical Psychology* 68(4):624–40.

Sapon-Shevin M 1986 Teaching cooperation. In G Cartledge and JF Milburn (eds), *Teaching social skills to children: innovative approaches*, 2nd edn. Pergamon, New York, pp. 270–302.

—— 1999 *Because we can change the world: a practical guide to building cooperative, inclusive classroom communities*. Allyn & Bacon, Boston, MA.

Sayal K, Goodman R, Ford T 2006 Barriers to the identification of children with attention deficit/hyperactivity disorder. *Journal of Child Psychology and Psychiatry* 47(7):744–50.

Scarr S, Eisenberg M, Deater-Deckard K 1994 Measurement of quality in child care centres. *Early Childhood Research Quarterly* 9(2):131–51.

Schaeffer CM, Petras H, Ialongo N, Poduska J, Kellam S 2003 Modeling growth in boys' aggressive behavior across elementary school: links to later criminal involvement, conduct disorder, and antisocial personality disorder. *Developmental Psychology* 39(6):1020–5.

Schmuck RA, Schmuck PA 2001 *Group processes in the classroom*, 8th edn. McGraw-Hill, Boston, MA.

Schuetze P, Lewis A, DiMartino D 1999 Relation between time spent in daycare and exploratory behaviors in 9-month-old infants. *Infant Behavior and Development* 22(2):267–76.

Schulting AB, Malone PS, Dodge KA 2005 The effect of school-based kindergarten transition policies and practices on child academic outcomes. *Developmental Psychology* 41(6):860–71.

Schwartz D, Dodge KA, Pettit GS, Bates JE, Conduct Problems Prevention Research Group 2000 Friendship as a moderating factor in the pathway between early harsh home environment and later victimization in the peer group. *Developmental Psychology* 36(5):646–62.

Schwarz JC, Krolick G, Strickland RG 1973 Effects of early day care experience on adjustment to a new environment. *American Journal of Orthopsychiatry* 43(3):340–6.

Scott S, Spender Q, Doolan M, Jacobs B, Aspland H 2001 Multicentre controlled trial of parenting groups for childhood antisocial behaviour in clinical practice. *British Medical Journal* 323(7306):194–7.

Scott-Little MC, Holloway SD 1992 Child care providers' reasoning about misbehaviors: Relation to classroom control strategies and professional training. *Early Childhood Research Quarterly* 7(4):595–606.

Seifer R, LaGasse LL, Lester B, Bauer CR, Shankaran S, Bada HS, Wright LL, Smeriglio L, Liu J 2004 Attachment status in children prenatally exposed to cocaine and other substances. *Child Development* 75(3):850–68.

Sekowski A 1995 Self-esteem and achievements of gifted students. *Gifted Education International* 10(2):65–70.

Selekman MD 1997 *Solution-focused therapy with children: harnessing family strengths for systemic change*. Guilford, New York.

Seligman MEP 1975 *Helplessness: on depression, development and death*. WH Freeman, San Francisco, CA.

Seligman MEP, Reivich K, Jaycox L, Gillham J 1995 *The optimistic child*. Random House, Sydney.

Shamir-Essakow G, Ungerer JA, Rapee RM, Safier R 2004 Caregiving representations of mothers of behaviorally inhibited and uninhibited preschool children. *Developmental Psychology* 40(6):899–910.

Sharp S, Thompson D 1994 The role of whole-school policies in tackling bullying behaviour in schools. In PK Smith and S Sharp (eds), *School bullying: insights and perspectives*. Routledge, London, pp. 57–83.

Shaw DS, Bell RQ, Gilliom M 2000 A truly early starter model of antisocial behavior revisited. *Clinical Child and Family Psychology Review* 3(3):155–72.

Shaw DS, Gilliom M, Ingoldsby EM, Nagin DS 2003 Trajectories leading to school-age conduct problems. *Developmental Psychology* 39(2):189–200.

Shaw DS, Lacourse E, Nagin DS 2005 Developmental trajectories of conduct problems and hyperactivity from ages 2 to 10. *Journal of Child Psychology and Psychiatry* 46(9):931–42.

Shaw DS, Owens EB, Giovannelli J, Winslow EB 2001 Infant and toddler pathways leading to early externalizing disorders. *Journal of the American Academy of Child and Adolescent Psychiatry* 40(1):36–43.

Shaw DS, Winslow EB, Flanagan C 1999 A prospective study of the effects of marital status and family relations on young children's adjustment among African American and European American families. *Child Development* 70(3):742–55.

Sheldon KM, Elliott AJ, Kim Y, Kasser T 2001 What is satisfying about satisfying events?: testing 10 candidate psychological needs. *Journal of Personality and Social Psychology* 80(2):325–39.

Shelton TL, Barkley RA, Crosswait C, Moorehouse M, Fletcher K, Barrett S, Jenkins L, Metevia L 1998 Psychiatric and psychological morbidity as a function of adaptive disability in preschool children with aggressive and hyperactive-impulsive-inattentive behavior. *Journal of Abnormal Child Psychology* 26(6):475–94.

Sheridan J, Dwyer SB, Sanders MR 1997 Parenting and family support for children with ADHD. *Australian Journal of Early Childhood* 22(4):15–23.

Sheridan SM 2000 Considerations of multiculturalism and diversity in behavioral consultation with parents and teachers. *School Psychology Review* 29(3):344–53.

Shields A, Ryan RM, Cicchetti D 2001 Narrative representations of caregivers and emotion dysregulation as predictors of maltreated children's rejection by peers. *Developmental Psychology* 37(3):321–37.

Shiu S 2001 Issues in the education of students with chronic illness. *International Journal of Disability, Development and Education* 48(3):269–81.

—— 2004 Maintaining the thread: including young children with chronic illness in the primary classroom. *Australian Journal of Early Childhood* 29(1):33–8.

Shonk SM, Cicchetti D 2001 Maltreatment, competency deficits, and risk for academic and behavioral maladjustment. *Developmental Psychology* 37(1):3–17.

Shute R, Owens L, Slee P 2002 'You just stare at them and give them daggers': nonverbal expressions of social aggression in teenage girls. *International Journal of Adolescence and Youth* 10(4):353–72.

Siegel B 2003 *Helping children with autism learn: treatment approaches for parents and professionals.* Oxford University Press, Oxford, UK.

Silverman LK 1994 Perfectionism. *Gifted and Talented Children's Association Newsletter.* 96:8.

—— 2002 *Upside-down brilliance: the visual-spatial learner.* DeLeon, Denver, CO.

Sims M, Guilfoyle A, Parry T 2005 What children's cortisol levels tell us about quality in childcare centres. *Australian Journal of Early Childhood* 30(2):29–39.

Siren-Tiusanen H, Robinson HA 2001 Nap schedules and sleep practices in infant–toddler groups. *Early Childhood Research Quarterly* 16(4):453–74.

Sklare GB 2005 *Brief counseling that works: a solution-focused approach for school counselors and administrators*, 2nd edn. Corwin Press, Thousand Oaks, CA.

Slaby RG, Roedell WC, Arezzo D, Hendrix K 1995 *Early violence prevention: tools for teachers of young children.* National Association for the Education of Young Children, Washington, DC.

Slee PT 1995a Bullying: health concerns of Australian secondary school students. *International Journal of Adolescence and Youth* 5(4):215–24.

—— 1995b Peer victimisation and its relationship to depression among Australian primary school students. *Journal of Personality and Individual Differences* 18(1):57–62.

Slee PT, Rigby K 1994 Peer victimisation at school. *Australian Journal of Early Childhood* 19(1):3–10.

Smidt S 1998 *Guide to early years practice*. Routledge, London.

Smith AB 1990 Early childhood on the margins. *Australian Journal of Early Childhood* 15(4):12–15.

—— 2004 How do infants and toddlers learn the rules? Family discipline and young children. *International Journal of Early Childhood* 36(2):27–41.

Smith CA, Farrington DP 2004 Continuities in antisocial behavior and parenting across three generations. *Journal of Child Psychology and Psychiatry* 45(2):230–47.

Smith CL, Calkins SD, Keane SP, Anastopoulos AD, Shelton TL 2004 Predicting stability and change in toddler behavior problems: contributions of maternal behavior and child gender. *Developmental Psychology* 40(1):29–42.

Smith JR, Brooks-Gunn J 1997 Correlates and consequences of harsh discipline for young children. *Archives of Pediatrics and Adolescent Medicine* 151(8):777–86.

Smith PK, Sharp S 1994 The problem of school bullying. In PK Smith and S Sharp (eds), *School bullying: insights and perspectives*. Routledge, London, pp. 1–19.

Smyth J 1989 Developing and sustaining critical reflection in teacher education. *Journal of Teacher Education* 40(2):2–9.

Snowling MJ, Bishop DVM, Stothard SE, Chipchase B, Kaplan C 2006 Psychosocial outcomes at 15 years of children with a preschool history of speech–language impairment. *Journal of Child Psychology and Psychiatry* 47(8):759–65.

Snyder J, Cramer A, Afrank J, Patterson GR 2005 The contributions of ineffective discipline and parental hostile attributions of child misbehavior to the development of conduct problems at home and school. *Developmental Psychology* 41(1):30–41.

Snyder J, Prichard J, Schrepferman L, Patrick MR, Stoolmiller M 2004 Child impulsiveness-inattention, early peer experiences, and the development of early onset conduct problems. *Journal of Abnormal Child Psychology* 32(6):579–94.

Socolar RRS, Amaya-Jackson L, Eron LD, Howard B, Landsverk J, Evans J 1997 Research on discipline: the state of the art, deficits and implications. *Archives of Pediatrics and Adolescent Medicine* 151(8):758–60.

Soden Z 2002a Daily living skills. In L Porter (ed.), *Educating young children with additional needs*. Allen & Unwin, Sydney, pp. 117–39.

—— 2002b Daily living skills. In L Porter (ed.), *Educating young children with special needs*. Paul Chapman, London; Sage, Thousand Oaks, CA, pp. 117–39.

Sohr-Preston SL, Scaramella LV 2006 Implications of timing of maternal depressive symptoms for early cognitive and language development. *Clinical Child and Family Psychology Review* 9(1):65–83.

Solomon CR, Serres F 1999 Effects of parental verbal aggression on children's self-esteem and school marks. *Child Abuse and Neglect* 23(4):339–51.

Soodak LC, Erwin EJ, Winton P, Brotherson MJ, Turnbull AP, Hanson MJ, Brault LMJ 2002 Implementing inclusive early childhood education: a call for professional empowerment. *Topics in Early Childhood Special Education* 22(2):91–102.

Spence SH, Najman JM, Bor W, O'Callaghan MJ, Williams GM 2002 Maternal anxiety and depression, poverty and marital relationship factors during early childhood as predictors of anxiety and depressive symptoms in adolescence. *Journal of Child Psychology and Psychiatry* 43(4):457–69.

Spieker SJ, Larson NC, Lewis SM, Keller TE, Gilchrist L 1999 Developmental trajectories of disruptive behavior problems in preschool children of adolescent mothers. *Child Development* 70(2):443–58.

Spieker SJ, Nelson DC, Petras A, Jolley SN, Barnard KE 2003 Joint influence of child care and infant attachment security for cognitive and language outcomes of low-income toddlers. *Infant Behavior and Development* 26(3):326–44.

Spinrad TL, Eisenberg N, Harris E, Hanish L, Fabes RA, Kupanoff K, Ringwald S, Holmes J 2004 The relation of children's everyday nonsocial peer play behavior to their emotionality, regulation, and social functioning. *Developmental Psychology* 40(1):67–80.

Spira EG, Fischel JE 2005 The impact of preschool inattention, hyperactivity, and impulsivity on social and academic development: a review. *Journal of Child Psychology and Psychiatry* 46(7):755–73.

Spirito A, Stark LJ, Grace N, Stamoulis D 1991 Common problems and coping strategies reported in childhood and early adolescence. *Journal of Youth and Adolescence* 20(5):531–44.

Stams GJM, Juffer F, van Ijzendoorn MH 2002 Maternal sensitivity, infant attachment, and temperament in early childhood predict adjustment in middle childhood: the case of adopted children and their biologically unrelated parents. *Developmental Psychology* 38(5):806–21.

Stauffacher K, DeHart GB 2006 Crossing social contexts: relational aggression between siblings and friends during early and middle childhood. *Journal of Applied Developmental Psychology* 27(3):228–40.

Steelman LM, Assel MA, Swank PR, Smith KE, Landry SH 2002 Early maternal warm responsiveness as a predictor of child social skills: direct and indirect paths of influence over time. *Journal of Applied Developmental Psychology* 23(2):135–56.

Stein MA, Efron LA, Schiff WB, Glanzman M 2002 Attention deficits and hyperactivity. In ML Batshaw (ed.), *Children with disabilities*, 5th edn. Elsevier, Sydney; Brookes, Baltimore, MD, pp. 389–416.

Steinberg L, Elmen JD, Mounts NS 1989 Authoritative parenting, psychosocial maturity, and academic success among adolescents. *Child Development* 60(6):1424–36.

Steinberg L, Lamborn SD, Darling N, Mounts NS, Dornbusch SM 1994 Over-time changes in adjustment and competence among adolescents from authoritative, authoritarian, indulgent, and neglectful families. *Child Development* 65(3):754–70.

Steinberg L, Lamborn SD, Dornbusch SM, Darling N 1992 Impact of parenting practices on adolescent achievement: authoritative parenting, school involvement, and encouragement to succeed. *Child Development* 63(5):1266–81.

Steinhausen H-C, Juzi C 1996 Elective mutism: an analysis of 100 cases. *Journal of the American Academy of Child and Adolescent Psychiatry* 35(5):606–14.

Steinhausen H-C, Wachter M, Laimböck K, Metzke CW 2006 A long-term outcome study of selective mutism in childhood. *Journal of Child Psychology and Psychiatry* 47(7):751–6.

Sterling-Turner H, Watson TS 1999 Consultant's guide for the use of time-out in the preschool and elementary classroom. *Psychology in the Schools* 36(2):135–48.

Sternberg KJ, Baradaran LP, Abbott CB, Lamb ME, Guterman E 2006a Type of violence, age, and gender differences in the effects of family violence on children's behavior problems: a mega-analysis. *Developmental Review* 26(1):89–112.

Sternberg KJ, Lamb ME, Guterman E, Abbott CB 2006b Effects of early and later family violence on children's behavior problems and depression: a longitudinal, multi-informant perspective. *Child Abuse and Neglect* 30(3):283–306.

Sternberg RJ 1999 *Cognitive psychology*, 2nd edn. Harcourt Brace College, Fort Worth, TX.

Stipek DJ, Feiler R, Byler P, Ryan R, Milburn S, Salmon JM 1998 Good beginnings: what difference does the program make in preparing young children for school? *Journal of Applied Developmental Psychology* 19(1):41–66.

Stipek DJ, Feiler R, Daniels D, Milburn S 1995 Effects of different instructional approaches on young children's achievement and motivation. *Child Development* 66(1):209–23.

Stonehouse A 1991 *Opening the doors: child care in a multi-cultural society*. Australian Early Childhood Association, Canberra.

—— 1994 *Not just nice ladies: a book of readings on early childhood care and education*. Pademelon, Sydney.

Stonehouse A, Gonzalez-Mena J 2004 *Making links: a collaborative approach to planning and practice in early childhood services.* Pademelon, Sydney.

Stoneman Z 1993 The effects of attitude on preschool integration. In CA Peck, SL Odom and DD Bricker (eds), *Integrating young children with disabilities into community programs: ecological perspectives on research and implementation.* Paul H Brookes, Baltmore, MD, pp. 223–48.

Stoolmiller M 2001 Synergistic interaction of child manageability problems and parent-discipline tactics in predicting future growth in externalizing behavior for boys. *Developmental Psychology* 37(6):814–25.

Stormont M 2002 Externalizing behavior problems in young children: contributing factors and early intervention. *Psychology in the Schools* 39(2):127–38.

Stormshak EA, Bierman KL, Bruschi C, Dodge KA, Coie JD, Conduct Problems Prevention Research Group 1999 The relation between behavior problems and peer preference in different classroom contexts. *Child Development* 70(1):169–82.

Strain PS, Hoyson M 2000 The need for longitudinal, intensive social skill intervention: LEAP follow-up outcomes for children with autism. *Topics in Early Childhood Special Education* 20(2):116–22.

Strain PS, Joseph GE 2004 Engaged supervision to support recommended practices for young children with challenging behavior. *Topics in Early Childhood Special Education* 24(1):39–50.

Straus MA, Sugarman DB, Giles-Sims J 1997 Spanking by parents and subsequent antisocial behavior of children. *Archives of Pediatrics and Adolescent Medicine* 151(8):761–7.

Strein W, Simonson T, Vail L 1999 Convergence of views: self-perceptions of African American and White kindergartners. *Psychology in the Schools* 36(2):125–34.

Sturge-Apple ML, Davies PT, Cummings EM 2006 Impact of hostility and withdrawal in interparental conflict on parental emotional unavailability and children's adjustment difficulties. *Child Development* 77(6):1623–41.

Sumsion J 2005 Male teachers in early childhood education: issues and case study. *Early Childhood Research Quarterly* 20(1):109–23.

Sundell K 2000 Examining Swedish profit and nonprofit child care: the relationships between adult-to-child ratio, age composition in child care classes, teaching and children's social and cognitive achievements. *Early Childhood Research Quarterly* 15(1):91–114.

Swick K 2005 Preventing violence through empathy development in families. *Early Childhood Education Journal* 33(1):53–9.

Sylva K 1994 School influences on children's development. *Journal of Child Psychology and Psychiatry and Related Disciplines* 35(1):135–70.

Sylva K, Siraj-Blatchford I, Taggart B, Sammons P, Melhuish E, Elliot K, Totsika V 2006 Capturing quality in early childhood through environmental rating scales. *Early Childhood Research Quarterly* 21(1):76–92.

Szatmari P, Bryson SE, Boyle MH, Streiner DL, Duku E 2003 Predictors of outcome among high functioning children with autism and Asperger syndrome. *Journal of Child Psychology and Psychiatry* 44(4):520–8.

Tamis-LeMonda CS, Bornstein MH, Baumwell L 2001 Maternal responsiveness and children's achievement of language milestones. *Child Development* 72(3):748–67.

Theimer CE, Killen M, Strangor C 2001 Young children's evaluations of exclusion in gender-stereotypic peer contexts. *Developmental Psychology* 37(1):18–27.

Thompson RA, Wyatt JM 1999 Current research on child maltreatment: implications for educators. *Educational Psychology Review* 11(3):173–201.

Tizard B, Philps J, Plewis I 1976 Staff behavior in pre-school centers. *Journal of Child Psychology and Psychiatry* 17(1):21–33.

Tollefson N 2000 Classroom applications of cognitive theories of motivation. *Educational Psychology Review* 12(1):63–83.

Trawick-Smith J 1988 'Let's say you're the baby, OK?' Play leadership and following behavior of young children. *Young Children* 43(5):51–9.

Tremblay RE 2004 Decade of behavior distinguished lecture: development of physical aggression during infancy. *Infant Mental Health Journal* 25(5):399–407.

Trickett PK 1998 Multiple maltreatment and the development of self and emotion regulation. In BBR Rossman and MS Rosenberg (eds), *Multiple victimization of children: conceptual, developmental, research and treatment issues.* Haworth Press, New York, pp. 171–87.

Trzesniewski KH, Moffitt TE, Caspi A, Taylor A, Maughan B 2006 Revisiting the association between reading achievement and antisocial behavior: new evidence of an environmental explanation from a twin study. *Child Development* 77(1):72–88.

Tucker CM, Zayco RA, Herman KC, Reinke WM, Trujillo M, Carraway K, Wallack C, Ivery PD 2002 Teacher and child variables as predictors of academic engagement among low-income African American children. *Psychology in the Schools* 39(4):477–88.

Turnbull A, Turnbull R, Erwin EJ, Soodak LC 2006 *Families, professionals, and exceptionality: Positive outcomes through partnerships and trust,* 5th edn. Pearson Merrill Prentice Hall, Upper Saddle River, NJ.

Tyler JS, Colson S 1994 Common pediatric disabilities: medical aspects and educational implications. *Focus on Exceptional Children* 27(4):1–16.

Vallerand RJ, Gagné F, Senécal C, Pelletier LG 1994 A comparison of the school intrinsic motivation and perceived competence of gifted and regular students. *Gifted Child Quarterly* 38(4):172–5.

van Boxtel HW, Mönks FJ 1992 General, social, and academic self-concepts of gifted adolescents. *Journal of Youth and Adolescence* 21(2):169–86.

van den Boom DC 1995 Do first-year intervention effects endure? Follow-up during toddlerhood of a sample of Dutch irritable infants. *Child Development* 66(6):1798–816.

van Goozen SHM, Cohen-Kettenis PT, Snoek H, Matthys W, Swaab-Barneveld H, van Engeland H 2004 Executive functioning in children: a comparison of hospitalised ODD and ODD/ADHD children and normal controls. *Journal of Child Psychology and Psychiatry* 45(2):284–92.

Vandell DL, Henderson VK, Wilson KS 1988 A longitudinal study of children with day-care experiences of varying quality. *Child Development* 59(5):1286–92.

Vartuli S 1999 How early childhood teacher beliefs vary across grade level. *Early Childhood Research Quarterly* 14(4):489–514.

Vaughn BE, Azria MR, Krzysik L, Caya LR, Bost KK, Newell W, Kazura KL 2000 Friendship and social competence in a sample of preschool children attending Head Start. *Developmental Psychology* 36(3):326–38.

Vaughn BE, Colvin TN, Azria MR, Caya L, Krzysik L 2001 Dyadic analyses of friendship in a sample of preschool-age children attending Head Start: correspondence between measures and implications for social competence. *Child Development* 72(3):862–78.

Vaughn BE, Vollenweider M, Bost KK, Azria-Evans MR, Snider JB 2003 Negative interactions and social competence for preschool children in two samples: reconsidering the interpretation of aggressive behavior for young children. *Merrill-Palmer Quarterly* 49(3):245–78.

Veenman S 1995 Cognitive and noncognitive effects of multigrade and multi-age classes: a best-evidence synthesis. *Review of Educational Research* 65(4):319–81.

—— 1996 Effects of multigrade and multi-age classes reconsidered. *Review of Educational Research* 66(3):323–40.

Vernon-Feagans L, Manlove EE 2005 Otitis media, the quality of child care, and the social/communicative behavior of toddlers: a replication and extension. *Early Childhood Research Quarterly* 20(3):306–28.

Verschueren K, Marcoen A 1999 Representation of self and socioemotional competence in kindergartners: differential and combined effects of attachment to mother and to father. *Child Development* 70(1):183–201.

Vickers M, Parris M, Bailey J 2004 Working mothers of children with chronic illness: narratives of working and caring. *Australian Journal of Early Childhood* 29(1):39–44.

Vigil JM, Geary DC, Byrd-Craven J 2005 A life history assessment of early childhood sexual abuse in women. *Developmental Psychology* 41(3):553–61.

Vitaro F, Barker ED, Boivin M, Brendgen M, Tremblay RE 2006 Do early difficult temperament and harsh parenting differentially predict reactive and proactive aggression? *Journal of Abnormal Child Psychology* 34(5):685–95.

Vitaro F, Brendgen M, Tremblay RE 2002 Reactively and proactively aggressive children: antecedent and subsequent characteristics. *Journal of Child Psychology and Psychiatry* 43(4):495–505.

Vizard E, Monck E, Misch P 1995 Child and adolescent sex abuse perpetrators: a review of the research literature. *Journal of Child Psychology and Psychiatry* 36(5):731–56.

Vuijk P, van Lier PAC, Huizink AC, Verhulst FC, Crijnen AAM 2006 Prenatal smoking predicts non-responsiveness to an intervention targeting attention-deficit/hyperactivity symptoms in elementary schoolchildren. *Journal of Child Psychology and Psychiatry* 47(9):891–901.

Wachs TD, Gurkas P, Kontos S 2004 Predictors of preschool children's compliance behavior in early childhood classroom settings. *Journal of Applied Developmental Psychology* 25(4):439–57.

Wagner P, Gillies E 2001 Consultation: a solution-focused approach. In Y Ajmal and I Rees (eds), *Solutions in schools*. BT Press, London, pp. 147–62.

Wakenshaw M 2002 *Caring for your grieving child*. New Harbinger, Oakland, CA.

Walker LJ, Hennig KH, Krettenauer T 2000 Parent and peer correlates for children's moral reasoning. *Child Development* 71(4):1033–48.

Wangmann J 1992 Accreditation: a right for all Australia's young children or a waste of time and money. In B Lambert (ed.), *Changing faces: the early childhood profession in Australia*. Australian Early Childhood Association, Canberra, pp. 46–57.

Warren SL, Huston L, Egeland B, Sroufe LA 1997 Child and adolescent anxiety disorders and early attachment. *Journal of the American Academy of Child and Adolescent Psychiatry* 36(5):637–44.

Watamura SE, Donzella B, Alwin J, Gunnar MR 2003 Morning-to-afternoon increases in cortisol concentrations for infants and toddlers at child care: age differences and behavioral correlates. *Child Development* 74(4):1006–20.

Waters E, Cummings M 2000 A secure base from which to explore close relationships. *Child Development* 71(1):164–72.

Waters E, Hamilton CE, Weinfield NS 2000a The stability of attachment security from infancy to adolescence and early adulthood: general introduction. *Child Development* 71(3):678–83.

Waters E, Merrick S, Treboux D, Crowell J, Albersheim L 2000b Attachment security in infancy and early adulthood: a twenty-year longitudinal study. *Child Development* 71(3):684–9.

Waters J 1996 *Making the connection: parents and early childhood staff*. Lady Gowrie Child Centre, Melbourne.

Watzlawick P, Weakland J, Fisch R 1974 *Change: principles of problem formation and problem resolution*. WW Norton, New York.

Weber-Schwartz N 1987 Patience or understanding? *Young Children* 42(3):52–4.

Webster RE 2001 Symptoms and long-term outcomes for children who have been sexually assaulted. *Psychology in the Schools* 38(6):533–47.

Webster-Stratton C 1998 Preventing conduct problems in Head Start children: strengthening parenting competencies. *Journal of Consulting and Clinical Psychology* 66(5):715–30.

Wehmeyer ML, Baker DJ, Blumberg R, Harrison R 2004 Self-determination and student involvement in functional assessment: innovative practices. *Journal of Positive Behavior Interventions* 6(1):29–35.

Weiner B 2000 Interpersonal and intrapersonal theories of motivation from an attributional perspective. *Educational Psychology Review* 22(1):1–14.

Weinfield NS, Sroufe LA, Egeland B 2000 Attachment from infancy to early adulthood in a high-risk sample: continuity, discontinuity, and their correlates. *Child Development* 71(3):695–702.

Wentzel KR 1994 Family functioning and academic achievement in middle school: a social-emotional perspective. *Journal of Early Adolescence* 14(2):268–91.

Wesley PW, Buysse V 2003 Making meaning of school readiness in schools and communities. *Early Childhood Research Quarterly* 18(3):351–75.

Whalen CK, Henker B, Dotemoto S 1981 Teacher response to the methylphenidate (Ritalin) versus placebo status of hyperactive boys in the classroom. *Child Development* 52(3):1005–14.

Whalen CK, Henker B, Jamner LD, Ishikawa SS, Floro JN, Swindle R, Perwien AR, Johnston JA 2006 Toward mapping daily challenges of living with ADHD: maternal and child perspectives using electronic diaries. *Journal of Abnormal Child Psychology* 34(1):111–26.

Wheeler JJ, Richey DD 2005 *Behavior management: principles and practices of positive behavior support.* Pearson Merrill Prentice Hall, Upper Saddle River, NJ.

Whitebook M, Sakai L 2003 Turnover begets turnover: an examination of job and occupational stability among child care centre staff. *Early Childhood Research Quarterly* 18(3):273–93.

Wien CA 1996 Time, work, and developmentally appropriate practice. *Early Childhood Research Quarterly* 11(3):377–403.

—— 2004 From policing to participation: overturning the rules and creating amiable classrooms. *Young Children* 59(1):34–40.

Willis CA 2002 The grieving process in children: strategies for understanding, educating, and reconciling children's perceptions of death. *Early Childhood Education Journal* 29(4):221–6.

Wilson BJ 1999 Entry behavior and emotion regulation abilities of developmentally delayed boys. *Developmental Psychology* 35(1):214–22.

Wiltz NW, Klein EL 2001 'What do you do in child care?' Children's perceptions of high and low quality classrooms. *Early Childhood Research Quarterly* 16(2):209–36.

Winslade J, Monk G 1999 *Narrative counseling in schools: powerful and brief.* Corwin Press, Thousand Oaks, CA.

Winsler A, Caverly SL, Willson-Quayle A, Carlton MP, Howell C, Long GN 2002 The social and behavioral ecology of mixed-age and same-age preschool classrooms: a natural experiment. *Journal of Applied Developmental Psychology* 23(3):305–30.

Wishard AG, Shivers EM, Howes C, Ritchie S 2003 Child care program and teacher practices: associations with quality and children's experiences. *Early Childhood Research Quarterly* 18(1):65–103.

Wodrich DL 1994 *Attention deficit hyperactivity disorder: what every parent wants to know.* Paul H Brookes, Baltimore, MD.

Wolchik SA, Tein J-Y, Sandler IN, Ayers TS 2006 Stressors, quality of the child–caregiver relationship, and children's mental health problems after parental death: the mediating role of self-system beliefs. *Journal of Abnormal Child Psychology* 34(2):212–29.

Wolery M, Werts MG, Holcombe A 1994 Current practices with young children who have disabilities: placement, assessment, and instruction issues. *Focus on Exceptional Children* 26(6):1–12.

Wolfgang CH, Bennett BJ, Irvin JL 1999 *Strategies for teaching self-discipline in the middle grades.* Allyn & Bacon, Boston, MA.

Wunsch MJ, Conlon CJ, Scheidt PC 2002 Substance abuse: a preventable threat to development. In ML Batshaw (ed.), *Children with disabilities*, 5th edn. MacLennan & Petty, Sydney, pp. 107–22.

Wyman PA, Cowen EL, Work WC, Hoyt-Meyers L, Magnus KB, Fagen DB 1999 Caregiving and developmental factors differentiating young at-risk urban children showing resilient versus stress-affected outcomes: a replication and extension. *Child Development* 70(3):645–59.

Yoon JS, Hughes JN, Cavell TA, Thompson B 2000 Social cognitive differences between aggressive-rejected and aggressive-nonrejected children. *Journal of School Psychology* 38(6):551–70.

Young ME 1992 *Counseling methods and techniques: an eclectic approach.* Merrill, New York.

Young S, Heptinstall E, Sonuga-Barke EJS, Chadwick O, Taylor E 2005 The adolescent outcome of hyperactive girls: self-report of psychosocial status. *Journal of Child Psychology and Psychiatry* 46(3):255–62.

Young SK, Fox NA, Zahn-Waxler C 1999 The relations between temperament and empathy in 2-year-olds. *Developmental Psychology* 35(5):1189–97.

Zahn-Waxler C, Radke-Yarrow M 1990 The origins of empathic concern. *Motivation and Emotion* 14(2):107–30.

Zaslow MJ, Oldham E, Moore KA, Magenheim E 1998 Welfare families' use of early childhood care and education programs, and implications for their children's development. *Early Childhood Research Quarterly* 13(4):535–63.

Zhou Q, Eisenberg N, Losoya SH, Fabes RA, Reiser M, Guthrie IK, Murphy BC, Cumberland AJ, Shepard SA 2002 The relations of parental warmth and positive expressiveness to children's empathy-related responding and social functioning: a longitudinal study. *Child Development* 73(3):893–915.

Ziegert DI, Kistner JA, Castro R, Robertson B 2001 Longitudinal study of young children's responses to challenging achievement situations. *Child Development* 72(2):609–24.

Zimet DM, Jacob T 2001 Influences of marital conflict on child adjustment: review of theory and research. *Clinical Child and Family Psychology Review* 4(4):319–35.

index